DATE DUE

‖‖‖‖‖‖‖‖‖‖‖‖‖‖‖

D1596761

Antje Jackelén

Time & Eternity

The Question of Time in Church,
Science, and Theology

Templeton Foundation Press

Philadelphia and London

Templeton Foundation Press
300 Conshohocken State Road, Suite 550
West Conshohocken, PA 19428
www.templetonpress.org

10|0⁵ Translation by Barbara Harshaw

Designed and typeset by Kachergis Book Design

Templeton Foundation Press helps intellectual leaders and others learn about science research on aspects of realities, invisible and intangible. Spiritual realities include unlimited love, accelerating creativity, worship, and the benefits of purpose in persons and in the cosmos.

Library of Congress Cataloging-in-Publication Data
Jackelén, Antje.
[Zeit und Ewigkeit. English]
Time and eternity : the question of time in church, science, and theology /
Antje Jackelén.
Xii, 34 5 p. cm.
Includes bibliographical references (p.   ) and index.
ISBN 1-932031-89-8 (pbk. : alk. paper) 1. Time—Religious aspects—Christianity. 2. Religion and science. I. Title.
BT78.J3313 2005
236—dc22
2005005325

Printed in the United States of America

05 06 07 08 09 10   10 9 8 7 6 5 4 3 2 1

To my teachers and my students

Contents

Preface to the English Edition

Even when one has a lot of support, there is still a long journey from a book published in German to a readable English text. Translation is often not acknowledged as the art it really is. I am aware that the use of several languages and terminology from hymnody, theology, physics and philosophy increased the challenge in this case. I want to express my gratitude to all who have contributed to this edition.

Special thanks to the Templeton Foundation Press, especially Laura Barrett and Joanna Hill, for making the translation possible and for guiding the project toward completion; April Wilson, Chicago, for her impressive perseverance in editing text, quotes and references; Professor Neil Spurway, Glasgow, for his thoughtful comments on the whole text; Professors John Albright, Mark Bangert, Ralph Klein and Audrey West, Chicago, and Dr. Stefan Vogt, Argonne National Laboratory, for their helpful suggestions on parts of the text.

Now it is up to the reader to judge the result. It is my hope that both the poetry and the prose as well as the sober figures in some places will be enjoyable enough to nourish both interest and insights into a theme that continues to captivate almost everyone's imagination.

I dedicate this book to those who taught and mentored me and to those who keep the challenge of teaching and learning alive—i.e., to my teachers and my students.

Chicago, February 2005

Preface to the German Edition

The aim of this book is to explore the possibilities of relationally determined and eschatologically qualified concepts of time and eternity. By doing this, I would like to contribute to the dialogue between theology and science, as well as to an appropriate theology of time.

This study is based on a doctoral dissertation which I submitted to the Theological Faculty of the University of Lund, Sweden. I have revised the text for publication. In the course of working with the topic of *time*, the concept of *relation* became increasingly important to me. Yet, it was not only the word itself that revealed its significance for my project; diverse real relations also made major impacts on its progress. Without a rich relational tapestry of human and academic contacts, this book would never have been completed.

For multiple support, advice, and help, I would here like to express my heartfelt thanks to: Bishops Krister Stendahl and KG Hammar, for their encouragement to begin a doctoral study program while being in parish ministry; Professor Werner G. Jeanrond of Lund, for his good and decisive advice during the writing of the dissertation; hymnologist Elisabet Wentz-Janacek of Lund, for her stimulating ideas and suggestions for the first chapter; Professor Gösta Gustafson of Lund, for his critical reading of the chapter on science; Professor Jürgen Hübner of Heidelberg, for many helpful discussions and access to the library of the Forschungsstätte der Evangelischen Studiengemeinschaft (FESt); Rev. Dr. Wolfgang Achtner, Giessen, for valuable perspectives on the entire study; Professor Michael Welker of Heidelberg, for making an exchange of ideas with other academics possible;

Professor Rainer Zimmermann of Munich, for reactions and comments, particularly with regard to the third chapter; my colleagues in the systematic theology doctoral seminar at the University of Lund, as well as Lund professors Gösta Hallonsten, Manfred Hofmann, and Rune Söderlund for numerous interesting discussions; Professor Ulf Görman, Rev. Dr. Charlotte Methuen, and all colleagues and friends in the *European Society for the Study of Science and Theology* (ESSSAT) who offered stimulating suggestions and advice; the Neukirchener Verlag, especially Mr. Starke and Mr. Hegner, for publishing this book; Joanna Jackelén, for the proofreading and layout; the IT team of the Lutheran School of Theology at Chicago, for assistance in resolving conflicts between German, Swedish, and American computer cultures; my parents, Marianne and Werner Zöllner, for their manifold support during the entire project; my husband Heinz and our daughters, Joanna and Andrea, for their understanding and occasional—but usually beneficial—lack of understanding; and, finally, also those dialogue partners outside of the university who followed the development of this study with sympathy and enthusiasm. Their questions often forced me to reformulate my thoughts in a more generally intelligible manner. They also continually made it clear to me that the topic of time is captivating and fascinating— and that the discussion of time will probably never come to an end.

A. J.
Chicago, December 2001

Time & Eternity

Abbreviations

AHB	*Australian Hymn Book with Catholic Supplement*
Cor.	Corinthians
Dan.	Daniel
Deut.	Deuteronomy
Eccles.	Ecclesiastes
EG	*Evangelische Gesangbuch* (1995 ed.)
EG1996	*Evangelische Gesangbuch* (1996 ed.)
Eph.	Ephesians
Exod.	Exodus
Gal.	Galatians
Gen.	Genesis
GL	*Gotteslob*
Isa.	Isaiah
Macc.	Maccabees
NRSV	New Revised Standard Version of the Bible
Pet.	Peter
Phil.	Philemon
Ps.	Psalm
Ps90	*Psalmer i 90-talet*
Rev.	Revelation
Rom.	Romans
SA	*Sing Alleluia. A Supplement to the Australian Hymn Book*
Sv ps	*Den Svenska Psalmboken* (1986 ed.)
Svps1937	*Den Svenska Psalmboken* (1937 ed.)
Thess.	Thessalonians

Introduction and Hermeneutical Approach

   This study deals with the relationship between faith and knowledge, between natural science and theology. There are essentially two different methods for dealing with this subject. On the one hand, there is the path of principle discourse, in which the presuppositions and methods of science and theology are compared to each other and brought into dialogue—preferably with the mediation of philosophy. On the other hand, there is also the possibility of allowing science and theology to enter into a dialogue on one specific topic.

   In this study, I have decided on the second alternative. My purpose is to bring concrete theological symbol systems—and not theology per se—together with science, and then to see what happens.

   I have selected time as the subject of my study. The question of time appears to represent an inexhaustible topic. Augustine's often-quoted remark from the eleventh book of the *Confessions*—that if no one asks him what time is, he knows, but if he wants to explain it to someone who asks, he does not know—seems to be valid even today. In spite of the lack of a clear and definitive definition of time, theologians and natural scientists often treat time as if such a definition had been given once and for all. Nevertheless, the concept of time that a person holds due to his or her profession can be considerably different from the concept of time that the same person has in all other aspects of life. The relevance of the subject of time can also be seen, not least of all, in the amount of literature currently being published on this topic (e.g., Achtner, Davies, Fagg, Gimmler, Sandbothe and Zimmerli, Gronemeyer, Mainzer, Reheis, Weis).

The question of time is important for theology because the conception of time has consequences for a large number of theological topics, not only for the entire field of eschatology, but also for the concepts of God, the understanding of the Incarnation, and numerous other fields. To be sure, theologians have considered the concept of time again and again, but they have done so primarily in the language of metaphysics. My study will take a different path. Fundamentally, I will proceed from the observation that, up until now, theological reflection has not dealt very explicitly with twentieth-century theories of physics. It is therefore quite possible that theological reflection has overlooked crucial insights.

This hypothesis and the decision to begin not with philosophy, but rather with concrete symbol systems, have also influenced the contents of my study and my methods of working. Stimulated by Paul Ricoeur's thesis that appropriate talk of time must be conveyed by narrative, I will start by searching for "narrated time" in chapter 1 in order to approach a theological concept of time. My quest will lead to the quantitative and qualitative analyses of German-, English-, and Swedish-language hymns. For example, the texts of the hymns are examined with respect to what they have to say about the relationship between God and time, about eternity, about the future, and about the relationship of human beings to time.

Chapter 2 begins with the concept of time in the Bible. In a critical discussion, primarily of Gerhard von Rad's work, I cast doubt upon the distinction between linear and cyclical time, arguing that it is oversimplified. The notion that an appropriate concept of time must be relationally shaped takes form at this point—in agreement with Carl Heinz Ratschow. This means that, when choosing between a definition of time and a description of it in terms of relationships, I give preference to the examination of relations. Along with Ingolf U. Dalferth, I argue against a static and dualistic concept of time that declares God and time, and time and eternity, to be fixed pairs of opposites. With the aid of three distinct models for differentiating the relation of time to eternity, I will attempt to approach a dynamic and relational concept of time. I will explain the three distinct models—the quantitative, the ontological, and the eschatological—by using the theological concepts of time of Oscar Cullmann and Augustine, as well as those of Karl Rahner and Wolfhart Pannenberg.

A dynamically and relationally shaped concept of time suggests the inclusion of the Trinitarian concept of God. I will discuss the strengths and weaknesses of the connection between time and the Trinity in a dialogue with Dalferth, Pannenberg, and Karl-Josef Kuschel. The second chapter concludes with an analysis of death within the perspective of a theology of time, which is oriented primarily toward the theologians Eberhard Jüngel and Werner G. Jeanrond, as well as the sociologist Zygmunt Bauman. The analysis concentrates primarily on two points of view: "eternalized time and eroded eternity," on the one hand, and "irrelevant eternity and dead time," on the other. A summarizing preliminary appraisal describes the relationship of time and eternity by characterizing eternity as "the other" of time. This is done independently of, but nevertheless in general agreement with, Emmanuel Lévinas.

Following a brief introduction to the problems of the dialogue between science and theology, in chapter 3 I deal with the theories of physics that are most important for an understanding of time. The first major topic in this chapter is the concept of absolute time, as it is found in Isaac Newton's works and in the correspondence between Gottfried Wilhelm Leibniz and Samuel Clarke—no doubt shaped by theological influences. "Dualisms" and "deism" are the summarizing concepts of this section. An examination of Einstein's theories of relativity follows; this then leads to a discussion of the independence of time. After considering the question of how quantum physics deals with time, I discuss the role of language in its relationship to physical reality, primarily using texts by Werner Heisenberg and Niels Bohr.

Then, after considering the very fast (theories of relativity) and the very small (quantum physics), my study turns to the very large, namely, to cosmological perspectives, to singularities and black holes, to the limits of time and space. From thermodynamics and research on chaos theory, the question of the directedness of time has gained new force. Can thermodynamics prove the irreversibility of time? Does chaos research necessarily reduce the determinism of a natural occurrence or, conversely, does it lead determinism to new triumphs?

Some summarizing reflections lead up to the fourth and final chapter. From the critical examination of physics theories, I conclude that the most appropriate understanding of time is as a relational and diverse phenomenon. An adequate understanding of time is not limited to an analysis of single elements, but rather includes structures and relationships, being and becoming. It considers a temporal openness, the articulation of which must necessarily reach beyond physics.

The concluding chapter 4 summarizes the various aspects of a theology of time. This summary is in harmony with, but goes beyond, the discussion in the first three chapters. Following a deeper reflection on statics, dynamics, and relationality in the concept of time—with John Polkinghorne and Thomas F. Torrance as the most important dialogue partners—I continue the discussion of time and the Trinity that was begun in the second chapter.

Here I turn toward more recent theological thinking, which can be found, for example, in the works of Colin Gunton, Kevin Vanhoozer, Elizabeth Johnson, Robert Jenson, and Christoph Schwöbel. These concepts are instructive in elucidating the change or transition from substance to relation, but they have definite limitations regarding their ability to make a relational concept of time explicit. Eschatology proves to be a more productive key to a relational concept of time, and it receives much of my attention in the fourth chapter. The train of thought moves from the role of eschatology in theology through a discussion of scientific eschatologies as formulated by Frank J. Tipler and Freeman J. Dyson, and then to a reflection—especially inspired by Georg Picht—on the different modes of time in the light of eschatology.

As already discussed in the second chapter, the category of the new is indispensable for an eschatological concept of time. It brings up the question of the continuity and identity of a creature and of creation in both individual and cosmic perspectives. Does "a new heaven and a new earth" mean the destruction or the transformation of the old? And how can we comprehend the rhetoric of eternal life if death means radical discontinuity? The latter appears to make continuous identity impossible. In a critical discussion of Theodor Mahlmann's thought, I attempt to show how an exclusively linear-chronological concept of time necessarily makes the question of identity a question of continuity, whereas a relational concept of time proceeds from the notion of alterity, in which identity is primarily constituted by relationships, liberating the identity understood in this manner from its tie to chronological continuity. A window is thus opened into the heart of a relational theological concept of time: the tension between the already and the not-yet as the eschatological disruption of linear chronology.

Narrative, dynamics, alterity, openness, and eschatologically qualified relationality—these are the major aspects of a theology of time. Can a system, an applicable theology of time, be constructed from these elements? Within the framework of a critical acknowledgment of Jürgen Moltmann's theology of time, I will clarify the problems that must be dealt with in any attempt to construct a theology of time. Accordingly, I believe a theology of time conceived as an abstract construct to be impossible; when formulated as a narrative about the relation to the other, however, I consider it to be a central concern of theological reflection.

Every evaluation of the possibilities for interdisciplinary dialogue is shaped by preconceptions regarding the presuppositions of communication and understanding. This naturally also applies to my study with regard to the question of time in Church, science, and theology. For this reason, let me say something here about the hermeneutical aspects of this study.[1] Essentially, there are two guiding principles that should be explained at this point, namely, *the self-evidence of the discussion* and *the desire for contact.*

The first principle grew out of my observation that this self-evidence is anything but self-evident! Rather, in many cases it must first be attained. This is especially true for the contact between theology and the natural sciences, for numerous difficulties are obvious here. The relationship between science and theology is greatly burdened with tensions and mistakes from the past; science basks in the glory of a spoiled baby in the lap of society, whereas theology, the once favorite child now abandoned, is still at times preoccupied with pitying itself and licking its wounds. It is readily supposed that physics belongs a priori in the most comfortable easy chair at the discussion table, possibly subjected to the malicious glares of biology and its related disciplines, who wish to compete for its position. Ethics then has the easiest time finding a place at the discussion table—it has become increasingly obvious that the self-sufficiency of science and technology was a deceptive myth. Philosophy should also easily qualify for a place at the table, despite occasional postmodern identity crises. For it, there is only the difficult question of which chair it should occupy—it can choose between the high-level meta-chair and a practical "observer chair." At times, philosophy strives for the higher level, on which, in fortunate cases, antitheses are reconciled. At other times, it is supposed to determine the items on the agenda, or sometimes it monitors compliance with the points of order. But theology? Is anything left over for it other than a footstool? Frequently, it must begin by securing its place as self-evident in the discussion, which can equal a new "escape from self-inflicted immaturity." In a certain sense, the Age of Enlightenment has never ended—and it never can. The conditions of rationality must be considered repeatedly, both critically and self-critically. This also requires clarification regarding which expectations can be linked to a dialogue.

I begin with the assumption that central theological contents can receive new illumination in dialogue. In the sense of a correlation theory,[2] I thereby presuppose two things for theology, namely, an awareness of one's own limitations and an openness to the potential contribution of nontheological thought to the constructive work of the theologian. An increase in knowledge and insight is therefore attained not simply within the boundaries of one's own discipline, but rather, to a large degree, precisely in dialogue with others.[3] This dialogue deals with reciprocal, critical correlations.

This means, first, that I consider an uninvolved side-by-side existence unacceptable. Ethical problems in research and the full assessment of the consequences of technological innovations are only two examples of how the natural sciences are dependent upon a dialogue with other parties. From the perspective of theology, the necessity for dialogue is grounded, among other things, in the theology of creation. That which, as nature, is the object of the so-called natural sciences is, as creation, also the object of theology. Even with all of their differences, the common ground shared by science and theology is large enough to be able to open up previously untapped opportunities for dialogue. The fact that, in this context, one can no more assume *a single* theology than one can assume *a single* natural science—but is rather confronted on both sides with various branches and perspectives—increases both the variety and the demands of dialogue.

Second, a justifiable expectation related to the dialogue can be seen in a spontaneous gain on the purely linguistic level. There is a constant need for new images, metaphors, and analogies in theological language. In this sense, one might hope to achieve from the dialogue a kind of linguistic alliance. This seems highly enticing, above all for theologians who strive for renewal of preaching. The transfer of scientific concepts such as complementarity and black holes to theological issues can initially appear to be refreshing. It can lead to elegant homiletic artifices that rightly elicit admiration because they can actually foster insights and generate new knowledge. However, homiletic functionality is something quite different from solid hermeneutical work. Even if there are nomadic concepts[4] that circulate quite freely among different branches of science, all of these crossovers require caution. Rash borrowing or incorporation is a risk not only for theology; other disciplines are also subject to the danger of using theological concepts indiscriminately. Newton's concept of God is not at all identical to the concepts of God that are used in early twenty-first-century theology.

For this reason, thirdly, one is warned against quick conclusions and premature attempts at harmonization. The obvious goal of dialogue is not synthesis; rather, it initially concerns the clarifying process. Alterity and differences should be respected. The most impressive syntheses justifiably elicit mistrust, for they can easily develop totalitarian and dictatorial tendencies. There can be no talk of a new "marriage" between science and theology, as was the case, for example, during Newton's time. In this context, apologetics in the traditional sense is also a poor adviser. A certain dualism or pluralism, in which two or more perspectives of the same reality complement, antagonize, and perhaps also correct each other, is preferable. From time to time, the most basic task of the dialogue may be to expose a conflict. Beneficial tension, eutonia, is a more worthwhile goal than a great synthesis, at least as long as the *unio mystica* remains unattainable.

I thus come to my second hermeneutical principle, the desire for contact. It is linked to the fact that theoretical agreement—even if it were possible to reach perfection in this respect—would not suffice as the only goal.

One must also always be concerned with practical social life, and life is not livable without contact.

Both science and theology speak of infinity and of space and time as dimensions of reality. With which goal, from which ascribed meaning, do they do this? In this world, people search in wretched places for edible trash just to stay alive—how then can one speak of infinity? People have accidents, die, and suddenly no longer come home to dinner—how then can one speak of a continuum of curved space-time? People cannot speak properly of infinity, either theologically or scientifically, without touching upon the finite nature of existence and allowing it to touch them. For the physicist, the discovery of relative time may have meant an intellectual revolution; for the mother and father who have no food for their children, time has always been relative to the space they have at their disposal.[5] In the case of theologians and cosmologists who sympathize with the Anthropic Cosmological Principle, the question of why something exists at all—and is not just nothing—may provoke enthusiasm for the world and its origins; for slum-dwellers, however, the question of why almost nothing of all that exists is in their home evokes despair of the world.

This means that one cannot limit oneself to the securing of the self-evident. The desire for contact must follow. Neither science nor theology can or may work in a vacuum. Both need the desire for contact. Constructs of ideas created in a clinically clean atmosphere are just as deficient as particle tests in a sterile testing facility if the knowledge is not brought into contact with the lives of those for whom these ideas and experiments were (supposedly) made and who are affected by their consequences. Contact in this case means two things, namely, to contact and to be contacted, to touch and to be touched.

Various fears of contact follow closely on the heels of the desire to make contact. Such fears emerge because, during contact, boundaries are transgressed or even shifted; and this causes insecurity about where the boundaries are actually located. So much theological work has been exhausted in the discussion of where boundaries should properly be drawn—so that there was then no more strength or interest for making contact and for crossing boundaries. Yet the God who was witnessed to in the Bible was decisively concerned with making contact and crossing boundaries. It was not only the Christology of the early church that had problems with God's crossing of boundaries. A lot of effort was expended before the achievement of the Chalcedonian formulations, which can be understood as an attempt to conceive relatedness and diversity in dynamic unity. Also in the theological concept of *communicatio idiomatum*, one finds the attempt to structure conceptually the meeting of differences. In the attempt to conceptualize relation and difference together, then, one is not dealing with a structure of thought that is new to the history of theology.

The primary concern need not necessarily be to eliminate the fears of contact to the greatest degree possible, but rather to live with the tension that is created by these fears. Theological reflection is challenged to be a theology of contact beyond and at the point of boundaries, regardless of whether they are the boundaries between God and humankind, between human beings themselves, or between human beings and nature. This means conflict and even a questioning of one's own self-understanding. Here, one's own identity is more a constant task than the unchallenged starting point. The fear of loss is offset by the awareness of new possibilities. In the words of David Tracy: "Conversation in its primary form is an exploration of possibilities in the search for truth. In following the track of any question, we must allow for difference and otherness. . . . Otherness and difference can become, however, genuine possibility: the *as* other, the *as* different becomes the *as* possible."[6]

In this context, I wish to emphasize especially two tasks of theology, namely, criticism of reductionism and advocacy for public dialogue. Criticism of reductionism is appropriate, first of all, where theology reduces itself and retreats into itself, regardless of whether this is done for elitist reasons or due to a lack of trust in its own competence. Such criticism is also appropriate whenever a person elevates himself or herself and proclaims a self-confident "nothing but." In this respect, reductionism in the presentation of research results is frequently easier to expose than the initial reductionism that, through the selection of material and methods, often incorporates a narrowness into the entire process that is seldom accounted for. The satisfaction of having formulated something exclusively superior is thereby bought with a more or less violent reduction of the starting material. Scholars of the humanities and the natural sciences are both subject to these risks. The more or less successful singling out of the thing per se is neither the only, nor always the best, path to knowledge. Shifting emphasis from definitions to relations can lead to significant gains in insight and knowledge.

The advocacy for public dialogue belongs to the correlative method.[7] In this role, theology also attempts to maintain continuity in the public dialogue. To consistently oppose the slide into the private sphere at the expense of public dialogue can at times be a terribly difficult undertaking; in several places—certainly at least in part as a reaction to an objectivism that is felt to be inflexible and rigid—a subjectivism, increasingly getting out of hand, thinks it is justified in and of itself and that it need not necessarily be responsible to any forum of public truth.

This subjectivism poses a problem for the dialogue between science and theology that should be taken seriously. It is accompanied by a waning interest in overlapping questions of truth, because truth is no longer primarily that which is generally perceived or understood, but rather that which is individually experienced as true. Truth that is publicly discussed thereby forfeits part of its relevance, and the question of truth becomes the question of many truths, the communication of which threatens to splinter into private milieus. Truth becomes a private matter, whereby it is worthwhile to remember that "private" is derived from the Latin *privare* (= to rob, to deprive of). What is gained here privately is lost there by the community. As a consequence of this privatization, dialogue cannot simply be conducted as if there were a public community of values and as if belief and knowledge, theology and science, were self-evident, major actors on the public stage. They are not—and, with this knowledge, they are in the same boat. Together they can discover that they are, not least of all, at the mercy of the power of economic forces, whose workings are occasionally influenced by very opaque rationalities. In this situation, they can demonstrate their competence by opening a forum, a public space for intellectual and social contact.

No Concept of
Time without Narrated Time

Narrated Time in Hymns

Motivation—Why Hymns?

This study considers the notion that time is accessible to human beings only to the extent that it is articulated in narrative form. My decision has been influenced by the theory of Paul Ricoeur, that appropriate talk of time cannot occur in direct discourse. It must instead be conveyed by the indirect discourse of narrative.[1] According to Ricoeur, each attempt to analyze time directly only multiplies the problems that occur anyway. For this reason, there is no conception of time without narrated time.[2] Narrative understanding deserves precedence over narratological rationality.[3] Ricoeur compares this narrative understanding to a picnic to which the author contributes the words, while the reader contributes the meaning.[4] In this way, the narrative can attain its highest degree of effectiveness: The readers find a solution to which they themselves must find the suitable questions.[5] Resorting to narrative is thus not a simplifying reduction. Quite to the contrary, it is necessary to do justice precisely to the complex difficulties related to the problematic nature of time.[6]

If Ricoeur's theory is correct, namely, that the poetics of narrative unite that which speculative philosophy separates, then it should be reasonable to begin a study of the theology of time with narrated time. From a consideration of narrated time, questions should be formulated whose treatment can deepen a theological concept of time in relation to the insights of modern science.

Narratives often occur in stylized, poetic form, and they must also be able to be repeated. This belongs to their essence, and, in this way, the particularity of the Church—"being a community of memory and narrative"[7]—comes to complete fruition. The characteristic form and repeatability of the narrative make the worship service in particular an appropriate venue for theological narrative—and also for the narrative of time.

Narrations have always occurred in special ways in hymns. One can even maintain that, at the very beginning, the Christian church began by singing.[8] One only has to think of the echo of numerous "psalms and hymns and spiritual songs" (Eph. 5:19) in the epistles of the New Testament. The hymns recorded in Luke—Gloria in excelsis, Benedictus, Magnificat, and Nunc dimittis—have accompanied the Christian community throughout the centuries. Following this tradition, current hymnals represent a collection of human, Christian, and theological experiences gathered over centuries. Even when denominational differences on church music and liturgy are taken into account, it is undeniable that the study of music, songs, and hymns often facilitates a better understanding of the thoughts and feelings of the Church than the study of the writings of its theologians.[9]

To some extent, hymns live their own lives in a borderland between experience and theological reflection. Precisely this aspect makes them so interesting in this context. In the words of a twentieth-century songwriter, the hymnal is the experienced Bible, and the hymns are works of art that have arisen from the encounter between the biblical message and the experience of life.[10] As poetry, the hymns are concentrated experience, and they therefore also achieve a kind of universality. Furthermore, they attempt to express experience in a forward-looking manner.[11] It would be astonishing if this treasure house of experience did not have something essential to say about experiencing and understanding time.

Surely, both more recent texts and those that have accompanied congregations for decades and even centuries exert a formative and normative influence upon life's meaning for those who read or sing them. Even without official canonization, the hymn collections of the churches tend, in practice, to attain canonical status.

It would have been conceivable also to include liturgical prayer texts in this study. In these texts, however, time is primarily spoken of in set phrases, so that one can speak less of narrated time in relation to such texts. Additionally, it is more likely the voice of the clergy that emerges from liturgical texts, whereas in the hymns, the path to the voice of the people should be at least somewhat shorter than in the inflexible liturgical portions.

Furthermore, the use of liturgical texts is concentrated in the church service, while hymns should have a broader application, "not only in the shaping of formal worship, but also as an enrichment of spiritual experience, both in private reading and memory and in meditation."[12] The editors of *The Australian Hymn Book* were determined to maintain the "intimacy and immediacy that would carry it [a hymn] out of the time of formal worship as a source of daily guidance and inspiration."[13] Similarly, the *Evangelische Gesangbuch (Protestant Hymnal)* also aims to fulfill the "tasks of a Christian family and parish book" [Aufgaben eines christlichen Haus- und Gemeindebuches].[14] Against the backdrop of the way in which the Swedish people practice piety, which is based more on the hymnal than directly on the Bible, *Den Svenska Psalmboken (The Swedish Hymnbook)* is indeed intended for private devotions as well as for public worship, as stated in its foreword.

Finally, the entire range of the centuries is easily accessible in the hymnals. Here, the new and the old—"the new to stimulate and extend us, the old to comfort and confirm"[15]—stand side by side. Methodologically, a study of hymns enables access "from below." Here, the starting point is not the abstract and historical development of dogmatic concepts, but rather the search for phenomenological access. This is not to say that dogmatics would not have been important in the creation of hymns. It is merely maintained here that this was not the *primus motor*. Finally, it may be noted that this study is less concerned with tracking down the *Zeitgeist* of different epochs than with listening to concentrated life experience.

Material

In the following discussion, several hymnals will be examined with respect to their treatment of time and the experience of time. To be relevant, the materials should be current hymnals that mirror a certain ecumenical breadth. They should also have general validity in numerous congregations and represent at least three different languages. Viewed from this standpoint, two German, two Swedish, and two English hymnals have been chosen.

The German hymnals include the 1995 provisional edition of the *Evangelische Gesangbuch*,[16] which was published for the Protestant Church in the Rhineland, the Protestant Church of Westphalia, and the Lippian Church, as well as the Catholic prayer and hymn book, *Gotteslob (Praise of God)[17]* (including the Supplement for the Archdiocese of Paderborn), which was published in 1975.

The two Swedish hymnals include the hymnal of the Church of Sweden, *Den Svenska Psalmboken*,[18] published in 1986, and the small book entitled *Psalmer i 90-talet*,[19] which was published in 1994. With its 123 hymns, the latter constitutes a supplement to the former, but without possessing its official status.

Both English-language hymnals come from Australia. They are *The Australian Hymn Book with Catholic Supplement*,[20] which appeared in 1977, and *Sing Alleluia. A Supplement to The Australian Hymn Book*,[21] which was published in 1987. Australia was selected because the use of hymnals in English congregations is very inconsistent, and it seemed enticing to leave the European continent. Above all, the two Australian hymnals show promise for discovering a melting pot of representative English-language hymn material. The selection thus remains largely focused on the context from which modern science has evolved.

The *EG* consists of a main portion—hymns 1 to 535—that was adopted following a ten-year decision-making process. The regional church portion, which has not yet been officially adopted in the edition I examined, extends from number 550 to number 691. Numbers 701 to 959 include prayers, confessions, orders of worship, a reference companion, and details on the ecclesiastical year. Except for the hymnological information, this portion was not considered in the current study.

The edition of the *EG* examined here is intended for use in two united churches and one reformed church within the Protestant Church in Germany, as well as for the Protestant Reformed Church in Germany. In Germany, 28.9 million[22] people are affected by the main portion, which is obligatory for the entire Protestant Church of Germany (EKD).

The *GL* also consists of a main portion and a local portion. In Germany alone, the main portion is obligatory for approximately 27.7 million Roman Catholics. Furthermore, 6.84 million Catholics in Austria and the Catholic congregations in German-speaking Switzerland use the main portion of the *GL* in their services. The Supplement, which begins with number 808, is intended for the Archdiocese of Paderborn, which has about 1.85 million Catholic parishioners.

The *Sv ps* consists of 700 hymns and songs. Of these, the first 325 are jointly used by fifteen different Christian churches and communities.[23] The entire hymnal is used both in the Church of Sweden (Svenska kyrkan, Lutheran) and in the Swedish Protestant Mission (Evangeliska Fosterlands-Stiftelsen). The hymns of the small book entitled *Psalmer i 90-talet*, which are numbered from 801 to 923, were published as complementary material for services in the Church of Sweden. Texts and melodies are intended as ways of expressing Christian belief "in our times," for singing "in time, on the path to eternity."[24] This raises the hope that not only is something new in time being said, but also something new about time. A large majority of the texts in the *Ps90* were written after 1970.[25]

The *AHB* emerged from work performed by a committee constituted by Anglicans, Congregationalists, Methodists, and Presbyterians in 1968. Collaboration begun in 1974 with the Roman Catholic Archdiocese of Sydney resulted in the publication of the hymnal in two formats, *The Australian Hymn Book* and *The Australian Hymn Book with Catholic Supplement*, which has been examined in this study. The committee assigned itself the task of preserving the best and most characteristic contributions of various denominations to the entire life of the Church throughout the centuries. The results are 624 hymns and songs that reflect a considerable breadth of English-language hymn material. The main emphases are on Charles Wesley (1707–1788) and Isaac Watts (1674–1748), who, with fifty-eight and thirty-five hymns respectively, were the most frequently represented hymn writers.

The editorial board for the *SA* consisted of representatives of the Anglican Church of Australia, the Catholic Archdiocese of Sydney, the Presbyterian Church of Australia, and the Uniting Church in Australia.[26] The *SA* contains biblical psalms, chorales primarily from the forty years preceding the edition, and hymns of diverse character, for example, songs from Taizé. The editors aimed to achieve international breadth. Among the 105 hymns, they have therefore included contributions from the Philippines, from China, from the area of the former Czechoslovakia, and from France, Great Britain, America, Africa, and New Zealand. Aboriginal hymns are also included in the Australian material.

Methods

How then is narrated time manifested in hymns? In the following discussion, the passages in which time concepts are articulated are analyzed for frequency and content, although the qualitative analysis is given priority. Selection criteria for relevant passages include the occurrence of the nouns "time(s)" [*Zeit(en)*], "future" [*Zukunft*], "day" [*Tag*], "night" [*Nacht*], "morning" [*Morgen*], "evening" [*Abend*], "year" [*Jahr*], and "hour" [*Stunde*], as well as the adjectives derived from these nouns. Time adverbs, such as "today" [*heute*] and "yesterday" [*gestern*], as well as seasonal concepts, have been taken into consideration. Compound nouns, such as "time on earth" [*Erdenzeit*] and "time of grace" [*Gnadenzeit*], have naturally also been discussed. Furthermore, all passages that center on the idea of "eternity" [*Ewigkeit*] have been included in the study. In this case, words such as "eternity/eternities" [*Ewigkeit(en)*], "eternal one" [*Ewiger*], and "eternal" [*ewig(lich)*] were decisive.

Frequently, recurring phrases and refrains have been considered only once. In order to prevent the number of passages being examined from becoming boundless, the expression "forever" [*all(e)zeit*] in the sense of "always" [*immer*], as well as other time adverbs in primarily unstressed passages, were not given particular attention.[27]

In the following discussion, the expression *time indication* [*Zeitindikation*] generally characterizes words and word combinations that articulate a concept of time and/or eternity, whereas *time terminology* [*Zeitterminologie*] means words or word combinations that speak explicitly of "Zeit" or "Zukunft," "tid" or "framtid," or "time"/"age" or "future." Correspondingly, *eternity terminology* [*Ewigkeitsterminologie*] includes the concepts "eternity or eternities" [*Ewigkeit(en)*] and "eternal" [*ewig(lich)*] or different forms of "eternal" [*ewig*] and "eternity" [*Ewigkeit*]. In the English hymns, a distinction is made between strictly literal eternity terminology, which contains the concepts "eternal," "everlasting," "endless"/"unending," and "eternity," and other eternity terminology that includes "ever" and "evermore." Concepts such as "day" [*Tag*] and "night" [*Nacht*], "morning" [*Morgen*] and "evening" [*Abend*], "year" [*Jahr*], "hour" [*Stunde*], "today" [*heute*] and "yesterday" [*gestern*], as well as the names of the seasons, are occasionally grouped together under the concept *everyday terminology* [*Alltagsterminologie*] or *seasonal terminology* [*Jahreszeitterminologie*].

The function of the quantitative analysis is to provide orientation. The inclusion of numerical figures should help the reader to see emphases and proportions. The quantitative analysis thus also helps to ensure that the text examples selected for the qualitative analysis are representative to a certain degree. The quantitative analysis was done nonelectronically. No guarantee can be made for 100 percent accuracy, although the results should be considered sufficiently solid. When I speak of "passages with time indications," this is generally synonymous with "stanzas with time indications." Numerous stanzas contain several time indications that are combined with one another, repeated, or juxtaposed; these appear in the overall calculation, however, as a respective single passage. Nevertheless, during the individual analysis of time terminology, eternity terminology, everyday terminology, and seasonal terminology, as well as in the analysis of final stanzas, several time indications within the same stanza have been considered individually.

In the qualitative analysis, I occasionally depart from the semantic fields established in the quantitative analysis. Translations have been kept as literal as possible, and closeness to text is given priority over rhyme and rhythm.

The qualitative analysis does not supply a hymnological study, that is, it does not attempt to perform a musical[28] or literary scientific analysis or to demonstrate church-historical or dogmatic peculiarities. It also does not seek to analyze intent in order to reconstruct original wording or uncover the sociological meaning of different hymns. Instead, it is driven by a phenomenologically motivated interest in retelling what the hymns of different epochs have to say about time and eternity. For traditional poetry in general, as well as for the poetry of hymns in particular, a phenomenological working method appears to me to be appropriate, since it stays close to the text and still allows freedom for ongoing interpretation. Thus, in the attempt to narrate the history of time in the hymns of the church, new history arises. The retelling occasionally borders on new narration and elicits questions, some of which will be touched upon more closely in the theological discussion in the next chapter.

Quantitative Analysis
Indications of Time

Comparison of Frequencies

I analyzed 3,682 passages containing indications of time in a total of 3,146 hymns. The *EG* contains 677 hymns.[29] In the texts of these hymns, there are about 885 passages containing indications of time, that is, there are approximately 1.3 indications of time per hymn. A portion of the hymn material is ecumenical and is also found in *Gotteslob*. In *GL*, 579 passages referring to time occurred in 917 hymns, songs, texts, and prayers. The numerical ratio shows a significantly higher occurrence of time indications in the *EG*. The two books are not entirely comparable in this respect, however, because in *GL*, diverse types of prayers and texts are integrated into the hymn portion, whereas the *EG* has a separate text and prayer portion that will not be discussed here. Also in the Catholic portion of the *AHB*, time indications certainly occur much less frequently than in the main portion. These two facts could show that references to time play a lesser role in traditional Catholic hymn material.

In the 700 hymns of *Sv ps*, I found 1,128 passages mentioning time, which I subsequently examined. This means approximately 1.6 indications of time per hymn, which represents a higher frequency than in the two German books. In *Ps90*, 166 passages containing indications of time occur in 123 hymns, i.e., 1.3 indications per hymn. This frequency corresponds precisely to that of the *SA*, in which 142 passages referring to time occur in 105 hymns. Indications of time appear somewhat less frequently in the *AHB*. Here, in 624 hymns, one finds 782 such passages, which is quite similar to the ratio in the *EG*.[30]

Indications of Time in Final Stanzas

Within the hymns, indications of time occur more frequently in the final stanzas. In the 264 hymns of *GL* that contain such passages,[31] indications of time are found in the final stanzas of 96 hymns. This figure is much higher for the *EG*. Of the 452 hymns mentioning time, 202 hymns contain such indications in the final stanza. Here, 17 percent and 23 percent respectively of all indications of time are found in final stanzas.

This trend is even more pronounced in *Sv ps*. Of the 550 hymns referring to time, 280 have such an indication in their final stanza. Here, therefore, at least half of all such hymns mention time in their final stanzas. Almost one-fourth of all time indications in *Sv ps* are in final stanzas. In *Ps90*, around one-third of all passages mentioning time appear in the final stanzas. Here, at least 63 percent of all hymns with time indications refer to time in the last stanza.

The prevalence of time indications in final stanzas is also high in the Australian books. More than half of such hymns mention time in the final stanza. Approximately 30 percent of all indications are found in the final stanzas.[32]

In keeping with the spirit of the strong medieval hymn tradition, doxological expressions appear, not surprisingly, in the final stanzas of numerous hymns in all three languages. A classical example that occurs in numerous variations is: "Der Heiligen Dreieinigkeit . . . sei Lob und Preis in Ewigkeit"[33] (To the Holy Trinity . . . be praise and honor for all eternity).

In the German books, a vast majority of the time indications in final stanzas consist of eternity terminology. The ratio of eternity terminology to time terminology in final stanzas is about 3:1 in the *EG* and about 2:1 in *GL*. For example, eternal life, eternal joy, and eternal peace are frequent themes.

Several passages also connect time and eternity to one another; thus, for example, a passage in a hymn about Christ reads: "Du unser Glück in dieser Zeit, du Sonne unsrer Ewigkeit" (You, our happiness in this time, you, the sun of our eternity).[34] All stanzas do not deal with time and eternity as freely as does this hymn, however. Particularly in the final stanzas—but not only there—a relatively high portion of time indications occur in set phrases. This is particularly true for many of the passages that combine *time, temporal* with *eternity, eternal*, for example, *EG* 114.10: "Sei hochgelobt in dieser Zeit . . . und ewig in der Herrlichkeit" (Be highly praised in this time . . .

and eternally in glory).[35] Here it should also be noted that the formulation of the *Gloria Patri* is different in the two books. In *EG*, the wording is "wie es war im Anfang, jetzt und immerdar und von Ewigkeit zu Ewigkeit" (as it was in the beginning, now and for evermore and from eternity to eternity), while in *GL*, one sings "wie im Anfang, so auch jetzt und alle Zeit und in Ewigkeit" (as in the beginning, thus also now and for all time and in eternity). In this case, the expressions "now and for evermore" and "now and for all time" should be considered synonymous. The significant difference lies in the simple "in eternity" and in the doubled "from eternity to eternity."

In the final stanzas of the hymns in *Sv ps*, the subject of eternity occurs twice as frequently as the subject of time.[36] When compared to *EG* and *GL*, however, it is striking that here most of the references to time in the final stanzas consist of concepts such as *day, night, morning, evening, hour, summer*, and *winter*, among which *day* and *night* are by far the most commonly used terms.[37] In *EG* and *GL*, on the other hand, the total amount of everyday terminology corresponds to only one-third of the amount of eternity terminology.

In *Ps90*, the relation of time to eternity in the final stanzas is clearly different. Here, time terminology and eternity terminology are balanced.[38] As in *Sv ps*, in *Ps90*, the largest number of time indications in the final stanzas is also made up of everyday terminology.

A look at the final stanzas of the *AHB* shows a clear predominance of terminology regarding eternity. Time terminology is represented less than half as frequently as eternity terminology in the strict sense. When considering eternity terminology in the broad sense, there are even 4.25 passages with eternity terminology for each passage containing time terminology.[39] Here, eternity terminology also occurs more frequently than everyday terminology.[40] Seasonal terms are not represented. In the *AHB*, a noticeably large number of final stanzas contain two, three, or even four indications of time.

Compared to the *AHB*, however, the *SA* presents an entirely different picture. Here, the dominant group of concepts is everyday terminology,[41] although even here there are not any seasonal terms. Eternity terminology appears only about half as often.[42] The passages with time terminology amount to the same number as those containing eternity terminology in the strict sense.

As collections of predominantly more recent hymns, *Ps90* and *SA* are distinguished from the classical hymnals, which contain hymn material from many centuries. In the more modern hymns, eternity terminology has clearly declined; the decrease in eternity terminology has not simply given way to time terminology, however. Particularly as compared to *EG* and *GL*, the area of everyday terminology has become more important.

Indications of Time in the Different Subject Areas

One can expect the frequency of time indications to vary according to subject area. For this reason, those subject areas that occur in a way comparable in all hymnals were examined with regard to the frequency of references to time.[43] These were the topics of Advent, Christmas, Lent, Passion or Holy Week,[44] Easter,[45] Ascension Day, Pentecost, and the theme of death.[46] In the case of *EG, Sv ps,* and *AHB,* the sections "Trinity" and "Epiphany" were compared. It was even possible to compare the section entitled "End of the church year" for *EG* and *Sv ps,* whereby *Sv ps* and *Ps90* were combined for this aspect of the study.

In the subject areas considered, *GL* has a generally lower frequency of time indications than *EG* and *Sv ps/Ps90.* On average, the Swedish hymnals have a higher rate than the *EG.* The *AHB* fluctuates at a level between *Sv ps/Ps90* and the *EG.*

GL shows the highest frequency for the topic "Tod und Vollendung" (death and consummation), although its rate still lies significantly below that of the other hymnbooks. The *GL* has the lowest number of time indications for Lent, lagging significantly behind the other books even in this regard. In the *EG,* the section "Ende des Kirchenjahres" (end of the church year) has the most occurrences, while the "Passion" section has the least. The subject of "Sterben und ewiges Leben, Bestattung" (death and eternal life, burial) assumes second place. Completely in agreement with these findings, the section "End of the Church Year" in *Sv ps/Ps90* also exhibits the highest frequency, followed by "The Gift and Limitation of Life, Heaven, Illness, Suffering, and Death." Here, however, the hymns for Epiphany have the lowest incidence.

For the most part, the *AHB* follows the characteristic profile of the other books, with one significant exception, namely, the Easter hymns. In the *AHB,* these have a significantly higher prevalence of time indications than in the other books. Also in the *AHB,* the highest incidence appears toward the end of the Church year, under the category "All Saints' Day and All Souls' Day." The *AHB* has the lowest values for Pentecost and Lent.

The other subject areas that were studied are situated in a solid middle field that exhibits no remarkable differences or deviations.

The analysis according to subject areas therefore offers few surprising results. It was to be expected that hymns dealing with the end of the church year, with dying, with death, and with eternal life contain a greater number of references to time. The low incidence for Lent, which is common to the two German books, may be surprising, however.

Plotted graphically, the coefficients derived from the number of passages

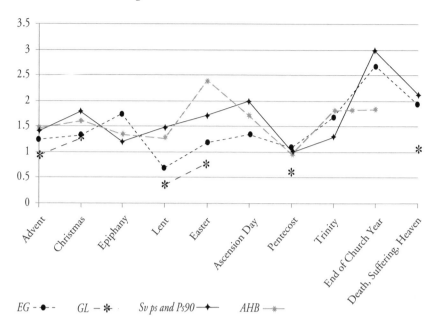

EG - ●- -   GL - ✱·   Sv ps and Ps90 ━✦━   AHB ━✳━

with time indications and the number of hymns in the individual subject areas can be seen in the chart above.

Time Terminology

Of those passages that were examined, 217 (*EG*) or 147 (*GL*) mention the word *Zeit(en)* (time[s]) or one of its derivatives or compound words, or the term *Zukunft* (future). This results in percentage incidence rates of terminology regarding time of 24.5 percent or 25.4 percent in all time-indicating passages. Because this slight variance can certainly lie within the margin of error, no quantitative differences with regard to time terminology can be verified here.

The *EG* mentions *Zeit* (time) 181 times, 25 of which are in the plural. In *GL*, the corresponding figures are 128 and 23, respectively. One thus sees the word *Zeiten* (times) relatively more often in *GL* than in *EG*. *Zukunft* (future) is mentioned six times in each of the hymnals. Some representative passages containing the words *zeitlich* (temporal), *beizeiten* (in good time), and *jederzeit* (at any time) have also been examined. The following concepts, which are expressed by compound (time terminology) terms, should be mentioned: *Gnadenzeit* (time of grace) (4/2),[47] *Erdenzeit* (time on earth) (1/6), *Leidenszeit(en)* (time(s) of suffering) (3/1), *Morgenzeit* (morning time) (1/1), *Weihnachtszeit* (Christmas season) (1/1), *Sommerzeit* (summertime)

(3/0), *Lebenszeit* (lifetime) (2/0), *Freudenzeit* (time of celebration) (1/0), *Erlösungszeit* (time of redemption) (1/0), *Erquickungszeiten* (times of comfort) (1/0), *Prüfungszeit* (time of testing) (1/0), *Abendzeit* (evening) (1/0), *Nachtzeit* (nighttime) (1/0), *Folgezeit* (time to come) (1/0), and *Gezeiten* (tides) (1/0).

According to this comparison, the *EG* contains a larger spectrum of time terminology; times of grace and times of suffering are also represented more frequently in the *EG*, which can perhaps be attributed to the influence of Protestant theology. In *GL*, on the other hand, the expression *Erdenzeit* (time on earth) is relatively over-represented.

In the passages of the *Sv ps* that were studied, there are 285 occurrences of time terminology expressions. This means that such terminology occurred in 25.3 percent of all passages examined, which corresponds amazingly well to the findings in the German hymnbooks. *Tid* (time) is mentioned 208 times in definite or indefinite form; "tid" occurs seventeen times in the plural. *Framtid* (future) appears fifteen times, three times of these being compound terms, namely, *framtidsdag* (day in the future), *framtidstro* (belief in the future), and *framtidsland* (land of the future). Different combinations of the word *tid* (time) appear forty-five times. The most frequent occurrences here are *prövotid* and *prövningstid* (time of testing), a total of seven passages. *Summer* is mentioned five times, *winter* twice, and *spring* once. There are three incidences of *tidevarv* (age), another three occurrences of Christmas season, and two occurrences each of *fastetid(er)* (Lent), *väntetid* (time of waiting), *arbetstid* (time of working), *sorgetid* (time of mourning), and *högtid* (time of celebration). We find one mention each of *urtid* (primeval times), *levnadstid* (lifetime), *ungdomstid* (youth), *vårfrudagstid* (Annunciation), *blomningstid* (time of flourishing), *vandringstid* (time of wandering), *rusningstid* (rush hour), *skördetid* (time of harvesting), *vilotid* (time of rest).

In *Ps90*, forty-nine passages contain time terminology in the 166 passages containing time indications, which, at a rate of 29.5 percent, represents the greatest concentration up to now. The concepts are distributed as follows: *time*, thirty times; *times*, twice; and *future*, nine times. The distribution of the compound terms are as follows: *blomningstid* (time of flourishing), four times; *väntetid* (time of waiting), twice; and once each for *vintertid* (wintertime) and *mognadstid* (time of maturity). In contrast to *Sv ps* and, above all, to *EG* and *GL*, one is struck here by a drastic increase in the usage of *Zukunft* (future).

The numerical ratios in the *AHB* and the *SA* are entirely different. Here, the proportion of time terminology to the total number of time-indicating passages amounts to 12.3 percent or 14.8 percent. It is true that even here the frequency in the *SA*, which is composed primarily of more modern hymns, is higher, but it nevertheless lags significantly behind that of the German and Swedish hymnals. Compound time terminology is rare in the two English-language books. The *AHB* mentions *seed-time* once, and the *SA* speaks once of *dreamtime*. *Timeless* occurs twice in each of these two books. Moreover, in the *AHB*, *ageless* occurs twice, and *age-long* appears once. In the 624 hymns of the *AHB*, *time* occurs thirty-eight times, seven of which are in the plural. *Age* is mentioned a full forty-three times, and *future* appears nine times. In the *SA*, *time* appears twelve times, three in the plural. The terms *age* and *future* occur three times each. In all of the ninety-six or twenty-one passages that contain time terminology in the *AHB* and the *SA*, the use of *future* in the *SA* is, proportionally, at least four times as high as in the *AHB*. The most striking observation, however, is the difference in the use of the word *age*. While the usage ratio between *age* and *time* was still 1.1:1 in the *AHB*, it had changed to 1:4 in the *SA*. This represents a significant reduction in the usage of *age* in favor of *time*.

For the *EG*, I also studied how the occurrences of time terminology were distributed over the centuries. The passages containing time terminology come from 182 hymns. Of these, fifty-seven—that is, almost one-third—have texts from the twentieth century, which represents a comparably high proportion. Random sampling in different subject areas of the *EG* show a relatively small proportion of hymns from the twentieth century.[48] Thus, it is evident that the topic of time has become more prevalent in recent times, at least in the *EG*.[49] This trend is supported by the fact that *Ps90*, with its texts coming primarily from the second half of the twentieth century, exhibits the highest frequency of time terminology in all the material I have analyzed.

Eternity Terminology

Compared to time terminology, eternity terminology occurs much more frequently in the two German hymnbooks. In *EG*, eternity is mentioned 1.6 times more often than time. In *GL*, there are even two passages containing eternity terminology for every one passage containing time terminology.

In contrast to time terminology with its numerous compound expressions, eternity terminology is limited to only a few concepts. The area is covered well by the words *Ewigkeit(en)* (eternity, eternities) and *ewig(lich)* (eternal). Apart from these words, only the terms *der/das Ewge*[50] (the eternal) and *allewig*[51] (eternal) occur.

The adjectival, adverbial, and substantive uses of *ewig* (eternal) occur much more frequently than the use of *Ewigkeit* (eternity). In the *GL*, *ewig* (eternal) appears 1.6 times more often than *Ewigkeit* (eternity); in the *EG*, the corresponding figure is actually 2.1 times as high.[52] The plural usage of *eternity* occurs, but it is rare.[53]

The spectrum of everything that can be eternal is large. In *GL*, one finds *ewig* (eternal) as a description of divinity: *eternal God, Father, Son,* and *High Priest;* in divine predicates, such as *splendor, radiance, on high, wisdom, throne, power, realm;* as a description of that which emanates from God: *word, counsel, covenant, gospel, goodness, salvation, redemption, comfort, gleam* (of light); and finally, as a description of things that can be eternal from a human perspective: *death, suffering, darkness, imprisonment, time, paths, good, light, rest, bliss, life,* (divine) *joy, love, home, fatherland, stone, community, the eternal purity* (= Mary), and even *eternity* itself.[54]

With few exceptions, the terms mentioned above also occur in the *EG* in combination with *ewig* (eternal). Furthermore, the *EG* also speaks of other things that could be "eternal": truth, honor, favor, mouth, compassion, fount, foundation, treasures, faithfulness, need, pain, ransom, reconciliation, freedom, gratitude, joy, church, beauty, paradise, the Lord's Supper, nuptial bliss, Advent, and the present.

In contrast to *EG, Sv ps* is more economical in its references to eternity terminology. Its usage here is not significantly higher than that of time terminology, the ratio between the two being 1.14:1. From a total of 325 passages containing eternity terminology, 225 mention *evig* (eternal), three speak of *den evige* (the Eternal), and nine mention *evinnerligen* (everlasting). *Evighet* (eternity) appears eighty-eight times, mostly in the singular,[55] and occasionally in a genitive construction.[56] The range of what is considered to be eternal is diverse. The concepts that are most frequently considered eternal are *time*[57] and *life*,[58] as well as *light, well-being,* and *peace*.[59] *Rest, grace, joys, need,* and *death* are also presented several times as being eternal.[60] Furthermore, one encounters eternity in connection with statements about God: *Father, God, king, the Good, power and honor, glory, compassion, counsel, law, covenant, throne,* and *cross*.[61] The hymn of praise, the hallelujah, jubilation, joy, comfort, wealth, the fruit, and the Word can also be eternal.[62] Hope for the future is directed toward *eternal reconciliation, eternal paradise, eternal dwelling place, eternal joy, eternal joys of summer,* and *eternal banquet hall*.[63] Some time concepts are also immersed in the dimension of eternity: *now, day, morning, spring, New Year,* and *church year*.[64] *Service, goal, foundation,* and *harm* can also be eternal.[65] The Holy Spirit is actively creating with eternal breath.[66] An eternal sign of love[67] occurs at the Communion table.

Ps90 turns all previous proportions upside down. Here, one finds almost twice as much time terminology as eternity terminology; to be exact, the ratio of eternity terminology to time terminology is 0.55:1. Of the twenty-seven passages containing eternity terminology, fifteen contain *evig* (eternal) and eight contain *evighet* (eternity). Eternity formulations containing double usage of the noun *eternity* occur four times, all under the category *Psalms and Canticles*.[68] Eternal time is mentioned twice. The adjective "eternal" is used once each for God's day and God's love, for heaven, for the fount, and for spring.[69] Something can also be in eternal agreement with God's calendar.[70] When considering eternity terminology in the literal sense, *SA* is very similar to *Ps90*, since here one also finds almost twice as much time terminology as strictly literal eternity terminology. In this case, the exact ratio of eternity terminology to time terminology is 0.57:1. The picture changes radically, however, when one considers eternity terminology in a more general sense. Then the ratio becomes 1.67:1. In other words, this means that the major portion of eternity terminology in *SA* consists of *ever* and *evermore*. Twenty-three passages contain these two terms, while *eternal* and *everlasting* occur only eight or four times. The noun *eternity* does not appear at all. *Eternal life*[71] is mentioned three times. The divine name,[72] God's love, and the signs of this divine love[73] are also eternal. Finally, it is also said that the Son, the heavenly feast, and the goal are eternal.[74]

Of all the hymnbooks studied, the *AHB* incorporates the most terminology concerning eternity. Eternity terminology in the most literal sense of the word occurs in approximately the same ratio to time terminology as it docs in *GL*.

In the *AHB*, the ratio of time to eternity is 1:2. When eternity in a more general sense is included, it rapidly increases to 1:3.75. *Ever* and *evermore* occur 164 times.[75] In the case of literal eternity terminology, most of the 112 occurrences consist of *eternal*,[76] *co-eternal*,[77] *eternally*,[78] and *the Eternal*.[79] The remaining eighty-four incidences are distributed among *everlasting*,[80] *endless/unending*,[81] and *eternity*.[82] Here, the list of everything that can be "eternal" is also long and complex. The words *God, Father, Son, Spirit, Lord, The One or Three in One, Savior, King, Ruler*, in combination with *eternal,* are used as direct terms for God. A certain triumphalism cannot be ignored: eternal *decree, honors, strength, Head, arms, righteousness, splendor, glory, rock, throne, praise*, and *rays of resurrection*. Of course, one also mentions the eternal *word, name, light, life, peace, love, grace, mercy, rest, truth, loving kindness,* and *joy*. Some concepts of time can even be eternal, for example, *day, night, spring, years, ages*, and *Eastertide*. Furthermore, eternity can also appear as an attribute of *house and home, gates, doors*, and *gifts of Christ*.

The terms *hymn, merit, covenant, purpose, bread, fount of love, thought, theme, seat, woe, ransom*, and *things*, and things "in general," are also combined with "eternal."

	Time Terminology in % of All Passages Containing Time Indications	Eternity Terminology in % of All Passages Containing Time Indications	Ratio of Time Terminology to Eternity Terminology
EG	24.52	39.66	1:1.62
GL	23.39	49.74	1:2.13
Sv ps	25.27	28.81	1:1.14
Ps90	29.51	16.27	1:0.55
AHB[83]	12.28	25.58	1:2.04
		46.04	1:3.75
SA	14.79	8.45	1:0.57
		24.65	1:1.67

The above table offers an overview of the occurrences of time and eternity terminologies.

Everyday and Seasonal Terminologies

In the hymnals that were analyzed, the most frequently used terms for the remaining time indications are generally the same. They are the concepts of *Tag/dag/day, Nacht/natt/night, Morgen/morgon/morning, Abend/afton, kväll/evening, Jahr år/year, heute/i dag /today, Stunde/stund, timme/hour*.[84] As one might expect, everyday terminology is found quite often in hymns dealing with the New Year and with times of day. Christmas and Easter hymns also exhibit a high frequency of everyday terminology. In all of the books, *day* is by far the word used most often, and *night* is the second most frequently used expression. Both terms are used primarily in a qualitative manner, whereby *day* has an entirely positive meaning, while *night* quite often symbolizes everything that is negative. Throughout the centuries, one encounters many variations of *white day* and *black night*.[85] With few exceptions,[86] night is the place that is considered to be remote from God, whereas the light of day signals closeness to salvation.

In all of the hymnals, *morning* is also used more frequently than *evening*. With the exception of *Ps90*, *evening* is the least used term of all those listed here. The most striking numerical difference with respect to the use of the terms *morning* and *evening* is found in the Australian books; in these hymnals, *morning* occurs six or nine times more frequently than its antithesis. Except for the two Swedish books, *today* appears more often than *year*. On the other hand, in *Sv ps* and *Ps90*, *hour* is clearly over-represented in comparison to the other books.

The relatively frequent use of seasonal terminology[87] in the Swedish books is striking. The *EG* contains twenty-three hymns dealing with the topic of "nature and the seasons." Distributed over five of these hymns, the seasons are specified by name only eight times.[88] Seasonal terminology is even rarer in the other songs of the *EG* and in the *GL*. The terms *winter, spring*, and *summer* are mentioned a few times in the *AHB*.[89] The seasons appear approximately ten times more frequently in the *Sv ps*, with *vår* (spring) and *sommar* (summer) being used more than three times as often as *vinter* (winter) and *höst* (autumn). Both in this book and in *Ps90, höst* (autumn) is the season that is mentioned least.[90] *Ps90* exhibits the greatest concentration of seasonal terminology[91] of all of the hymnals; however, in this hymnal, *vinter* (winter) is the most frequently occurring term. It is mentioned as much as summer and spring combined.

In addition to the words already mentioned, everyday terminology is also illustrated by the following terms that appear less frequently: *täglich* (daily), *gestern* (yesterday), *morgen* (tomorrow, in the morning), *Mittag* (midday), *Sekunde* (second), *Minute* (minute), *Woche* (week), *Jahrhundert* (century), and *Jahrtausend* (millennium).

Everyday and seasonal terminologies are often combined with time terminology or eternity terminology.[92] Overall, those passages that contain everyday and seasonal terminologies in either pure or combined form are predominant in all of the books—except for the *GL,* in which eternity terminology, which makes up approximately half of all time indications, constitutes the largest portion. *Ps90* contains the largest proportion (90 percent) of pure and combined everyday terminology and seasonal terminology.

The following diagram illustrates the relation of time terminology to eternity terminology, as well as to everyday and seasonal terminologies, in the hymnals that were examined:

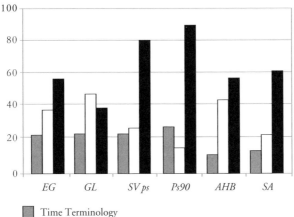

Time Terminology
Eternity Terminology (in the broad sense for *AHB* and *SA*)
Everyday and Seasonal Terminologies (in pure and combined forms)

Qualitative Analysis

"Die Zukunft ist sein Land"[93]—The History of
the Future as *Surrendering and Grasping*

Even if my quantitative analysis of the hymnals clearly indicated that explicit mention of the future is relatively rare, these passages nevertheless tell their own history of human expectation regarding the future. I propose to define this history with the words *surrendering* and *grasping*. In this context, *surrendering* means confidently entrusting the future to God. *Grasping*, on the other hand, involves the active attempt to ensure that, in the face of a threatening and threatened future, one can still believe that a livable future is possible. A classical example of *surrendering* is found in the following lines:

> Be still, my soul: your God will undertake
> to guide the future as he has the past.
> Your hope, your confidence let nothing shake,
> all now mysterious shall be clear at last.
> Be still, my soul: the tempests still obey
> his voice, who ruled them once on Galilee.[94]

The future is not at the disposal of human beings. One can possess the past, but, conversely, the future is the "great unknown."[95] In light of this, trusting surrender to a God who has been experienced as powerful in the past is recommended as the appropriate human response. It even appears that it would not be beneficial for human beings to concern themselves further with the future that is beyond their range of action. In any case, one can understand the devout desire in this way:

> Lead, kindly light . . . lead thou me on.
> Keep thou my feet; I do not ask to see
> the distant scene—one step enough for me.[96]

At any rate, the thought of a future that includes an imminent judgment can encourage moral improvement. In 1653, Paul Gerhardt provided such an exhortation:

> Richt unsre Herzen, dass wir ja nicht scherzen
> mit deinen Strafen, sondern fromm zu werden
> vor deiner Zukunft uns bemühn auf Erden.
> Lobet den Herren![97]

With this single use of the word *Zukunft* (future), Gerhardt is an exception among hymn writers from past centuries. Particularly in the German and Swedish hymnals, it is striking that *future* belongs almost exclusively to the vocabulary of modern hymns.[98] The majority of these were written after 1960.[99]

In the modern revision of a hymn written around the end of the seventeenth century, one can see how thoughts of the future begin to appear. In place of the more or less passively awaited and secured heavenly future, one increasingly finds the attempt to grasp an earthly future that is influenced by the heavenly future. One is no longer concerned merely with a future in the hereafter but, to a greater extent, with a future of the here and now. A comparison of the version of a stanza that was revised by Johan Olof Wallin in 1816 and the newly revised wording by Britt G. Hallqvist from 1983 illustrates this development:

> Herre, var de trognas styrka
> Och din smorde hjälp beskär.
> Fräls ditt folk och stöd din kyrka,
> Som ditt arv och eget är.
> Låt dem här i dig förnöjas
> Och till evig tid upphöjas.[100]

> Herre, var de trognas styrka,
> främja rätten i vårt land.
> Fräls ditt folk och stöd din kyrka,
> tag vår framtid i din hand.
> Giv oss glädje här i tiden,
> slut till sist oss in i friden.[101]

Instead of praying for "help for your Anointed One,"[102] one now prays for "furtherance of justice in our land." Instead of praying for "a church that is your inheritance and your property," one now prays, "take our future in your hand." What has happened? On the path from the seventeenth century to the most recent decades, the future has become a problem. It is no longer sufficient to see that the future is indeterminate, to call for an individually devout way of life in the face of a coming day of judgment, and, for the time being, to submit to God's faithful guidance. The future, though admittedly from God, is no longer something that simply happens to the human being on earth and in heaven. Human beings are included in the shaping—or at least they assist in the shaping—of either a life-affirming or a death-bringing future. Something must happen here and now, so that the future becomes possible at all. One must pray for the future. One needs assurance that the future is possible, since the question of the future has increasingly become a question of whether hope is possible at all.

Even if Nils Frykman could sing the following words in 1883 with relatively little concern:[103]

> Min framtidsdag är ljus och lång,
> den räcker bortom tidens tvång,
> där Gud och Lammet säll jag ser
> och ingen nöd skall vara mer,[104]

and look forward to heaven and see the struggle of earthly life as a time of testing, the situation had changed significantly for his colleagues nearly a century later :

> Ich steh vor dir mit leeren Händen, Herr; . . .
> mein Los ist Tod, hast du nicht andern Segen?
> Bist du der Gott, der Zukunft mir verheißt?
> Ich möchte glauben, komm mir doch entgegen.[105]

When the future is no longer taken for granted, one tries to assure oneself through prayer and to grasp it through faith. In the *GL*, one finds in the litanies prayers like: "Be our future"[106] and "for our children be you the future."[107] Thoughts about the future no longer lead directly to heavenly peace. The future increasingly becomes the partner of hope:

> Gottes Wort ist wie Licht in der Nacht;
> es hat Hoffnung und Zukunft gebracht; . . .[108]

In some passages, *future* even appears as a synonym for hope. One speaks of children in slums and in desolation, who are suffering and living without a future,[109] and of songs of praise that do not cease as long as eyes shine brightly with hope and faith in the future[110] and as long as children still dare to hope for a future land.[111]

The fear of the unknown future of a young child being baptized[112] refers not only to eternal salvation, but especially to the dangers and uncertainties of earthly life.[113] In this situation, the act of baptism becomes the inauguration of an assurance of the future in the midst of earthly life and beyond life on earth.[114] The future is grasped through faith and is believed to be permeated with God's Spirit. Only in this way can its threats and dangers be endured. Brian Wren may have had similar thoughts while writing these words:

> Christ is alive! No longer bound
> to distant years in Palestine,
> he comes to claim the here and now,
> and conquer every place and time.
>
> Christ is alive! His Spirit burns
> through this and every future age,
> till all creation lives and learns
> his joy, his justice, love, and praise.[115]

When hymns from the second half of the twentieth century speak of the future, then they generally do not distinguish between an earthly and a heavenly future. The heavenly future is not only seen side by side with earthly time, but God's future is envisioned as also already being realized in the present. Jonas Jonson writes that, in God's Spirit, heaven is present on earth. According to this hymn, one does not even need the anticipatory power of the sacrament in order to make the future of God perceivable by means of one's senses:

> Himmel på jorden, här får vi leva, . . .
> Öva er barn, att leva i Anden,
> våga idag smaka Guds framtid![116]

Apart from this, Jonson praises the Lord's Supper as precisely the place where, in the shared sacramental meal, one celebrates an anticipated taste of the future:

> . . . Vi reser ett tecken, rättvisans tecken, måltid delad med alla.
> Vi smakar den framtid de fattiga hoppas, tid då murar skall falla.[117]

In a third hymn by the same author, the Eucharist again appears as a sign of the future in the face of threatened hope:

> Kring detta bord församlas mänskligheten,
> med hoppet vänt mot honom som skall komma.
>
> Ett hotat hopp, som längtan håller uppe.
> En enda värld.
>
> I detta bröd är tecknet för vår framtid.
> Det delas ut och räcker åt oss alla. . . .
>
> På detta bord möts himmelen och jorden. . . .
> Befriat folk kan föregripa freden.
> En enda värld.[118]

Quite often, older hymns base their trust in the future on the experience of God's faithfulness in the past.[119] In more recent hymns, the direction of one's thought is less from the perspective of the past into the future than from the more or less distant future of God (back) toward our immediately imminent future. The following lines provide an example of such thinking:

> Vertraut den neuen Wegen,
> auf die uns Gott gesandt!
> Er selbst kommt uns entgegen.
> Die Zukunft ist sein Land.
> Wer aufbricht, der kann hoffen

in Zeit und Ewigkeit.
Die Tore stehen offen.
Das Land ist hell und weit.[120]

Thus, surrendering before the future has gradually given way to the effort to grasp it. In the process of grasping, people have been increasingly forced to experience the threat of the future. To the same extent that a person wishes to grasp the future, it eludes that person by moving into the realm of the threatened and the threatening. For this reason, the struggle to grasp the future increasingly became a struggle to seize on hope. During the 1990s, much thought was given to the unity of hope and the future. Svein Ellingsen's hymn on the topic of "responsibility for the earth" exemplifies this beautifully:

Ännu är hoppet en brinnande gnista . . .
Drömmen och hoppet slår rot i vårt hjärta . . .
Framtiden lever: En framtid för jorden!
Hopplöshet viker och dag följer natt.[121]

In another hymn, the hopeful grasping for the future of a healed world paradoxically leads back to the beginnings of time:

En gång i tidens morgon är jorden ny,
luften är renad och sjöbottnen synbar . . .[122]

It is unclear why the morning of time coincides here with the fulfillment of God's saving grace, which, in the world's view, is still to come. Nevertheless, there appears to be a blending of the past and the future in a vision of salvation.

"Heut schleußt er wieder auf die Tür"[123]
—Contemporizing the Past

Christmas and Easter hymns treat time in a particularly striking way. In these hymns, the past event of Christ's birth or resurrection is contemporized by an emphasis on "today."

"Uns zum Heil erkoren, ward er heut geboren, heute uns geboren"[124] (Elected to be our salvation, he was born today, born to us today)—this message in the refrain of a Christmas hymn from the mid-nineteenth century is echoed in numerous other hymns. Although many Christmas carols were written during the nineteenth century, the programmatic "today" is also found in hymns and carols of other epochs. "Heute geht aus seiner Kammer Gottes Held, der die Welt reißt aus allem Jammer"[125] (Today, God's hero, who saves the world from all misery, leaves his chamber) and "[h]eut schleußt er wieder auf die Tür zum schönen Paradeis [sic]"[126] (Today he reopens the gate to the beautiful Paradise). "Yea, Lord, we greet thee, born this happy morning"[127] is sung with great rejoicing in the English rendition of *Adeste fideles, laeti, triumphantes*, a hymn that was also translated into German and Swedish. The occasion for joy is described in a hymn from the previous century:

> . . . Jesus Christ is born today,
> ox and ass before him bow,
> and he is in the manger now;
> Christ is born today,
> Christ is born today.[128]

This carol shows that theological conclusions are drawn from the contemporization of the past—the heavenly door is now open, and the fear of death is no longer necessary.[129] But the question of whether the today of the birth has altered time in some basic way remains largely unanswered. Typically, stanzas two and three of this carol switch to the imperfect tense: "Christ was born for this . . . Christ was born to save."

Jochen Klepper treats time in a much more complex manner in his Christmas text from 1938.[130] This text also speaks of the *today* of the birth of Christ. This is evidenced in the "Du Kind" (you, child) in the salutation of the carol, as well as in the statement, "Du . . . liegst im armen Stall" (you . . . lie in a lowly manger). This *today* of the past birth, however, is different from that of today's Christmas joy, which is experienced when singing the carol. The two "todays" appear to lie on two different levels that are in tension with each other. The joyful reverberations and the joyful light of today's world are contrasted with the poverty and harshness of the manger. The reason for this tension is expressed in an interlocking of times. The death sentence that was still in the future at the time of Jesus's birth does indeed precede the birth of today.

> Die Welt ist heut voll Freudenhall.
> Du aber liegst im armen Stall.
> Dein Urteilsspruch ist längst gefällt,
> das Kreuz ist dir schon aufgestellt.
> Kyrieleison.[131]

> . . . Dein Elend wendet keiner ab.
> Vor deiner Krippe gähnt das Grab . . .[132]

Facing the manger is the grave. Within the framework of the "interlocking of time," particularly in the second stanza, the "before" can be understood not only as a location, but also in the sense of time. There is also a parallel interlocking of time between the manger and human sin. Viewed from the time of Christ's birth, the punishment that is a consequence of the sin of future human beings is already now being heaped upon the newly born child in the manger.

> . . . gedenken wir auch an dein Leid,
> das wir zu dieser späten Nacht
> durch unsre Schuld auf dich gebracht . . .[133]

> Die Welt ist heut an Liedern reich.
> Dich aber bettet keiner weich
> und singt dich ein zu lindem Schlaf.
> Wir häufen auf dich unsre Straf.
> Kyrieleison.[134]

Mary and Joseph, as well as the stars, the angels, and the shepherds that populate so many Christmas hymns, have been forced to make room for this double interlocking of time. It seems reasonable that the phrase "zu dieser heilgen Zeit" (at this holy time) of the first stanza is not only the rhyming partner of *Leid* (suffering), but is also the primary hermeneutic key to the understanding of time in this hymn. The quality of time as holy enables the interlocking of times. The sorrowful tension of this interlocking of time, which is expressed in the *Kyrie eleison*, is relieved only by the *some day* of a new simultaneity:

> Wenn wir mit dir einst auferstehn
> und dich von Angesichte sehn,
> dann erst ist ohne Bitterkeit
> das Herz uns zum Gesange weit.
> Hosianna.[135]

"Jesus Christ is risen today,"[136] "[h]eut triumphieret Gottes Sohn, der von dem Tod erstanden schon"[137] (today, the Son of God, who is already risen from the dead, is triumphant), "[d]etta är den stora dagen"[138] (this is the great day), "[d]enna dag stod Kristus opp"[139] (on this day Christ is arisen)—in the Easter hymns, it is not difficult to find formulations for contemporizing the past. Thus, just as one can sing of the *today* of the birth, the *today* of the resurrection is also celebrated. If there it was the holy night that brought salvation, then here it is the wonderful day that brings triumph.[140] If there one spoke of the opening of paradise, then here, it is "der Höllen Pfort"[141] (the gate to Hell) that is destroyed and the heavens that are opened.[142] At Christmas and, above all, at Easter, the motif from Ps. 118:24— "This is the day that the Lord has made"[143]—occurs in numerous hymns.

A few words should also be said regarding the contemporization of the Passion. Its actualization as a past event is classical;[144] however, its contemporization as a current event, illustrated in the following lines, is a more recent idea:

> . . . Today we see your Passion
> spread open to our gaze; . . .
>
> Wherever love is outraged,
> wherever hope is killed,
> where man still wrongs his brother man,
> your Passion is fulfilled . . .
>
> The groaning of creation . . .
> these are your cries of pain; . . .[145]

Even today, Christ is still being crucified:

> Even today
> we crucify still,
> and drive in the nails of apathy's will. . . .
>
> Living with us,
> he penetrates pain,
> our death he defeats
> and rises again.[146]

Here, one notices that the presence of the Passion changes the contemporization of the resurrection. The unique, triumphant resurrection does not occur in the now. What we can experience now is a kind of repeated resurrection, in the penetration of suffering and in the victory over our (!) own deaths.

There are also hymns that create a contemporizing effect by projecting the now into the past of the Passion. Robin Mann does this when he ends his depiction of the arrest and trial with the words: "We were in the crowd that day when our life began again."[147] The crucifixion is spoken of in a similar way: "I was the one who nailed your hands when our life began again."[148]

Sacraments as a Special Example of Contemporization

What role do the sacraments of *Baptism* and *Eucharist* play in the contemporization of the past? Initially, one notices that only a few baptismal and Communion hymns explicitly include aspects of time. We find only a meager basis for the notion that something happens to time in the celebration of the sacraments. Take the following ritual words of praise, for example:

> We praise you that this child now shares
> the freedom Christ can give,

> has died to sin with Christ, and now
> with Christ is raised to live.[149]

These words do not mean to imply that the *now* (the moment they are spoken) is simultaneous with the death and resurrection of Jesus, which were documented as a historically unique occurrence in the Gospels. Participation in this event is certainly occurring now, but the hymn does not reflect upon how the time between the *then* of that event and the *now* of the baptismal ceremony is bridged.

A baptismal hymn translated from English into Swedish suggests the notion that Baptism entails a universal simultaneity with the past:

> Med Noa, räddad ur sin ark
> från stormigt hav till vårlig mark,
> med Mose, lyft ur floden opp,
> vi firar fest med nyfött hopp.[150]

This stanza of a baptismal hymn originally in Norwegian is also similar:

> Över tidens gränser lever alltjämt
> dina löftesord vid dopets vatten.
> Dopets ljus förblir när livet slocknar.[151]

In this hymn, however, one is dealing with the future instead of the past. The sacramental event breaks through the boundary, toward the future, more than it moves backward, between present and past.

One also finds the same outlook in some of the Communion hymns. In the meal that is praised in song as a mystery, the bread that we break makes us one with Christ, the brother who died for us on Golgotha; the wine that we share unites us with God; the meal of the reign of Heaven gives us joy and hope for facing tomorrow, certain of the faithfulness of Christ, who once promised to return.[152] Here, one is not dealing with the simultaneity of a salvation experience in the past, but rather with the arrival of Christ/God in the present, in order to create the anticipation of a redemptive future. An even clearer orientation toward the future is found in the previously mentioned Communion hymn by Jonson.[153] It deals with the threatened hope of humanity, which, in the bread of the Lord's Supper, receives a sign of the future, by virtue of which the peace that is still to come can be realized.[154]

On the other hand, the notion of a universal simultaneity is suggested in the lines:

> Du som med livets bröd
> går genom tid och rum,

> giv oss för varje dag,
> Kristus det brödet.[155]

We find one of the rare, explicit examples of contemporizing the past in a Communion hymn in *Sv ps* 392. It speaks of an altar ready laid on which the bread rests, as Jesus himself once rested in Bethlehem:

> Här krubban är—jag faller ned, tillbeder . . .
> O, sakrament, som oss i nåd bereder
> att Gud, den evige, på jorden se.[156]

In conclusion, there is another clear but unique example of the sacramental power of the Lord's Supper that influences time:

> Inga avstånd mer, ej främlingskap,
> och tiden genomträngd av Guds "i dag,"
> med Abraham är du och jag kamrat.
> Gud är en av oss vid detta bord.[157]

Here, more than contemporization is at stake. Later, we will discuss this *more* as the permeation of time by something that is qualitatively different.

"bis ich dich nach dieser Zeit lob und lieb in Ewigkeit"[158] —Time and Eternity

"Nur ein Hauch trennt Zeit von Ewigkeit"[159]—in spite of, or perhaps precisely because of this proximity, the relationship of time to eternity is not entirely simple to describe. One cannot find dogmatically sound definitions of time and eternity and of the relationship of the two to each other in the hymns analyzed; and yet, both concepts are used in a variety of ways. Particularly in the German and Swedish hymns, the terms *time* and *eternity* occur in both singular and plural forms, but the plural of *eternity* occurs much less frequently. In the Swedish hymnbook, it is largely limited to Psalms,[160] while in the *EG*, it occurs only for the purpose of rhyming.[161] Factors such as tune and rhyme will often have influenced the selection of singular and plural more than theological reflection. Furthermore, the meaning appears to become more blurred in the plural forms. Thus, at least in the translations of the *Te Deum* from the fourth century, one can find an example in which, in the same hymn, the meaning of *always* is conveyed once in the same passage with "zu allen Zeiten" (for all times) and, another time, with "durch alle Ewigkeiten" (through all eternities).[162] In the singular, however, the difference in meaning between time and eternity is guaranteed. As I will show, eternity is interpreted as endless time, as well as something qualitatively different from time, in the sense of timelessness.[163]

In expressions such as "at all times," the plural of time has the meaning of "always" in all three languages. Furthermore, "times" characterizes the change and the succession of different periods, such as old, difficult, stormy, changing, and new times. Particularly in German, the plural often appears, even at this point, to be a result of the requirements of rhyme. In Swedish, one likes to speak of eternal time and also of eternal times,[164] which corresponds to the occasional use of "eternal ages"[165] in the *AHB*.[166] "New times" can have a time-immanent as well as a time-transcendent meaning, that is, either they are new periods within time, or they signal a complete transition into eternity.[167]

If time is placed in relation to eternity, it often occurs according to a clear pattern. Time does not necessarily have a negative character, but its temporary nature is seen more or less as a comfortable prelude to heavenly peace and songs of praise.[168] This time-eternity perspective based on the pattern "here the (preparation) time—there the peace" has a long tradition in classical hymns. It is based upon a distinction between time and eternity that is not always strictly expressed in the terminology, but which can be verified by the comparison of the characteristics of time and eternity. Time is short and fraught with difficulty; eternity means peace.[169] In time, one is encouraged to "watch, pray, and fight,"[170] while in eternity, one speaks of coming home, of songs of praise, of restfulness and peace.[171] While time can signify torment, eternity is comfort.[172] In eternity, no one ages; and, indeed, there is simultaneity with God.[173] Darkness, coverings, and veils belong to time, whereas clarity is the mark of eternity.[174] In short, time corresponds to night;[175] eternity symbolizes morning, day, and summer.[176]

However, I do not wish to give the impression that time has been described in a purely unfavorable manner. The classical hymns certainly know how to distinguish between good and splendid times on the one hand, and evil and bad times on the other; but, due to their preliminary nature, both are defined by eternity, and each, in its own way, is at its service.[177] The bad times, on the one hand, strengthen eternity's dimensions of comfort and hope: The more wretched one's time is in the vale of tears, the brighter the brilliant glow of eternity.[178] Good times, on the other hand, vastly increase the expectations for eternity: If it is so lovely now, just imagine what it will be like then![179]

A feature common to many hymns, particularly older ones, is therefore the primacy of eternity. The quality of time is not defined in reference to itself, but rather by its subordination to eternity.

> Ein Tag, der sagt dem andern,
> mein Leben sei ein Wandern
> zur großen Ewigkeit.

> O Ewigkeit, so schöne,
> mein Herz an dich gewöhne,
> mein Heim ist nicht in dieser Zeit.[180]

This stanza by Tersteegen—like the quote from Gerhardt in the title of this section—expresses something that can also be found in other hymns. The eternal home awaits the pilgrim who has dwelt on earth like a stranger from a better land.[181]

This alternative relatedness of time and eternity under the primacy of eternity is expressed in three different types of relations. First, one finds the relation of a successive movement of time to eternity with the more or less clearly expressed desire for time to make room for the dawning of eternity.[182] Second, one can also observe an interaction of time and eternity, which, in turn, is realized in two different directions. At times, this interaction travels from time in the direction of eternity; at other times, it moves from eternity toward time. In the first case, time exhibits tendencies to merge into eternity. Something happens that, either by blocking or transforming, brings time to an end.

> För domsbasunens gälla ljud
> skall rummets murar falla.
> All tid skall bli ett enda nu,
> ty tidens ur skall stanna . . .[183]

The interaction in the other direction causes an event that allows time to progress, but enriches it with eternity.

> In die Wirrnis dieser Zeit
> fahre, Strahl der Ewigkeit;
> zeig den Kämpfern Platz und Pfad
> und das Ziel der Gottesstadt.[184]

This entrance of eternity into time is also described in less warlike metaphorical language. At times, such talk is linked to the Incarnation,[185] and, at other times, to the Resurrection[186] of Christ. Love is described as eternal life amidst all of the change here on earth.[187] This means that the filling of time with eternity can occur constantly without a connection to specific key events.[188] This type of interaction leads to an adjustment of the perspective of life in time and to an assurance of the goal and meaning of temporal life.

In the third type of relation between time and eternity, one encompasses the other. Eternity surrounds time,[189] which, like an island, lies in the sea of eternity or, conversely, as an inland sea is surrounded by the shores of eternity.[190] Time is born of eternity and returns to it:

Du Schöpfer aller Wesen,
du Lenker aller Zeit,
die Woche, die gewesen,
kehrt heim zur Ewigkeit.[191]

As noted earlier, in the two books that contain primarily more recent hymns, there is a noticeable lack of interest in eternity. In the *SA*, the theme of eternity hardly appears at all.[192] Instead, the here and now is more important. If, in the past, earthly life was subordinated to otherworldly eternity, eternity is now categorized as being in this world.[193] Whereas the unrest of the times was previously contrasted to the peacefulness of eternity, now we are dealing with peace in a time that is running out:

Jesus, hjälp oss finna tid . . .
I vår brådska skapa frid . . .[194]

The emphasis is on "hope for today."[195] Hymns that deal with suffering are not content to wait for eternity; instead, they seek hope and assurance in the present.[196] The heavenly feast is less the goal in itself than the model for shaping the present-day world:

In praise of God meet duty and delight,
angels and creatures, men and spirits blest:
in praise is earth transfigured by the sound
and sight of heaven's everlasting feast.[197]

The experience of being part of a threatened creation has contributed to an enhanced importance of this-worldliness. Eternal salvation can no longer be thought of exclusively as the eternal life of Christians who have died. In order for it to be salvation, it must also include the liberation of a frightened creation. Hope is not oriented toward otherworldly eternity, but rather toward an eighth day of creation, a flourishing future for the earth.[198] Thus, one achieves a kind of reconciliation of differences in the concepts *eternity* and *time*. Eternity enjoys an increasing level of immanence; it is increasingly at the service of time, in order to improve or ennoble it:

Minns att var sekund
är en liten stund
av evigheten hos Gud,
och när dagen lång
du hör fåglars sång,
hör du himmelens egna ljud. . . .
. . . minns att rätt och frid
i vår egen tid
ska få spegla Guds kärleks lag.
Så lev Guds nu. . . .[199]

The passages cited here do not provide a definitive verdict on the question of whether they represent an expression of the trivialization of the relationship between time and eternity or a carefully considered theological position. However, this stanza is not an isolated case. In a hymn of springtime, for example, it says that we small creatures stand before greatness and humbly see eternity in all things.[200]

Time appears to swell, and even to absorb eternity into itself. The sovereign privilege of interpreting life in time is something that has apparently been lost from eternity. One might even question whether a reversal in correlations has taken place. If, in the past, eternity was the authority to which time had to answer, then now, eternity is forced to give an account, before the forum of time, of what it is capable of performing.

From this perspective, the words *bis ich dich nach dieser Zeit lieb und lob in Ewigkeit* (until, after this time, I will love and praise you in eternity) by Paul Gerhardt appear to belong to a completely different world. An eternity seems to lie between his view of the world and the enthusiasm of Jonas Jonson:

> Himmel på jorden, här får vi leva,
> älska och ge, burna av glädje . . .
> Öva er barn, att leva i Anden,
> himlen är här, evig i tiden![201]

Here, there is little to remind us of the endless, qualitative difference between eternity and time for which dialectical theology had once argued.[202] It remains to be asked: What was and is the function of the rhetoric regarding eternity? And how does God relate to time and eternity?

"ihm gehört der Raum, die Zeit, sein ist auch die Ewigkeit"[203]—Space, Time, and Eternity

Before turning to the question of the relationship of God to time, I will look at the relationships between space, time, and eternity. First, one notices that the combination of time and space occurs almost exclusively in hymns of the twentieth century.[204] It does not occur at all in *GL. Ps90* speaks repeatedly of space and frequently of time, but it does not combine the two concepts.[205]

In Swedish, there are two terms for space, namely, *rum*, which means *space* and *room*, and, *rymd*, which refers to *space* and *outer space*. This corresponds more or less to the use of *place* and *space* in the two English-language books. *Rymd* is used primarily in hymns that were either written between 1960 and 1984 or revised during the same period to include the word *rymd*.[206] What was originally only an earthly and inner-temporal perspective is expanded by such a revision into a cosmic perspective.[207] Surprisingly, this expansion appears to have been revoked in *Ps90*. Instead of using the cosmological perspective, here we see a focus on the interior world of the individual.[208]

Otherwise, the intensification of space travel during that period has surely also contributed to the shift of perspective in the direction of the cosmic. The following lines are based on the hymn "Great God, Our Source and Lord of Space," which was finished by the American George Utech during the year when the first human being landed on the moon:

> Gott, unser Ursprung, Herr des Raums,
> du schufst aus unbegrenzter Macht
> den Stoff, darin sich Feuer regt.
> Du hast der Sterne Glut entfacht . . .
>
> Du selbst bist Flamme, Gott, du bist
> die Liebe, die in Christus brennt.
> Sie wacht, wenn der Gedanken Lauf
> das All durchmißt, das Element.
> Führ uns an atomarer Nacht
> vorüber, hilf der Hoffnung auf.[209]

The content is related to a hymn in the *AHB:*

> God, who stretched the spangled heavens,
> infinite in time and place,
> flung the suns in burning radiance
> through the silent fields of space,
> we thy children, in thy likeness,
> share inventive powers with thee:
> great Creator, still creating,
> teach us what we yet may be.
>
> We have conquered worlds undreamed of
> since the childhood of our race,
> known the ecstasy of winging
> through uncharted realms of space,
> probed the secrets of the atom,
> yielding unimagined power,
> facing us with life's destruction
> or our most triumphant hour.[210]

Our entrance into the atomic and space ages opened up new aspects of theology and anthropology. Thus, when one speaks in numerous doxological contexts of the "Lord of space and time," rather than of the "Lord in eternity," this may well be due to the topicality of (outer) space:

> Father, Lord of all creation,
> ground of Being, Life and Love;
> . . . yours is every hour's existence,
> sovereign Lord of time and space.[211]

One finds the doxological function of space and time in both christological and Trinitarian contexts.[212] Of the Son, it says:

> Creation sings a new song to the Lord,
> the universal energies rejoice,
> through all the magnitudes of space and time
> creatures proclaim the grandeur of Christ.[213]

If the mention of "space and time" here serves to replace traditional eternity terminology, then we encounter the expression "place and time" in Brian Wren in the opposite context. In the hymn "Christ Is Alive," the risen Christ, who comes here from the distant past in Palestine and triumphs over every place and time, claims the here and now. He is not enthroned in the distant heavens, but is rather present in the midst of daily life, in order, in his Spirit, to realize his joy, justice, and love throughout this and all future ages[214]—a kind of immanent Christology from the past.

Jerusalem is the city that stands high above space and time, with joys beyond measure and transcendent peace, as is recounted in the Swedish rendition of Pierre Abélard's hymn, "O quanta, qualia sunt illa sabbata."[215] A look at the Latin text[216] shows that the sublimity over space and time does not have a direct correlation here. Instead, we are dealing with an interpretation set against the horizon of a modern worldview, just as is found in Olov Hartman's revised version of *Dies irae,* the Day of Wrath, where there is neither time nor space.[217] In Hartman's version, the universe and the sea tremble, the walls of space fall, the clocks of time stop, and time becomes a single now.[218] The thirteenth-century Latin text, which can probably be traced back to Thomas von Celano, knows nothing of this.[219]

Hartman is not entirely consistent, however, with regard to the end of time. In a text from 1979, he makes God the one who, in death, recreates life for ages and worlds to come.[220] How these new ages and worlds will react on the day of the big collapse of space and time is a question that must remain open here. It may be that Hartman, who died in 1982, did not have enough time to think through, and poetically express, the theme of "(outer) space and time," a topic that he frequently mentioned, though it was so new. His basic intent, however, was clearly expressed in his creed from 1970:

> Vi tror att Gud är mer än världen och rymd och tid,
> den förste och den siste av allt som finns.
> När världen störtar samman är han vårt liv.[221]

In summary, one can say that, as existential conditions of the world, space, and time occur more frequently in more recent texts, where they occasionally replace eternity terminology; that God has a different relationship to space and time than God has to human beings; and that, at some point, something highly dramatic will happen to space and time. Apart from this, one cannot say anything more precise. Hoping for greater clarity, let us therefore now ask about the relationship of time to God, who, in the words of Rudolf Alexander Schröder, ". . . prepares the world according to an inscrutable plan . . . who behind time and measures, which awe the mind, prepares the beautiful streets . . . that lead to the eternal present, where perfect clarity is revealed to all . . ."[222]

"Der du die Zeit in Händen hast"[223]—God and Time

Is God beyond time and not influenced by it? If so, then is God's timelessness a flaw? Can God be God without time? Or conversely, can a God having time be God at all? Does God's divinity not presuppose a transcendence of temporality? Is God's eternity an endless temporality or a timelessness? Hardly any passages can be found in which God's relationship to time and eternity is actually a topic. As already previously observed, the hymns do not deal with a carefully considered dogmatic statement, but rather with the formulation and processing of faith and life experiences. There is basically no doubt that the eternal God is related to earthly reality. As the eternal Father, God is also the Lord and Ruler of creation[224] and the one who structures time.[225] The acting presence of an eternal God in the temporal world per se is not seen as a logical problem.

Even if the hymns themselves do not actually deal with timelessness versus God's temporality as a theological question, there are nevertheless two types of narration, namely, one that moves eternity and God's unchangeability into the foreground and one that presupposes the experience of time and looks at God's existence and actions in time. Let us first turn to the former, the foundation of which Gerhardt described as follows:

> Die Morgenröte war noch nicht mit ihrem Licht vorhanden;
> und siehe, da war schon das Licht, das ewig leucht, erstanden.
> Die Sonne war noch nicht erwacht,
> da wachte und ging auf voll Macht
> die unerschaffne Sonne.[226]

"As you were before all time began, so you will remain in eternity."[227] This interpretive translation of the *te aeternum Patrem* in the *Te deum* stresses the unchanging nature of God, which nevertheless does not prevent God from guiding God's people through this age, so that they can be admitted into eternity.[228] That God, as Wallin said, has placed God's throne high above time, emphasizes that God's being is unalterable, unchangeable, and unending.[229] The same God, however, arranges a coming and going in earthly reality, as well as a succession of different ages, and God's grace is new each and every morning.[230] The thought that the daily newness of grace actually presupposes a discontinuous relationship with what has gone on before—which in turn must stand in a certain contradiction to God's unchanging nature—does not bother Wallin. His explanation in the final stanza of the hymn says merely:

> . . . han alltid allt allen förmår . . .[231]

That God's throne was established from the beginning of time and that God has existed since all eternity has remarkable consequences for the world. A free rendering of Psalm 93 says: "Before him, the world stands unchangeable, since it is held in his hand."[232] It is not necessary for God to intervene in order to silence the powers that fill all living things with mortal fear—a mere glance at the highly elevated Lord makes them sink into oblivion.[233] In the power of divine majesty from all eternity, God guarantees steadfastness and the continuation of world order, as well as the constancy of the divine Word.[234] All of science cannot shake God's majesty, because "science's remotest probe feels but the fringes of your robe."[235]

A significant part of this train of thought is the often-asserted foreknowledge attributed to God. The God who existed before time and who "beyond all changes [is] still the same,"[236] who thought "mit Erbarmen schon an mich von Ewigkeit" (of me with compassion from time immemorial);[237] even before our birth, God knew our names;[238] and God sees the worlds of which we as yet know nothing.[239] "God everlasting through eternity,"[240] "the First, the Last, beyond all thought his timeless years"[241]—formulations of the eternal sovereignty of God can be found in great variation. The Trinity is also included here:

> Laud and honour to . . .
> ever Three and ever One,
> consubstantial, co-eternal,
> while unending ages run.[242]

If, on the one hand, God's foreknowledge precedes human life, then, on the other hand, communion with God beyond time and space is enticing:

> Där får till sist vi svar på alla frågor,
> vi blickar in i Guds mysterium,
> och efter ensamhet och död vi lever
> i hans gemenskap bortom tid och rum.[243]

This waiting for consummation beyond time, however, expresses a tension between the *already now* and the *not-yet*. As a God who is hidden in the divine unattainable eternity, God is nevertheless present in time, something that is seen most clearly in the sacrament of the Eucharist. Here, as previously shown, not only is the past contemporized, but the wall between time and eternity is also momentarily penetrated. Thus, as it says in a Sanctus hymn from 1965: "Preis ihm, der kommt in unsre Zeit" (Praise him who comes into our time).[244] The grace of the sacrament enables human beings to see the eternal God on earth.[245] "Er [Gott] nimmt sich für uns Zeit" (He [God] devotes time to us).[246] It is true that the day of God is yet to come, but because God's eternity is already present in the hidden form of God's reign, "like water below the ground and like wind in the treetops,"[247] human beings can prepare for the long-awaited arrival of that day through their actions.[248] Therein lies a dimension of hope,[249] which distinguishes itself from the passive longing for eternity found in many of the older hymns in that it leads to a loving involvement in the created world.[250]

These thoughts about the hidden presence of eternity in time form a bridge to the second way of narrating, namely, the one that addresses God's being and actions in time from the perspective of the experience of time. Its basic motif is expressed in the words of Klepper:

> Der du die Zeit in Händen hast, Herr, . . .
> Der Mensch, sein Tag, sein Werk vergeht:
> nur du allein wirst bleiben.
> Nur Gottes Jahr währt für und für,
> drum kehre jeden Tag zu dir, . . .
> Der du allein der Ewge heißt
> und Anfang, Ziel und Mitte weißt
> im Fluge unsrer Zeiten:
> bleib du uns gnädig zugewandt . . .[251]

The Eternal has a relation to time that, on the one hand, is directed toward the orientation of time to eternity (*kehre jeden Tag zu dir* [turn toward you every day]), and, on the other hand, also describes the turning toward human beings in time (*bleib du uns gnädig zugewandt* [continue to be merciful to us]). The latter becomes even clearer in another hymn by Klepper:

> Aus seinem Glanz und Lichte
> tritt er in deine Nacht:
> Und alles wird zunichte,
> was dir so bange macht.[251]

Whenever the eternity of God and temporality collide, something happens: The future is opened up,[253] God is eternal and present,[254] God the Father creates an internal eternity, God the Son opens up an eternity from the inside, and God the Spirit breathes into eternity and opens up an inner space.[255] Especially modern hymn writers are eager to communicate the experience that God "[ist] aus seiner Höhe unter uns erschienen, daß er sei nahe jeder Zeit und Zone, hier aber wohne" (appeared among us from on high, to be close to all times and places, yet to reside here).[256] As on pp. 37–41, one also sees here an attempt to make eternity inherently accessible. God is not merely God because God is eternal; rather, God is the God who will come in time,[257] who will take time for us,[258] and who has time.[259] God is no longer only the God beyond time, who cannot be affected by time's consuming powers. God is rather the God who voluntarily enters into time and who has enough time to show human beings, who are tormented by time, new perspectives of eternity.

> Alla har brått, ingen har tid . . .
> Gud har ju tid.
> Evighet, ja,
> tid till att lyssna stilla . . .[260]

God even seeks God's own image in human beings; when the time has come, God will shower blessings upon those who have remained faithful in their doubts and despair.[261]

Whoever has followed these two directions in the narratives about God and time has also been able to experience a historical development. The God who reigns on high, far above time and space, in a place that is also called the eternal home;[262] the god who holds time in the divine hand has, over the course of time, become more present in time. God's eternity is not questioned in any way, but the dynamics in creation and time become more the center of attention for hymn writers than the continued existence of the eternal rules. As a result, the metaphor of the dance surfaces:

> Called now at all times to wait on the Father,
> follow his lead as he partners our dance;
> brolga bird dances, retreats and, returning,
> bowing at last to his partner, the Lord.[263]

"Das Wort geht von dem Vater aus und bleibt doch ewiglich zu Haus . . ."[264]—Christ and Time

Apart from *Ps90* and *SA*, references to the preexistence of Jesus are found in all of the hymnals. The formulation "du gingst vor aller Zeiten Lauf in unerschaffner Klarheit auf" (You appeared before the beginning of time in uncreated clarity)[265] is rather unusual, however, because the existence of Jesus Christ before time is generally seen in relation to the parenthood of God, e.g., "Jesus Christus, du ewiges Wort, aus dem Vater geboren vor aller Zeit" (Jesus Christ, you eternal word, born of the father before all time),[266] "wir glauben Christum, Gottes Sohn, aus Gott geboren vor der Zeit" (we believe in Christ, the Son of God, born of God before time began),[267] and "vom Vater her vor allen Zeiten" (coming from the Father before time began).[268] "Bevor das Licht geworden ist, hat dich der höchste Vater schon gezeugt als wesensgleichen Sohn" (Before there was light, the most divine Father had already begotten you as Son identical in nature),[269] which is why

> [e]ine Jungfrau den gebar,
> der ihr eigner Schöpfer war,
> Gott vor allen Zeiten.
> Und das Kindlein, das sie stillt,
> hat mit seinem Glanz erfüllt
> alle Ewigkeiten.[270]

Jesus is the name of salvation, "which for many a generation hid in God's foreknowledge lay."[271] He is the "eternal" or "co-eternal Son."[272] At this point, the text is not always clear whether the eternity of the Son is an eternity directed toward the future, which could very well signify a beginning in time,[273] or whether it is an eternity before and after all time. However, *GL* provides an unmistakable message when it says in the translation of the expression *Tu Patris Sempiternus es Filius:* "Du bist des Vaters allewiger Sohn" (You are the Father's all-eternal son).[274] Other passages also appear to presume the eternal nature of the Son. Thus, one speaks of the eternal Son, before the worlds began,[275] of our King before creation, of the Lord of history,[276] and of "the Lord of years, the Potentate of time, Creator of the rolling spheres."[277] Nevertheless, the preexistence of Jesus is oriented toward his coming in this age:

> When at length the appointed fullness
> of the sacred time was come,
> he was sent, the world's Creator,
> from the Father's heavenly home
> and was found in human fashion,
> offspring of the Virgin's womb.[278]

We may suppose that Jesus Christ's coming in this age also has significance for the structure of time, but there is not a consensual opinion about this. Thus, on the one hand, one hymn says, "im Zenit der Zeiten kam sein Sohn zur Welt" (At the zenith of time, his Son was born);[279] and another, Jesus was "für uns ein Mensch geboren im letzten Teil der Zeit" (born as a human being for us during the last period of time),[280] and his coming signifies the fullness of heavenly time.[281] Furthermore, the hymn tradition also says that the day began with his birth,[282] and that the manger is associated with the time of creation.[283] There may be uncertainty about where to place the Incarnation event within the earthly progression of time, but, in any event, it is indisputable that the coming of Jesus brings something dramatically new into time:

> Christus ist erschienen.
> Seht, die Zeit des Heils begann . . .[284]

The earthly time of Jesus has affected human time:

> Vad ingen sett, vad ingen hört,
> det har Han in i tiden fört.[285]

It sanctifies human life into days of grace, and it makes all time the time of Christ.[286] Above all, modern hymns know how to report on a continuous coming of Jesus into time. Again and again, he enters time in order to travel through the world.

> Der durch die Welt geht und die Zeit,
> ruft nicht, wie man beim Jahrmarkt schreit.
> Er spricht das Herz an, heute . . .[287]

> Damit aus Fremden Freunde werden,
> kommst du als Mensch in unsre Zeit . . .
> . . . gehst du als Bruder durch das Land . . .[288]

Wherever God's Spirit wafts through the world, "[d]a schreitet Christus durch die Zeit in seiner Kirche Pilgerkleid" (There Christ strides through time in the pilgrim's dress of his church).[289] Yet, for the sake of contemporizing the past, one can also sing of the coming of Christ in human form as an event that will take place in the future:

> God in time, God in man,
> this is God's timeless plan:
> he will come, as a man,
> born himself of woman,
> God divinely human.[290]

To what extent the coming of Jesus in time could or must entail the renunciation of his eternity does not appear to be a frequent question in the lyrical composition of Church hymns. To be sure, the Son of God comes from a place of eternal joy, leaving his crystal throne, in order to begin his earthly life on straw in a stable.[291] But does this becoming human also mean that he has exchanged his eternity for the state of temporality? What does *kenosis* mean in this case? At least Johan Åström and Britt G. Hallqvist appear to plead for the idea that Jesus' relationship to God's eternal time was not cancelled by his coming in human form; his humble birth does not put an end to his eternal nature—it merely conceals his majesty.[292]

In addition to statements regarding the preexistence of Christ and Christ in time, all the hymnals I have examined also contain formulations referring to the future coming of Jesus. The Christ of the future is no longer primarily the Son of the Father, but rather the coming Lord who will end time:[293]

> He is coming like the glory of the morning on the wave; . . .
> so the world shall be his foot-stool, and the soul of time his slave:
> our God is marching on.[294]

The day of the Second Coming is the Day of Judgment and, from an inner-worldly and inner-temporal perspective, it is the day on which eternity definitively arrives.[295] Statements are made about this day that cannot easily be reconciled with each other. On the one hand, the day is predetermined,[296] but, on the other hand, its arrival can also be hastened by prayer and faith.[297] Furthermore, it is the continually approaching day. The Judge stands at the door; he is already among us; nevertheless, no one can know when the day will arrive.[298]

The returning Lord will come unexpectedly some day, but he also allows himself, even now, to be discovered within the world:

> Look not for his presence in heaven's dark space:
> by the light of our living on earth we'll discover his face.
> The face of the master is always at hand . . .
> —in the face of a man.[299]

People raised from the dead will finally see Jesus Christ as the last and the first.[300]

Numerous passages address the topic of a "post-worldly Christ." This Christ is the King of the Universe, the King of all times,[301] and the victor over death and time.[302] But here, once again, irreconcilable statements are found. Thus, the risen Christ lives beyond the borders of time,[303] but he also lives today,[304] in time, and even a normal day can be a day of Jesus.[305] He is the one who has risen from the dead and, at the same time, the one who can never die.[306] He is always new and yet unchangeable.[307] He comes every year and every day, though he was never gone.[308] He lives and walks in our midst,[309] and yet he lives in heaven and sits at the right hand of God.[310] The primary concern of the hymns with regard to this topic is and remains above all the assurance of the redemptive proximity of the living Christ. An oft-cited hymn by Wren provides a good example of this:

> Not throned above, remotely high,
> untouched, unmoved by human pains,
> but daily, in the midst of life,
> our Saviour with the Father reigns.[311]

Christ is the bright day whose brilliance penetrates the dark night.[312] Wherever he goes, eternal spring blossoms,[313] or at least the hope of spring for the wilderness.[314] His resurrection allowed the sun of righteousness to rise over time and eternity.[315] He is the fulfilment of the past and the promise of what is to come.[316] The limbs of his mystical body live in the presence of a then and a now:

> Once were seen the blood and water:
> now he seems but bread and wine.
> Then in human form he suffered,
> now his form is but a sign.[317]

Here an increasingly intense meshing of the post-worldly reality and eternity of Jesus Christ with the earthly dimensions is taking place. So it is no wonder that again in this context—as was previously the case with notions of God—the metaphor of the dance appears. Not only during the celebration of Jesus' birth are midwives, carpenters, tax assessors, police, and scientists asked to dance,[318] but also, according to Matthew 25, when the stranger seeks refuge for the night, "there'll be a homecoming, with dancing and singing within."[319] For the Lord of the Dance says:

> I danced in the morning when the world was begun . . .
> and I danced on the earth . . .
> They buried my body and they thought I'd gone;
> but I am the dance and I still go on . . .
> I am the Lord of the Dance, said he:
> Dance then, wherever you may be;
> I am the Lord of the Dance, said he;
> and I'll lead you all wherever you may be;
> and I'll lead you all in the dance, said he.[320]

"Höchster Tröster in der Zeit"[321]—Spirit and Time

The Spirit is discussed only rarely in connection with time and eternity. Nevertheless, one can determine four different time-eternity relations of the Spirit. First, according to Gen. 1.2b, there are allusions to the presence of the Spirit at the time of creation. Second, the eternal communion with the Father and the Son is mentioned. The presence of the Spirit in time is the Spirit's third task, which is followed, fourth, by the Spirit's work on the Day of Judgment.

At the beginning of time, God's Spirit lay over the night of chaos.[322] The Spirit's presence at that time is the reason and the occasion for also requesting its work in the present. The Spirit is eternal and powerful,[323] it emanates eternally from the Father and the Son,[324] and it is one in an eternal bond of love with the Father and the Son.[325] In time, the Spirit acts to cleanse, to heal, and to give life.[326] It provides comfort,[327] brings near that which is becoming, that which is, and that which was;[328] and it connects times and human beings in a never-ending fellowship.[329] At last, the Spirit's works are directed toward eternity in the distant future: The Spirit awakens on the Day of Judgment[330] and helps us to inherit "des ewgen Lebens Haus" (the house of eternal life).[331]

"sie eilt dahin, wir halten nichts in Händen"[332]
—Human Beings and Time

The basic human experience of time is its flowing away. In all three languages, the image of the stream occurs.

. . . Wie ein Strom beginnt zu rinnen
und mit Laufen nicht hält innen,
so fährt unsre Zeit von hinnen.[333]

Transitoriness is the basic theme of human existence, for: "Hin geht die Zeit, her kommt der Tod" (Time flows away, and death approaches);[334] and the human day in time is but a fleeting dream.[335] This experience causes a trace of resignation to resonate in some of the hymns; it even elicits terror.[336] Faith processes the experience of life as an existence predetermined to die in three ways. It finds security in that which is constant within the changes of time, it longs for time to be superseded by eternity,[337] or it approaches the ethical challenges of this age in the conscious realization that all time is always God's time.[338] In addition to Godself, the Church can also be constant.[339] The longing for eternity is primarily a solution provided by older hymns, whereas twentieth-century hymns instead tend to draw ethical conclusions.

One of the main problems of time for the modern person is the lack of time. A contemporary who feels hurried and stressed asks for time for the essentials of life.[340] For his or her ancestors, the big problem was, primarily, evil, dangerous, aimless, and faithless times. They did not ask for more time, but rather for shorter times of testing, protection from epidemics, and from periods with high costs of living.[341] For this reason, devout submissiveness is depicted as the ideal image of previous ages; one submits to the fate of the times and entrusts time to God.[342]

Hymns of various periods tell of the change from bad to good times.

Time becomes good because the day of salvation, the time of grace, dawns brightly in the heart of the believer.[343] Goodness does not appear to be a characteristic of time per se; rather, it is something that time is granted through divine promise and divine action.[344] Only divine activity can qualify time as truly good time. The flowing away, that is, time's transitoriness, which is basically experienced as negative, appears, on the other hand, to belong to the essence of time itself. What human beings experience as the destructive power of time is thus made relative—from the human perspective—by the subsequent qualification of time as a time of grace. This qualification accomplished by the saving acts of God in Christ also finds a partner in a preexistent qualification of time by divine foreknowledge:

> Lang, ehe wir geboren,
> hast du uns angesehn!
> "Sie sinds, die vor den Toren
> des Lebens wartend stehn.
> Gebt ihnen Raum . . ."[345]

Divine, loving foreknowledge lends time a connection to eternity, so to speak, from the very beginning, and thus creates trust in the beings who are subject to all the destructive powers of transitoriness. On this basis, on the one hand, hope for an increasingly better understanding of divine truth is possible;[346] and, on the other hand, an ethically responsible management of time is provided. It is necessary to be watchful,[347] to make use of the brief time that one has,[348] and to use it properly,[349] as well as to heed the "signs of the times."[350] Those who are rushed and pressed should take time to stop[351] and live in God's now.[352] Daily life should be a liturgy that celebrates the victory of Jesus each and every day.[353] As already mentioned, in more recent hymns, times of suffering are no longer dealt with by being content to wait for eternal peace; rather, one strives to search and find meaning in the present.[354]

Two hymns from the Catholic tradition mention a special time that serves as a place of purification, namely, the interim state of purgatory.[355]

As already established, the otherworldliness of eternity has moved increasingly into the background during the twentieth century. It does not disappear, but time, growing in significance at its side, distinguishes itself as the habitat of human beings. Kurt Marti expresses an extremely radical this-worldliness in his text from 1986:

> In uns kreist das Leben,
> das uns Gott gegeben,
> kreist als Stirb und Werde
> dieser Erde.[356]

It is a matter of hope for life, hope for the time that is and will come,[357] for "Gott hat uns diese Erde gegeben, dass wir auf ihr die Zeit bestehen" (God gave us this earth on which to stand the test of time),[358] and "[w]enn wir heute mutig wagen, auf Jesu Weg zu gehn, werden wir in unsern Tagen den kommenden Frieden sehn" (if today we courageously dare to follow the path of Jesus, we will see the coming peace in our days).[359] Here, however, one must act in faith, since feelings allow us to enjoy for only brief moments that which, in reality, we possess all the time.[360] Contrary to appearances, the future is already now real:

> Redan är du
> den du en gång skall bli:
> dömd och benådad,
> död och uppstånden . . .[361]

For "[d]er Himmel, der kommt, grüßt schon die Erde, die ist, wenn die Liebe das Leben verändert" (the heaven to come already greets the earth that exists, when love transforms life).[362]

When their sojourn in the habitat of time is finally over, then people "går ur tiden" (they will leave time)[363]—as the Swedish language expresses it in a synonym for "dying." Until that time, however, the shaping of a lifetime is, to a great degree, the responsibility of human beings; and this also entails special risks. Human self-assertion leads, namely, to an attack on God's sovereignty. A hymn from the 1960s speaks of this dilemma:

> Wir wollen leben und uns selbst behaupten.
> Doch deine Freiheit setzen wir aufs Spiel.
> Nach unserm Willen soll die Welt sich ordnen.
> Wir bauen selbstgerecht den Turm der Zeit.[364]

As a consequence of such Babylonian tower-building, we are dependent upon God's grace again and again:

> . . . Laß deine Gnade, Herr, vor Recht ergehen;
> von gestern und morgen sprich uns los.[365]

Thus, a person set free from the past and the future could then finally live in the now of the present, which in turn, according to Augustine,[366] would be tantamount to a life in eternity.

Summary and Preview

The examination in this first chapter began with a hypothesis based on Paul Ricoeur, namely, that time is tangible only as narrated time. Its aim has been to trace the central motifs of the narration of time in church hymns in order to glean formulations of questions for the rest of this study.

The narration of time becomes tangible primarily in the time indications that occur in the hymns. These include everyday and seasonal terminologies, as well as eternity terminology and explicit time terminology.[367] As the centuries have progressed, talk of eternity has receded into the background, while narration about everyday affairs and time has gained in importance. According to the classical hymn tradition, talk of eternity frequently occurs in set phrases within the context of doxology. Only rarely is *eternity* itself the subject, and even rarer are the phrases in which *time* occurs as the main actor. Nevertheless, both are present in various ways as a frame of reference.

The *future* is primarily a theme of the twentieth century. Here, in the face of a threatening and threatened future, human beings stand between calm surrendering and hope-seeking grasping. It remains unclear whether they desire to take hold of an earthly or a heavenly future, for complete salvation is no longer conceivable without including the entirety of suffering creation. In their vision of hope, human beings appear to blend not only goals, but also the past and the future.

Christmas carols and Easter hymns in particular tend to portray the past as the present. Thus, they relativize the distance to the historical event and signal the importance of the past event for the present. Within the framework of *contemporization*, an interlocking of times may occur that will finally be revoked in a new simultaneity. In recent times, the Passion of Christ has been contemporized as an event in the present. Consequently, the Resurrection is not only mentioned as a unique occurrence, but rather, by overcoming suffering and gaining victory over human death, it is unfolding as a continuous process.

Especially more recent baptismal and Communion hymns are less interested in contemporizing the past than the future. The strong motif of remembrance is almost superseded by the idea that in the sacrament, time is imbued with something qualitatively different.

Eternity means endless time as well as timelessness, that is, something that has a quality different from time. Traditionally, time derives definition from the primacy of eternity. Eternity and time can be related to each other in three ways, namely, as a succession, as an interaction in one direction or the other, or as an encompassing of time by eternity. In more recent hymns, the main emphasis has been shifted in a significant way: Eternity appears to be categorized as this-worldly and must give an accounting before the forum of time. This change must be taken into account when we endeavor to understand the hermeneutics of the various perceptions of time and eternity.

In more recent texts, *space* and *time* occur more frequently as existential conditions of the world. Although they have a provisional character, they occasionally replace terminology of doxological eternity.

Narrations about *God and time* represent two different perspectives, partially from the perspective of eternity and the unchanging nature of God, and partially from experience of God's action in time. The two perspectives cannot easily be reconciled with each other. Tensions continue to exist, but when God's eternity and temporality collide, a movement—similar to a dance—occurs that opens up the future.

Without expressly distinguishing between the divine and the human (or eternal and temporal) nature, Christ's preexistence is assumed. The classifying of his birth within the structure of time is to some degree contradictory; however, Jesus gives earthly time, human time, its character as a time of grace. The Christ of the future comes as Lord, in order to prepare the end of time. As the post-earthly Christ, he is always near, bringing salvation; and as the "Lord of the dance," he brings his eternity into earthly dimensions.

The Spirit was present at the time of original creation, lives eternally in the Trinity, comforts and gives life in time, and awakens on the Day of Judgment. Although the Spirit is not often directly connected to time and eternity, its place as the connecting link between God's time and human time appears to be self-evident.

Human time is, above all, transitory time. People of past centuries often longed for the constancy of eternity, whereas contemporaries are plagued by a lack of time. Good times alternate with bad times, but it appears that goodness comes to time only through divine promise and divine action. Time increasingly distinguishes itself as the habitat of human beings. Divine imbuement makes it the time of grace. The longing for eternity that was common in past ages has been replaced in modern hymn lyrics by hope for life and the world, partly through a believing anticipation of the future and partly through the desire to live a good life in the present.

The hymns of the church narrate time, but they hardly ever do so in a way that gives time the solo part in the narrative. Rather, time—as accompanying music—is always present in some way. Life takes place "in, with, and under" time. Time has many faces[368] and relates to eternity in different ways. Inspired by the repeatedly occurring metaphor of the dance, time and eternity could be seen as a pair in a cosmic dance, who, turning and pulsing, move with and against each other. The strength of this metaphor lies in the fact that—assuming that the dance is not over-choreographed—it allows space for movement and spontaneity.

Whenever time is narrated, there is always some concern about overcoming its negative aspects, controlling its destructive powers, and creating an order in which one can live. Thus, a worldview defines itself to a great extent by its underlying concept of time or eternity. The most significant change that the study of church hymns has clearly shown is the *decline of the perspective of eternity*. Eternity has been forced to relinquish its privileged position. Thanks to its dominance, it once made time a more or less comfortable prelude to actual reality, namely, life in an eternity beyond time. Now it instead has the task of making time worth living. Eternity lends hope to time. One of the reasons for this development can surely be found in the fact that a hope for eternity that naturally limits itself to saving of the souls of Christians who have died becomes suspicious at the moment when people become more conscious of the totality of creation. The observation of cultural and religious diversity in the human sphere, as well as the knowledge of the connection between the spirit and the body and also between culture and nature—not least of all that forced upon us by the experiences of nuclear and ecological threats—altered the perspective. If eternity is no longer merely a question of the future for Christian souls, but rather must also include the liberation of all of creation, of the entire universe, then a new perspective arises. All simple before-and-after schemes must be eliminated. In their place, the *relations* between time and eternity are increasingly becoming the subject of hermeneutical interest. The sense that this entails not merely a single relation, but rather a variety of relations, is becoming more pronounced.

The time-eternity relation thereby appears richer. Eternity is more than simply that which comes after time. It can also be conceived of as something that affects time and lends it a new quality. However, the attempts to bring time and eternity together conceptually go in such different directions that the confusing impression that readily arises can hardly be conveyed by my attempts at systematization. In spite of this ambiguity, it is theologically important to make the interaction between time and eternity into a central theme. Precisely with respect to the changing of eternity into an inner-temporal factor of hope, one must reflect upon its possible significance: Wherein lies the authority of eternity today? How sharp must the distinction between time and eternity be in order to attain an appropriate concept of time? Can one understand time without considering the relationship to "an other" of time, i.e., to eternity? What does it mean when eternity becomes essentially meaningless?

Losing the perspective of eternity leads to a concentration on time as the only reality. This fixation can result in time's being forced to accomplish more than it actually can. It simply has to provide *everything*. If it is unable to do so, however, one quickly feels that there is never enough time. Thus, there appears to be a correlation between the experience of a lack of time, on the one hand, and the observed diminishing of eternity's importance, to the benefit of time, on the other hand. The contemporary who is plagued by the fear of missing out on far too much in his or her short lifespan is interested in living as quickly as possible and knowing that the future—in our case, including eternity—has been exhausted as much as possible, so that as little as possible will be left undone. Marianne Gronemeyer calls this radical contemporization a maltreatment of time.[369] What Gronemeyer says about the relationship of the future to the present harmonizes well with what is expressed in numerous modern hymns about the relation between eternity and time: "*Homo accelerandus* had a serious argument with the future, at least with that future which rightly bears its name because it contains that which, unmade and unplanned, 'comes toward' us. He issued a draft notice to the unpredictable and unforeseeable Not-Yet: The future must appear in the present."[370]

Eternity must appear in time and give an account of itself. The loss of meaning for eternity leads to an increased significance for the individual life in the here and now, whose youth, in any case, must be preserved as long as possible. If the notion of an eternity beyond time has become irrelevant, then the realization of the dream of eternal life in the here and now must be sought. Thus, middle age as the apex of the accelerated and self-realizing life becomes more important than life's end; one's fortieth or fiftieth birthday is more important than one's seventieth or eightieth. A highly relevant eternity, however, can go hand in hand with respect for old age, with careful preparation for death, and with a general relativization of the temporal. A reference to the meaning of the death penalty in the early medieval *sub specie aeternitatis* can emphasize this.[371]

In a time that does not relate to eternity, speed can quickly become a value in itself. Acceleration is good; a delay—or even a standstill—is bad. Fast speed and quick solutions are preferable, while farsightedness approaches boredom. In this setting, boredom can no longer be experienced as a potential for creativity, but rather only as sheer misfortune. Change and instant gratification, on the other hand, signify happiness and good fortune. The problem is that the constant speed record ultimately leads to precisely that which was to be avoided from the very beginning—boredom and discontent. Rhythms and differences fall victim to the constant push for faster speeds. Resistance is largely eliminated so that, in the final analysis, a standardization and leveling occurs. This, in turn, creates a feeling of emptiness.

Relationships that require time to develop are impeded. Encounters with the unfamiliar, the foreign, which are dependent upon the ability to accept differences and the will to deal with them patiently, are prevented.

The most extreme consequence of such a concept of time can be found in increasing violence and in the inability to encounter the unfamiliar.[372] The lack of time has then become, in the most literal sense, *chronic*— caused by time itself, which has lost its relationship as partner to eternity.

The relationship between time and eternity has become unclear and problematic. The relation between time and eternity, which once appeared to be so self-evident, now seems to be shattered. With this knowledge as its point of reference, the following chapter discusses biblical and theological concepts of time.

[2]

Biblical and Theological Conceptions of Time

The second chapter of this study is devoted to an examination of the complex meaning inherent in "time" in biblical and theological perspectives. In the course of reflection, a reference framework will be developed for problems and questions that will then be revisited—following an excursion into the world of natural scientific models of time in chapter 3—in the concluding fourth chapter. The question of time as a relational concept, as discussed in chapter 1, will guide my research.

The results of the study of time concepts in the Bible are summarized in theses on pp. 80–81. I believe two features of the biblical conception of time are most essential. First, there is the multilayered presence of time within the context of a simultaneous absence of an antithesis between time and eternity. Second, there is the primacy of the fullness of time in terms of its content over and against the formal designation of time.

The theological considerations of *time* are oriented toward neither a history of theology nor a history of dogma, because, after all, one cannot speak of a dogma of time in the proper sense. Instead, the relationship of the theological concepts of *God, time, eternity*, and *death* is examined with respect to its inherent potential for relationality. My argument for a relational rather than an antithetical relationship of time to God/eternity is supported by the depiction of three different ways of distinguishing between time and eternity. Based on this analysis, I will suggest that, although a time-eternity

61

relation can in no way establish a doctrine of the Trinity, conceptions of time marked by Trinitarian differentiation could nevertheless be most appropriate for developing a dynamic, relational model of time. These thoughts will be expanded beginning on p. 97.

Finally, these theological investigations will be completed by reflections on death as the place where, from an anthropological perspective, time and eternity collide with each other, and relationality thus experiences its deepest crisis.

"Eternity as the Other of time" constitutes the preliminary summarizing formula for this second chapter, a formula that is still open in many ways. The formula should indicate that time is to be conceived primarily as a relational concept and that a static dualism is as inappropriate as schematic subject-object relations would be.

On the Theological Understanding of the Problem of Time

In order to work out a framework for theological reflection on time, I shall start with Carl Heinz Ratschow's *Anmerkungen zur theologischen Auffassung des Zeitproblems.*[1] Ratschow distinguishes among three different meanings of the word *time.* First, he deals with time as temporality and thus transitoriness; then, he turns to time as the ages, i.e., historical time; finally, he explores time as the experience of lack of time.

From the human perspective, temporality as *transitoriness* is seen as a demon,[2] as destiny, or as an a priori concept.[3] Human beings react to this understanding by postulating eternity: They "free themselves from the terror of time and jump over the *via negationis* to the intransitory, the unchangeable and the invariable."[4] Thus, humans wish to understand temporality and transitoriness in light of the antithesis of eternity. Ratschow explains that this antithesis lends itself at best to a very rudimentary understanding of what biblical theology is about, however. Instead of understanding transitoriness from the standpoint of temporality, biblical thought speaks of it from the perspective of guilt or sin. For this reason, the poles are not temporal/transitory versus eternal/intransitory, but rather world/human/sin versus God/"Last Things"/life.[5] Accordingly, in those Old Testament passages in which one would expect to find mention of an eternal God, one instead finds the loyal, jealous, or angry God. An antithetical concept of absolute eternity retreats, giving way to a relation-oriented concept of a God who, in relation to guilt and faith, influences time and the world.[6] We already noticed a parallel development when we were examining the hymns on pp. 37–41: The rather antithetical model "here in time—there in eterni-ty" [*hier in der Zeit—dort in der Ewigkeit*] has increasingly given way to more integrated and interactive descriptive models of the relationship of time to eternity.

Even with respect to *historical time*, Ratschow sees a difference between antithetical thinking and a relation-oriented biblical theology. Human be-ings do not move in time (singular) as such, but rather they come from past times (plural), which they concretize as history, and they direct their atten-tion towards the future. The *pluraletantum* time, that is, the concrete, avail-able periods and aspects of time, then faces *singularetantum* eternity.[7] Ac-cording to this scheme, eternity is no longer perceived as invariability, but rather as infinity. The antithesis to time as the ages that have become con-crete is therefore eternity as infinity.

Here, biblical thinking is again taking a different path. For historical times, it frequently uses the term *days*. The opposite of this, however, is not an eternity without days, but rather, above all, the darkness of night. A word pair filled with qualitative meaning is thus created, which also occurs frequently in the hymns of the Church. The end of all things is not infinity, but rather, "the coming days," the "day of Yahweh," or the "day of salva-tion."[8] Once again, we are not dealing with the antithesis of time/eternity, but rather with relation: "Between our days, the days of primeval times, and the day of Yahweh, there is a basic connection, namely, in being a day."[9]

Corresponding with my findings in chapter 1, Ratschow determines that the third range of meaning of the word *time*, namely, the one dealing with the *lack of time*, lies closest to people of modernity: ". . . modern people are modern to the extent that they live with the sense of having no time."[10] The having-no-time is always oriented towards a "for"; people experience that they have no time *for* something, with respect to something. With regard to that for which people have no time, they are closed, so that the person who has no time at all is "the completely closed human being."[11] To-close-oneself therefore means a loss of time, whereas every instance of being open causes one to gain time. Behind the openness of having-time-for, the being-time-for—and thus the freedom to wait for the right time to come—becomes vis-ible. The opposite of being free to have-time-for is the state of being-closed, which, once again, in no way means eternity.

Even here, Ratschow again proposes a relational, rather than an anti-thetical, solution. The time characterized as having-time-for "can be neither drawn out into permanence nor chained together to reach infinity. . . . What eternity can mean here has nothing to do with the long duration or brevity of this time, but rather with the depth of its facilitation."[12] Thus, time understood as "time-for" is always accompanied by its eternity; the moment has a relationship to eternity. In biblical thought, Ratschow sees this dimension of time expressed by the terms *ʿēt* and *kairos*.

The most interesting and potentially fruitful aspect of Ratschow's *Anmerkungen zur theologischen Auffassung des Zeitproblems* is his overcoming of a dualistic and antithetical way of thinking about time and eternity, which was accomplished by his presentation of relational and interactive models for the relationship of time to eternity. The filling of the formal, *philosophical* dualism of time and eternity with relational and dynamic content emerges as a major *theological* accomplishment.

I consider Ratschow's thoughts to be a good foundation for the discussion with modern natural science, a discussion in which we also will be dealing with dynamics and relationality. Before we can begin this discussion, however, theological reflection on time must first be placed in a broader context. Therefore, I will now look more closely at what the biblical texts are saying about concepts of time.

Time in the Bible

The Bible certainly does not provide a theory of time, but in the Bible, time is narrated, for the things that the Bible describes take place "in, with, and under" the experience of time. It will become evident that such an experience of time is influenced by its particular cultural context. I will examine the biblical findings with respect to the concepts of linear and cyclical time. Furthermore, I will also attempt to render the individual semantic fields, as well as the overarching concepts—primarily that of eschatology—fruitful for the question of a theology of time.

Time and *eternity* are not often explicit topics in theological literature about the Old and New Testaments, as can easily be confirmed by looking at the subject index of relevant books and the terms appearing in dictionaries and lexicons. The two terms are frequently not dealt with as such, but instead, references are made to key words such as *eschatology, eternal* or *everlasting life*, and *apocalypticism*.[13] This in itself indicates that the working out of a comprehensive biblical theory of time cannot be an appropriate task for this section. The section will instead discuss various features of the biblical attitude toward time. I will first turn to the Hebrew Scriptures. The division into "Time in the Old Testament" and "Time in the New Testament" is made for practical purposes. I do not wish to give the impression that it is possible to develop one specific Old Testament or New Testament conception of time. To the extent that one can speak at all about conceptions of time, one must also stress that these understandings can differ considerably from each other, depending upon the specific biblical passage and individual traditions.

Time in the Old Testament
On the Concept of Time in the Hebrew Scriptures

There is general agreement that Old Testament thought "has no natural tendency to abstractions."[14] Israel never understood time as something separate from the respective event; in this sense, it knew only "filled time,"[15] that is, "every event has a definite place in the time-order; the event is inconceivable without its time, and *vice versa*."[16] As a rule, there is no reflection about the nature of time. What happens within time is much more interesting.[17] The earliest period in which more abstract ideas about time are found is the post-exilic period, as, for example, in the Priestly account of creation or in the reflections on time in Ecclesiastes. Due to this reason alone, one cannot speak of a uniform Old Testament concept of time. Furthermore, Hebrew has more than one word for the Western term *time*. Therefore, an analysis of the passages in which the most closely related words—*ʿôlām* and *ʿēt*[18]—occur leads only to a partial understanding of the Old Testament concept of time.[19]

In the Old Testament, one seeks in vain for *eternity* as an antonym to *time*. The Hebrew word *ʿôlām* is not used in as exclusive a manner as is the concept of God's holiness; mountains, sun, and moon can also be eternal.[20] Nevertheless, just as God, the Lord over time and space (Isa. 40:28), is the ultimate source of holiness, God also appears to be the final source of eternity.

The eternity of God should not be understood as timelessness, but rather as the fullness of time and power over time.[21] This notion of God's sovereignty over time may also have moved the author of the Priestly account in Genesis 1–2 to have the creation event culminate in holy time: "So God blessed the seventh day and hallowed it" (Gen. 2:3; cf. also Exod. 34:21, which is probably the oldest version of the Sabbath commandment, and Exod. 20:8–11).[22] The climax of the first biblical creation story is therefore the creation of holy time with social and cosmic dimensions.[23] It is worth noting the difference between this version and the Babylonian creation epic, *Enuma elish*, which ends with the founding of a city and a temple—thus, in holy space.[24]

The Old Testament deals frequently with land, with space. This cannot hide the fact, however, that it was not ultimately space, but rather time, that decisively determined Israelite identity. The best known but least understood aspect of Jewish civilization may well be the fact that, following the destruction of Jerusalem, Jews had a common calendar for almost two thousand years, although they did not have a common land.[25] Different from most other peoples, whose identity manifested itself in structured space, Jewish identity was manifested in the structures of time. Whereas in Christianity and Islam the main focus was on a religious geography and a control over space, Judaism achieved a spiritualization of time: "the Jewish vocation became the creation of a spiritual calendar constructed of timeless moments, sacred events, and religious imperatives, these largely ordered by the cycles of time, the passing of seasons, and even the hours of each passing day."[26] Étan Levine believes that only Judaism has been successful in transcending space and, in this sense, has become truly universal.[27] The Jerusalem in time was always nearby, but the resurrection of a Jerusalem in space during the twentieth century led to manifold unforeseen ethical, social, and domestic/foreign policy problems for Jewish identity: "for nearly twenty centuries Jews have survived spacelessness; they must now learn to survive space."[28]

A Linear Concept of Time?

Let us now look at the question of how the structuring of time appears in the Old Testament world. From the standpoint of cultural history, it would be natural to see a relation between the calendar of festivals and the development of a consciousness of time. The rhythm of festivals and periods without festivals structures people's lives. For this reason, according to Gerhard von Rad, time per se is not an absolute given, but rather the festivals are the conditions of absolute holiness.[29] These festivals originally had an agrarian nature, but they were interpreted by Israel within the horizon of its history in such a way that the celebration becomes a participation in the particular historic situation that had become the basis for the festival. One therefore enters into a "vivid experience of the contemporaneousness of the divine saving acts"[30] (cf. Deut. 5:3). Israel's God is not a nature god; above all, Yahweh is the God of Israel's history who becomes the God of world history. In light of such historicism, von Rad maintains that one could "scarcely overestimate the importance of such changes, brought about as they were by a unique understanding of the world and of human existence."[31] From the individual historical facts, he sees here the growth of a consciousness of historical sequence that results in the conception of a linear view of history. History is guided by Yahweh (Deut. 26:5–9 and other passages). According to von Rad, the idea that Israel owes its existence not to an event but rather to divine historical guidance is "an epoch-making step."[32] For a period of time, cultic and chronological contemporizations of history ran parallel. Finally, however, with increasing temporal distance, a crisis occurred in the cultic contemporization of the divine saving acts, which, together with other factors, led to the eschatologization of historical thought by the prophets.[33] Even if the concept of eschatology is ambiguous here, von Rad's thesis nevertheless drew attention to two important components of prophetic proclamation, namely, its relatedness to secular history and its claim that the new historical acts are superseding everything that has happened in the past. This then completes a turn toward the future, within whose horizon the cosmic expansion of the tradition of the Day of Yahweh needs to be considered.

In his account, von Rad emphasizes the unique quality of the Israelite conceptions of time, which, in his opinion, are in contrast to an ancient oriental worldview shaped by a mythical-cyclical way of thinking that resulted in a sacred and essentially nonhistorical understanding of the world. In this cyclical concept of the world, there is no room for the uniqueness of the inner-historical divine acts of God. Nevertheless, in his desire to distinguish Israel as totally *other* and *unique,* von Rad rushed prematurely to the view that Israel's linear concept was unequaled. It was surely no "ugly ditch" that separated Israel's understanding of time from that of its neighbors,[34] as can be seen, for example, in Siegfried Morenz's account of the Egyptian understanding of time. Morenz states that in Egypt there were certainly distinctions among different times, both terminologically[35] and in terms of consciousness; in fact, the timeline of human beings is geometrically located on a straight line, whereas natural phenomena and cult are assigned to a circle.[36] The circle of periodicity has its actual point of reference in the recurrence of the Nile flood and vegetation. The straight line running into in-finity is oriented toward the goal-directed existence of the individual, which can be illustrated by the official career track of Egyptians and their striving for eternity that finds its highest expression in the symbol of the mummy.[37]

Even the quality of "being filled," which von Rad develops as a feature of the Israelite concept of time, is actually related to Egyptian thought, for, according to Morenz, Egyptians "did not envisage it [time] as an absolute quantity, or at least only as this, but related it to something else and thereby gave it quality."[38] "Time becomes a receptacle for a fulfilled present."[39] Corresponding to the Greek *kairos,* things always have their assigned opportune moment. Morenz presents numerous examples from Egyptian literature for the motto "For everything there is a time," which reminds one of Eccles. 3:1ff., just as the sentence "The years are in his hand,"[40] from a hymn to Amun-Re, causes one to think of Ps. 31:16 and of Klepper's "You who hold time in your hands."[41] Egyptians also were familiar with the notion of time planned down to the last detail[42]—"all have their nourishment, and their days are numbered."[43]

The Egyptologist Eberhard Otto also believes that, very early on in the ancient Near East, cyclical and linear concepts of time existed side by side. He sees a compromise between cyclical and linear time concepts in the calculation of time according to the years of rule of the respective reigning monarchs.[44]

For the ancient Near Eastern cultures of Mesopotamia and the Hittite kingdom, Hartmut Gese has shown that one can also not assume a cyclical, ahistorical understanding of time.[45] In Mesopotamia, the view of history as a noncausal sequence of good and evil times in keeping with the unfathomable will of the gods developed into the concept of a succession of ages characterized by a cause-and-effect principle. When Israel developed its conception of history as judgment, it could tie into this ancient oriental conception of history as sequence.[46]

In the Hebrew Scriptures, one can find traces of at least three different systems for naming months: names having a Canaanite origin, Babylonian month names, and designation of months by ordinal number. We learn nothing about the length of the individual months or years, and nothing about the probable intercalary procedure that was needed for holding lunar and solar years together.[47] Even these facts speak for the hypothesis that Israel's concept of time is not as unique or independent of its surroundings as von Rad claims. In contrast to what we know about Babylonian, Assyrian, and Egyptian calendars, we can glean little information on the nature of the Jewish calendar from the Hebrew Scriptures.[48] This also indicates that the development of a special concept of temporal structuring was not a primary concern.

Instead of assuming that the development of a linear concept of time in Israel was relatively direct and unique, as von Rad has done, one should conclude that cyclical and linear conceptions of time coexisted and interfered with each other.[49] This is confirmed by a look at Genesis 8 and 9, where different experiences of time are redactionally linked to each other. The text describes a new beginning following the Flood, which the Yahwist explains cyclically: "As long as the earth endures, seedtime and harvest, cold and heat, summer and winter, day and night, shall not cease" (Gen. 8:22).[50] The Priestly material, on the other hand, marks the new beginning with a historical event: God blesses Noah and his sons and establishes a covenant with them that includes "every living creature" on earth and is sealed by the sign of the rainbow (Gen. 9:1–17).[51] Von Rad does not comment on this difference in the understanding of time; he sees both accounts of the history of the Flood from the viewpoint of maintaining order. Thus, for the Yahwist, "[i]t is not yet . . . that grace which forgives sins . . . , but a gracious will that is . . . effective and recognizable in the changeless duration of nature's orders,"[52] whereas in the Priestly material, one is dealing with "a solemn guarantee of the cosmic orders which were disturbed by the temporary invasion of chaos."[53]

Claus Westermann, on the other hand, interprets this by starting with the aspect of time. In the expression *as long as the earth endures* (literally: all days of the earth, Gen. 8:22), he sees a probable Yahwist innovation, by means of which for the first time in human history "the cosmic event is seen as a whole in its extension in time."[54] Rolf Rendtorff understands Gen. 8:22 as a polemic against Canaanite religion. The change of seasons, which is understood there to be a battle among the gods and precipitated by ritual acts, is demythologized; from this point on, Yahweh alone guarantees order.[55] According to Walther Eichrodt, the Priestly material provides a historical outline of the dispensational teaching of the ancient oriental worldview and illustrates, with the establishment of the covenants, the ordered evolution of history that is progressing according to plan.[56]

In my opinion, it is significant that the redactional combination of J and P in Genesis 8–9 places side by side cyclical time (in the course of nature and objective order) and linear time (in human and salvation history). Since this combination also brings together sources from different time periods, it is reasonable to assume that the linear concept of time developed from the cyclical one. However, this development should not be looked upon too schematically or interpreted exclusively within the category of progress. It is simply not enough to define the understanding of time in the Old Testament as a single-sided linear one.[57] How else could one explain, for example, the post-exilic institution of the Jubilee Year, which, in its regular recurrence, represents a cyclical phenomenon?

Even within the Priestly tradition, one can observe a multilayered complexity to which a simplified contraposition of linear and cyclical time in no way does justice. In his study entitled *The Ideology of Ritual*, Frank H. Gorman concludes that the different concepts of time that are found in the ritual Priestly material of the books of Leviticus and Numbers could not be reduced to the antithetical pair of cyclical/linear; rather, time must be seen to express various modalities and nuances that are determined in part by the ritual situation. This suggests that time should not be graphically spoken of or depicted as either a straight line or a circle, but should be understood in terms of qualitative tone or texture.[58]

Accordingly, in order to do justice to the complexity of the material, one needs to accept a certain parallelism in the concepts of time rather than presupposing an underlying hierarchy. It is therefore worthwhile to consider, for example, the scheme of promise and fulfillment under two aspects: from a linear and salvation-historical perspective[59] and from the viewpoint of a large-scale circularity.[60]

It is surely correct to consider the "transformation of religious structures of the cosmic type into events of sacred history" as characteristic of Yahwistic monotheism.[61] It may also be argued "that the Hebrews were the first to discover the significance of history as an epiphany of God."[62] However, this does not mean that a linear and completely unique development occurred here,[63] because, for a long time, new and old concepts existed side by side.[64] It is reasonable to assume that, finally, the two perspectives—the historical-linear and the cosmological-cyclical—supplement each other in various ways.[65] Nevertheless, in apocalypticism, things come to a head: World history is moving toward a goal that lies outside history. This can either be interpreted as the victory of an exclusively linear understanding of time,[66] or it can be understood on the basis of the totality of world history as a single cycle that, in turn, is divided into cyclical periods.[67] One should also not prematurely exclude the possibility that, even within apocalypticism's essentially deterministic view of history, underlying cyclical thinking is still present. It could be that a cyclical conception of time is participating in the *vaticinia ex eventu*. When there is an exclusive predominance of a linear concept of time, *vaticinia ex eventu* are actually illogical because they are completely useless, whereas under the condition of a double perspective— for example, linear time with cyclical undertones—they move into the range of the meaningfully possible: a potential aid to do better next time around.

Far too many Old Testament studies follow without comment, and perhaps inadvertently, the conviction that salvation history is superior to mythology; linear time to cyclical time; and eschatology to apocalypticism. This evokes a pressure to impose clear distinctions on a complex textual material, and suggests an overemphasis on a linear conception of time in the Old Testament. The more appropriate hypothesis, however, is to consider the cyclical as a constant companion, from the promise of the continual return of sowing and harvesting, of summer and winter, and of day and night in primal history, to popular expressions like the "every year once more"[68] in a popular German Christmas carol.

The criticism I have expressed here pertains basically to every hermeneutical perspective claiming uniqueness and exclusivity. As the comparison of linear and cyclical time shows, such a viewpoint always tends to construct dualisms, which disqualify, so to speak, half of life: Linear time is linked to Yahweh, the one, masculine God, exclusively for Israel and its striving for religious and ritual purity. The opposite is cyclical time, which is identified with the fertility gods and goddesses and the syncretism of the nations. In similar fashion, myth is supplanted by history, and apocalypticism becomes a kind of degenerate eschatology.

Eschatological Dynamics

The consideration of linear versus cyclical time should not divert our attention from other aspects of the Old Testament concept of time. Interesting observations can also be made by using distinctions between dynamic and static concepts of time as an analytic tool.[69] A dynamic view of time is found in classical prophecy. It sees history as a battlefield on which evil powers attack the reign of God. The present is therefore often viewed critically: It is the place of decision. The perspective is oriented toward the future, toward the end of history and the dawning of a new eon. God is above all the God who is coming. In contrast, in the tradition of the priesthood we encounter primarily a static view of time. Here, the present is understood from the perspective of the past. The present relatedness to God has existed forever and is tied to the fixed order of the Law. God is the supreme ruler, even if the world rejects God. God is always the God who has come. Thus, a tension arises between the present that is interpreted in light of the future (as in the prophetic tradition) and the present that is understood in light of the past (as in the Priestly tradition). A one-sided, dynamic understanding can degenerate into enthusiasm, complete relativism, or pessimism with respect to the present. A one-sided, static understanding runs the risk of a deistic dissociation of God from the world, a rationalization springing from an overestimation of order, or a complacent conservatism that is certain of eternal truths.

As the considerations about linear and cyclical time have already suggested, the interesting question is less whether time should be conceived either dynamically or statically; it is the interplay of the different perspectives that is much more instructive. How do the divergent perspectives in the different traditions relate to one another? What happens when emphases shift or when a specific outlook becomes predominant? How do historic events affect the concept of time? Do crises always promote a dynamic understanding of time, while "normal situations" more likely go hand in hand with a static view?

The dynamic nature of time emerges particularly in conjunction with eschatological ideas. Here once again, it becomes clear that time is primarily understood in terms of its contents, because Old Testament eschatology deals less with the end of the world, time, and history than it does with the end of evil brought about by God's transformation of human beings, society, and nature.[70] For this reason, Donald E. Gowan prefers to conceive of the core of eschatology as being spatial rather than temporal, since its central concern is with Zion, God's city, not with a return to the garden of Eden; its primary concern is with the realization of the full complexity of human society.[71] Thus, Old Testament eschatology says almost more about space than about time, and more about the past and present than about the future, since it tells about the present and past by selecting the language and images from the past that most closely approach the anticipated ideal.[72] It would be erroneous, however, to pit time against space in this context. Eschatological space and eschatological time are more appropriately classified as being relative to each other.

Regarding the various aspects of the concept of time, it is an improper stricture to claim one perspective at the expense of the Other. Rather, each model is to be seen as a complement to the Other. The tension between the God who has come and the God who is coming, between past and present orientations, must be considered constitutive. It will also accompany us in our explorations of "time" in the New Testament.

Time in the New Testament

The Greek Frame of Reference

The New Testament concept of time is often portrayed against the backdrop of the Greek understanding of time.[73] Prominent here is the evaluation of the eternal—based on Parmenides and Zeno—as the true,[74] and the temporal as having an ontological deficit. Without true being, time is merely *onoma*, a concept set forth by human beings; yet people are dependent upon its actuality.[75] Mere becoming is hopelessly inferior to immutable being. If time is conceived in a Platonic sense, as a moving image of eternity, i.e., an image that is eternal but moving according to number, while eternity itself rests in unity,[76] then a cyclical concept of time seems desirable for at least two reasons. First, as an emulation, a cyclical concept of time most closely approaches the ideal of timelessness. This is supported by the fact that the circle, and especially the sphere, correspond best to the Greek ideal of harmony. Second, in the cycle, "time [can be] more or less captured by circulatory repetitions of processes that permit unavoidable temporal movement but prevent an 'outpouring' caused by an eruption into linear infinity."[77] It succeeds in "cyclically taming time."[78] Furthermore, the idea of rhythm also serves to tame time, which is dangerous because it is so unpredictable. Rhythmicity, as one finds it in poetry, music, and dance, "cultures" the natural flow of time.[79]

Within the horizon of such thought, neither the temporal beginning nor the final goal of things is of interest. Instead, we find an "orientation toward the present, indeed, a joyfulness in the present"[80] that is expressed in the *kairos* and comes along "with an especially powerful expression of spatial consciousness that rivals linear, future-oriented time consciousness."[81] The Aristotelian inference of time from place and movement, as well as the generally high estimation of geometry among the Greeks, point in the same direction. Seen this way, it does not surprise that in Greece the act that is performed at sacred sites becomes decisive, whereas in biblical thinking the pendulum seems to swing in the direction of an understanding of time as the place of purposeful divine action in history.

While Greek thought sees the world primarily as space, Israel rather accentuates time and, based on this presupposition, relates time and space to each other.[82] In this respect, James Muilenburg speaks even of a basic difference between Israel and its neighbors, for "in Israel the mystery and meaning of time is not resolved by appeal to the cosmic world of space; among the other nations, the heavenly bodies are deified and *chronos* spatializes time into extension and duration";[83] and in Israel, "time is grasped in terms of purpose, will, and decision."[84] The Jewish prohibition of pictures and polemic against graven images should also be understood in light of the primacy of time to space: "The God of Israel is active, active in time and event; he cannot be transformed into space."[85] Accordingly, time does not become concrete within the context of the spatial, but rather, in the language of the Word. If Greek culture is primarily a culture of the eye, then Hebrew culture is rather a culture of the ear[86] (cf. Isa. 50:4f; 55:10f.).

Even if such stylized comparisons of one people to (almost) all other peoples should be met with a healthy skepticism,[87] Muilenburg's emphasis on the primacy of time over space in biblical thought is noteworthy. It brings up the interesting question of how the primacy of time has been managed theologically and to what extent, for example, it led to the neglect of space or to the escalation or dissolution of time in eternity.

The difference between New Testament and Greek thinking can also be shown—as was done in the context of existential interpretation—by pointing out dissimilarities in views of the "moment." While Greek thought springs from "a basic transcendental disposition in which people—driven by their fears—fail to realize the demands of the moment,"[88] the New Testament is often concerned precisely with the event of the eschatological moment that is breaking into time. While the former is striving, by means of ideas and ideals, to overcome being at the mercy of time, the latter is concerned with the eschatological time that seizes actual persons in their temporality and that opens up a new history. Thus, we have two poles of thought, namely, space, fixed orders, and eternal ideas, on the one hand, and time, event, and eschatological happenings, on the other.

On the Understanding of Time in the New Testament

In the following sections I will discuss how thought about time unfolds in the New Testament. Gerhard Delling's study from 1940, with the very promising title *Das Zeitverständnis des Neuen Testaments* (The Understanding of Time in the New Testament), can be consulted only with reservations, however.[89] I will instead refer to a later essay[90] by the same author.

Delling starts from the basic concept of time as a natural condition. Along with Oscar Cullmann, he sees New Testament time completely in light of the Christ event. "Initially, time runs toward the Christ event. This is the absolute center of meaning and core of time."[91] Accordingly, a distinction is made between the time that moves toward Christ and the time that comes from the Christ event. But this differentiation does not result in a true division of time, for, even if the Christ event is final, unique, and an eschatological fulfillment of time,[92] it is true that: "The saving action of God is one in past, present, and future, in anticipation, fulfillment, and consummation."[93] For the primitive Church, the Christ event does not become an event in the past, but rather remains present, a "now event" in which the Church participates.[94] This does not prevent the Church from portraying the Jesus event as a historical event in time and space, however. In the end, it is the identity of the Crucified and Exalted One that does not make the present time of Christians "the time 'after Christ' in the chronological sense, but rather the time of Christ, the time that is conditioned by the crucified and exalted Christ."[95] The time of Christ is the End Time. Between Easter and the final consummation, however, time is characterized, particularly in Pauline thought, by "a factually grounded simultaneity"[96] of the "already" and the "not-yet." Christians have already been liberated from the power of sin, but they still stand "in the struggle between self-will and the Holy Spirit."[97] Even in the realized eschatology of the Gospel of John, the difference between the present time of grace and the future time of consummation is preserved.[98] Life that is lived in the not-yet of final consummation is at the same time marked by the certainty of the already of God's unique and final act of salvation. If this is a correct portrayal of Christian life, waiting for the *parousia* does not pose a problem. Martin Werner's theory that the delay of the *parousia* was the cause for the development of dogmas in the early church can therefore be criticized.[99]

In the New Testament, time is set teleologically by God. God is the One acting in time; a timeless essence is not ascribed to God. For Christ, an eternal being in God prior to his becoming human is suggested. Again, following Cullmann, Delling does not consider the New Testament's notion of eternity to have been pondered philosophically, but rather describes it as based upon linear, unlimited time.[100] Nevertheless, God is conceived as the one who is superior to time and who controls it.[101] For the person who is drawn into the salvation event, time is the possibility granted by God for the purpose of realizing a new existence based on salvation.[102] A constitutive mark of New Testament time is its eschatologically determined "openness to the future."[103] As in the Old Testament, time is considered less in the formal sense than with regard to its content.

Time Terminology in the New Testament

Of the New Testament terms for time—*aiōn, kairos, chronos*, and *hōra* —*aiōn* and its derived adjective *aiōnios* occur most frequently.[104] The term occurs primarily in prepositional phrases, but also as an independent noun both in the singular and the plural.[105] Only from the particular context can one decide whether *aiōn* means "eternity" or only "distant, long, uninterrupted time." Basically, eon means a long time, limited or unlimited, which actually leads to the contradictory expression *chronoi aiōnioi* (Rom. 16:25, etc.). However, its meaning can also be extended in the direction of "world time," so that the same word is used for two profoundly contrasting meanings, namely, for the eternity of God and for the time of the world. Under the influence of apocalypticism, *aiōn* can even designate the world in the spatial sense.[106] *Aiōn* does not describe a uniformly endless sequence of events, but instead marks courses of time in a structured history that can be restructured again and again. Along with the preposition *eis, aiōn* can mean both the inner-temporal and the post-temporal future. The most graphic depiction of eons is found in Matthew, who distinguishes between two successive periods of world time, the present one and the future one. A doctrine of eons, however, such as one can find in Gnosticism,[107] is not developed in the New Testament. In Paul, "this eon" is the sin-determined course of the world without Christ. In the Synoptics, eternal life, *zoē aiōnios*, as the life belonging to God, is also the life that is expected within the framework of a future resurrection of the dead. In John, by contrast, belonging to Christ in faith is the eternal life, which is therefore already possessed by those who have entered into communion with Christ.

In general, the future is mentioned only with a certain reservation; it is the present that is of primary concern. Eternity is described mainly in temporal categories. It is neither understood as pure timelessness nor in terms of a dualism between time and eternity. Answering the question of whether eternity is to be understood as everlasting time or as timelessness is not the subject of the New Testament. This assessment is important because it prevents us from reading the New Testament through the glasses of the Greek philosophy of time. It also provides the explanation of why Cullmann is wrong, even though his theory in *Christ and Time*, namely, that the New Testament does not contain any notion of a timeless eternity, is correct in principle.[108] The New Testament does not know of any timeless eternity because it is not concerned with the nature of eternity. When the New Testa-

ment deals with time and eternity, it deals instead with the relationship of
the spheres of the eternal and the temporal.

Kairos is the second most frequently used term referring to time. The
advent of Jesus marks the fulfillment of the *kairos* (also the *kairoi*), when the
reign of God is coming near (Mark 1:15). Based on this, kerygmatic interpretation emphasizes the present and presence of Jesus' *kairos:* The *now* of
Jesus Christ's having-already-come corresponds to the *now* of the proclamation of the Word as the *now* in which the decision between death and life is
made. The *kairos* of decision is followed by a time of struggle and of prov-
ing oneself, until salvation is revealed *en kairō eschatō*. It is not possible to
distinguish *aiōn* and *kairos* consistently. The term *aiōn* in fact never means
"moment/point in time," whereas in some passages, *kairos* takes on the
meaning of "period of time."[109]

Chronos, as a designation for a period of time and also occasionally for a
point in time, occurs most frequently in the writings of Luke. In terms of
content, the concept is construed from the Jesus event. *Chronos* is not an
absolute entity, but rather the space and visual form for the historical action
of God and the time-structuring response of the believer. Against the backdrop of apocalyptic messianic expectations, the Jesus event can, on the one
hand, be regarded as the end of time or of the old eon; on the other hand,
however, it can be understood, in terms of Luke, as the center of time. This
creates an ambiguity very much like the one we encountered in the examination of the hymns on pp. 47–51. The New Testament does not distinguish
between *kairos* and *chronos* nearly as rigorously as one would like to assume.
In some passages, the two terms are directly interchangeable.[110]

The word *hōra* is found primarily in the Gospels, sometimes providing
more or less exact information about time and, in other places, as a description of limited, measurable periods of time. The term also serves to give emphasis to special events, such as, e.g., the hour of glorification (John 12:27f.).

Jesus' Understanding of Time—An Example of the Difficulty of Speaking about Time

From what has previously been said, one can see that "time" in the New
Testament is a phenomenon shimmering with many nuances—a fact that
time and again leads to considerable difficulties in theological discussions. A
few remarks on Jesus' understanding of time will illustrate some of the
problems.

Regarding the notion of time in Jesus' proclamation, Eta Linnemann[111]
remarks—in contrast to Joachim Jeremias, Werner Georg Kümmel, and
Erich Grässer—that there is no evidence for a near expectation of the
parousia in Jesus himself. Rather, she says, in the Gospels, words of Jesus

that presuppose the futurity of God's reign and those that proclaim its presence appear to contradict each other. Linnemann wants to resolve this contradiction not by playing down the presence of God's reign, as she believes is done in Hans Conzelmann, Ernst Fuchs, Günther Bornkamm, and Kümmel.[112] Rather, influenced by Martin Heidegger and Fuchs, she believes that the aporia of the juxtaposition of the present and future qualities of God's reign are to be resolved in the concept of time itself. For a traditional concept of time, which allows only for continual, ongoing time, present and future reigns of God cannot be conceived of simultaneously. On the other hand, an understanding of time "as time for, being with, as present"[113] permits a correspondence between relating and withdrawing, between granting and withholding, between present and future.[114] Wherever the traditional concept of time acts in a way that is excluding, the more original understanding of time, as "time for," creates new correlations. Thus, Jesus encountered "the concept [of the *basileia tou theou*] in a conceptual framework that implied the vulgar, improper concept of time and related it to an understanding of time that conceived of time more originally as time to."[115] Linnemann therefore thinks that the concept of God's reign proves to be "the split switch that connects the track of traditional Jewish eschatology to the path of Jesus' specific announcement of time."[116]

Behind this distinction of time concepts, which Linnemann sees in Jesus' proclamation, one can of course recognize the difference between *chronos* and *kairos*. Whether the chronological concept of time should be seen as improper and exclusive while the kairological concept is seen as original and integrative, as Linnemann seems to suggest, remains questionable, however. In spite of this objection, Linnemann's attempt to provide an integrative account of Jesus' understanding of time seems to be an interesting alternative to antithetical frameworks, such as those found in Fuchs.

In the debate with Cullmann, Fuchs is concerned (in 1949) with presenting Christ as the end of history and the Law.[117] In his opinion, God did not reveal a plan of salvation, but rather a "new" age.[118] On the cross, Christ was the end of history, or in other words: Jesus' cross itself was the *eschaton*, the moment between the ages.[119] This "time between the ages" reappears in Fuchs's 1960 essay on Jesus' understanding of time, namely, as the description of Jesus' presence as a "chronologically impossible time":[120] "Jesus claims his time as the presence prior to God's coming, in a way that contrasts it to every other time."[121] Thus, Jesus distinguishes between the two miracles of the call to freedom and the coming of God, a distinction that is ultimately identical with the knowledge of God. Present and future hereby relate to each other as the miracle of the call relates to the miracle of God's coming.[122] What remains decisive for the understanding of time is that Jesus' cry on the cross was an eternally valid act of love upon which our entire time/age depends.[123] It seems that this statement about Jesus' cry sheds light on Fuchs's claim that "His word *was* then *word-of-time*, nothing else."[124]

The very condensed way in which I have presented some of Linnemann's and Fuchs's thoughts may create confusion, but in fact, the arguments themselves are at times opaque and appear to take place on several levels at once. The lack of clarity about what is meant by "time" whenever the term is used makes it difficult to grasp the content of the discussion. The various emphases and characteristics of the New Testament writings cause additional problems for a comprehensive account of Jesus' understanding of time.

Time and Eschatology

Because of the problems just discussed, I would like to describe some of the nuances of New Testament concepts of time in light of various eschatological concepts.

Mark conceives of Jesus' proclamation of the nearness of the reign of God in such a way that, in spite of its eschatological character, this reign already begins to be realized in the work of Jesus. "The future determines the present, but in a way that that which is consummated in the future can be partially experienced in the present."[125] Things are indeed judged in light of the end, but the emphasis is on the Christian way of coping with the present.[126] Mark narrates his story for this purpose.[127]

The connection between eschatology and ecclesiology is primarily found in Matthew.[128] Jesus' lifetime on earth, "obviously in the state of still ambiguous lowliness," and the time of the Holy Spirit, which dawns with Jesus' exaltation, as the time of decision, belong to this eon.[129] The time between the Resurrection and Jesus' *parousia* is the time of the Church, which exists as *corpus mixtum* until the separation at the Last Judgment. The coming eon then begins with the Last Judgment. The strength of this concept is its account of the paradoxical presence of salvation under the conditions of time, as a dynamic interlocking of *kairos* and *chronos*.

In Luke, the end of the world is energetically pushed into the distance. Luke deals more with the past than with the future. In Luke's conception of salvation history, the *Una sancta apostolica*[130] conclusively replaces the *eschaton* for an indefinite period. Jesus' absence is the normal state; proclamation is remembering the history of Jesus as the central epoch of salvation history. This is no longer about the two eons, but rather about a plan of salvation in two phases (age of promise and age of fulfillment) or three phases (age of Israel, age of Jesus, and age of the Church).[131] Entrance into eternal life is depicted as an individual event.[132] Eyewitnesses and apostolic succession guarantee the truth of Jesus' history in the present. Only in this way can the salvation situated in the past become the center of time.[133] Thus, of all of the evangelists, Luke has the most chronological concept of time.

In John, the eschatological crisis occurs as a present event. "His eschatological confession of faith is the unique and tremendous protest against the trivialization and emptying of the present, that is qualified as eschatological by the coming of Jesus."[134] What elsewhere is expected as future fulfillment is here already present, as individual appropriation of salvation. "The eschatological crisis is thus already decided in *faith*."[135] This, of course, does not end the discussion about the future; but if eternal life has already been realized in this manner, then at least the delay of the *parousia* is no longer a problem. Wherever else eternity is thought of in light of (the consummation of) time, it is threatened by a quantifying definition presenting it as a magnified projection of time. In avoiding this train of thought, John promotes an understanding of eternity in terms of quality instead of quantity. Eternity can enter into time in transformative fashion precisely as—and only as—something qualitatively different from time (John 5:24).[136]

In Paul, eschatology is shaped christologically.[137] Christ came when time was fulfilled.[138] The present and the existence of Christians is defined eschatologically by Christ's having already come. When Paul refers to the Law as *paidagōgos . . . eis Christon* (Gal. 3:24), this definitely includes a temporal determination.[139] Paul "fundamentally sees the present as the time of the beginning, eschatological saving activity of God."[140] Those who are in Christ have already died with Christ, but their resurrection is still to come.[141] Apocalyptic concepts of the eons hardly play a role here. The present eon does in fact still exist, and it threatens those who live in it, but in Christ the decisive redemptive act has already taken place. This is why, even now, the believer lives in the glory of Christ. Old and new, present and future not only touch each other; they even overlap to some degree. What is still to come, then, is not a new eon, but rather the reign of God,[142] Christ's *parousia*,[143] the revealing of the Lord,[144] and of the children of God.[145] An apocalyptic time scheme is replaced by the final salvation, that is, the communion with Jesus Christ that is no longer endangered or coming to an end.[146]

The Pauline "already" and "not-yet"[147] describes not only the eschatological tension between present and future in Christian life. It can also explain the apparent contradiction between near expectation of the *parousia* and the anticipation of death. While Paul considers the impending *parousia* and the simultaneous reception of the spiritual body,[148] he also speaks of individual death as the date when one receives final salvation;[149] or he possibly contemplates a temporary waiting by the dead[150] for the final appearance of

Christ.[151] This seeming contradiction can be explained by the fact that Paul neither speaks antithetically of time and eternity nor permits eternity to appear as endless time. The breaking through of the new into the old, which is thematized as the tension between the "already" and the "not-yet," interests him more than the abstract forms of time and eternity.

In the later writings of the New Testament, we can see attempts to link eschatology, apocalypticism, and Christology to one another. With increasing temporal distance to Jesus' life on earth, thoughts about the events that are expected at the end of time are turned into a doctrine of the "Last Things," which moves to the margin of ecclesiastical instruction.[152] Colossians and Ephesians replace eschatological expectation with spatial concepts and, in contrast to Romans, allow the resurrection with Christ to take place in Baptism.[153] End-time expectation is less oriented toward the resurrection of the dead than toward the revelation of the *doxa*. Until then, the extended time of waiting is used for exhortation. The most obvious connection of eschatology, apocalypticism, and Christology can be encountered in the Revelation of John: "The wealth of apocalyptic images is embraced by the Christological confession. Thus, the apocalyptic material has experienced a link to history that alters its character in a basic way, so that it now serves to illustrate the universality of the Christ event."[154]

Spatial and temporal conceptions in eschatological thought cannot simply be isolated from each other. Rather, a combination of the two ways of thinking should be assumed, although in apocalypticism the spatial components are more salient.

Summarizing Theses

1. The concept of time is not a specific concern in the Bible. In the Old Testament, as in the New Testament, one does not deal with notions of the essence of time and/or eternity per se.

2. A dualism of time and eternity cannot be discovered in the Bible. Time and eternity do not encounter each other as an antithesis, but rather relate to each other in various ways.

3. There is general agreement in biblical research that the Bible deals more with the content than with the form of time. Time is not an empty category; instead, time is filled time. It is granted by God, and it is oriented toward a goal. Correspondingly, eternity is also not encountered as an endlessly extended form of time, but rather as something qualitatively different from time.

4. Contrasting cyclical and linear time proves to be inadequate. Generally speaking, the inadequacy and provisional nature of spatial expressions

for time must be given careful consideration[155] because, on the one hand, the static character of spatial conceptions hides the dynamic character of time and, on the other hand, the spatialization of time leads almost inevitably to generalizations that can hardly be substantiated.[156]

5. The ambiguity of biblical language and the conception of time cause considerable problems for theological discourse. Theological work must live with the aporia of not being able to clearly define, in the light of the biblical sources, what would need to be defined for a successful dialogue. On the other hand, this multiplicity of meanings ensures an openness that facilitates the discussion of various models.

6. The scope of the biblical, and particularly the New Testament, concept of time is most clearly expressed in eschatology. The tension between "already" and "not-yet," which occurs in various degrees in the New Testament writings, is constitutive for a New Testament understanding of time.

7. In order to do justice to the multilayered dynamic nature of the biblical concept of time, one should strive for the most plural time concept possible. This concept should have room for *chronos* and *kairos*, for eons whose meanings vacillate, for near and remote (time), and for extended and concentrated time; and it should be expressed narratively in a variety of images: in straight lines and wavy lines, in circles and spirals, in points and crosses, in islands and seas.

8. Against the horizon of the New Testament, the development found in chapter 1 toward a stronger contemporization of the future in hymns appears to be a shifting of the "not-yet" toward the "already."[157] This is a change from what is more nearly a Lucan focus in theology and tradition to one that is more strongly Johannine. In the remainder of this study I will keep in mind the dynamic nature of the relationship between "already" and "not-yet," between new and old ages.

Time in Theological Conceptualization

At the beginning of the second chapter of this study, I dealt with Ratschow's *Anmerkungen zur theologischen Auffassung des Zeitproblems*. Our examination of biblical concepts of time found that he was correct in saying that the Bible was not concerned with a dualism of time and an eternity that is considered unchangeable and endless or timeless. Instead, Ratschow proposed a relational model: God behaves like a loyal, jealous, angry God vis-à-vis the world and human time; God's coming days, which are also called the "day of salvation," are linked to the day and night of human and world time; time as moment relates to eternity in much the same way as the "closedness" of insufficient time relates to the openness of having-time-for.

Against the backdrop of our findings on how time in the Bible is understood not as form but rather from the perspective of its content—as filled time, Ratschow's model seems conclusive. Just as abstract time is not an issue in the Bible, there is also no abstract eternity. Rather, the Bible evidences an active relationship between the two, as is most clearly expressed in the New Testament in the tense eschatological relationship between "already" and "not-yet." Because time is not conceivable as an abstract entity, I would now like to address the question of the relationship of God, time, and eternity.

God, Time, and Eternity—Theological Approaches

In terms of a correct distinction between Creator and creation, the theological answer to the question of God's relationship to time seems to have been taken for granted for centuries:[158] God is beyond time, since time means finiteness and changeability, whereas God is distinguished from creation by being infinite and immutable.[159]

One can change perspective, however, and ask: Can a God who is exclusively beyond time truly be God? Would the unrelatedness herein implied not be understood as a deficiency? Thus, Paul Tillich writes: "If we call God a living God, we affirm that he includes temporality and with this a relation to the modes of time."[160] There was much argument in this direction during the twentieth century, in order "to liberate the concept of God from its Babylonian captivity as an abstract contrast to the concept of time."[161]

God in Contrast to Time?

Because it has become increasingly more evident in the course of this study that the question regarding the relationship of time to eternity necessitates the search for dynamic relational models, an article by Ingolf W. Dalferth sparks particular interest, because Dalferth pleads for a revision of the idea that God and time are mutually exclusive. His most important arguments for rejecting the notion of God and time as exclusive alternatives can be summarized as follows:[162]

1. The notion of God's timelessness is not of Judeo-Christian origin; it rather entered Christian theology by way of Neoplatonism.
2. The purely negative category of timelessness is not found in the Bible, and it in no way does justice to the acts of God that are therein described.

3. One can speak of life in a theological way, even of divine life, only when one speaks also of time.

4. If God is timeless in the sense that God has neither a place nor extension in time, then, according to the analytical philosophy of religion, all statements that relate God to time, in terms of place or duration, are meaningless or necessarily false. The notion of a Creator interacting with creation is then impossible.

5. In the view of process theology, God is not only related to time, but is even conceived as a temporal process.

6. From a christological perspective, God proves God's divinity precisely by becoming temporal without thereby ceasing to be God.

7. A doctrine of the Trinity (for example, that of Jürgen Moltmann) that is based on a theology of the cross presents the Trinitarian history of God as the *perichoretic* interlocking of all ages, which means that God should be thought of in terms of a Trinitarian history of time.

Such, or similarly stated, arguments for a revision of the notion of God's timelessness have been variously received. Duane H. Larson[163] argues for temporality within the Trinity, whereas Paul Helm[164] and Brian Leftow[165] hold fast to the timelessness of God, and Alan G. Padgett[166] presents the hypothesis of God's relative timelessness.[167] Both the position of timelessness and that of temporality pose problems that must be overcome. Dalferth approaches these problems by initially choosing a christological and Trinitarian concept of God over a traditionally theistic one because, in his view, without the christological foundation and Trinitarian structure, God's existence as Creator cannot be properly conceived in keeping with a Christian understanding.[168] In the next step, Dalferth supports the thesis that time exists only in the plural: not *the* time, but rather only a multiplicity of times, since the fact of our temporal existence does "not in any way result in a universal structure of time in which all causal sequences of events are localized in a clear and irreversible order."[169]

With respect to the structuring of time in the Christian tradition, Dalferth introduces a basic distinction[170] between "the ontological time difference between eternity and time" and "the eschatological time difference between the old and new ages."[171] Whereas the first deals with the mythical time difference between archaic time and present time, the other concerns the apocalyptic time difference between present time and end time. In the first case, the concern is with a reference back to primeval times, which must always be reenacted through rites and festivals. Current events are understood in light of what has always been. The second model of time is marked by a forward-looking perspective, by the interpretation of events "in light of that which does not yet exist but which, unyieldingly will come."[172] It is this eschatological difference between the old and new ages that comprises the orienting principle of the Church year. Whereas in apocalypticism the tension between the present time and the soon-to-be-dawning end of time is constitutive, Christian theology stresses the tension between the old age and the new age: In the Christ event, the new age has already dawned once and for all, as Paul in particular emphasizes. Jesus' death on the cross brought the old age, the age of Adam, to an end; his resurrection allowed the new age, the age of Christ, to begin. That part of the old age that is now still effective is overlapped by the new age that has already arrived. The "voluntary eschatological changeover to the new age" (2 Cor. 5:17) takes place in human beings through faith.[173]

If this interpretation of the Christ event in terms of a theology of time is correct, then the eschatological time difference would also have to be the decisive interpretation of time in the Christian context. However, as I have shown in my analysis in chapter 1, one must conclude that this is only partially the case, and in a rather weak manner. Dalferth notes that the ontological difference between eternity and time has been superimposed on the eschatological difference. This shift leads to a "neutralizing of the basic contrast between old and new ages into an epochal sequence in the continuum of a presumed world history."[174] As a consequence, the tension between the old and new ages is first reduced to a temporal sequence. Then old and new ages are jointly compared to eternity. As a result, most of the eschatological tension is lost. This preference for the time-eternity contrast in the Christian reflection on time, at the expense of eschatological difference, "does not originate in the basic Christian experience, but it has nevertheless dominated the main tradition of theological reflection on time since the Ancient Church."[175] According to Dalferth, the ensuing way of thinking has contributed successfully to the dissolution of a specifically Christian consciousness of time.[176]

Using three models as examples, Dalferth explains the extent to which descriptions of God's relationship to time, which are based on the ontological difference between time and eternity, are unsatisfactory.[177] The first example is provided by Christian Platonism. There, in timeless eternity, God has a relationship to an eternal world that is the foundation and archetype of the temporal world. The breach between time and eternity is thereby shifted to the world. This means that the relationship between eternal and temporal worlds and the relationship of God to the temporal world remain unclear. If God is related to the temporal world only via the devious route of the eternal world, then the question remains whether anything genuinely new can happen at all in the temporal world. The Platonic model thus invites a conservative position, which hardly leaves room for an eschatological breakthrough into the temporal world.

The second model differentiates the conception of God rather than the conception of the world. Here, by distinguishing between a timeless-eternal God and a temporal God, God—rather than the world—is considered dipolar. The "timeless-eternal" describes the "possible" as the primordial nature of God. The "temporal" describes the "real" as the consequent nature of God. It remains questionable, though, how eternal primordial nature and temporal consequent nature relate to each other. Because God cannot be conceived in this model without a relationship to the world, the thought of a *creatio ex nihilo* becomes problematic. If it was difficult to imagine a true innovation in Platonically oriented thought, then in this model of process theology it is difficult to think of anything other than change. Both examples strive to overcome the gulf between time and eternity by introducing a third party. They are distinguished from each other in that, in the first case, the third instance is introduced as eternal world on the side of eternity; and, in the second case, it is introduced as temporal God on the side of time.

In an apparently elegant manner, a third model avoids the difficulties of the first two by consistently contrasting God and eternity, on the one hand, and world and time, on the other. But then the question immediately arises of how one should conceive of God's acts within this conception. Timeless action appears contradictory, because "action" is always related to time. Consequently, either God could not act at all as Creator, or God could act in God's own time without any temporal relationship to world time, or God appears as the timeless enabling ground for events in time, which, however, undermines the talk of a living God, as appears to me to be the case in Leftow.[178] All three alternatives have one element in common: They basically render God irrelevant for the conception and structuring of time.

The difficulties of Christian Platonism, process theology, and modern theism show that it is insufficient to simply claim that there is "some kind" of relatedness between God and world. Instead, the *how* of the relatedness of God to the world must be discussed in theological terms. For this reason, Dalferth believes that his task is "to emphasize theologically the nature of this relatedness as the nearness of God that makes all things new and gives everything a new quality."[179] He believes that this cannot be achieved by dualistic thought about the world or God. "In order to correct the self-inflicted loss of relevance of the God-concept, we need a new elaboration of the concept of eternity."[180]

Before I discuss Dalferth's suggested solution (see pp. 98–101), the characteristics and consequences of various types of distinctions between time and eternity require further and more detailed analysis.

The Quantitative Difference between Time and Eternity

Whenever models oriented toward Platonism or process theology get into trouble because they build, in different ways, on a qualitative difference between time and eternity and are then unable to demonstrate the relationship of time and eternity conclusively, the opposite path seems tempting. Namely, when one asserts merely a quantitative difference, instead of the qualitative distinction between time and eternity, then further polarization within the concept of world or the concept of God is no longer necessary for describing a time-eternity relationship.

Cullmann's approach offers a good example for the application of a quantitative difference between time and eternity. When reflecting upon some sixteen years of *Wirkungsgeschichte* [history of effect] from *Christus und die Zeit*,[181] Cullmann in fact says that he—irrespective of the title of the book—had not been primarily concerned about time because time is just a screen for his central concern, namely, salvation history.[182] He also would not wish to be understood as a systematic theologian, but rather consciously as a Bible scholar deeply involved with New Testament exegesis.[183] Despite these admissions made within the context of his response to the massive criticism of *Christ and Time*, he nevertheless strongly emphasizes "that because the New Testament speaks only of God's saving acts and nowhere reflects upon God's eternal being, it does not make a philosophical, qualitative distinction between time and eternity and, consequently, knows only linear time."[184]

Precisely this sentence illustrates some of Cullmann's most basic presuppositions, to which he repeatedly returns. He considers a qualitative difference between time and eternity to be philosophical, whereby he understands philosophical as a synonym for Platonic. Cullmann wants to strictly avoid such a philosophical way of looking at New Testament theology because he believes it is completely foreign to the New Testament. In fact, he says that in order to understand the original Christian conception of eternity, one must even think "in *as unphilosophical a manner as possible*."[185] The lack of a qualitative difference between time and eternity then leads him to conclude that the New Testament understanding of time is exclusively linear. Why a qualitative distinction between time and eternity is philosophical/Platonic per se and why the lack of such a distinction necessarily leads to an exclusively linear and—thus—quantitative[186] concept of time remains largely unexplained, however.

Cullmann considers the New Testament concepts of time and history as "the *basic presuppositions of all New Testament theology.*"[187] He emphasizes two characteristics of these conceptions. First, "salvation is bound to a *continuous time process* which embraces past, present, and future. Revelation and salvation take place along the course of an ascending timeline."[188] Second, he asserts that "it is characteristic of this estimate of time as the scene of redemptive history that all points of this redemptive line are related to the one *historical fact* at the mid-point . . . : the death and resurrection of Jesus Christ."[189] Thus, as Cullmann claims, the so-called Christian calendar, which calculates backwards and forwards from the birth of Christ, corresponds to the conceptions of time and history of early Christianity.[190] Cullmann apparently fails to notice here, however, that he himself starts from Jesus' death and resurrection as the center, whereas, already by the sixth century, the West had replaced the old Passion and Resurrection era with the era of the Incarnation.[191]

In contrast to the Greek qualitative distinction between time and eternity, according to which eternity is timelessness, Cullmann says that, for the early Christian view, it turns out "that eternity, which is possible only as an attribute of God, is time, or, to put it better, what we call 'time' is nothing but a part, defined and delimited by God, of this same unending duration of God's time."[192] Early Christianity did not know a timeless God. Time and eternity are both temporal,[193] so that "eternity can be conceived in Primitive Christianity only as endlessly extended time."[194] Temporality is not an exclusive mark of creation.[195] Even if human beings cannot grasp the extent of the timeline, there is no doubt about its measurability.[196] The God who is not timeless reigns over time. God's sovereignty expresses itself in predestination and preexistence, and this, in turn, "signifies nothing else but that he, the Eternal One, is in control over the entire time line in its endless extension. . . ."[197]

Time can be divided into both three and two parts. The tripartite division encompasses the eon prior to creation, the present eon, which lies between creation and the end, and the coming eon, which will contain the New Creation. This tripartite division, however, is overlapped by a two-part division that separates time—as a red line at the zero point of a thermometer scale of infinite expansion—into eons before and after the midpoint of time, that is, an eon before and an eon after Christ's death and resurrection.[198] In this scheme, the Holy Spirit is "nothing else than the anticipation of the end in the present."[199] The Church is included in the divine rule over time as the place where the Spirit is active, and it "takes, so to speak, part in it,"[200] Cullmann claims. He immediately appears to change his mind, however, when he says: "the thing in question is not a sharing by the believer in the Lordship of God over time."[201]

In his chapter on time and eternity, it is striking how frequently Cullmann uses the expressions "nothing else but/than" and "only." Such use of
language generally signifies a reductionist *modus operandi*. In fact, there are
passages where Cullmann reduces to such an extent that alternatives are cut
short and unnecessary dualisms arise. Thus, for example, the inevitability of
the dualism between philosophy in general (and Platonism in particular)
and the New Testament conception is not really plausible. Does the New
Testament then float in space that is void of philosophy? Does every qualitative distinction between time and eternity lead then inevitably to Platonism? Is the contrast of infinite time to timelessness then the only possible alternative? No room remains in Cullmann's system for conceptual attempts
that utilize concepts such as multi-temporality, other-temporality, and
supra-temporality. In my view, this lack of openness for options of qualitative otherness is the most important objection to Cullmann's presentation
of time and eternity.[202]

Cullmann is quick and rigorous in reaching his conclusions. Because
time is conceived as a circle in Greek thought, being bound to time must be
experienced as a curse.[203] Since the New Testament knows only a line of
eons that runs in a consistent straight line from beginning to end, time is
like a straight line.[204] In fact, Cullmann calls it an ascending timeline,[205] although the ascent appears to me as a smuggled-in fruit of Western notions
of progress rather than the result of an exegetical examination of the New
Testament. The combination of line, straight line, and infinity leads to a
problem left unsolved by Cullmann. The problem is intensified by the
measurability that he postulates.[206] When a straight line has a beginning
and an end, it is not infinite, but measurable. A line can be infinite if it has
neither beginning nor end, but then it can hardly be measured. Moreover,
these geometric models are incapable of expressing what actually matters to
Cullmann, namely, the salvation-historical tension between the "already"
and the "not-yet." In retrospect, he recognized this problem correctly.[207] In
Heil als Geschichte, he also finally changed the rigid model of straight lines
to one of wavy lines, though admittedly without changing anything basic.[208]

If eternity is an exclusive attribute of God,[209] but is simultaneously
nothing but (infinite) time, then the concept of eternity is already undermined as soon as it is introduced. This results in what Friedrich Schleiermacher calls the obscuring equating of God's eternity with "what seems to
be eternity, namely, with infinite time," which he combats with the words:
"We must therefore reject as inadequate all those explanations which abro-
gate for God only the limits of time and not time itself, and would form
eternity from time by the removal of limits, while in fact these are oppo-

sites."²¹⁰ Nevertheless, Cullmann ultimately embraces the equation: eternity = time. Then, however, the God who is thought to have power over time and to rule over time is, in the end, a temporal God who can at best be distinguished from creation only in terms of a Feuerbachian projection. The purely quantitative difference between time and eternity essentially renders the concept of eternity superfluous. Because only God is granted eternity and because this eternity is understood as God's power over time, one can actually do without the concept of eternity. What remains is time, of which we know little except that it is the screen for salvation history,²¹¹ that it is "the means of which God makes use in order to reveal his gracious works."²¹²

In my analysis of the New Testament (pp. 72–80), I did not find any self-contained time-eternity model that would come anywhere close to the one that Cullmann develops. Therefore, one must ask: What if Cullmann's scheme is more an interpretation of the Newtonian model of absolute time than an interpretation of a New Testament concept of time?²¹³ Chapter 3 will show how a quantitative time-eternity model of the Cullmann type looks in light of twentieth-century physics.

The Ontological Difference Between Time and Eternity

According to Cullmann, the quantitative difference between time and eternity derived from the need to find a comprehensive framework for his concept of salvation history. This resulted in an alienation of time and eternity from time consciousness because of the definition of time and eternity as *external* categories of the redemptive event. Concurrently, the distinction between time and eternity almost disappeared. The opposing movement, a positioning of the distinction between time and eternity in the *internal* world, is usually ascribed to Augustine's concept of time: Writing 1,500 years before Cullmann, "he moved time into the soul, in order to bring it back home, out of its externalization and diffusion in the world."²¹⁴

If I deal at this point with Augustine, it is not because I am concerned with an overall account of Augustine's doctrine of time. This has been covered in various ways by others and has resulted in vast amounts of literature.²¹⁵ An account of Augustine must also struggle with the fact that it is easier to read something into his writings than to interpret them. To a shockingly high degree, the major preconception of a particular reader of Augustine seems to determine the outcome of the reading. Thus, Karl Hinrich Manzke, for example, proceeds from a time-eternity relationship in which eternity is understood as the truth of time, and he therefore finds a relational time-eternity model in Augustine.²¹⁶ Arguing from the premises of the overall conception of the *Confessions* and Greek ontology, Ulrich

Duchrow concludes that "Augustine's so-called psychological concept of time" does not represent any essentially new solution to the problem of time.[217] Duchrow faults Augustine's lack of interest in connecting physical time to his psychological theory, which resulted in the abandonment of nature. He also criticizes the inconsistency of Augustine's statements on salvation history. Thus, on the one hand, the past tends to dissolve into nothingness; on the other hand, however, it establishes salvation. The future does then indeed promise eschatological redemption, but this redemption is simultaneously defined as the eternally existing present.[218] Duchrow understands both shortcomings as the disastrous fruit of the combining of important elements of Greek ontology and Roman rhetoric; and, due to the pressures of this combination, Augustine was "not innocent in the development toward a modern *diastasis* between the subject and a world abandoned by the Spirit."[219]

Dalferth, in turn, deals with Augustine by proceeding from his preconception of the fateful superimposition of the ontological time difference on the eschatological. He accuses Augustine of domesticating the eschatological time difference, which in fact makes the timeless God irrelevant for orientation in time and abandons the world to a secular notion of progress.[220] By contrast, Gilles Quispel, who believes that it is clearly evident in the church fathers "that the pathos of progress is a secularization of primitive Christian ideas,"[221] describes Augustine's theology as just the opposite. Augustine's theology, he says, is "demythicized eschatology,"[222] because Augustine's key terms for his theology of time—*distentio* and *intentio*—are "the primordial words of Judeo-Christian eschatology."[223] Quispel is not concerned with a relation of eternity to time, as Manzke is, but rather with the individual human soul, which can come into contact with eternity by means of withdrawing from the external world via *intentio*.[224]

Four interpreters and four interpretations: I do not wish to add a fifth here, but rather ask how Augustine may have understood the ontological difference between time and eternity. Linked to this is the question of whether, or to what extent, it is adequate or fruitful to consider time and eternity as having different natures. For this purpose, I shall concentrate on the eleventh book of the *Confessions*.

For Augustine, eternity is *semper stans*, that is, unlimited stability.[225] It is also *totum esse praesens*, complete simultaneity.[226] Furthermore, as the constant present, it is the timeless foundation of all temporal things because time cannot create unity and wholeness out of itself.[227] No possibility exists for comparing eternity to the *temporibus numquam stantibus* (the times that never stand still).[228] Time as the past exists no longer; time as the future does not yet exist; time as the present becomes time only when it moves into the past, for a lasting present would be eternity. For this reason, it belongs to the essence of time that it "flows toward non-existence" [*tendit non esse*].[229] This tendency toward nonexistence is evident when time appears as memory of an earlier present and as the expectation of a future at hand in the actual present. The present is at the heart of Augustine's doctrine of time,[230] yet, even the present is constantly threatened by nonexistence. Given this characteristic, it is understandable why Augustine initially translates the question of the essence of time into the question of its place and its measurability.

Strictly speaking, the separate existence of time as past, present, and future cannot be expressed. Instead, one should say: "there are three times, a present of things past, a present of things present, a present of things to come."[231] As *memoria* (memory), *contuitus* (observation, attention), and *expectatio* (expectation), these three are in the soul.[232] Thus, Augustine finally concludes that time is a kind of extension,[233] namely, an extension of the mind itself [*distentio animi*].[234] Along with creation, time was created by God, the *operator omnium temporum* (operator of all times).[235] Time is not the movement of a body.[236]

Measured against eternity, the *distentio animi* takes on the negative taste of a shortcoming or a defect. The *distentio* is then no longer simply the solution to the problem of the measurability of time in the sense of extension; it is also, simultaneously, a synonym for fragmentation and being scattered. Temporality appears as the malady of scatteredness, and eternity, as the perfection of calmness. Only *secundum intentionem*, "in the manner of tense composure,"[237] does a consoling hope for a less fragmented life open up. From this perspective, *intentio* is then no longer only the anticipation of an entire hymn before it is sung[238] and the power that moves what is still in the future into the past;[239] rather, it is hope in the "Last Things."[240] Thus, *intentio* and *distentio* fall into a dialectic of praise and lament that can be resolved only through mystical language: "The storms of incoherent events tear to pieces my thoughts, the inmost entrails of my soul, until that day when, purified and molten by the fire of your love, I flow together to merge into you.[241]

This view of Augustine's hardly leaves room for an optimistic notion of progress. Augustine does not expect something from a future within time, but rather from a present. Only in the *praesens attentio* of the soul can a person, by means of a combination of memory (*memoria*), present attention (*contuitus, attentio*), and expectation (*expectatio*), establish a unity of temporal events.[242] And only in moments of fulfilled present, when time opens itself to eternity, so to speak, in a *rara visio* (a rare vision) of enlightenment,[243] is it possible for human beings to access, though fragmentarily, the transcendent, the connectedness of time and eternity, and the experience of eternity.[244] Apart from such mystical moments—he may have been thinking of the vision of Ostia[245]—Augustine does not anticipate a future fulfillment of time in eternity: "For Augustine, in human history, a person always remains the same distance from God's eternity."[246] Thus, for Augustine, the essential difference between eternity and time continues to be the prevailing one. A dynamic relationship of the two to each other, which may entail a relationship to eternity that has implications for the concrete shaping of one's time, remains out of question. For this reason, Duchrow and Dalferth have correctly concluded that nature and the world are left to their own devices. If de-temporalization is the goal of life, questions regarding the concrete shaping of time lose their urgency.[247]

The strength of the ontological distinction between time and eternity lies in its prevention of an idolization of time, by qualifying time as being created vis-à-vis uncreated eternity, and in its presentation of God's eternity as the condition for the possibility of time. Whether the ontological distinction must necessarily lead to a description of time as nothing more than a deficient mode of being, however, remains questionable. At any rate, the ontological distinction is not sufficient for a theological reflection that takes seriously the specific eschatological tension between the already and the not-yet observed in the New Testament. Above all, it does not suffice when the "already" is taken to imply more than merely a momentary glimpse into eternity in the *praesens attentio* of the individual soul, when this "already," for instance, is taken to have consequences for how the person in whom this soul resides relates to other humans and to the world.

The ontological difference between time and eternity causes difficulties not only for anthropology. There are also problems with respect to Christology: Given the ontological difference, is it conceivable that the Incarnation introduces something qualitatively new, or does the static nature of the ontological difference prohibit such dynamics? If the Incarnation also means in-temporization of the eternal, does it then alter the ontological distinction? Would it not then be necessary to modify, in a relational direction, the notion of God's immutability, absoluteness, and impassibility that is implied by the ontological distinction? Thus, the *that* of the ontological distinction presses toward the *how*, and not primarily toward the *how* of the *difference* between time and eternity, but rather, and above all, toward the *how* of the *relationship* between the two. The merely negative *other* seeks a positive *other*.

The Eschatological Difference between Time and Eternity

The eschatological difference between time and eternity needs to be understood in light of the tension between that which was and is, and that which is yet to come. It manifests itself in the difference between old and new time. It does not work with an extrapolation of the existing as the idea of progress does. Instead, the eschatological difference between time and eternity focuses on the new that breaks into the existing. In contrast to the quantitative difference, the eschatological distinction does not presuppose infinite continuity; it builds on daunting discontinuity instead. In contrast to the ontological difference, time is not measured in relation to its opposite (eternity) in order to ascertain what and how much it lacks with regard to complete being. Rather, eternity itself initially moves into the background, giving way to the question of what makes time old or new. Because this question cannot be answered without considering the Jesus event, this differentiation model is essentially linked to Christology, which was not at all true of the ontological model, and was only partially true of the quantitative model.

Apart from Dalferth's scheme, which has already been introduced, it seems that examples for consistent eschatological differentiations between time and eternity are more difficult to find than examples for the other two models. Nevertheless, one can recognize tendencies toward an eschatological differentiation in Karl Rahner's reflections on a theology of time. Rahner complains of the apparent lack of a theology of time.[248] He is also intentional about linking his thoughts on a theology of time to a scientific pluralism,[249] which makes his ideas particularly interesting within the context of this study.

The key concept in Rahner's remarks on the concept of time is the history of freedom.[250] Time is the condition for the possibility of a history of freedom. The concern is not a freedom *from* something, but rather—in eschatological terms—a freedom oriented toward fulfillment in God. In the framework defined in this way, time must be recognized as the determination of the world, which, however, should not be confused with the statement that the world is in time.[251] Transitoriness as experienced temporality is the condition of freedom. This becomes especially clear in relation to death, for there is a yearning for the end as consummation. Accordingly, manifested in death is "that towards which the will of the free person tends at its deepest and most ultimate, because this free person must seek the end of that which merely prolongs itself in time in order to achieve his consummation."[252] Rahner considers the fear of death consistently as a phenomenon of the surface of human consciousness only, whereas at the foundation of our existence we hunger for the end of that which is unconsummated in order that consummation may be achieved.[253]

The history of freedom is conceived individually; it is granted to "the human existence of the individual."[254] Rahner sees time as a characteristic not only of the material world, but also of "the spirit as such,"[255] so that "the time inherent in material reality is not, in the last analysis, the power which dominates human history, but on the contrary remains one particular and subordinate element in the time that belongs to personal freedom."[256] Thus, Rahner does not speak of a new time that transforms existing time into an old time. He misses these dynamics by choosing the distinction between the time of the spirit and the time of matter. It is therefore not surprising that Rahner finds the decisive argument for asserting the temporal finiteness of the world precisely in the human being's limited capacity for freedom:

we can and must positively assert that the time of the world is finite . . . , if, and to the extent that, we regard the time belonging to the world as the material for the finite freedom of man as related to the totality of the world. For in that case to postulate an infinitude of the world's time would imply that it was of such a kind that in principle it could not be the material of man's finite freedom in this sense.[257]

Against this backdrop, Rahner's premises are clear: The human being considered as an individual has precedence over nature,[258] the spiritual over the material,[259] and the internal over the external.[260]

A suspicion of Platonism is aroused here. Rahner seems to adopt a dualism that applies not only to the relationship of the personal spirit to its material environment, but also to the relationship between the history of salvation and physical time in general. The latter can then be determined only negatively, "And, this negative character, considered as a negative inherent in the time of material being, is precisely that negativity which prevents this time as such from being raised in itself to any definitive and final state of being brought to an end in this."[261] For its consummation, time therefore needs an Other.

With this concept, however, Rahner is at the same time far removed from a concept of time as an absolute, constantly and uniformly flowing given. "Manifestly, time is not a modality which is present in a univocal sense everywhere where anything takes place, but rather a modality which admits of intrinsic variations, and hence is analogously applied to the various realities of which it is predicated."[262] At this point, Rahner therefore sees a dynamic nature that enables him, in analogy of the relationship between grace and nature, to express an explicit relationship between the time of the spirit—now called the supernatural understanding of time—and the profane understanding of time.[263] Thus, in the final analysis, the accusation of dualism does not stick, and one must instead speak of a duality. The scheme, which is basically hierarchical, is repeatedly eclipsed by a complementary understanding in which the lower is the distinct condition for the possibility of the higher.

In the manner of existentialist theology, the eternity of God is understood in light of the experience of time, not merely of physical time, but rather *via eminentiae* in light of time understood as the event of the free self-communication of God. God is nontemporal, but God experiences history in the Other of the world.[264] God makes divine eternity the true meaning of time. Time is separate from eternity, but eternity is not actually separate from time, i.e., eternity can include the temporal, but not vice versa. The latter does not work because time is constituted by the loving self-communication of God to God's Other.[265] Rahner does not see an actual difference between time and history because, for him, time shows up only as human history.

Here, the eschatological time difference remains implicit, so to speak. It is true that Rahner speaks of *kairos* and *ephapax*,[266] but, strangely enough, he does not mention the eschatological problem of the "already" and the "not-yet" within the context of his theological remarks on the concept of time. The "already" of consummation as a result of God's self-communication in the Incarnation seems curiously "timeless"; it more closely resembles an abstract principle than it does an event. This may well be due to the fact that Rahner does not really understand eschatology in light of the future, but rather primarily from statements of the past that are interpreted in the present. He does indeed emphasize that Christian eschatology "really bears on the *future*, that which is still to come, in a very ordinary, empirical sense of the word time" and may not be de-eschatologized into "something that takes place here and now in the existence of each individual and in the decision he takes here and now."[267] Then, however, Rahner identifies "a forward-looking draft of existence oriented toward the fulfillment of the end of time"[268] as the source of revelation of the *eschata*. Accordingly, the future occurs less as the breakthrough of the new than as an extrapolation of the consummation that has already been granted: "[B]iblical eschatology must always be read as an assertion based on the revealed present and pointing towards the genuine future, but not as an assertion pointing back from an anticipated future into the present. To extrapolate from the present into the future is eschatology, to interpolate from the future into the present is apocalyptic."[269] This, however, puts the eschatological discontinuity in danger of complete dissolution. It is therefore not surprising that Rahner can call eternity the "fruit of time" and that, in the context of Johannine eschatology, which he understands as "in-existence of eternity in time," "eternity emerges out of time."[270]

Given this method of extrapolation, the question arises: Can there be anything really new? How much innovation can be expected in this framework? Well, Rahner expects the dissolution of time, because the final realization of the consummation that has already happened cannot take place on this time axis;[271] and he anticipates the individual event of consummation in human death, by means of which ultimate consummation, as Philip Geister expresses it, "is gradually 'ratified.'"[272] "Eschatological consummation appears to be like a cosmic puzzle into which a new part is added every time a person dies, until finally it is completed—at the end of time and the cosmos."[273] Later, I will return to alternative ways of understanding death. In the meantime, it should suffice here to say that Rahner's implicit eschatological time difference definitely overcomes a static dualism, but its way of juxtaposing time and eternity largely remains hostage to an anthropocentric and individualistic approach.[274]

Wolfhart Pannenberg's method is more explicitly eschatological. Pannenberg repeatedly stresses that God's eternity enters time along with the eschatological future and, from there, is creatively present to every temporal thing that precedes this future.[275] This creative presence means that that which exists in time—based on that which will emerge as its true identity at the end of time and history—is already now participating in eternity.[276] An event that has not yet occurred thus determines the present as if it were already a historical fact. That which will not fully occur until the eschatological future is already manifest: "the truth of things that will be revealed in the future, their true essence that will come to light in the *eschaton*, generally defines already their present existence."[277] How is this possible? Pannenberg does not provide a direct explanation. The biblical reference that he cites (". . . what we will be has not yet been revealed," 1 John 3:2)[278] admittedly emphasizes the "not-yet," but it says nothing about the powerful "already" that is related to participation in eternity. Instead, Pannenberg resorts to the historical past by saying that only in the history of Jesus of Nazareth did the eschatological future, and, with it, the eternity of God, actually enter into the historical present.[279] Pannenberg offers contradictory information regarding the degree of discontinuity between that which is and that which is to come. On the one hand, the eschatological future faces present reality, which should already be conceived as its own eschatological manifestation in the process of becoming, "not as a totally different reality."[280] On the other hand, because of sin, the participation of created beings in the eternity of God is "possible, however, only on the condition of a radical change."[281]

Like Rahner, Pannenberg also does not make use of the terminology of old and new time. Upon closer examination, it is also evident that one cannot really expect anything genuinely new in his eschatology, because, ultimately, nothing is newly created. Instead, that which has always existed is restored, something that brings to mind the return of eternal ideas to their timeless source rather than a new heaven and a new earth: "The resurrection of the dead and the renewal of creation may be seen as the act by which God through his spirit, *restores* to the creatures' essence that is preserved in his eternity *the form of being-for-themselves*."[282] Inspired by Pannenberg's frequent use of the term *future*, one had hoped that the eschatological distinction between old and new time would have rendered the relation of time and eternity in Pannenberg's theology more dynamic. It seems, however, that the dynamic hoped for has been eclipsed by a rather conservatively oriented constancy of essence.

Models based on the distinction between old and new times probably often fail because of their difficulty in accounting for the concept of eternity. Is in this scheme eternity being replaced by the new time? Will it be absorbed by the concept of future? The answer to these questions depends, first, upon whether the eschatological difference excludes, includes, or even surpasses the ontological difference, and, second, upon how successful one is in taking seriously the specificity of the time that is qualified as old time even after the new time has dawned.

The ontological differentiation is included in the eschatological one to the extent that the coming of new time is not a penetration of two ontological spheres, but is instead an interaction that does not destroy the respective character of the interacting entities but strengthens it. Through the breakthrough of new time, old and new times are essentially linked to each other and related to each other, although they remain different from each other. This is the relationship of tension described with the words "already" and "not-yet."

God, Time, and Eternity—
Trinitarian Perspectives

The attempt to describe the relationship of time to eternity theologically must also consider the question of the understanding of God. As soon as one is concerned not only with the *that* of the distinction between time and eternity, but rather with the *how* of the relationship of time and eternity, then one cannot deal only with the *that* of a concept of God. If time and eternity are distinguished from each other and if God relates to both of them, then the question also arises regarding a differentiation in this divine relationship, because every relationship implies differentiation. I am thus confronted with the question of how God's relationship to eternity is different from God's relationship to time. Consequently, one cannot presume a God who is like a monolith, but rather, one must speak about God as an internally differentiated unity. A relational concept of time appears to presuppose differentiation in God.

The idea of the differentiation between time and eternity consequently suggests differentiation in God. Initially, however, this brings up only the idea of a two-part differentiation, i.e., a doctrine of the Trinity cannot necessarily be derived from the time-eternity relation. Trinitarian dogma must be substantiated elsewhere and therefore is presented only secondarily within the context of the time-eternity discussion. Dalferth,[283] in particular, is not sufficiently clear at this point, which is why he must accept the reproach that he does not provide enough justification for his imposition of a Trinitarian scheme onto the eschatological time-eternity difference that he accurately outlined.[284]

After having addressed this caveat, I will now nevertheless turn my attention to an examination of Trinitarian conceptions of time. This is motivated by the central place that the doctrine of the Trinity occupies in Christian theology.

Trinitarian Differentiation of Time and Eternity

First, I would like to return to Dalferth's suggestion of how the relationship between God and time can be conceived.[285] I have already introduced Dalferth's revision of the view that God is eternal and therefore timeless. God's eternity cannot simply be "the negative Other of time"[286] if God's relation to time is to be perceived as positive. Conversely, God also cannot simply be conceived as being temporally eternal in the sense of *sempiternitas,* because this does not permit the idea of a positive relation of God to time that maintains the difference between God and creation. In other words, mixing time and eternity by eternalizing time and temporalizing eternity is not a solution. It jeopardizes both the relatedness of God to the world and the difference between Creator and creation.

God's eternity is temporal, not in the sense of infinite duration, but rather in the sense of a multi-temporality: "God is close at all times in every time sequence."[287] This multi-temporal presence of God would inevitably lead to a fragmentation of the idea of God, however, if we did not also simultaneously assume God's timeless presence: God's "co-presence with the multitude of times requires that God's eternity be conceived not merely as infinite temporality, but rather as a unity of timelessness and multi-temporality."[288]

An acceptable concept of eternity therefore requires a twofold correction of the view of eternity that has been common since Augustine. First,

God should not be viewed as merely timeless; and, second, the ontological difference between eternity and time should be interpreted in light of the eschatological difference between old and new times, and not vice versa. In light of the eschatological difference, the timeless and temporal eternities of God are no longer mutually exclusive. Rather, the two should be considered together, "because God, based on the concrete event of God's temporal self-revelation, is seen in Trinitarian differentiation as Father, Son, and Spirit; and, correspondingly, God's relationship to time should also be viewed in a Trinitarian manner—that is, always different in the horizon of God's action of creation, of salvation, and of consummation."[289] These differences are expressed as the timeless eternity of God the Creator, the multi-temporal eternity of the Spirit, and the temporality of the Son.

As Creator, God relates to creation as the divine Other, which, in turn, means "that God defines Godself as timeless in relation to time, i.e., to the timeless actualization of certain temporal possibilities."[290] This describes the ontological difference between timeless eternity and time. The temporal eternity of the work of the Spirit is rooted in the intent of the Creator, namely, that creation exists *coram deo*, in the presence of the God who remains nearby. The multiplicity of times that are specific to events in creation determines the temporal eternity of the work of the Spirit as multi-temporality. Subsequently, the eschatological difference between old and new times is manifested in the temporality of the Son. Here, God's eternal temporality is made known as God's "timeless readiness to concede time to creation and to take time for creation eternally and temporally."[291] Dalferth thus expresses the same time-eternity understanding of the Incarnation that we have already seen in a Christmas hymn by Martin Luther. The literal translation of the stanza reads like this:

> The eternal Light enters there,
> gives the world a new glow;
> it shines in the middle of the night
> and makes us children of the light. Kyrieleis.[292]

Eternal temporality (eternal Light) enters into time (shines in the night), which lends that which is located in time something new (makes us children of the light).

The main thrust of Dalferth's article is thus a time-eternity conception marked by a Trinitarian differentiation. This highlights the eschatological difference between old and new times to the disadvantage of the ontological difference between time and eternity. Dalferth himself summarizes his solution as follows:

God is related to creation, in triune fashion, as a differentiated unity of Father, Spirit, and Son: as the timeless foundation of everything, as the multi-temporal companion of everyone, and as the temporal mediator of salvation in the specific lifetime of Jesus Christ and of all who believe in him. God's eternity is the epitome of these time relationships and cannot be identified with any one of them as such.[293]

Dalferth's reflections lead us further at some important points: First, he frees theological discourse from the fetters of philosophy. Then, he is successful in overcoming exclusive alternatives, and he achieves a certain relationality. He does this by creating relationships without being guilty of mixing concepts. Thus, relationality emerges within retained differentiation, as Dalferth himself subsequently formulates: "God does not simply belong to a realm above and beyond our world, but God is also not merely wrapped up in it [our world] and thus destroyed by its contradictions, ambivalences, congenialities, and horrors. Rather, God distinguishes Godself from it by establishing differences in it. . . ."[294]

What one misses in Dalferth's theory, however, is a more exact explanation of how the economic Trinity relates to the immanent Trinity. Without more clarity on this point, it is difficult to decide whether or not the Trinitarian differentiation of time is, in the end, more than an elegant phrase. Dalferth must also face the question of whether he does not ultimately give up the primacy of the eschatological difference when he anchors the ontological time difference in the Creator and the eschatological time difference in the Son. With respect to the Holy Spirit, the question of the Spirit's own role is sparked; it is not at all clear to what extent the Spirit's multi-temporal role is still necessary and constitutive after the positions of the Father and Son have been determined. This promising view of the Trinitarian differentiation thus falls short of its own claim. The new concept of eternity that is called for remains somewhat fuzzy; nevertheless, the proposed unity of timelessness and multi-temporality seems promising.

Pannenberg also wishes to think of the relationship of God's eternity to time in a Trinitarian perspective. Furthermore, he uses scientific models such as the field concept in his theology, which makes him an especially interesting dialogue partner. With respect to the philosophy of time, Pannenberg starts with Plotinus and Boethius.

According to Pannenberg, a genuine relationship of God to time can be conceived only "if the reality of God is not understood as undifferentiated identity but as intrinsically differentiated unity."[295] According to Pannenberg, this is precisely what the doctrine of the Trinity accomplishes: "in virtue of trinitarian differentiation God's eternity includes the time of creatures in its full range, from the beginning of creation to its eschatological consummation."[296] Pannenberg hereby assumes the unity of the immanent and economic Trinities.[297]

Thus, even here we have a concept that abandons the notion of eternity as nothing more than the opposite of time.[298] Instead, we find a model that differentiates eternity and time, and still allows eternity to encompass the entire course of time. Pannenberg is interested in an inclusive definition of eternity, since an exclusive definition of eternity—as the negative Other of time—would wind up in the dead end of finiteness:

> The thought of eternity that is not simply opposed to time but positively related to it, embracing it in its totality, offers a paradigmatic illustration and actualization of the structure of the true Infinite which is not just opposed to the finite but also embraces the antithesis. On the other hand the idea of a timeless eternity that is merely opposed to time corresponds to the improper infinite which in its opposition to the finite is defined by it and thereby shows itself to be finite.[299]

The end of time is to be understood in analogy to the death of the individual as the event when time is dissolved into eternity, whereby, according to Pannenberg, neither the characteristics of created reality nor the distinctiveness of time's moments and modes simply disappear. They are instead transposed into a kind of simultaneity.[300] Eternity is the condition of the coherence in the sequence of temporal moments and should therefore be considered as the boundary[301] and "structural foundation of time."[302] The future, however, also plays a constitutive role for the essence of time, "because only in terms of the future could the totality be given to time which makes possible the unity and continuity of time's process";[303] the future excludes a simultaneity of all times with eternity and thus creates a dynamic process that moves towards the end.[304] These two statements about eternity and future are not contradictory only because, in the future of God's rule—that is, in the coming of God's reign— Pannenberg sees the beginning of God's eternity in time, as well as the place of eternity itself in time, and the place of God in God's relationship to the world.[305]

In the following sections, I will continue to focus on how Pannenberg portrays the time-eternity relation of the individual persons of the Trinity in his theology. I will now discuss the concepts of the eternal Father, the eternal Son, and the eternal Spirit.

The Eternal Father

Pannenberg says that "God is eternal because he has no future outside of himself. His future is that of himself and of all that is distinct from him."[306] This means that "the eternal God as the absolute future—in the commun-

ion of Father, Son, and Spirit—[is] the free origin of himself and his creation."[307] One difficulty posed by the depiction of the temporal relation of
the eternal Father is immediately evident in these sentences. Statements
about the eternal God who does not exhibit Trinitarian differentiation are
often hardly distinguishable from statements about the eternal Father as a
person within the Trinity. In Pannenberg's work, it becomes very clear how
the talk of Father and Creator becomes possible only in the reciprocal relation especially between Father and Son, because the starting point for the
otherness and the independence of creation lies in the Father's devotion to
the Son and the Son's humble self-differentiation from the Father.[308]

The creative act of God is to be conceived as an eternal act. It is inadequate to think of creation as an act in time; it can be adequately conceived
only as the construction of the finite reality of created beings together with
time as their form of existence. In contrast, God's preservational act as *creatio continua* is structured temporally. In preserving and ruling, God becomes involved with time as the existential form of creation.[309] There need
be no contradiction between the historicity and contingency of divine action in preserving creation and the eternity of God in the act of creation.
Both can be asserted under the condition that God's immutability be interpreted as an expression of God's faithfulness. This interpretation allows
room, on the one hand, for an evolution, a becoming, in Godself, as the dynamic nature of the Trinitarian relationships; on the other hand, God's eternity is expressed over the course of time as the faithfulness of divine creative
love. Furthermore, this concept enables one to conceive of a process overarching creation that allows eternity and time to coincide only in the eschatological consummation of history.[310]

Holding together conceptually the eternal act of creation and the temporally structured, preserving, and ruling acts of God paves the way for "an
attempt to think of the eschaton as the creative beginning of the cosmic
process."[311] This also solves the problem that God's foreknowledge, from
the time of creation forward, would rob the world of its contingency and
necessarily lead to determinism. If, namely, "the eschatological future of
God in the coming of his kingdom is the standpoint from which to understand the world as a whole,"[312] then the beginning of the world can no
longer be thought of as a self-contained, unchangeable foundation of the
entire world; it is then "merely the beginning of that which will achieve its
full form and true individuality, only at the end."[313]

If God's eternity were appropriately and adequately described as timelessness or infinite time, then a philosophical, undifferentiated concept of
God would suffice. If, however, incorruptibility and pre-temporality, as well
as omnipresence[314] and temporal powerfulness, belong to God's eternity,

then the discussion quickly turns to the eternal Spirit and, even more quickly, to the eternal Son. The latter is probably connected to the fact that the difference between the Son and the Father seems clearer than the difference between the Spirit and the Father. While either the Father or the Spirit alone seems to be able to represent divinity as a whole, the Son participates in the eternal Godhead only through his relationship to the Father and, thus, through his differentiation from this Father.[315]

The Eternal Son

The question of the eternal Son is twofold. It involves the question of the eternal future of the Son and the question of the Son's eternal past. The first question concerns the post-existence of the eternally Exalted One, and it also includes the question of the presence of this Exalted One. The second question leads to reflections on preexistence, which is formulated in the Nicene Creed with the words "eternally begotten of the Father."

In his extensive work entitled *Geboren vor aller Zeit?*,[316] Karl-Josef Kuschel examines the *topos* of the preexistence of Christ. He traces the treatment of this topic—from Adolf von Harnack to Karl Barth, Rudolf Bultmann, Wolfhart Pannenberg, Karl Rahner, Eberhard Jüngel, Jürgen Moltmann, among others, and, finally, to Walter Kasper and Edward Schillebeeckx—and gives an account and an interpretation of christological statements in the Bible having to do with preexistence. Kuschel then tries to provide starting points for a fruitful interreligious dialogue on this topic, and for the dialogue with scientific cosmology, with art and literature, and also—within theology itself—with liberation theology and feminist theology.[317] Unfortunately, Kuschel's perspectives for dialogue, especially with regard to the natural sciences, are basically limited to text references and to admonitions "to think situationally and contextually";[318] apart from that, however, he presents a wealth of valuable material.

Kuschel initially notes: "The New Testament does not know of pre-existence [of Jesus Christ] as a speculative theme."[319] Rather, in light of the New Testament texts, a preexistence Christology would have to be relativized. Jesus himself never spoke of his own preexistence. In twenty New Testament writings, Jesus as the Son of God is mentioned without this being tied to notions of preexistence. In the places where statements about preexistence appear, for example, in Colossians and Hebrews, as well as in the Johannine writings, they are relativized by statements rooted in a theology of the cross and a theology of the Incarnation.[320] Above all, however, one should remember that statements on preexistence have a retrospective character. They are eschatological statements that originated in the Easter experience and are therefore secondary in relation to resurrection Christology or exaltation Christology.[321] Thus, just as one dared in the Old Testament to draw conclusions from the exodus experience for creation history,[322] "so too now Christians argued back from the experience of the God who creates anew (indeed he had liberated Jesus from death) to the God of primal creation."[323] It is therefore also clear that there can be no statement about preexistence that "can pass over the figure of the historical Jesus."[324] Jesus of Nazareth is the eternal Son. The assertion of preexistence has a clear function, namely, "to make comprehensible it's the historical depth and universal significance of the 'event of Jesus.'"[325]

Against this background, the eternity of the Son means that Jesus himself is the way God relates to human beings. This statement expresses the fundamental experience that the source of all existence lies in the concrete person of Jesus; and it makes clear that the person, the purpose, and the fate of Jesus Christ belong definitively to the definition of the eternal essence of God.[326] This makes the reality of God dynamic.[327] "If, in Jesus Christ, God revealed not only a part of divinity, but rather God's very essence in a definitive and unconditional manner, then Jesus Christ—as spirit and in the Spirit— is also present at all times, simultaneous with all times, and free from all times. Nothing else is expressed when we use the words 'preexistence of Christ.'"[328] According to this, preexistence then implies that God's humanity has always belonged to God's divinity.[329]

Precisely this interpretation of preexistence is also found in Jüngel's work: "God does indeed come from God and only from God, and he is determined by nobody and nothing other than by himself; however, he determines himself to be God, not without man. That is the sense of the New Testament statements about the preexistence of the Son of God identified with Jesus."[330] At this point, however, Jüngel does not include the Spirit, but rather argues exclusively in light of the self-definition of God as an expression of divine freedom. This self-definition of God, namely, not to be God without human beings, should be seen in the context of God's self-definition as the one who, through divine initiative, is both lover and loved one,[331] namely as God and as the dead Jesus.[332] In a critical response, Kuschel complains to Jüngel that this self-definition is not actually necessary and that, by suggesting it, Jüngel widens the gap between exegesis and dogmatics.

But when Kuschel pleads both from the viewpoint of biblical theology and dogmatics for a process for reaching conclusions, he has a similar problem: Is his necessity for reaching conclusions (about the self-consistent essence of the eternal God) a better necessity than Jüngel's theological necessity (of the self-definition of God)? Kuschel is unable to completely escape the problems that he himself apostrophizes—citing Karl Hermann Schelkle,[333] namely, that it is questionable to use the formula of preexistence in order to relate divine eternity to human time and then to calculate from that point. In such a process, he says, the phase of salvation history is extended backwards and drawn out into infinity. But the preexistent "before" and the time of salvation history should neither be separated nor added on to each other; instead, they are present in each other, Schelkle states. In light of the self-determination of God, Jüngel's approach indeed avoids this before-and-after difficulty, but is this advantage perhaps gained at the price of a neglected theology of time? Would a theology of time elevate Jüngel's formulations above the suspicion of clever play on words?

This suspicion of puns is not expressed frivolously or ironically at all; Kuschel also remarks that the language here has reached its limitations: "Holding Jesus' preexistence, existence, and post-existence together conceptually . . . requires a *language of simultaneity*, which is perhaps possible for the ciphered language of modern poetry, the tonal language of music, or the color-filled language of painting, but it is not possible for the language of reflection and discourse."[334] Modern science may be able to contribute metaphors and/or models that can be helpful for formulating a theology of time.

In Pannenberg, the eternity of the Son becomes conceivable primarily in his role as mediator of creation. The origin of everything that is different from the Father lies within the Son. "[God's creatures] become the object of the Father's love because the eternal Son is manifested in them."[335] With respect to his creaturely existence, Jesus remains different from the eternal Son. The eternal Son is the ground of his own being and the being of all created things.[336]

Otherwise, Pannenberg sees the life of the earthly and resurrected Jesus—his post-existence—closely tied to the work of the Spirit. In the act of the Incarnation and Resurrection, which, from the perspective of eternity, is one and the same event, the Son was merely an object of the creative dynamic work of the Spirit. The Spirit also participates in the return of Christ, but now in such a way that the work of the Spirit is consummated in Christ's *parousia*.[337] The Incarnation is already the dawning of God's future, the dissolution of the opposition of time to eternity,[338] and the entrance of eternity into time. Essentially, neither the Resurrection nor the *parousia* can add anything to this. Only from the human perspective is there an escalation: The Resurrection provides the foundation for the confession of the Incarnation; the *parousia* ultimately provides the public confirmation of the Easter event. Just as the Resurrection is the prolepsis of eschatological salvation, so is the pre-Easter work of Jesus the prolepsis of the coming reign of God.[339]

The Eternal Spirit

For Pannenberg, a major concern is the emphasis on the relationality of
the persons of the Trinity. In the development of his thinking, he borrows
the concept of field from physics[340] in order to describe the triune God as a
dynamic force field. Distancing himself from the Platonic-Origenic tradition of interpreting the divine spirit as *nous*, Pannenberg opts for interpreting "God is spirit" (John 4:24) as a field that can be conceived as occurring
equally in all three persons of the Trinity.[341] "The divine persons, then, are
. . . individual aspects of the dynamic field of the eternal Godhead."[342] The
Spirit is hereby given a double meaning, as the shared essence of God and as
its own *hypostasis* in the Trinity.[343] It is therefore understandable that the
role of the Spirit changes depending upon whether the Spirit is understood
as an expression of the divinity as a whole or as an entity that is differentiated from Father and Son. This creates some confusion regarding the profile
of the Spirit. According to Pannenberg, God's relation to time in the preservation of creation and in world rule is ultimately based on "the self-differentiation of God in his Trinitarian life" as "the self-differentiation of the Son
from the Father. The Son's moving out of the unity of the divine life makes
independent creaturely existence possible."[344] Here, the Spirit seems to have
run out of work, whereas in other places the participation of the Spirit in
every act of God, from creation to the eschatological consummation of salvation, is emphasized.[345] The consummation of both the individual and the
community is the work of the Spirit. As the eschatological gift, the Spirit is
not only involved in the future still to come; it precedes itself and, by overcoming sin and death, already determines the present of the believers.[346]

According to Pannenberg, "[O]n the one side the Spirit is the principle
of the creative presence of the transcendent God with his creatures; on the
other side he is the medium of the creatures in the divine life, and therefore
in life as such."[347] The dynamic nature of the work of the Spirit consists,
both within the Trinity and in creation, of positive relatedness in the sense
of a communion of the differentiated; however, in time it expresses itself
differently than within the eternal, inner-Trinitarian communion.[348] Even
though Pannenberg himself speaks only of a doubling of the salvific work of
the Spirit in the tension between the future and the present of the eternal,[349]
it appears that the temporal relationship of the Spirit intended here is probably quite consistent with the multi-temporality that Dalferth ascribes to
the Spirit.

Pannenberg relates the multi-temporality of the Spirit to the independence of the creatures. In the differentiation and relatedness of the Spirit
with respect to the present and the future (what has happened here to the

past?), he sees the guarantee that created beings will not be completely absorbed by the presence of God, but will rather continue to exist independently even in their eschatological consummation.[350] It remains unclear whether the work of the Spirit in believers is different from the work of the Spirit in creation as a whole, and if so, to what extent.

One should consider the possibility that multi-temporality contributes to the ambiguity of the role of the Spirit to the point of inconsistency. Thus, Pannenberg can say, for example, that the work of the Son is fulfilled only through the work of the Spirit in the hearts of the believers, that the Spirit thus testifies to Christ,[351] and that, without the Spirit, the Son cannot be the Son.[352] In Kuschel, on the contrary, the emphasis is on the Christ who works through the Spirit in the present and who is not restricted to space and time.[353] With regard to their respective temporal relationships, Christ and the Spirit seem here to be interchangeable.

Generally, multi-temporality can be understood as the constant simultaneity of the dynamic effectiveness of the divine Spirit. In this manner, it can be conceived, from an inner-worldly perspective, as the expression of an eternity that is "the undivided present of life in its totality,"[354] whereby *present* here should be understood as "a present that comprehends all time."[355] Pannenberg does not understand eternity to be anything like the essential nature of time, the "epitome of time"; rather, "we are to think of time with its sequence of events—future, present, past—as proceeding from eternity and constantly comprehended by it."[356] However, he does not think that time can be derived from the concept of eternity, and he sympathizes with Plotinus's conception of the transition from eternity to time as a leap.[357] Time that manifests itself as a time sequence is a precondition for the independence of the created beings. For this reason, one should not expect eschatological consummation to mean the disappearance of differences that have evolved during cosmic time, but rather the dissolution of the separation of ages into past, present, and future.[358]

Pannenberg also examines the theories of quantum physics and thermodynamics when he speaks of the divine Spirit, understood here as the totality of God, as a temporally structured force field of that which is possible in the future. He ventures to identify this force field as the constantly restructuring formative force that is counteracting entropic decay, and ultimately as the source of all events.[359] At the beginning of the unfolding of the creative dynamic nature of the Spirit stands "the emergence of contingent individual events from the possibility field of the future"; its apex attains this dynamic nature "in the integration of events and life's moments into unified form."[360] The goal of the Spirit's work is "to give the creaturely forms duration by a share in eternity and to protect them against the tendency to disintegrate that follows from their independence."[361] "The Spirit, then, is the creative source of resurrection life both in relation to the resurrection of Jesus and in relation to others."[362] In conjunction with the Judgment, which is understood as a purifying fire, the Spirit is granted a judging role. Thus, it unites several functions within itself: It "is the source of salvation, of the new and eternal life, but also the organ of judgment."[363] These functions are held together by the notion of glorification. The Spirit is a participant in the reciprocal glorification of the Father and the Son; and, as the light of divine glory in the fire of purification, it glorifies believers by including them, transformed, in the eternal communion of the Father and the Son.[364] Thus the Spirit moves quite freely beyond the boundaries of time and eternity.

Upon closer examination, one sees that several of Pannenberg's key concepts are clouded by ambivalences that do not appear to have particularly bothered him. At best these ambivalences can be interpreted as the expression of the eschatological tension between the "already" and the "not-yet." Here are some examples of unsettled issues. The independence of the created beings is a gift guaranteed by the self-differentiation of the Son from the Father; however, it is also an evil to be overcome by the Spirit as soon as creatures become too independent. Must the Spirit then be deployed to iron out possible shortcomings and irregularities in the work of the Son? Although eternity allows time to emerge from it, and it constantly encompasses time, the eternity of God nevertheless enters time as future.[365] Time cannot be derived from eternity, yet, in time, eternity is foreboded.[366] Only in relation to the future does Pannenberg himself address ambivalent aspects: For the created being, the future is the possibility for consummation as well as the impending end and disintegration.[367] On the one hand, the future is the expression of the possible that is always coming and successively crystallizes into present fact; it is always that which is yet-to-come. On the other hand, from the perspective of the creature, it is—as the "source of all events"—also that which has already been, i.e., the past.[368]

For Pannenberg, *future* is much more than a grammatical concept and the chronological marker of what is yet to come. In his thinking, it develops into a category *sui generis* that contains significantly more than a chronology: It is the guarantee for the totality of the temporal, including all humankind; it is the dawning of God's eternity in time; it is the unification of time and eternity; and it is even eternity inasmuch as the eternal God is the future of God's own self.[369] However, one must ask whether such rich content does not overstretch the concept of the future to the point that it ultimately becomes an empty cipher. Is Pannenberg's concept eschatological in a way that causes everything to dissolve (prematurely) in the future?

The description of the eschatological difference tells us that when the new time breaks through, the time that thereby becomes old time does not simply disappear. Precisely in its discovery of time that has become old lies an important fact to which, in this respect, Pannenberg is denied access. Jüngel, however, has emphatically referred to this dynamic by insisting on the ontologically positive nature of perishability—namely the primacy of possibility over reality.[370] Because Pannenberg identifies the possible with the future, "old time," for him, is absorbed by the future, without his being able to interpret constructively, from the human perspective, the ambivalent nature of the future that we have just discussed.

The Pros and Cons of Trinitarian Differentiations of Time and Eternity

If at this point my deliberations on Trinitarian differentiations of time and eternity lead to some preliminary conclusions, then I can register both positive and negative results. Trinitarian models enable us to conceive of multi-temporality and relational dynamics between time and eternity. However, unsolved problems have arisen when the persons of the Trinity were assigned to different aspects of time and various ways of distinguishing between time and eternity. Because an account of time/eternity relationships cannot in and of itself justify a doctrine of the Trinity, the Trinity runs the risk of being considered fundamental, although, in reality, it is secondarily superimposed upon a theology of time. The question still remains whether the assigning of aspects of the Trinity to various aspects of time/eternity can occur only more or less arbitrarily or whether tenable criteria for such an assignment can be formulated.

Models of Trinitarian differentiation between time and eternity emphasize the relational dynamics that exist between time and eternity; but, until now, they have been unable to express these dynamics in conclusive models. I will return to these problems in chapter 4.

Before I can turn to models of time in science, however, I would like to examine a phenomenon that so far has received little attention but that is nevertheless of great import for an understanding of time and eternity. We must now supplement the thoughts concerning the relationship of God, time, and eternity with some considerations on death, which, from the human perspective, can be called the event of absolute transitoriness and absolute unrelatedness.

Time and Death—A Human Perspective

In the phenomenon of death, my three previous key concepts—time, eternity, and relation—come together. Death throws important light particularly on the definition of the concept of relation, for the meaning of relation becomes especially clear wherever relationship becomes problematic. Relation can thus be understood precisely in light of its crisis. The most extreme crisis of relation is death, as the event of a very special unrelatedness. The essential nature of death is non-relationality or "relationlessness."[371] "Death is the absolute *other* of being, an *unimaginable* other, hovering beyond the reach of communication."[372]

In the following sections, various aspects of death will therefore be addressed as they relate to time and eternity. I will proceed here from an understanding of human life as a wealth of life relationships that are always in process. With Jüngel, I hold that this non-negotiable relatedness does not constitute an anthropological deficiency. Rather, it is the expression of the true richness of human life: Human beings can live only in relationship; they cannot relate to themselves without already and always being related to others and, above all, to God.[373] Relation is thus understood as a positively loaded word; non-relationality, on the other hand, is understood as a negatively defined word.

The impulse toward non-relationality that terminates relationships in order to have life, so to speak, as a private possession for oneself, . . . is the impulse toward death. And death itself is the result of this impulse toward non-relationality: the event in which even the last relation dissolves and even the last relationship collapses—namely, the relation that I have with myself, self-relationship.[374]

Death is therefore also the event in which the significance and meaning of a relation between time and eternity occurs most succinctly. Every interpretation of death is simultaneously an interpretation of the relation of time and eternity. The following sections should show how modern conceptions of death can illustrate the collapse of the relation of time and eternity that was already observed in the first chapter of this study.

Death as Transition—Eternalized Time and Eroded Eternity

The Hebrew Scriptures say little about what can be expected after death. They speak of *sheol,* the world of the dead, as a shadow world where one does not praise God.[375] The hope for an individual eternal life is a rather late phenomenon.[376] In the New Testament, the theme of resurrection is discussed in light of Jesus' resurrection. The experience of the Resurrection of Jesus does not immediately trigger the individualistic interpretation "if he, then also I." Far more important was the fact that God did not allow the shame of Jesus' horrible death to persist. The Resurrection means that God did justice. Luke presents this testimonial in Peter's sermon at Pentecost (Acts 2:22–36). It takes considerable theological reflection in order to arrive, like Paul, at the insight that the Resurrection of Jesus as the beginning of a new order has significance for the death of the individual and that its goal is "that God may be all in all" (1 Cor. 15:28).

This theology makes it possible to see the biological span of individual life embedded in a larger context. The time of earthly life stands in relation to eternity. That this relation has been foundational for centuries and has been expressed in various ways was shown clearly on pp. 37–41. In such a worldview, death is not the last stop, but rather an intermediate stage and the entrance into a new phase of being.

The connection to eternity relativizes the significance of time in at least two ways, in both cases in two respects. First, the perspective of eternity has the power to relativize the suffering in time. It fulfills a consoling function that can inspire a serene calm, but also can evoke a mindless submissiveness or carelessness. Karl Marx rightly inveighed against the latter form of consolation when he criticized religion as the opium of the people. Second, the perspective of eternity can relativize the merits and good things of life through the knowledge that all things, all knowledge, and all efforts are temporary. When nothing in this world can be the ultimate, but rather, at the most, the penultimate, power structures are seen in a different light. When, from the perspective of eternity, the temporary nature of all hierarchies becomes clear, this can encourage people to be more radical in their critique of society and more daring in trying out alternatives. However, such a perspective of eternity can also be misused repressively in the attempt to grant existing hierarchies eternal and divine sanction or to force human beings, under threat of eternal punishment, to render blind obedience.

The conception of death as transition to something else thus relativizes the importance of life by placing it in a larger context. It therefore makes the event of transition an important happening, for which the individual must prepare and which the community must surround with appropriate rituals.

The notion of death as transition, however, also tends to reduce the significance of death itself. It does this in a way that separates it from Pauline thought. One could say that here a popularized interpretation of Pauline theology comes to fruition that tries to circumvent death rather than suffer it. This interpretation was supported by the Greek idea of the mortal body and the immortal soul and by dualist thoughts in Gnosticism. The body indeed dies, but the soul escapes death, so to speak, through the back door. The notion of the immortality of the soul is incompatible with Pauline theology because, in the final analysis, it does not take death seriously.[377] Whoever does not take death seriously is also unable to take the death of death seriously, that is, Christ's resurrection—which, for Paul, is the center of all thought about death and resurrection. The New Testament is not about conjuring away death, but rather about suffering and overcoming death.[378]

"As the event of accomplished non-relationality, death is the exact opposite of the release of a kind of indestructible personal core and, even more so, the exact opposite of a human act of self-perfection or self-essentification. In death, the human being *is annihilated*."[379] The reference to the immortality of the soul[380] as an answer to the question of the preservation of identity in death and resurrection is to be met with skepticism.[381] It raises more questions than it answers.[382] Furthermore, the notion of the immortality of the soul expresses an exclusively anthropocentric understanding of death. Animals, plants, and stars also die—a reality that is not considered in any of the theological schemes on death that have been mentioned here.

To the extent that the conception of death as transition relativizes death per se, the character of eternity, as something radically different from time, is eroded. Eternity becomes a kind of prolonged time, an eternalized time. This outlook lacks the possibility of making eternity conceivable as the Other of time.

Death as End—Irrelevant Eternity and Dead Time

The study in chapter 1 showed that the significance of eternity decreased over the course of the centuries until eternity finally became part of time. It was also observed that the notion of dying as an exit or escape from time occurs only in modern hymns.[383] These findings agree with the description of the sociologist Zygmunt Bauman in his analysis of the deconstruction of mortality in the modern age: Death has been reduced to an absolute withdrawal, to a moment of cessation, an end of all goals and all plans. Death has become a completely private end of the completely private affair that is called life.[384] What led to this reduction may for the moment remain undefined—whether it was modernity's concentration on the humanly possible and humanly feasible, coupled with its simultaneous distancing of itself from everything supra-human; whether it was the huge expansion of the time horizon from thousands to billions of years brought about by discoveries in geology, biology, and cosmology that caused the contours of time and eternity to disappear into infinite distance; or whether it was the materialism that arose in the nineteenth century.

If death is no longer a transition to something new and different, but is merely the last episode of life, then this shift of course has consequences for the conception of time, death, and eternity. Because it proves to be impossible to abolish death, the modern age chooses the path of deconstructing mortality. Death becomes the result of human action. Human beings no longer die because they are mortal; rather, they die from various causes.[385] This presupposes that, in principle, it is possible to eradicate these causes. Death is then basically considered a failure of medicine.[386] It is no longer looked upon as a natural and necessary phenomenon; it is a defeat, a "business lost."[387] All kinds of measures are taken in order to avoid this defeat and to secure the individual life span. Eschatology is successfully absorbed by technology.[388] The unanswerable question of the great exit is split into minor questions that appear to be technologically answerable by using hygiene and medicine.[389]

In its enthusiasm for deconstruction, modernity does not stop with the deconstruction of death, however. Eternal salvation is also subjected to a process of deconstruction and thus split up into smaller and constantly attainable moments of bliss, so that, in light of the many ecstatic pleasures, the grand consummation is completely lost from sight.[390] The modern world becomes a filled world, a closed system that allows no openings or holes in time and space and that permits no deviation from the unstoppable and continuous course of time, since there is no such thing as the extra-temporal.[391]

A system that permits no extra-temporality accordingly has no interest in a perspective of eternity. Consequently, eternity then becomes completely irrelevant. Gronemeyer has shown how the experience of time that has no perspective of eternity leads to a shortage of time and an acceleration of life's tempo, to the point of completely leveling all differences and being unable to tolerate the strange and the different.[392]

If time occurs as exclusive inner-temporality within the structure of a closed system and remains void of any relation to something eternal and supra-temporal, this then has at least two consequences. First, individual intervals or moments of time are related to each other only immanently; and, second, time as continuum thus disintegrates into fragments. Metaphorically expressed, in a closed system, time suffocates itself; given the loss of eternity, time dies the death of non-relationality. The loss of a relation to eternity could therefore ultimately lead to a disintegration of time. Only death would remain.

A look at Bauman's reflections on the deconstruction of immortality in the postmodern age confirms these thoughts. Bauman says that Protestant pilgrims on the journey through life have become postmodern nomads on the path between places that have no connection. The identity of the nomads is documented in the disconnectedness of time and space, whereas that of the pilgrim was embedded in the connectedness of time and space.[393] Simultaneity replaces history as the location of meaning; the power to define and shape is no longer vested in the past; it resides only in the here and now.[394] Even the future is dissolved into the now.[395] Life therefore consists of moments of equal value. It becomes senseless to speak of directions, long-term projects, and implementation. Immortality—the goal of the modern age—basically becomes boring: "[N]ow, . . . it is *immortality* that has been 'tamed'—no more an object of desire, distant and alluring; no more the remote and high-handed God, commanding ascesis, self-immolation and self-sacrifice."[396] Concepts such as *mortality* and *immortality* lose relevance. "With eternity decomposed into a Brownian movement of passing moments, nothing seems to be immortal any more. But nothing seems mortal either. Not in the old—supra-human, sinister, awesome—sense of 'once-for-allness,' of irrevocability, of irreversibility."[397] The only constancy is transitoriness; the mortality that is repeated daily becomes immortality;[398] and recycling becomes the ideal. Identities no longer exist; there are only transformations.[399] The belief in the Western variant of reincarnation that seems to grow in attraction can clearly be understood as an attempt to tame the constancy of transitoriness by changing it into a transformation that has a certain degree of continuity, but no actual obligation.[400]

Life does not resemble a carefully constructed novel with a plot of numerous layers of relationships in time and space; rather, it disintegrates into disconnected episodes.[401] Sacrifices for the sake of the future are not worthwhile. Equality is attained when everyone enjoys the present to the maximum, since the *now* is the only place of happiness.[402] The collapse of time as a totality and the splintering of the constant into an infinite series of transitory moments make both self-identity and authority a problem. Nothing lasts "for an entire lifetime" anymore, neither skills and the place of residence, nor work and one's partner.[403] What remains is death: "The paradoxical outcome of modernity's project is that the work of modernity is being undone. Death is back—un-deconstructed, unreconstructed. Even immortality has now come under its spell and rule. The price of exorcising the spectre of mortality proved to be a collective incapacity to construct life as reality, to take life seriously."[404]

If the description of death as transition could result in the eternalization of time and the eroding of eternity by its loss of character as time's Other, then the conception of death as exit and end would lead to a complete loss of eternity, causing time to disintegrate within itself and, ultimately, permitting only death to remain. The end appears to be a dead end. Both understandings of death highlight the questions that a theology of time must confront if it wishes to formulate and establish a dynamic relation between time and eternity. Both of them suffer from the fact that they, in different ways, absolutize time and therefore remain incapable of conceiving eternity as the Other of time.

Before I attempt to deepen our understanding of eternity as the Other of time in the last section of this chapter, I would like to conclude this analysis of death by providing a sketch of some criteria for a Christian understanding of death.

Theological Criteria of a Christian Understanding of Death

First: Death is death—nothing more, nothing less. That death is not less than death means that death cannot be avoided by postulating an immortal soul. Death is the collapse of all relations; it is the beginning and the event of absolute non-relationality,[405] and, as such, it must be taken seriously[406] and suffered as the "anthropological passive."[407] That death is not more than death, however, means that it has to be reduced to that limit which humans cannot set, for humans cannot abolish it.[408] Thus, death must be and become what Jesus Christ made of it: the limit to human beings that is set by God alone, who, in our total powerlessness, never abuses divine power.[409]

Second: Space, time, and language as the factors limiting human existence prevent us from knowing what is in and after death. Liberation from these boundaries can be achieved only by paying the price of death.[410] In the condition of not knowing, images fulfill a function; they are the mythological fruit of human fantasy, however, and, as such, should not be used as "signposts in a supernatural geography."[411]

Third: Because death is death and because not knowing shrouds human existence prior to death, death is the radical collapse in which God becomes all in all (1 Cor. 15:28). A new, eternal order of relations is established on God's ultimate faithfulness and God's eternal will to establish lasting relationships with human beings.[412] Talk of eternal life that has already begun is possible only in light of God's desire to relate.

Fourth: Collapse and transformation must be understood in light of the death and resurrection of Jesus Christ. Christian faith in the resurrection of the dead can therefore be proclaimed "as a new beginning out of the devastating nothingness of death."[413]

Fifth: The connection of human beings–time–relation/communication–history needs to be related to an Other in order not to fall apart. For a theology of time, this means: The lifetime of a person becomes genuinely historical only when it is understood as a moment of God's history with all people.[414] An understanding of eternity as the effective Other of time is in the offing here.

Sixth: A Christian conception of death cannot be limited to reflections upon the death of human beings. The anthropocentric boundary should be abolished by applying a cosmic perspective.

The criteria that have been briefly discussed here elicit questions that we must pursue: How can something be radical discontinuity and a complete end and nevertheless, at the same time, be continuity and a new beginning? How can identity and individuality be maintained in this contradictory process? I will address this question again (see pp. 217–19) in order to show how a relational understanding of time can assist in clarifying the issue.

We have repeatedly seen that a static, dualistic explanatory model confronts a host of difficulties and is unable to offer intellectually satisfying answers to a series of questions. I therefore will intensify my search for dynamic, relational thought models.

Provisional Results—Eternity as the Other of Time

Before turning to the question of time in the formation of scientific theories, I will provide a summary and interpretation of what has been achieved in this chapter.

In the biblical material, we saw that the content gleaned from the non-antithetical relation of time to eternity is more important than the formal definition of time and eternity. Speculations about whether time should be conceived cyclically or linearly and whether eternity should be thought of as endless duration or timelessness recede into the background in light of the eschatological relation of the "already" and the "not-yet." For this reason, in agreement with Ratschow, I found it justified from the outset to put reflections concerning the theological notion of time into a relational context. It is precisely the relational aspects that are difficult to deal with satisfactorily within an abstract, theistic framework. Also, neither a model that dualistically contrasts the temporal world to an eternal God, nor a model that merges eternity and time, provides a meaningful description of a dynamic relationality between time and eternity. Time is more than a deficient eternity, and eternity is something other than multiplied time.

Because relation cannot be conceived without differentiation of the related partners, it was necessary to examine some differentiating models in detail. Of the three models studied, the quantitative model proved to be the most closed and the least capable of development; the ontological model, the clearest, but the least dynamic; and the eschatological model, the most dynamic, but also the most open—capable of development but also ambiguous. If the eschatological time difference is given preference, then the question of how God, in differentiated unity, can relate to old and new time becomes urgent. This makes the examination of Trinitarian models of relationship relevant. I saw their strength in the possibility of conceiving multi-temporal, relational dynamics, and their weakness in an inability to develop a consistent assignment of the persons of the Trinity and of the temporal relationships.

In order to create a sufficient basis for further reflections in chapter 4, the Trinitarian-theological outlook had to be expanded by an anthropological perspective. This occurred in light of the phenomenon of death, where time and eternity indeed confront each other most clearly, but where, simultaneously, that which holds the two together, namely, relation, experiences its deepest crisis.

Until now, questions of definition related to the concepts of time and eternity have hardly been addressed. I chose this path consciously, in order not to limit myself from the very beginning by using the conceptual definitions of classical philosophy, for example. I did not want to offer definitions of the concepts per se, but rather, I made the attempt to start from relationality. The ensuing process led to the emergent portrayal of eternity as the Other of time. Until now, this way of talking has admittedly been rather imprecise. Tentatively, I will now provide some further clarification.

Speaking of the Other does not imply a negative, but rather a positive Other. It is about a basic differentiation having simultaneous relatedness. This, in turn, suggests that one is dealing with an effective Other, that is, one is not concerned with a negative abstract, but with a positive concrete. Speaking of the Other may assist us in escaping the pressure of a static dualism, without our simultaneously falling into the other extreme, namely, into complete relativism. The static exclusivity of a Platonic or Cartesian dualism can be overcome without thereby forfeiting the clear possibilities for differentiation. In other words: Duality—yes; ontological statics—no. It appears that a static dualism of *res cogitans* and *res extensa* is by no means insurmountable if Augustine could already locate time as extension [*distentio*] in the mind.

The concept of the Other should help us to achieve a dynamic methodology that deals with relation and movement. The focus of interest is thereby shifted from the essence of the concepts to their relation to one another, from the ontological status to the dynamic nature of the interaction, from a subject-object relation to a subject-subject relation. As things now stand, the lack of clarity in the concept of the Other appears to be the price that must be paid for achieving this dynamism.

When I look back to the insights that we have gained until now and forward to the topics in the next chapter, I see a certain confirmation of my own reflections in Emmanuel Lévinas. In *Time and the Other*,[415] Lévinas does not describe time as a degradation of eternity, "but as the relationship to *that* which—of itself unassimilable, absolutely other—would not allow

itself to be assimilated by experience; or to *that* which—of itself infinite—
would not allow itself to be com-prehended."[416]

This incomprehensibility of the absolute Other[417] is not the consequence of human inability, but should rather be understood as an impossibility in principle, since the relation appears as follows:

It is a relationship with the In-visible, where invisibility results not from some incapacity of human knowledge, but from the inaptitude of knowledge as such—from
its in-adequation—to the Infinity of the absolutely other, and from the absurdity
that an event such as coincidence would have here. This impossibility of coinciding
and this inadequation are not simply negative notions, but have a meaning in the
phenomenon of noncoincidence *given* in the dia-chrony of time. Time signifies this
always of noncoincidence, but also the *always* of the *relationship*, an aspiration and
an awaiting . . .[418]

In Lévinas, time therefore not only stands in relation to something else,
it *is* relation: "The situation of the face-to-face would be the very accomplishment of time."[419] Time is the very relationship of the subject with the
Other.[420] The absence of time is solitude.[421] Time—understood as relation—enables a pluralistic existence, without merging everything into a single unity.[422] The relationship that is conceived as a relation between two
subjects "does not *ipso facto* neutralize the alterity, but preserves it."[423] One
is thus dealing with a relation that preserves the alterity of the Other,[424] and
therefore precisely that which I have just characterized as differentiation
with simultaneous relatedness.

Even if his motivation is somewhat different than mine (see pp. 109–16)
above, Lévinas also considers an analysis of death absolutely essential in the
context of a study of time. Without death, which is likewise understood as
an experience of passivity, as the moment when we are no longer capable of
doing anything, time as relation is no longer conceivable.[425] In his book
God, Death and Time,[426] death is not viewed simply as the end, however,
but is instead seen, in light of the desire for infinity, within the ethical context of the responsibility for the Other.[427] In order to understand this, one
must explain how Lévinas opposes an identity-oriented way of thinking. Instead of viewing time as the relation to the end (like Heidegger), he wishes
to conceive of time as the relation to the Other. Thus, he wants to abandon
a way of thinking that is oriented toward identity and, therefore, the stability of the self, since such a way of thinking constantly tries to assimilate the
Other to this self. Moreover, it neutralizes "becoming" into "a stability, apt
to present itself and to be represented, apt to hold itself together in a presence, and thereby to be taken in hand."[428] The metaphor that corresponds
to this understanding of time, Lévinas says, is the *flux*, the trickling away of
something fluid, of a stream of time loaded with moments as atoms.

Lévinas looks for other formulations for the restlessness of time, however, than those of continual movement. He likewise calls into question the analysis of all temporal phenomena based on their shortcomings and asks: "Is it not possible, in these phenomena, to think of their emptiness and their incompletion as a step beyond contents, a mode of relationship with the noncontainable, with the infinite that one could not say is a term?"[429] Time is to be conceived as this relation to infinity, and Lévinas again emphasizes that we only seemingly are dealing with a shortcoming; in fact, however, we are dealing with the positive turn of the self to the Other: "The search or the question [for the Infinite] would be not a deficiency of some possession but, from the outset, a relationship with what is beyond possession, with the ungraspable wherein thought would tear itself apart."[430]

Precisely this tearing-itself-apart in thinking explains the constant questioning of the I by the Other and the restlessness of time as awakening, the temporality. Lévinas is concerned with the ethical consequence of this fracturing of the same by the Other, namely, the impossibility of resting in distant complacency. He wants us to see, above all, the nominative in the accusative.[431] Contrary to all common sense and ontology, the goals of which are stability, self-identity, and contemporization as tangibility, the impossible becomes real in the desire for the non-comprehensible: "[T]he infinite, which places me in question, is like a more within a less."[432] "Time would thus be the explosion of the *more* of the infinite within the *less*."[433]

Whereas in *Time and the Other* the *future* appears as the absolutely incomprehensible and as the actual relation to the Other,[434] in *God, Death and Time*, the *infinite* is given a key position. Whether these philosophical assertions find their theological correspondence in the primacy of the eschatological relation of old and new time will still need to be considered.[435] How eternity can then be characterized as the "other" of time requires more precision. Also the question of whether—or to what extent—time finds itself by recognizing eternity as its Other may be explored. In any case, the reflections that issued from the analysis of the hymns in the first chapter already point to the fact that an adequate understanding of time cannot be found without considering a relation of time to eternity.

[3]

Time in the Formulation of
Scientific Theory

On the Dialogue between Science and Theology

For anyone seeking a dynamic relational model for the relationship of time and eternity, the words of the theologian Gabriel Daly must sound like sweet music: "The flowering of atomic and sub-atomic physics is revealing a cosmos of startling and beautiful complexity which is marked above all by motion and the wonders of systemic interrelationship."[1] I consider Daly's description both correct and auspicious for my study. His emphasis on motion and systemic interrelationship especially catches my attention because, over the course of this study, it is precisely motion, dynamics, and relation that have come forcefully to the forefront as the decisive fundamental concepts in the search for appropriate formulations related to a theology of time.

Such positive expectations for the dialogue with natural scientific disciplines are certainly not self-evident, however. There are also voices asserting the opposite: "If theology wishes to cling to *its* subject matter, then it should not concern itself with the diverse philosophical, scientific, and historical concepts of time and eternity . . ."[2]

With regard to the dialogue between natural sciences and theology/religion, a variety of fundamental directions can be observed. In general, however, this dialogue has experienced an exciting development over the course of the twentieth century. The natural sciences, which once sprang from the heart of the church, left their parental home following a stormy puberty, and began to live an autonomous adult life. The revolts caused theology to lose its firm footing and made it seek refuge in the internal sphere, but such an amicable separation could not be a successful permanent solution. Although it is unclear whether it was due to insight or necessity, during the twentieth century there was a growing desire to reassess the relationship between the two disciplines; and this led to a series of relatively productive attempts at dialogue.[3] Karl Heim must be regarded as one of the pioneers in the German-speaking world. Subsequently, works by Günter Howe, Günter Altner, and Jürgen Hübner provided important impulses for placing this topic on the agenda of public scientific discussion. Since theology, over the course of its history, has always been involved in a give-and-take relationship with the forces influencing contemporary culture, it is completely natural that the dialogue with science and technology has expanded in recent times. Over the past few years, numerous books have been published that illuminate the presuppositions, problems, and possibilities of the dialogue between science and religion.[4]

The dialogue between the natural sciences and theology has a broader foundation in the Anglo-Saxon than in the German-speaking world. In the former, it is oriented more toward integral plans than it is toward conflict, indifference, or separation models. It appears that a theology that is not required to see itself as heir to dialectic theology can deal more easily with the relationship between God and nature, on the one hand, and between faith, religion, and knowledge, on the other.[5] The connection of Newton's science to Anglican theology and the Boyle Lectures, which claimed reason and science as the basis for a natural religion, contributed to a more advantageous climate for the dialogue between science and theology in England. On the European continent, by contrast, there were negative repercussions, not least of all due to Kant's philosophy. Kant's questioning of the entire concept of a theology of nature complicated the relationships between science and theology that had been so important for the early Newtonians, and it undermined the notions about religion benefiting from science.[6]

In addition to treating specific problems of an ecological, ethical, and philosophical nature, over the past few decades, a series of general strategies dealing with the relationship between science and theology have emerged that outline different models.[7] Thus, for example, Ian G. Barbour designed a process-oriented model that includes the stages of conflict, mutual independence, dialogue, and integration.[8] Ralph W. Burhoe, longtime publisher of the journal *Zygon*, worked with a naturalistic evolutionary concept. While Arthur R. Peacocke and John Polkinghorne devote more attention to harmonization, Thomas F. Torrance,[9] writing in the Barthian tradition, places more emphasis on the distinctions between nature and God. In a model derived from Knud E. Løgstrup, Viggo Mortensen[10] also attempts to preserve the differences. He does not wish either to mix or to separate theology and science, but rather prefers seeing them in a lively, friendly interaction. Process philosophy, which is associated with the names of Alfred North Whitehead and Charles Hartshorne, has greatly influenced the development of the dialogue. Among the French-speaking intelligentsia, programmatic frameworks on the topic of science and theology can be found in Teilhard de Chardin and Jean Ladrière, among others.[11]

My own model is less a comprehensive attempt to synthesize different systems than an attempt to initiate a discussion between science and theology by asking specific questions. Here I assume that both are dealing with the same reality, but proceeding from different presuppositions and using different terminologies, so that although complete consensus is not possible, a meaningful discussion can be achieved within the context of a still unexhausted series of questions. I consider general models on the relationship of science and theology as *prolegomena* for this discussion. My greatest expectations, however, are linked to the dialogue on individual topics in which theological symbol systems are discussed directly. In the field of ethics, this method already has a long tradition. With respect to topics that are traditionally ascribed to dogmatics, the discussion of questions dealing with the theology of creation in light of the theory of evolution has the longest history.[12] In this area, one can also find numerous apologetic writings, especially of the fundamentalist-creationist type.[13] More recently, there have been attempts to bring about a discussion of the doctrine of the Trinity in relation to natural science.[14] The question of God's actions in the world has also been discussed repeatedly.[15] On the topic of time, there are at least three more recent proposals. From a theological perspective, there is a work by Duane Larson dealing with time, Trinity, and cosmology.[16] Lawrence Fagg attempts to integrate physical and religious time from the perspective of a nuclear physicist.[17] Two theologians, Wolfgang Achtner and Stefan Kunz, as well as physicist and mathematician Thomas Walter, have jointly discussed time, from anthropological, scientific, and theological viewpoints, as a so-called tripolar system.[18] Meanwhile, a new generation is also critically examining the models of the "Great Thinkers" who participated in the initial rounds of dialogue following the establishment of modern physics.[19]

There are primarily three reasons that make the dialogue between theology and natural science attractive in relation to the subject of time. First, in science, there seems to have been something like a "Copernican Revolution" from absolute to relative time, while in theology there is no evidence of a corresponding development within the discussion of time. Second, specialized physics terms such as *relativity* and *chaos* tend to become trendy words that have an ideological tone. For this reason, these terms also play an important role for the context of theology. Clarity on how fundamental concepts can be understood within their scientific context provides hope for gaining insight into this matter. Third, there is the question of whether it is possible to achieve relevant results for future theological research without following a substance-ontological path.

What role does this scientific chapter then play within the context of this study? Is it connected consistently to the first two chapters, or is it just being added to them in a loosely connected manner? To answer these questions, we must briefly review my work so far. It has been shown that theology is constantly in danger of working with an "old-fashioned" concept of time. This occurs primarily when time is viewed only as absolute and linear and when it is compared dualistically to an eternity that is conceived as timelessness. This view turns into a static system that should be understood in terms of dynamic relation instead. In this regard, one can legitimately expect that the time concept of modern physics would be able to assist theological thought. The idea that modern physics works with a relative concept of time has made my previous reflections more sensitive to certain characteristics in the theological treatment of time. These aspects include interest in relationality, the idea that fuzziness in the definition of concepts is the price of dynamics, multi-temporality as a possible conceptual model, and openness as a characteristic of time. With this, I am not claiming that in the two fields the same meaning is automatically assigned to concepts such as relativity and fuzziness. That would be a form of substance ontology that should be strictly avoided. However, the preconception of Einstein's theory of relativity, as well as that of quantum physics, has had an important heuristical function for what has been elaborated thus far.

The account of scientific conceptions of time that now follows is meant to reinforce and further develop this concept. In this manner, I hope to support previous ideas and to place them on a more solid foundation. However, I also anticipate the possibility of disillusioning or even disappointing my readers if, for example, my discussion of the openness of physical time proves not to enhance the study of theology, but rather confirms the limitations of physics.

However, let us turn first to the classical physical concept of absolute time as encountered in the works of Isaac Newton and illuminated by the criticism of Gottfried Wilhelm Leibniz. This is followed by an account of the theories of relativity, which concludes with the question of the independence of time. In the course of a brief description of quantum physics from the viewpoint of time, I will then discuss the role of the observer and the relationship of language and physics. Using cosmological theories, I will concentrate especially on the boundaries of time. Finally, in a section on thermodynamics and chaos research, among other things, I will discuss the irreversibility and openness of time.

The Concept of Absolute Time

"Experiments, or other certain truths"—Isaac Newton

The expression "experiments, or other certain truths" was penned by Isaac Newton (1642[20]–1727). His scientific method consisted of what he himself called experiments and observations from which conclusions can be drawn by means of induction and against which contradictions are tolerated only if they are also based on "experiments or other certain truths."[21] The certain truths can be understood in contrast to hypotheses, which are completely inappropriate for experimental philosophy.[22] However, this section will show how problematic the relationship between experimental results and predetermined certain truths was, even for Newton. Establishing a connection of absolute time and absolute space with the existence of God proved to be difficult and provocative.

In Newton's account of the basic principles of mechanics, *Philosophiae Naturalis Principia Mathematica*,[23] one finds sentences that are often cited by classical physics as the typical definition of time. Newton prefaces his definition with the comment that the generally well-known concepts of *time, space, place*, and *motion* actually would not require an explanation. Due to human perception, however, prejudices could easily arise that he thought he could eliminate by distinguishing between absolute, true, and mathematical, on the one hand, and relative, apparent, and common, on the other. Thus, he always distinguishes between absolute and relative space, absolute and relative place, and absolute and relative motion. Only in the case of time, which he defines first, does he list all three distinguishing criteria:

I. Absolute, True and Mathematical Time, of it self, and from its own nature flows equably without regard to anything external, and by another name is called Duration: Relative, Apparent, and Common Time is some sensible and external (whether accurate or unequable) measure of Duration by the means of motion, which is commonly used instead of True time; such is an Hour, a Day, a Month, a Year.[24]

Correspondingly, absolute space "without regard to any thing external, remains always similar and immovable," while relative space is "some moveable or measure of the absolute spaces," which we customarily perceive to be immovable space.[25] Place and motion are each defined in relation to absolute or relative space.[26]

Even though Newton favors an empirical, inductive method in a conscious distancing from Descartes' deductive method that is based on principles of reason, he is not completely successful in deriving absolute time. He says that, in astronomy, absolute time is measured by the motion of the heavenly bodies, but he concedes that it is possible that no uniform motion exists at all on which time could be precisely measured: "All motions can be accelerated or retarded, but the True or equable progress, of Absolute time is liable to no change."[27] Absolute time therefore remains a postulate or, at least, a theoretical value, which is indeed defined, but does not correspond to direct experience.

Likewise, the distinctions between relative and absolute with regard to space, place, and motion are not directly accessible.

For from the positions and distances of things from any body consider'd as immoveable, we define all places: and then with respect to such places, we estimate all motions, considering bodies as transfer'd from some of those places into others. And so instead of absolute places and motions, we use relative ones; and that without any inconvenience in common affairs: but in Philosophical disquisitions, we ought to abstract from our senses, and consider things themselves, distinct from what are only sensible measures of them. For it may be that there is no body really at rest, to which the places and motions of others may be referr'd.[28]

Absolute values are, at the most, only approximately accessible by means of observations and experiments. How then can a distinction be made between an absolute inert space and a system in motion? Newton gives an example: When a container filled with water revolves around its own axis, the water surface assumes a concave shape, i.e., a curve that rises towards the walls of the container, as a result of centrifugal force, while it forms a flat plane in a stationary container. Based on centrifugal force, an empirical distinction can thus be made between the system in motion and the inert system. This distinction remains relative, however, because it is impossible, by means of measurements, to distinguish the absolutely inert space from all other systems moving uniformly relative to inert space.

Newton admits that distinguishing true values from apparent ones is quite difficult, yet "not altogether desperate,"[29] since there are aids for properly distinguishing the causes and effects of true or apparent motions, the proper use of which is the instructional purpose of the *Principia*. To make

no distinction between absolute and relative values would be almost moral-
ly reprehensible; whoever confuses one with the other both violates the
Holy Scriptures and also sullies mathematics and philosophy.[30]

Newton distinguishes between eternity and infinity in the same way
that he differentiates between space and time. What eternity is for time,
infinity is for space. The value pairs appear to stand in extrapolative relationship to each other, so that eternity and infinity always appear to be the
highest powers of time and space. Correspondingly, God's duration lasts
from eternity to eternity, and God's presence from infinity to infinity.[31] Yet,
this conceptual separation is not always applied consistently. When he says,
as an exclusive property of stationary places, that they maintain the same
relative position "from infinity to infinity"—i.e., they always remain stationary[32]—then "infinity" should not be understood here only spatially, but
also temporally.[33] Both eternity and infinity are conceived as being in continuity with time and space; Newton does not consider the possibility of a
fundamentally different dimensionality.

From a further reading of Newton's works, one gets the impression that
his concern is actually more about the problems of absoluteness and relativity of space, whereas the concept of absolute time initially remains unchallenged. Indeed, the physical realization of absolute time appears to be
simpler than that of absolute space. By synchronizing the time-measuring
instruments of all observers, a coordination of time within different frames
of reference appears to be attainable. With regard to space, on the other
hand, the transition from one reference system to another requires a transformation. Mathematically, this corresponds to the conversion of the coordinates of one frame of reference to the coordinates of another frame of
reference. In classical mechanics, one uses the Galilean Transformation,
whose equations for rectilinear and uniform motion along the X-axis read
as follows:[34]

$$x' = x - vt \qquad y' = y \qquad z' = z \qquad t' = t$$

Time appears to avoid the problems that are associated with space. As
the factor t in the equations, it can be used for calculations without requiring a description of what absolute and relative time really are. The fact that
the equations of motion allow solutions with both positive and negative
time (t and $-t$), i.e., that they allow time to be considered as reversible, did
not harm classical mechanics. The differences between past, present, and future had to appear as an illusion in this system. This must have been considered to be only an insignificant shortcoming, however, when contrasted to
the huge gains of a mathematical description of the universe that includes

time, united Copernican and Keplerian astronomy with the Galilean concept of acceleration, and deterministically and causally explained the movement of earthly and heavenly bodies by means of a single force—gravity.[35]

Edwin A. Burtt points out that Newton's distinction of absolute and relative motion using the concept of force as criterion is untenable.[36] When Newton claims that wherever force is exerted, absolute motion occurs,[37] he inadmissibly presumes that one can also reverse the argument of an effect in the direction of a cause into an argument of a cause (i.e., force) in the direction of an effect.[38] Burtt sees the basis for this conclusion by Newton as being in the contemporary idea of force as a phenomenon having an autonomous existence that precedes all effects and is independent of them. Burtt speaks of animistic characteristics from which the scientific theory of force was only gradually cleansed. Because there is no doubt of Newton's theological ambitions, however, I believe it is more reasonable to assume that Newton defined the physical concept of force within the framework of the theological notion of divine action.[39]

Burtt, who assumes that Newton was influenced by the Cambridge Platonist Henry More,[40] sees another inconsistency in the fact that Newton relates the movement of bodies to absolute space and absolute time.[41] Because absolute space and absolute time are infinite and homogenous entities and thus cannot be distinguished within themselves, bodies can certainly move in absolute space and in absolute time, but the motion is only noticeable in relation to other bodies and not in relation to absolute space and absolute time. According to Burtt, mathematics and physics were not decisive here for Newton, but rather his theological conviction that, ultimately, time and space have religious significance. He substantiates this with quotations from the General Scholium, among other things, which Newton added to the second edition of the *Principia*—according to which God, existing forever and everywhere, constitutes time and space.[42] "Absolute space for Newton is not only the omnipresence of God; it is also the infinite scene of the divine knowledge and control."[43]

In *Opticks*, Newton speaks of a divine sensorium in connection with absolute space, which suggests an understanding of divine consciousness as the highest frame of reference for absolute motion. Whenever the connection to this divine frame of reference is abolished, however, absolute space and absolute time become empty categories. What remain are ideas of a mechanical universe that functions like a clock and a nature that is despiritualized. Burtt already foresees this development.[44] Within the framework of eco-theological concepts, it has been emphasized repeatedly that Newton's thoughts paved the way for the misuse and exploitation of nature. In my opinion, however, it was not Newton's thinking per se that necessarily resulted in damage to the environment. The threat to a nature that is understood mechanically by human beings ruling over it is more likely a consequence of the dissolution of the synthesis of science and theology that still existed in Newton.[45]

Natural scientific, as well as theological work, takes place in a social reality. The historian John Brooke describes what this means for Newton's work. On the one hand, Brooke points to the sociopolitical interpretative potential of Newton's ideas;[46] and, on the other hand, he examines the merging of science and theology in Newton's thinking.[47] He contradicts the idea that, by the end of the seventeenth century, a so-called scientific revolution caused the development of modern science, with a sharp division between philosophy and theology on the one side and natural science on the other. Indeed, Newton's century saw an increasing differentiation between theology and science, but scientific findings were still being presented in theological terminology, and divine characteristics were still being explained in physical terms.[48] Brooke elucidates this by using Newton as an example: Newton was concerned with explaining natural phenomena as mechanical processes as well as expressions of divine will. He rejected the alternative to the latter, namely that the cause of an event is inherent to physical matter. His thinking therefore adopted an ambiguity that could lead to both theistic and deistic interpretations.[49] In his laws, Newton saw proof of the constant presence of God; however, these laws could just as easily apply to the notion of an absent clockmaker.[50] In this ambiguity, Newton's theology also bears the seed of its own destruction: Against Newton's will, God becomes a "god of the gaps," who is finally dethroned by Pierre de Laplace. The fact that Newton thought the Trinitarian dogma was irrelevant[51] is consistent with the premises portrayed here. As he matured, his Arian conviction grew until he became convinced that true religion and world peace would be possible only when the doctrine of the Trinity was eradicated.[52] Correspondingly, Newton also did not develop a Christology that could have influenced his religious-philosophical thoughts in *Principia* and *Opticks*.[53]

The observation of societal and philosophical interconnections raises the difficult question of what actually caused what. Did the sociopolitical climate influence natural philosophy or did science influence politics? Did Newton's image of God leave its mark on mechanics or did mechanics shape his image of God? Brooke makes a plea for the latter alternative: Newton created a God for himself according to his own understanding[54]— "[t]he rationalism characteristic of his scientific work was not so much *deflected* as *reflected* in his biblical studies."[55] At the same time, Brooke concedes that theology influenced the concept of space and also fundamentally shaped the content of the concepts of law and force.[56] In any case, one should note that the purely mathematical consequences of Newton's laws could certainly be effective theologically: The equations of motion must be solved using differential calculus. In order to obtain in this process only one solution, instead of an infinite number, the initial conditions of the system must be defined. Similarly, the theological interpretation of a deterministic mechanics for the universe requires a God who is understood as the one determining the initial conditions.

How, then, is the concept of time to be understood against this backdrop? Burtt, who sees this as a linguistic question rather than one of physics, indeed attributes ambiguity to Newton's definition of absolute time, but he sees it as a brilliant use of language.[57] Whether or not time can actually flow remains unclear. Is it not instead the case that things and events flow in time? Does a river flow, or is it water molecules that flow? Two things are hidden within this uncertainty: On the one hand, absolute time appears to be a homogenous mathematical continuum that extends from an infinite past into an infinite future and is always conceived as a whole. Thus, however, it can hardly be distinguished from space. On the other hand, it is a sequence of moments of which only the prevailing *now* exists; time thus shrivels into a razor-thin mathematical border between past and future, a boundary that flows uniformly in time, but that cannot be time itself. Burtt advocates the idea that Newton wants to combine these two understandings of time by describing time as an infinite continuum with a language that belongs to the understanding of time as a boundary that is continuously moving forward.[58] Despite all of its brilliance, however, this scientific concept of time has lost contact with the duration that is experienced as being direct.[59]

I have given much attention to Newton's accounts of the relationship of God to absolute space and absolute time, as described in the General Scholium and in some sections of Queries 28 and 31 in *Opticks*. However, I do not wish to mislead the reader into thinking that it was Newton the theologian[60] rather than Newton the mathematician, the physicist, and the astronomer who accomplished pioneering scientific work. Thus, the General Scholium, which was based on the study of planets and gravitation and dealt with the role and necessity of God, was not part of the first edition of the *Principia*. Newton, who was over seventy years old at the time, wrote it only for the second edition in 1713, as a concession to those pious souls who were upset by a mechanical explanation of the universe that could be interpreted as being atheistic.

In the General Scholium, Newton uses a type of cosmological proof of the existence of God: "This most beautiful system of the sun, planets, and comets, could only proceed from the counsel and dominion of an intelligent and powerful Being."[61] This being is God in the sense that it rules over everything. The word "God" is understood relationally,[62] as Lord over servants: "It is the dominion of a spiritual being which constitutes a God."[63] God's duration lasts from eternity to eternity and God's presence from infinity to infinity; however, "he is not duration or space, but he endures and is present. . . . [H]e constitutes duration and space."[64] God is omnipresent, not only virtually, but also substantially.[65] God necessarily exists forever and everywhere. All bodies move in God without suffering resistance from the divine omnipresence.[66] From a human perspective, three attributes should be given to God, namely, "dominion, providence, and final causes."[67] Should God also therefore be identified as the cause of the gravity that determines the phenomena of heaven and earth? Newton expresses himself cautiously on this matter. Up to this point, he says that he has not been able to derive the causes of the properties of gravity empirically, and he rejects hypotheses. Here, one finds the sentence that is often cited out of context: "Hypotheses non fingo." (I do not manufacture hypotheses).[68]

Newton had already expressed the same thoughts towards the end of Query 28 in *Opticks*, where he described the main task of natural philosophy as being "to argue from Phenomena without feigning Hypotheses, and to deduce Causes from Effects, till we come to the very first Cause, which certainly is not mechanical . . ."[69] Even if natural philosophy does not provide direct access to this first cause, it does lead to close proximity and is therefore quite valuable. The consideration of natural phenomena suggests

that there is a Being incorporeal, living, intelligent, omnipresent, who in infinite Space, as it were in his Sensory, sees the things themselves intimately, and throughly [*sic*] perceives them, and comprehends them wholly by their immediate Presence to himself: Of which things the Images only carried through the Organs of Sense into our little Sensoriums, are there seen and beheld by that which in us perceives and thinks.[70]

There is a similar reflection at the end of Query 31. In a clear allusion to the biblical story of creation, Newton considers it to be probable that God "in the beginning form'd Matter in solid, massy, hard, impenetrable, moveable Particles, . . . no ordinary Power being able to divide what God himself made one in the first Creation."[71] These particles can indeed be combined into new shapes, but their stability is the basis for all continuity of natural phenomena. The particles are controlled by forces of natural laws, thanks to which the world is able to maintain itself, with the exception of a few irregularities that can increase "till this system wants a reformation."[72] God can change the natural laws and create worlds that have different natural laws in different parts of the universe.[73] An examination of the animal kingdom supports the sense that the ruling order there

can be the effect of nothing else than the Wisdom and Skill of a powerful ever-living Agent, who being in all Places, is more able by his Will to move the Bodies within his boundless uniform Sensorium, and thereby to form and reform the parts of the Universe, than we are by our Will to move the Parts of our own Bodies.[74]

Precisely those passages that speak of a *sensorium* of God[75] provided rich material for discussion. They repeatedly formed the background for the controversy concerning the absoluteness of space and time between Newton's disciple Samuel Clarke and the philosopher Gottfried Wilhelm Leibniz, which we will discuss in the next section.

The following concepts[76] are suitable for a summarizing characterization of Newton's concept of time: Absolute time is qualified as universality. Its uniformity (symmetry) makes it quantifiable and divisible.[77] On the one hand, time experiences an idealization in the sense of a lack of concrete content and an abstraction of the empirical experience of time. On the other hand, as the "arena" for the actions of the omnipotent and omnipresent God, it experiences a realization by being filled with determined (theological) content.

"Quelque chose de purement relatif: un ordre des Coexistences"—Leibniz's Criticism

"Something purely relative and an order of the co-existences"—with these words, Gottfried Wilhelm Leibniz (1646–1716) describes his concept of space. Something corresponding also applies to time, he adds. Time is also relative and to be understood as an order of succession.[78] Leibniz developed these ideas during a dispute with Samuel Clarke (1675–1729) over the interpretation of Newton's ideas.[79]

The argument between Leibniz and Clarke included five letters by each of the two adversaries and ended, without reaching any consensus, upon the death of Leibniz in 1716.[80] It began in November 1715, with a letter from Leibniz to Caroline, Princess of Wales, which was followed by Clarke's response.[81] The questions at issue, which are then repeatedly addressed in further correspondence, already surface in this first letter. The main accusations of Leibniz include materialism—"Many will have human souls to be material: others make God himself a corporeal being"[82]—a limitation of God's sovereignty—the discussion about space as God's *sensorium* makes God dependent upon this—and a false understanding of God's actions—

Newton's God is a poor clockmaker, for this God is constantly having to intervene and correct creation. On the contrary, Leibniz's God, from the beginning, put into motion the interplay of the natural forces according to "le bel ordre préétabli,"[83] so that miracles effected by God are not mandated by a nature needing correction, but rather can be understood solely as acts of grace.

The least reconciled issues are the differences in the question of the *sensorium Dei*. While Leibniz steadfastly defines *sensorium* as a perceptive organ and, for this reason, accuses Clarke and Newton of misunderstanding space as the sensory organ of God, Clarke explains over and over that Newton is concerned only with an analogous use of the concepts: space (and, correspondingly, also time) are only *like* sensory organs. Instead, the omnipresent God perceives all things "by his immediate presence to them, in all space wherever they are, without the intervention or assistance of any organ or medium whatsoever."[84]

To the accusation of making God look like an inferior craftsman, Clarke replies that God is more than just a mechanic. Precisely the assertion that God is the source *and* the constant preserver does justice to God's true greatness and prevents God's expulsion from the world; "'tis not a diminution, but the true glory of his workmanship, that nothing is done without his continual government and inspection."[85] At the end of this initial round of discussions, two features of the debate have already crystallized that will be reinforced over the course of the correspondence. First, the reader, who hopes for an intensive illumination of the phenomenon of absolute time, tends to be disappointed, because the discussion revolves primarily around space. It must be noted, however, that what is said about space also applies to time.[86] Second, different conceptions of divine action come to light. The contributions of the two adversaries to the discussion of this question are extensive and deal repeatedly with the role of God's intervention in natural occurrences in relation to divine perfection. I believe that physical, cosmological, or philosophical theses are not really the issue here, but rather that the core of the debate centers on a difference in theological outlook. An interpretation wishing to do justice to the character of the correspondence must devote great attention to the theological premises. A key to understanding lies in the consideration of what each author considers significant with regard to God's perfection. While Newton and Clarke each predominantly focus on the *power* of God,[87] Leibniz always argues from the standpoint of God's *wisdom*.[88]

The power of Newton's and Clarke's God is expressed especially in divine omnipresence.[89] This connection of power, eternity, and omnipresence forces Clarke to declare that absolute space and absolute time are necessary attributes of God's divinity. In contrast, the primacy of wisdom in Leibniz's concept of God leads to the idea of the beauty of preestablished harmony.[90] It is God's wise foresight that makes a corrective intervention in the mechanics of the world unnecessary. In divine wisdom, God does nothing unintentionally; all God's actions are well founded.[91] Leibniz's aversion to the existence of a vacuum should be understood in light of the principle of God's wisdom—namely, the less matter that exists, the fewer objects would be available for the goodness of God. God's work would then be incomplete, which would contravene God's wisdom and the axiom of sufficient cause that is asserted by Leibniz.[92]

In his second reply, Clarke concedes that the continual need to repair the world's mechanism can be understood only in relative terms. He says that what to human observation appears to be disorder is, in reality, the expression of God's perfect idea. In the same breath, he assures the reader that God is neither "a mundane intelligence" nor "a supramundane intelligence," but rather "an omnipresent intelligence, both in and without the world. He is in all, and through all, as well as above all."[93]

In his third letter, Leibniz directly attacks Newton's space-time concept. He considers the concept of space as "a real absolute being"[94] to be contradictory. Such space would have to be eternal and infinite, which is why it is also erroneously conceived of as God or, at least, as an attribute of God. However, because space consists of parts, it cannot belong to God in such a manner. For this reason, Leibniz explains: "As for my own opinion, I have said more than once that I hold space to be something merely relative, as time is; that I hold it to be an order of coexistences, as time is an order of successions."[95]

Accordingly, space and time are not things, but rather arrangements of things. In comparison to Newton's *Principia*, the emphasis of the inquiry has shifted in Leibniz and Clarke. If Newton was primarily concerned with the question of which space and time concepts are the most successful in physics, then Leibniz and Clarke are debating less about the physical implications than about the ontological question of what space and time are. All three are thus a long way from thinking that the setting of a standard for time is more a matter of convention or consensus than a question of truth or error.[96] With their assertion that space and time represent real and independent values, Newton and Clarke are in clear conflict with a conventional solution. The relativity of time and space in Leibniz, however, also should not be understood in the sense of a conventional model, because relativity does not exist in the mutual relationship of diverse possible reference systems, but rather in the relationship of the phenomena to one another in time and space.[97] Without phenomena there would be no space and time; thus, neither of the two is a real substance.[98] Absolute space and absolute time are chimeras and impossible fictions, Leibniz rails.[99]

Clarke objects that he is not defining space as a substance or being at all. Space, he says, is instead a property or consequence of the existence of an infinite and eternal being. It is the *immensity* of God, but not God per se. Space and time are not outside of God—otherwise, there could be absoluteness outside of God. Instead, they are the direct and necessary consequences of God's existence because, without them, God would be robbed of divine eternity and omipresence.[100] This train of thought appears paradoxical: The absoluteness of space and time are not separate from God; but, in turn, they are also not God. What leads Clarke to this aporia is his passion for establishing space and time as "media of God's effectiveness in the world."[101] Speaking figuratively, space and time appear as a divine theater in which God's eternal omnipotence and omnipresence are expressed, although the term *theater* here must mean place and event in equal measure. A one-sided understanding of theater as place would have dualistic consequences, while an exclusive understanding of it as event would identify God with time and space.

Clarke does not think that it is possible to refrain from quantifying space and time, for the Leibniz model has absurd consequences: If time were nothing more than "the order of succession," then God could have created the world millions of years earlier without it having been created earlier.[102] Then things could follow each other in the same sequence, but more quickly or more slowly, without Leibniz being in a position to determine a difference. Indeed, Newton's time has more structure in this regard, which is why Clarke concludes that "order of succession" is something other than time; and he crowns this thought with the conclusion: "If no creatures existed, yet the ubiquity of God, and the continuance of his existence, would make space and duration to be exactly the same as they are now."[103]

In Clarke's view, the perspective of the absoluteness of space and time therefore appears to shift to the absoluteness of God. Absolute space and absolute time do not emerge from themselves or from the world of phenomena, but rather God's absoluteness determines the absoluteness of space and time. In contrast, Leibniz alleges that Clarke is confusing God's will with God's power. In Leibniz, God's omnipotence is qualified by God's wisdom. For this reason, God can indeed do everything that is possible or that does not indicate any contradiction, but God wants to create only the best of everything that is possible.[104]

In his last letter, Leibniz also addresses the issues of the relationship of space and time as attributes and God's absoluteness. If space were an attribute of God, it would belong to the divine nature, which in turn means—since space is divisible—that God's nature disintegrates. Furthermore, if infinite space corresponds to the immensity [*immensitas*] of God and if infinite time corresponds to God's eternity, then that which is in space and time would also be in God's nature: "strange expressions,"[105] Leibniz says to such a notion. "And the analogy between time and space, will easily make it appear, that the one is as merely ideal as the other."[106] With words that are almost Kantian, Leibniz emphasizes the ideal nature of space (and time): The mind creates the idea of space without necessary correspondence to an external real and absolute being; abstract space is the order of situations that are recognized as possible and therefore it is ideal rather than real.[107] With regard to the question whether there would be time and space if creation did not exist, Leibniz therefore comes to a conclusion that is diametrically opposed to Clarke's. Because he considers the immensity and eternity of God to be independent of time and space, Leibniz can say: "If there were no creatures, there would be neither time nor place, and consequently no actual space. . . . And therefore I don't admit what's here alleged, that if God existed alone, there would be time and space as there is now: whereas then, in my opinion, they would be only in the ideas of God as mere possibilities."[108]

In his final reply, which was left unanswered, Clarke again tried to state God's relationship to time and space more precisely. God does not exist in them, but God's existence creates space and time in such a way that "boundless space and time" are necessary consequences of God's existence.[109] Clarke tries to repudiate the reproach that he is guilty of using *alloglossia*, a confusing manner of speaking, by charging that Leibniz's use of the concepts *immensity* and *eternity* is identical to asserting that words are meaningless.

Because of Leibniz's death, Clarke indeed had the last word in this dispute, but it would be premature to therefore declare him the victor. The motif of his battle for the absoluteness of time and space, for empty space and fixed atoms, was the proof of the power and omnipresence of God as the great *manager* of the world. He certainly did not foresee that this Clockmaker God would very soon be condemned to inactivity due to the excellent functionality of the clockwork mechanism.

Dualisms and Deism—The Significance of the Concept of Absolute Time

Whenever one speaks of Newton's accomplishments, the eighteenth-century English poet Alexander Pope is often quoted:

Nature and nature's law lay hid in night.
God said: "Let Newton be," and all was light.[110]

The rendering of Pope's words at this point is more justified as an expression of contemporary scientific optimism than as evidence of the illuminating insights of Newton for our questions regarding time. It is reflec-
tive of the enthusiasm for the simplicity, coherence, and functionality of the
mechanical system. Newton succeeded in uniting earthly and heavenly
mathematics. For two events, it seemed that one could make an objective
decision regarding whether they are absolutely simultaneous and occur at
the same location. Nature was embedded in the uniform flow of absolute
time and not vice versa; time was therefore not understood as a dimension
of nature. The proof of the universality of gravitation allowed nature to appear as a homogeneous whole. The vertical dualism of heaven and earth and
the polarization of time and eternity thus lost their footing.

With regard to time, one should note that Newton indeed distinguishes
between absolute and relative time; however, the concept of space dominates his later discussion. Time is treated analogously to space and not vice
versa. God's standing as the guarantor of absolute space appears to exceed
God's significance as the basis of absolute time. Evidently, the image of a
God whose principal predicates are power, ultimate cause, and providence
is well-suited to absolute concepts.

Newtonian science has been oriented toward the ideal of uniformity
and symmetry and is basically more space-oriented than time-oriented.
Both the study of hymns and the account of biblical findings (chapters 1
and 2) showed, in contrast, that Christian theology is more time-oriented
than space-oriented.[111] An increasing interest in space was clearly manifested only in the most recent hymns, which suggests the conclusion that the
interest in space grew when the traditional time-eternity model declined.[112]
This change seems to go hand in hand with a shift of emphasis from the notion of the impending Last Judgment to the call to realize the reign of God
here and now.

Space-oriented classical science and time-oriented classical Christianity—it is entirely possible that this opposing relationship, which has hardly
been considered until now, has contributed to the conflict-laden aspects of
the history of the dialogue between science and theology; and it is just as
possible that a greater time orientation of science and a more conscious
space orientation of theology during the twentieth century have favorably
influenced the preconditions for this dialogue.

Leibniz's relationally oriented concept of time does not mean that Leibniz had a more relational concept of God than Newton did. Instead, the re-

verse is true. While Newton's concept of divine power is expressly linked to a relation—God is always the Lord over servants[113]—in Leibniz, God is "determined by internal reasons";[114] God's wisdom is absolute. The taming of omnipotence by divine wisdom does indeed help Leibniz to get beyond Clarke's problem of the relationship of space/time and omnipresence/eternity with its aporia of the identification of God with absolute space and absolute time. But within his system, he is unsuccessful in conclusively conceiving of God's preservational activity, for the wisdom that is being expressed in the preestablished harmony not only makes a continuous preservation activity unnecessary, but it also renders any divine intervention at all problematic. Leibniz is in danger of contrasting a self-functioning world mechanism with an otherworldly God, while Clarke runs the risk of integrating an omnipotent God into a closed system.

In both Clarke and Leibniz, God is necessary for understanding space and time, as well as for comprehending the world. Both apportion to God the position of logical guarantor for the rationality of the world mechanism. Proof of this necessary God is thus also derived from the world's coherence, which brings God into a relationship of dependency with far-reaching consequences, although this certainly had not been intended. What still appears to be a valid mental construction on the horizon of the dawning eighteenth century is soon transformed into a pile of rubble: The God who is the necessary foundation of everything becomes a God who is constantly retreating and for whom smaller and smaller gaps remain within what is not yet explicable by the laws of nature. The modern theological discussion of the "more than necessary" God should be understood as a counterpart to this development. It claims that God cannot be proven to be the sufficient ground of being on the basis of the world's coherence; God always comes from Godself.[115]

The thoughts expressed here leave no doubt that, in Newton/Clarke and Leibniz, theology and physics have mutually influenced each other. I believe a decision cannot be made as to whether one can assign greater influence to theology or physics in specific cases. It remains to be emphasized that the distinctions worked out in the Leibniz-Clarke correspondence developed into a dualism not only between time and space and between absolute and relative, but also between space/time and matter and, finally, between God and the world. In my view, the theistic concept of a God who is absolute and static in divine majesty contributed to this process.[116] How would it have been if Newton had included—if not an elaborated doctrine of the Trinity—then at least a Christology? If it can be reasonably assumed that Newton did not intend a development toward a "God of the gaps," would the result have been different if he had included Christology? What, for example, could the Incarnation mean for absolute space and absolute time? How would the sentence in the General Scholium, "God suffers nothing from the motion of bodies; bodies find no resistance from the omnipresence of God,"[117] read if the death and resurrection of Jesus Christ had also been considered? These are certainly speculative questions that cannot be answered at this point. They open a path to an insight that is important for our further study, however: One can speak dynamically and relationally of time and eternity only if one also starts from a dynamic and relational concept of God. The theistic concept of God proves to be unsuitable here.

Expressed somewhat differently: Newton's God has two determining features—divine absoluteness and divine preservational activity, including occasional correcting intervention in cosmic events that are generally determined by the laws of nature. Giving God's absolute power supreme importance, however, deprives the preservational work of its legitimacy; it must always accept the reproach of implying that God is an inferior clockmaker. Nothing essential would have changed in this regard, however, if Newton, like Leibniz, had elevated wisdom to the position of a superordinate concept, since this construction also does not bypass deism. Thus, the reason for the dead end of deism should be sought less in the concept of absolute or relative time than in the absoluteness of the theistic concept of God, which effectively suppresses the idea of true relationality.

As might be expected, further development did not go in the direction of relationality of time and eternity.[118] On the contrary, the philosopher who took up both Newton's and Leibniz's thoughts and who was also familiar with *Reflexions sur l'espace et le temps* by the mathematician Leonhard Euler did much to increase the separation of time from its relation to the idea of eternity.[119] In Immanuel Kant (1724–1804), one finds, on the one hand, the same absoluteness in the concept of time as in Newton, with the crucial difference that in Kant, absoluteness turns "inward": Time is the subjective condition of all human ideas, "a necessary presentation that underlies all intuitions."[120] For the sake of preserving God's transcendence, absoluteness befits time itself as a medium of God's effectiveness less than it befits the finite subject.[121] On the other hand, the Kantian concept of time, particularly in its early stage, is also reminiscent of the type of ideality that one finds in Leibniz.[122] Finally, however, Kant rejects the notion of a relative time in the sense of an ordering of things, for time is, first of all, not a condition of things in themselves; it is neither substance, nor attribute, nor relation, but instead, it is a form for intuition [*Anschauungsform*] to order the material of sensory perceptions. As such a form, it must "altogether lie ready for the sensations a priori in the mind."[123] Within the framework of his transcendental aesthetics, Kant comes to the following conclusions with regard to time:

(a) Time is not something that is self-subsistent or that attaches to things as an objective determination, and that hence would remain if one abstracted from all subjective conditions of our intuition of it. For if time were self-subsistent, then it would be something that without there being an actual object, would yet be actual. But if, on the second alternative, time were a determination or order attaching to things themselves, then it could not precede the objects as their condition. . . .

(b) Time is nothing but the form of inner senses i.e., the intuiting we do of ourselves and our inner state. For time cannot be a determination of outer appearances . . . but rather determines the relation of presentations in our inner state. And, precisely because this inner intuition gives us no shape, do we try to make up for this deficiency by means of analogies. We present time sequence by a line continuing *ad infinitum*, a line in which the manifold constitutes a series of only one dimension. And from the properties of that line we infer all the properties of time . . .

c) Time is the formal a priori condition of all appearances . . . [I]t is the direct condition of inner appearances (of our souls) and precisely thereby also indirectly, a condition of the outer appearances.[124]

Thus, the unity of time is ensured by the unity of the self, which leads "to the contradictory 'idea' of a finiteness that posits itself as absolute."[125]

The lines of thought of Newton and Leibniz can also be recognized in Kant's double description that "time is *empirically* real i.e., objectively valid in regard to all objects that might ever be given to our senses," and of "the *transcendental ideality* of time. According to this view, if we abstract from the subjective conditions of sensible intuition, then time is nothing, and cannot be included among objects in themselves . . . either as subsisting [as such an object] or as inhering [in one]."[126]

Kant's concentration on the role of the self for the unity of time, as well as his description in terms of reality and ideality, is oriented more toward the static and the constant than it is toward a description of change and dynamics. Time remains the invariable and the permanent.[127] In this sense, Newton's absolute, reversible concept of time has prevailed. Seeking to discover how dynamics and time asymmetry are to be conceived, I will now turn to twentieth-century physics.

The Concept of Relative Time

Physics constitutes a logical system of thought which is in a state of evolution, and whose basis cannot be obtained through distillation by any inductive method from the experiences lived through, but which can only be attained by free invention. The justification (truth content) of the system rests in the proof of usefulness of the resulting theorems on the basis of sense experiences, where the relations of the latter to the former can only be comprehended intuitively. Evolution is going on in the direction of increasing simplicity of the logical basis. In order further to approach this goal, we must make up our mind to accept the fact that the logical basis departs more and more from the facts of experience, and that the path of our thought from the fundamental basis to these resulting theorems, which correlate with sense experiences, becomes continually harder and longer.[128]

The author of this physical declaration of principle is Albert Einstein (1879–1955), creator of the special and general theories of relativity in the years 1905 and 1915, respectively.[129] His words mirror both the intuitive, creative dimension of physical science and the constant struggle for a uniform conception of the world, in which theory and experience reach agreement. Both also are found in Einstein's biography.[130] The creative achievement of the twenty-six-year-old "third-class technical expert" at the Swiss Federal Institute of Intellectual Property in Bern and the recognition that the professor and member of the Prussian Academy of Sciences in Berlin received in 1919 following the official confirmation of the general theory of relativity (due to the publication of the data collected by a British expedition during a solar eclipse) brought him world fame and the reputation of being a genius.[131] Nevertheless, Einstein's big dream of achieving a uniform field theory that would summarize his conception of the world was left unfulfilled. His stubborn refusal to accept quantum mechanics with all of its "illogicality" appears to have finally led him to a dead end.[132]

Problematicized Simultaneity— The Special Theory of Relativity

If it was striking that Newton spoke more about space than about time, Einstein appears to have actually given time a crucial role,[133] since the key that opened his way to a new understanding of basic physical concepts was precisely an analysis of the concept of time. Einstein recognized that the concept of absolute time was useless because the presupposed synchronization of clocks using effects that expand at extreme velocity cannot be implemented due to the finite nature of the speed of light. He speaks of a relative simultaneity instead. This relative simultaneity means that, in reference systems that are inert relative to one another, the simultaneity determined by using light signals completely corresponds to the traditional conceptions.[134] The study of moving systems, however, resulted in entirely different findings, which makes it impossible to speak of a simultaneity of two events in a sense that is valid for all reference systems. In this case, relative simultaneity must be understood in such a way that a certain Observer A characterizes two events as simultaneous, while an Observer B, moved in relationship to A, calls these events nonsimultaneous. This makes it necessary to transfer not only the place coordinates, but also the time coordinates, during a transition from one inertial system[135] to another. In the everyday sphere of perception, that which is simultaneously observed also appears to happen simultaneously. However, consideration of the finite nature of the spreading speed of light forces one to distinguish between time and local time. This distinction nullifies the identity of simultaneous observation and simultaneous event.[136]

Thus, at the beginning of the special theory of relativity, there is an analysis of the concept of time with the insight that time cannot be defined absolutely, since there is an indissoluble connection between time and the speed with which a signal can travel.[137] In the end, Einstein says, "[t]he theory of relativity may indeed be said to have put a sort of finishing touch to the mighty intellectual edifice of Maxwell and Lorentz, inasmuch as it seeks to extend field physics to all phenomena, gravitation included."[138]

Initially, however, Einstein did not wish to have his theory characterized as a closed system, but rather as a heuristic principle. This means that individual laws are not contained in the theory of relativity and cannot be derived from it by means of deduction, but rather that the theory of relativity in the sense of a metatheory specifies correlations between laws and the presuppositions that are to be fulfilled by them.[139] Therefore, he spoke initially only of a "principle of relativity."[140] The term *theory of relativity*, which gained acceptance beginning in 1907, was proposed by other people and subsequently accepted only reluctantly by Einstein.[141] The term *theory* possibly led to a popular understanding in the sense of "everything is relative." Especially after the general theory of relativity became known, there was ample breeding ground for such a misunderstanding because of the political and cultural conditions of the times, although, with regard to contents, one is in fact dealing, quite the contrary, with the invariance and universality of the absolute speed of light;[142] the causality in Einstein's theory is no less rigorous than that in Newton's.[143]

In other words: The absoluteness of the speed of light has replaced the absoluteness of space and time. The boundary of the light barrier cannot be crossed from any side. Thus, the constancy of the speed of light in a vacuum determines the boundary for the expansion of every effect. The speed of light limits the observable universe, not only with regard to space, but also with regard to time, by permitting access only to a limited past. It also restricts the scope of knowledge that could, for example, reach us within a lifetime from extraterrestrial civilizations.[144] From the constancy of the speed of light follows the constancy of the four-dimensional space-time interval between two events; space and time can each vary, but the interval as a whole remains the same for all observers, independent of their relative speed. In this network of relationships and boundaries, time no longer has an independent existence; it appears—as in Leibniz—to be a way of ordering matter that has no physical meaning without changes in the relationships of objects.[145]

In addition to the constancy of the speed of light in the vacuum, Einstein built on the postulate of the validity of the same laws of nature in all systems moving uniformly towards one another.[146] However, even before then, in agreement with the Michelson-Morley experiment, the result of which "was a verdict of 'death' to the theory of a calm ether-sea through which all matter moves,"[147] Einstein had eliminated the "'*enfant terrible*' of the family of physical substances"[148] and basically dropped the ether concept. The two presuppositions for Einstein's special theory of relativity produce a contradiction to the classical transformation. For high speeds, it is easy to show that the Galilean Transformation of classical mechanics is inapplicable.[149] While the experiences gained through classical mechanics definitely retain their validity for low speeds compared to the speed of light, speeds that approximate the speed of light require the Lorentz Transformation. This transformation predicts that a rod moved at high speed will shrink in the direction of motion, and a clock moved in the same way will slow its pace (time dilatation). At the speed of light, the rod would disappear, and the clock would stop.[150] The equations of the Lorentz-Transformation[151]

$$x' = \frac{x-vt}{\sqrt{1-\left(\frac{v}{c}\right)^2}} \qquad y'=y \qquad z'=z \qquad t' = \frac{t-\frac{vx}{c^2}}{\sqrt{1-\left(\frac{v}{c}\right)^2}}$$

contain, as it were, the Galilean Transformation, since when the speed of light travels towards infinity, a transition from the Lorentz Transformation into the Galilean Transformation occurs (the denominator of the first equation approximates 1), i.e., if the speed of light is infinite, there would be an instant signal transmission, and thus absolute time. The discrepancy between the values of the classical transformation and those of the Lorentz Transformation is greatest for speeds approximating the speed of light.

A few months after the publication of the article "Zur Elektrodynamik bewegter Körper" (On the Electrodynamics of Moving Bodies) in the *Annalen der Physik*, Einstein concluded that there is a general equivalence of mass and energy, which was expressed in the well-known formula $E = mc^2$.[152]

In contrast to classical mechanics, the measurement of space and time in relativistic physics using the regularities of light clearly shows: "The means by which nature is recognized are nothing other than parts of precisely this nature."[153] Physics can therefore no longer be understood as natural philosophy in the sense of a theory of nature "as it is." Rather, one is dealing with a theory of nature "as it appears when it is tested using real standards and clocks."[154] Time can no longer be understood as a "container" for nature. Nature is not in time, but rather, time is in nature.

Space-Time Curvature—The General Theory of Relativity

The restricted application of the special theory of relativity to uniformly moving systems called attention to the fact "that the previous theory of relativity needed to be generalized so that the seemingly unjust preference for uniform translation, as contrasted to relative movements of a different type, vanishes from the theory."[155] The general theory of relativity[156] solved this problem of formulating physical laws for *all* systems. It contains the special theory of relativity as a limiting case. The great achievement of the general theory of relativity was the inclusion of gravity, which occurred by expanding the principle of relativity to coordinate systems accelerated relative to one another and by considering the gravitational fields that were caused thereby. The recognition of the invariance[157] of the speed of light made the idea of instant gravitational effects impossible and required the mathematical treatment of gravity according to a field theory. This is achieved by the general theory of relativity. The difference from the concepts of space and time in classical mechanics is obvious. In Newton, space and time were defined in advance as the solid stage on which the development of physical systems takes place, but space-time in the general theory of relativity is an essential part of this very development.[158]

The general theory of relativity makes use of the Gaussian method for the mathematical treatment of any continuum. In a four-dimensional continuum, it attributes four coordinates (x_1, x_2, x_3, *and* x_4) to each event, whereby no distinction is made between space and time coordinates. This method replaces descriptions that use a reference body and is therefore not limited to describing a continuum with a Euclidean character.[159]

The connection of local space and time coordinates, as is known by the special theory of relativity, is replaced by a more general relationship that contains a so-called metric tensor g_{ik} (x, y, z, t). The space-time continuum of the general theory of relativity corresponds to the shape of a four-dimensional curved space. The expression "curved space" implies that the spatial arrangement of material bodies does not agree with the laws of three-dimensional Euclidian geometry.[160] Instead, the theory uses Riemannian geometry,[161] the simplest illustration of which can draw upon the geometry of a spherical surface. The two-dimensional surface of a sphere is finite and yet unlimited. A three-dimensional space with similar properties must be thought of as curved back into itself. Since, in Riemannian geometry, Euclidian geometry is locally valid in infinitesimally small areas of the curved spaces, the latter is to a certain degree included in the former.

Einstein's gravity equations were initially confirmed empirically in three respects, namely, by the rotation of the ellipses of the planetary orbits around the sun (complete explanation of the deviations in the perihelion of Mercury), the light deflection in a gravitational field (using the solar eclipse photographs of the 1919 British expedition), and the gravitational redshift of light. In addition, the predicted consequences of Einstein's theory in the form of time dilation have since been empirically confirmed numerous times.[162]

If, according to the special theory of relativity, it was movement that slowed down the operation of clocks, then according to the general theory of relativity, the same applies to gravity. These facts are frequently illustrated using the well-known "twin paradox."[163] A twin who takes a journey into space at high speeds will be younger upon her return than the sister who remained at home. Similarly, one twin who was exposed to much stronger gravity on a heavenly body of higher density than the other was exposed to on earth finds on her return that the sister who stayed at home is older than she is.

Neither the special nor the general theory of relativity can define the direction of a time arrow; as in Newtonian mechanics, time here is also basically reversible. The theory of relativity did not falsify Newtonian mechanics, but rather specified the scope of its validity.

Merely a Shadow—The End of Independent Time?

On September 21, 1908, the mathematician Hermann Minkowski from Göttingen began his presentation entitled "Raum und Zeit" (Space and Time) at the Assembly of German Natural Scientists and Physicians in Cologne with suggestive words: "Gentlemen! The views of space and time which I wish to lay before you have sprung from the soil of experimental physics. Therein lies their strength. They are radical. Henceforth space by itself, and time by itself are doomed to fade away into mere shadows, and only a kind of union of the two will preserve an independent reality."[164]

These sentences did not fail to impress. In the literature on the theory of relativity, they are frequently quoted, and reference is regularly made to the "Minkowski World." In this four-dimensional world, space and time are thus, each for itself, sentenced to a shadowy existence. They survive only as a unity of four coordinates.

Does this signify the end of time as an autonomous entity? May one speak only of space-time? Does Einstein himself draw such a conclusion? In his presentation of the general theory of relativity, after initial skepticism, Einstein expresses[165] his admiration for Minkowski's interpretation of the special theory of relativity: "The generalization of the theory of relativity has been greatly facilitated by the form that was given to the special theory of relativity by Minkowski, the mathematician who first clearly recognized the formal equivalency of the spatial and time coordinates and used it for establishing the theory."[166] Without Minkowski, the general theory of relativity would have "perhaps remained stuck in infancy."[167]

Elsewhere, however, Einstein expressed himself much more cautiously:

From a formal point of view one may characterize the achievement of the special theory of relativity thus: it has shown generally the role which the universal constant c (velocity of light) plays in the laws of nature and has demonstrated that there exists a close connection between the form in which time on the one hand and the spatial coordinates on the other hand enter into the laws of nature.[168]

He therefore appears to presuppose a difference between space and time despite their arithmetical unification as coordinates of one and the same system. Or is this more an emotional assertion of an elderly man rather than of a scientist? For in "A London Speech," Einstein says when referring to Minkowski: "According to the special theory of relativity the four dimensional continuum formed by the union of space and time retains the absolute character which, according to the earlier theory, belonged to both space and time separately."[169] Mathematically, "no statement is more banal than that our familiar world is a four-dimensional time-space continuum,"[170] for it can be shown that the laws of nature, which correspond to the requirements of the theory of relativity, "assume mathematical forms in which the time coordinate plays exactly the same role as the three spatial coordinates."[171]

How, then, can this loss of autonomy of time and space be understood?[172] Classical physics could allow itself two equally valid interpretations of a space-time continuum, namely, first as a dynamic concept of positions that change in time, and, second, as a static concept of movement as something existing. In the first case, the continuum is broken down into space and time; in the second, it is viewed as a whole. In classical physics, the oscillation between the two concepts presents no problem inasmuch as, according to the idea of absolute time, the time coordinate always remains the same. When relating to another system, only the space coordinates, but not the time coordinates, are transformed. Within the special theory of relativity, on the other hand, a space-time continuum cannot simply be split into a space and a time dimension, since in two different systems, not only the space coordinates, but also the time coordinate, are different. For this reason, in the theory of relativity, the static, continuous conception of space-time is the more useful and objective one. Einstein concedes, "Indeed, we can, if we so desire, continue to work with the dynamic manner of representation also within the framework of the theory of relativity; but then we must always consider that splitting into time and space has no objective significance, since, for us, time is no longer absolute."[173] In the "Minkowski World," physics was transformed from an *event* in three-dimensional space into an *existence* in this four-dimensional world.[174] Because in this four-dimensional continuum there are "no more sections that objectively represent the 'now', the concept of the *event* and *becoming* is not completely abolished, but rather, is made more complicated."[175] For this reason, Einstein prefers "to think of the physically real as a four-dimensional existence, instead of, as previously, as the *becoming* of a three-dimensional existence."[176]

A distinction between space and time that likewise deviates from everyday understanding is linked to the constancy of the speed of light. The speed of light permits causality between two events only when the events lie within the particular area that light, with its finite speed, can reach at a certain time. Graphically, this area corresponds to a cone that, with infinite speed of light, would be opened up to the *x* level. Events that lie within a light cone are characterized as being situated timelike to one another. Events that lie outside a light cone are characterized as being situated spacelike to one another.

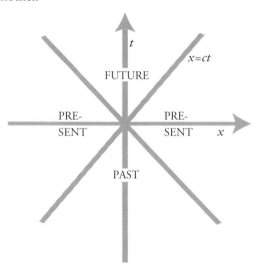

Light Cone and Ordering of Past, Present, and Future

Events having a spacelike position can have no interaction with one another at all. The boundary of the cone is termed an event horizon. Events that are situated spacelike and timelike can thus be distinguished from one another by the clearly defined boundary of the event horizon. On the one hand, this use of "spacelike" or "timelike" points to the change in meaning of the colloquial concepts of "space" and "time" within relativistic physics; on the other hand, it gives the impression that time and space are still strictly distinguishable variables. Furthermore, the descriptive model of the light cone enables a special definition of past, future, and present. For an event E, the past consists of all events that can have causally influenced E. The future consists of all events that can be influenced by E. The present then consists of all events that neither influence E nor are influenced by E. Conceptually, these definitions completely agree with the framework of classical physics. Mathematically, however, interesting differences result, especially for the description of the present. In relativistic physics, the lower portion of the light cone corresponds to the past, and the upper part, to the future. In classical physics, only the event points lying on the x-axis belong to the present, while in relativistic physics, all spacelike points must be thought of as belonging to the present.[177]

The question of autonomy, however, concerns not only the relationship of time to space and vice versa. In the general theory of relativity, an even more radical loss of autonomy takes place. If space (or space-time) had an autonomous existence vis-à-vis matter or field in classical mechanics and also according to the special theory of relativity, then, in the general theory of relativity, the "separate existence" of space disappears vis-à-vis that which "fills space"; there is no space without field.[178]

In summary, Einstein says: "The process of development here sketched [toward the general theory of relativity] strips the space-time coordinates of all independent reality. The metrically real is now only given through the combination of the space-time co-ordinates with the mathematical quantities which describe the gravitational field."[179] Thus, the requirements of the general theory of relativity take "from space and from time the last trace of physical concreteness."[180]

On the whole, from these considerations, it should be noted that according to Einstein, time and space are still distinguishable and that each by itself has significance, but not an objective significance. In terms of conception, both appear to be much less concrete than in classical physics. Nevertheless, they obtain an operational character, for it became clear that the definitions of physical concepts require the specification of measurement procedures. In this regard, the question "What is time?" receives the answer: "That which is measured with clocks." Both the special and the general theory of relativity allow the assumption of timelessness under certain physical conditions, but they do not allow its realization.

The assertion that time has been degraded to a function of space is inappropriate. Why speak of a spatialization of time when one can just as easily speak of a dynamization of space?[181] If the need for the transformation of spatial coordinates was already expressed in the Galilean Transformation, then with the theory of relativity, time has approached space in the sense that now its necessity for transformation also becomes clear. Time and space emerge together as entities tied to movement. Thus, they find themselves equally relativized, but not identified with each other: "Relativity has broken down the isolation of time and space but not their distinction."[182] It has thus become clear "that already within the framework of physics, time, space, and matter have a deep internal structural connection."[183] It is not autonomy in the sense of qualitative distinction that has thereby disappeared, but rather autonomy in the quantitative sense. Instead of a four-dimensional continuum, it would be better to speak "of a $(3 + 1)$-dimensional continuum,"[184] since one is dealing with differences within a framework of relatedness—not with absoluteness, but rather with relationality.[185]

The dualism between absolute space or absolute time and relative space or relative time, as well as between space and time, has become superfluous.[186] If there is something in the theory of relativity that is to be characterized as absolute, then it is the principle of the constancy of the vacuum speed of light. Light sets the "boundary and dimension" of space and time; as the basic variable of nature, it attains a unique metaphysical, though finite, status.[187] For this reason, it is not surprising that theologians using this interpretation have tried to see links here to the discussion of God's infinite light and that they look for connections, for example, to the Johannine symbolism of light.[188]

Time and the Quantum World

"Subtle is the Lord, but not malicious."[189] These oft-quoted words of Einstein give an impression of Einstein's passionate rejection of quantum theory. He would have preferred being a cobbler or a casino employee rather than a physicist, if he were forced to give up the strict requirement of causality and accept the notion "that an electron exposed to radiation should choose *of its own free will,* not only its moment to jump off, but also its direction."[190] For the person who had provided important impulses for the development of quantum theory, for instance with his 1905 hypothesis of light quanta, quantum mechanics certainly appeared to be "quite awe-inspiring"; it seemed to him "however, not the real thing": "The theory says a lot, but does not really bring us closer to the secret of the 'old one.' I, at any rate, am convinced that *He* is not playing at dice."[191]

Above all, the epistemological interpretation that Werner Heisenberg (1901–1976) and Niels Bohr (1885–1962)[192] gave to quantum theory between 1925 and 1927 was decisive for Einstein's lifelong aversion to quantum mechanics.[193] The criticism that initially sounded so irreconcilable, however, was mitigated by the discussions on the Einstein-Podolsky-Rosen Experiment of 1934, so that, in 1940, Einstein declared that the progress of the century consists of two theories that are basically independent of each other, namely, the theory of relativity and quantum mechanics. In his opinion, the two theories do not actually directly contradict each other, but they also do not appear to be suitable for merging into a uniform theory.[194] He sees the fundamental difference between quantum theory and all previous theories in the fact that, instead of a model description of actual events in time and space being given, probability distributions are now being provided for the dependency of possible measurements upon time. And this was not done on the basis of imaginative flights of thought, but rather due to the compelling power of empirical facts.

And Heisenberg has convincingly shown, from an empirical point of view, any decision as to a rigorously deterministic structure of nature is definitely ruled out, because of the atomistic structure of our experimental apparatus. Thus it is probably out of the question that any future knowledge can compel physics again to relinquish our present statistical theoretical foundation in favor of a deterministic one which would deal directly with physical reality . . . Some physicists, among them myself, can not believe that we must abandon, actually and forever, the idea of direct representation of physical reality in space and time; or that we must accept the view that events in nature are analogous to a game of chance.[195]

Accordingly, Einstein considered quantum physics to be a logical and consistent, though incomplete, description of a still unknown underlying theory, which would finally achieve an objective description of reality.[196] This deep skepticism of Einstein indicates the extent to which quantum physics challenged the established line of thinking that had been shaped to look for deterministic structures of causality.

Time Getting Blurred—Quantum Theory

If the theory of relativity dealt with the very large and led us to the spatially and temporally comprehensible "ends" of the universe, then quantum theory takes us into the realm of the very small, into the world of atomic nuclei and subatomic particles.[197] Important steps in the development of quantum theory included Max Planck's study of black-body radiation in 1900, his discovery of the quantum of action and the derivation of the so-called Planck's Constant connected with it, as well as Einstein's 1905 article on light quanta. After the wave theory of light had ruled for a century, the discussion then shifted to photons and light quanta, whereby individual atomic processes were ascribed a discontinuity that was foreign to classical physics.[198] It became clear that light, depending upon which measuring process is used, exhibits two different modes of behavior. It acts like a wave and like a small, solid object. The two modes of behavior cannot be observed simultaneously and apply not only to photons, but also to particles in general. Each object of quantum theory is therefore as much a particle as it is a wave. Bohr summarized these findings in the *complementarity principle*, which had a great impact, and not only on physics. The concept of complementarity that was new to physics had repercussions on philosophy as a model for understanding dichotomies.[199]

Complementarity thus describes two sides of one and the same object that contradict each other and never occur simultaneously, but that complete each other to create a structural connection: "The very nature of the quantum theory thus forces us to regard the space-time co-ordination and the claim of causality, the union of which characterises the classical theories, as complementary but exclusive features of the description, symbolising the idealisation of observation and definition respectively."[200]

Even if quantum physics has existed as a theory for over sixty years, its interpretation is still the subject of discussion. Thus, for example, the status of reality is interpreted in various ways. Positions range from the view that observations only describe already existing reality to the standpoint that reality is created only through observation or that only statements regarding phenomena and their behavior are possible, but not statements about reality as a whole. The Copenhagen interpretation of quantum theory, which was developed primarily by Bohr and Heisenberg, is thus not the only one, but it is certainly the most common.[201]

The heartbeat of quantum theory lies in the *indeterminacy principle*, which was formulated by Heisenberg.[202] It says that perfect precision in the measurement of the momentum (= velocity × mass) and position of a particle is impossible, and this is not because the measurement equipment is defective, but rather because nature is the way it is. If we know where a particle is, we cannot simultaneously know what it is doing and vice versa. Mathematically expressed, this means: The uncertainty of the measurement of the position of a particle multiplied by the uncertainty of the measurement of its velocity can never result in a smaller value than $h/4\pi m$, where h is Planck's Constant, and m is the mass of the particle in question. Thus, the larger the particle mass, the smaller the uncertainty; the smaller the particle mass, the larger the uncertainty.

What applies to the uncertainty relation of impulse or velocity and position is also valid for the relationships of time and energy or time and mass. Analogous to the minimum values in the relationship of position and impulse, minimum values also exist here, i.e., a value below which one cannot go, for the time that is interpreted as the measuring time.[203] The world of the very small thus confronts us, in relation to the expressive possibilities of concrete language, with a blurred image of reality. It is possible to conclude from this "that in the deep layers of the particle waves, the essence of space and time itself is imprecise and only vaguely defined."[204]

The quantum field theory developed by Paul Dirac in 1927 enabled a rational understanding of the duality of waves and particles. In contrast, the structure of the measurement process is still open to varying interpretations. As long as it is not measured, a system is in the state of superposition, i.e., a particle is in a state that is a mixture of "here" and "there." The mixture does not mean that the particle is somewhere between "here" and "there," but rather that its position can be determined only according to probability. Only the measurement forces a decision, which is the same as saying that the wave function suffers a collapse. The principle of superposition is therefore the cause for the statistical character of the quantum world.

In quantum physics, one is confronted with two different shapes of time. On the one hand, there are reversible quantum states and equations that do not define a direction of time. On the other hand, observations or measurements are performed that transform the quantum system, which is indifferent to directions of time, into an irreversible event, because conclusions cannot be drawn on the past of the quantum system based on an observational finding.[205] With regard to the measuring process, it should be noted that each measuring instrument is exposed to quantum physical processes. Even the most precise clocks are objects that are subject to quantum uncertainty.

Even if quantum theory appears to contradict the intuitive understanding of reality, it neither allows the interpretation that everything is possible, nor does it permit any indiscriminately far-reaching metaphysical conclusions.[206] In a direct sense, it concerns only the area of the subatomic order; the effects of quantum phenomena, however, affect the entire range from atom to cosmos.[207]

Initially, quantum theory appeared to cause radical disillusionment for the hopes that were linked to the progress in the field of atomic theory. With regard to lucidity and the description of causal correlations, it virtually led to resignation. This "resignation," however, was very soon regarded as epistemological progress,[208] and one of the reasons for the successful application of quantum theory lies precisely in this manner of viewing things.

Both Spectator and Actor in the Great Existential Drama[209]—
The Role of the Observer

The theory of relativity had already bestowed upon the observer a more important position than ever before by making time dependent upon the respective reference systems of one or another observer. Quantum theory increased this tendency into the almost unimaginable. First, it brought disorder into the distinction between "objective" and "subjective" that was apparently so self-evident in natural science. Thus, for example, the concept "objective observation" becomes contradictory in itself, because in quantum theory, it must be assumed that we can observe only that which cannot be separated from us.[210] Quantum physics also robbed empirical measurement processes of their innocence by asserting that any observation of a process represents an influence on that process. In the words of Bohr: "Now the quantum postulate implies that any observation of atomic phenomena will involve an interaction with the agency of observation not to be neglected. Accordingly, an independent reality in the ordinary physical sense can neither be ascribed to the phenomena nor to the agencies of observation."[211]

Bohr thus goes so far as to question the very existence of an independent reality. Neither the phenomena nor the observations can be described with a simple "that's how it is." Each observation requires an intervention into the course of phenomena in a way that deprives us of the basis for a causal description.[212]

It may sound improbable that the intense observation of a clock slows down its movement, but that is precisely what happens when the clock is regarded as a quantum system. It has been shown on atoms that normally disintegrate with regularity that continuous observation prevents these atoms from disintegrating.[213] During uninterrupted observation of a quantum system, time, then, principally stands still. For physicists, this is not entirely unproblematic: Their definition of time as being that which is shown by the clock works only when they do not look at the clock too often.

So far, this presentation of quantum physics has focused on probability and uncertainty only. The inclusion of the observer makes clear that, in quantum theory, one is dealing with a massive triad of probability, complementarity, and observation. Neither probability nor complementarity becomes clear without measurement. This means that even when uncertainty cannot be traced back to a fault of the observer and his or her equipment, but is rather a feature of nature per se, uncertainty becomes evident only through the act of measurement that is performed by an acting subject. The extent to which a distinction can be maintained between an observing subject and a quantum system as the observed object is the subject of an ongoing discussion.[214] Some interpretations can go so far that, finally, "everything" is dependent upon the observer. What "everything" means in this context can be clarified by the thought experiment with Erwin Schrödinger's famous cat. This is the attempt to work out the epistemological consequences of quantum theory by transposing a quantum system onto the macroscopic level. The thought experiment goes like this: A cat is in a closed, opaque crate together with an ampoule of lethal poison. A hammer is affixed above the ampoule and crushes the ampoule when it falls down, thus leading to the instant death of the cat. The release of the hammer is dependent upon the random disintegration of a radioactive atom. As long as no one looks into the crate, the cat is not, as would be assumed, either alive or dead, but it is rather in a "both dead-and-alive condition," which corresponds to a wave function that contains both possibilities. Only at the moment when an observer looks into the box does the one possibility disappear and the other become reality, which is synonymous with the collapse of the wave function for the unrealized possibility.[215]

Generally speaking, one can say that a measurement causes a collapse at a point when the condition of all possible measurement results passes into the state of a factual result. This condition then holds true at the same moment in the entire universe.[216] To what extent such measurements require the presence and activity of human consciousness continues to be debated.

The highly subject-oriented interpretation of the measurement process that is outlined here has significance for the conceptions of the beginning and end of the universe, or of time. It can be understood in such a way that an external observer causes the collapse of a wave function by measuring and thus calls a concrete reality into existence. Formulated differently: If this interpretation is correct, a universe without an external observer would be inconceivable. The mathematician Andrej A. Grib[217] goes so far as to characterize the universe as a creation out of nothing, a vacuum state, by an external observer who decided upon a special measurement. Somewhat in the manner of Frank J. Tipler,[218] he infers a general resurrection from quantum cosmology.

Understandably, such interpretations are extremely controversial in the scientific camp, for they go far beyond what can be called a general consensus. According to Grib, "All events in spacetime will be reorganized or 'resurrected' but not in such a way that they will be in time."[219] He thereby identifies neither God with the "Ultimate Observer" or the Resurrection with the collapse of the wave function in the great final collapse of the universe, but he postulates both as possibilities.[220] Another possible interpretation that dispenses with an external observer propagates the notion that all quantum physical possibilities are of equal value. Each of these possibilities is realized in its own universe, which leads to an infinite number of parallel universes.

These thoughts belong to the realm of what are, in part, highly speculative cosmological theories that will be discussed in more detail in 3.5.3. First, however, I shall consider the significance of quantum theory for the relationship between language and reality.

Playing with Different Images—Language and Physical Reality

What was largely ignored by Kant has been discussed deliberately by the fathers of quantum theory, namely, the fact that it is not only the perception of space and time that structures our concept of reality, but rather, language is also fundamentally involved. Both Bohr and Heisenberg have dealt with the relationship of language and reality and thus emphasized the hermeneutical character of the natural sciences in significant ways.[221]

In *Physics and Beyond*, "a type of memoir in the form of Platonic dialogues,"[222] Heisenberg reviews discussions about language that he had in an alpine hut during the 1933 Easter holidays, primarily with Bohr. The ideas revolve around the boundaries of language that are also inescapable in science. According to Bohr, "Language is, as it were, a net spread out between people, a net in which our thoughts and knowledge are inextricably enmeshed."[223] So, basically, it is not really surprising—even if it might initially appear contradictory—that quantum theory makes use of the same terminology as classical physics. The attempt in physics to bypass "this strange, fluid character"[224] of language by using a strictly mathematical mode of expression is not particularly successful. Though it is an imperfect instrument, language also remains a precondition for natural science: "For if we want to say anything at all about nature—and what else does science try to do?—we must somehow pass from mathematical to everyday language."[225] Imprecise, but brilliant, this, in brief, is the content of Bohr's insight about language, gained while washing dishes under the somewhat primitive conditions of an alpine hut: "Our washing up is just like our language . . . We have dirty water and dirty dishcloths, and yet, we manage to get the plates and glasses clean. In language, too, we have to work with unclear concepts and a form of logic whose scope is restricted in an unknown way, and yet we use it to bring some clarity in our understanding of nature."[226]

Heisenberg expressed a fundamental trust in the capacity of language in his essay entitled "Ordnung der Wirklichkeit" (Order of Reality), which was written before the end of 1942: "Every area of reality can ultimately be portrayed by language."[227] Heisenberg hereby distinguishes between a static and a dynamic use of language. Static linguistic behavior serves to sharpen the conceptual systems by means of which one can decide what is "true" and what is "false." This strength, however, is accompanied by a serious disadvantage, namely, "the renunciation of that infinitely diverse relatedness of words and concepts that first awaken in us the feeling of having understood something of the infinite richness of reality."[228] In order to do justice to this relatedness, one needs the "dynamic" application of language instead. Dynamic use of language is not primarily concerned with the accuracy, but rather with the fruitfulness of concepts. Static thinking explains; dynamic thinking interprets. The former is in danger of "degenerating into form without content," and the latter risks becoming "vague and incomprehensible."[229] Heisenberg sees a synthesis of the two ways of thinking in poetry: "Poetry stands, as it were, at the point at which extremes meet: the purely content-laden thinking that makes optimal use of the liveliness of the word, on the one hand, and the linking of concepts into a rigid mathematical schema, on the other."[230]

Essentially two figures of thought may have been the force behind this notion of Heisenberg's: Hegelian dialectic, on the one hand, and the uncertainty relation, on the other. Language is successful, but it cannot overcome a final deficit: "One cannot speak about the ultimate things."[231]

In at least three places, one can find direct points of contact between Heisenberg's thinking and the starting point of this study. In searching for a dynamic concept of time, I first made a conscious effort not to adopt conceptual definitions; I avoided the "static" use of language in order to direct the focus toward relationality. Second, I interpreted the lack of conceptual clarity that resulted from this choice as the price to be paid for the dynamics and fruitfulness of thinking that goes beyond a formal dualism of time and eternity. Third, my use of hymnal poetry in approaching questions of time and eternity seems even more justified. Poetry as the interface between static and dynamic uses of language once again appears to be a perfect starting point for the most precise and productive understanding of time.

Heisenberg treats the problem of language in detail and with specific reference to the requirements of science in his essay entitled "Sprache und Wirklichkeit in der modernen Physik,"[232] which appeared in 1960. In it he confronts the fuzziness of language, which simultaneously comprises its richness, with the requirements of scientific formulations. Because in science the special is derived from the general, the general laws must contain the fewest and most precisely defined concepts possible. Attaining such a level of precision is possible only within exact logic and aided by mathematical abstraction. Allocating mathematical symbols to concepts of natural language creates an "artificial mathematical language"[233] [*mathematische*

Kunstsprache]. Portions of this artificial language are gradually integrated into everyday language. This applies, for example, to the concepts of energy, impulse, entropy, and electrical field.[234] By its expansion into areas that are not directly accessible to sensory experience, modern physics has made the limitation or even failure of language at certain points even more obvious. One has been forced to rethink what were apparently simple concepts, for example, space, place, time, and velocity. The theory of relativity was rather successful in adapting the spoken language to the artificial mathematical language. By supplementing "simultaneous" with the qualifier "relative to a certain reference system," for example, the question of whether time dilatation is real or only apparent becomes irrelevant.[235] The insight "that the world is 'really' not the way that everyday concepts would lead us to believe" has made its way into general consciousness.[236]

There are much greater difficulties for language in the area of the very small—in atomic physics. When one and the same object can occur either as a particle or as a wave, depending upon the experiment, then it is hard to adapt everyday language successfully to the artificial mathematical language. Language does not have a word for something that is simultaneously a wave and a solid body. Instead, "word paintings" [*Wortgemälde*] are used, i.e., a manner of speaking in which one alternately uses different, mutually contradicting pictorial images.[237] Heisenberg has no doubt that one must speak of atoms and subatomic particles in (normal) language: "We must speak about them because, otherwise, we cannot understand our experiments."[238] For Heisenberg, therefore, scientific understanding is accomplished only by means of language, and indeed no less in everyday language than in artificial mathematical language. An adequate description of processes in the quantum realm is attained "first by playing with the different images."[239]

In the case of quantum physics, Heisenberg sees the reason for the difficulties in adapting the imprecise, metaphorical language of everyday speech to the artificial mathematical language in the fact that Aristotelian logic loses its validity in a language that tries to do justice to the mathematical formalism of quantum theory. A language responding to the demands of quantum physics requires a logic that allows not only the alternative "either right or wrong" for assertions, but also interim values that may not be interpreted as ignorance of the "true" state.[240] Heisenberg thinks that such a quantum logic[241] can be implemented if different logics are used for different linguistic levels (e.g., objects—statements about objects—statements about statements about objects), in which case Aristotelian logic would again have to be used on the highest level.[242] An ontological parallel to quantum logic would be the talk of coexisting conditions, or even better,

"coexisting possibilities." The concept of "possibility" deserves a central position, because it stands "in the right way in the middle between the concept of objective material reality, on the one hand, and the concept of the
purely intellectual, and thus subjective, reality, on the other hand."[243]

From these ideas, Heisenberg concludes that it is necessary to learn a
new language that is foreign to everyday language at numerous points. This
new language is also accompanied by a new way of thinking.[244] No doubt,
Heisenberg saw this as a lengthy process, since he ended a lecture in 1975
with the words: "I am afraid that it might take another century, before one
has become really well acquainted with all this new scientific material and
its practical, political, ethical and philosophical consequences."[245]

Compared to Heisenberg, Bohr expressed more restraint regarding a
new logic. In spite of all of the difficulties, he thought that the situation was
clearer than generally assumed: "[S]uch tools as three-valued logics I consider rather as complications, since a consistent representation of all ax-
iomatic and dialectic aspects of the situation can be given in simple daily
life language."[246]

Bohr thought that under no circumstances could one do without the
forms of perception within which ultimately all experience is expressed and
which give color to the entire language.[247] He is very cautious with regard to
a comprehensive logic for the natural sciences. Such a logic is best attainable
in mathematic symbolism, "which shows us an ideal of objectivity, the attainment of which is almost unlimited in every closed area in which logic is
applied."[248] It is different, however, in "the actual sciences": There, no strictly closed areas of application can exist, since one must always contend with
an increased number of facts requiring a revision of previous conceptual
aids.[249] Quantum phenomena demand the same caution in the use of expressive means that psychology, with its constant difficulties in identifying
objective content, needs to exercise.[250] Thus, there is no way to avoid the
aporia of the perception problem, namely

that, on the one hand, the description of our mental activity requires the comparison of an objectively specified content and an observing subject, while, on the other hand, . . . a strict separation between the object and the subject cannot be maintained . . . This situation results not only in the relative meaning of each
concept—or, even better, each word—that is dependent upon the arbitrariness in
the selection of viewpoint, but rather, we must generally be prepared for the fact
that an all-round examination of one and the same object can require different
points of view, which prevent an unambiguous description. Strictly speaking, the
conscious analysis of any concept has an excluding relationship to its direct application.[251]

In this sense, Bohr understood quantum mechanics as being an expression of the boundary that nature itself sets for us with regard to the possibility of speaking about the objective existence of phenomena. This boundary certainly does not prevent further intellectual progress, but it constantly requires increasing abstraction from the familiar concreteness in the description of nature.[252]

When one considers language, different basic positions become clear. Expressed simply, Einstein emerges as a pessimistic idealist: If no strict causality exists, then God is throwing dice, and that cannot be. On the other hand, with his question about a highly complicated quantum logic, Heisenberg is attempting to forge the link between idealism and realism, while Bohr instead assumed the viewpoint of an optimistic pragmatism: Reality is just as blurred, but its description works in spite of this; being conscious of uncertainty, one indeed cannot live with exact precision, but one can nevertheless live very well.

Stephen W. Hawking goes one step farther when he draws the conclusion that God is an inveterate gambler and throws the dice on every possible occasion.[253] In the game, God sometimes also throws the dice to a place where they cannot be seen.[254] However, at least in Hawking, this apparent vice of God stands in a constructive relationship with the virtue of the universe to let itself be explored. We will deal with the context of cosmological theories in the next section.

Cosmological Perspectives

If one is trying to understand what the theory of relativity and quantum physics can jointly contribute to the understanding of time, then one can hardly avoid dealing with the large questions of cosmology. At the forefront of the formation of cosmological theory, one deals with possibilities for uniting theories for the very large and the very small. One of the tasks of this section is to describe the challenges related to this matter. In this context, I will not deal with a systematic overview of various cosmological models, but will rather present some theories and thoughts that have significance for the understanding of time.

A Microsecond for One Person Is Infinite Time for Another—
Big Bang and Singularities

Up until now, it has not been possible to answer questions about the past of the universe or its distant future conclusively. According to the cosmological principle derived from observations, matter in the universe is evenly distributed, and the properties of the universe are invariable; the universe is homogenous and isotropic. Within the framework of the so-called Friedmann models,[255] which were developed with the help of this principle, cosmologists assume that the universe came into being approximately 2×10^{10} years ago as a result of the so-called Big Bang.[256] According to this scenario, a state dominated by quantum effects prevailed until approximately 10^{-43} seconds after the Big Bang began (= the so-called Planck Time). At this time (2005), there have been no theories available that can define space and time in this state, but it seems plausible to imagine the four forces as united in the very beginning. Then, gravity and the strong nuclear force broke away successively from this conglomerate, until after 10^{-10} seconds the electromagnetic and weak force had also separated from each another. Via the gradual development of quarks, protons, neutrons, and electrons, atoms emerged after approximately 300,000 years. Among other things, the average homogeneity of the universe and minimal fluctuations in the cosmic background radiation, which was somewhat accidentally discovered in 1965, support the expansion of the Big Bang model using the theory of an inflationary universe. According to this theory, an extremely rapid expansionary phase probably occurred between 10^{-35} and 10^{-30} seconds after the Big Bang.

Within the framework of the theories of relativity, the only thing that can be said about the beginning of time is that time begins with a singularity.[257] Because a theory cannot be mathematically defined in a singularity, this means that in terms of physics, one cannot speak of a "before" of this singularity or of a "how" of the genesis of time. Therefore, the general theory of relativity cannot explain the origin of space and time. "Thus, from the theory of relativity, an internal boundary of its explanatory potential is necessarily derived."[258]

Another singularity having significance for time that can be derived from the general theory of relativity is that of "black holes."[259] These occur when a star of sufficient mass "dies" as a result of a gravitational collapse. The gravitational field of a black hole then becomes so strong that, according to the general theory of relativity, it "swallows" all signals coming from the outside and does not emit any signals. According to the uncertainty principle of quantum mechanics, however, a black hole can nevertheless emit radiation. Hawking maintains that "black holes ain't so black," and he shows that black holes can indeed emit particles and radiation.[260] What is not possible within the framework of the general theory of relativity can be explained using quantum-mechanical fluctuations. Quantum fluctuations enable the emission of radiation from the strong gravitational field at the boundary of the black hole. The energy for this comes from the black hole, which thereby loses mass and finally disappears.

The boundary of a black hole is characterized as an absolute event horizon or Schwarzschild radius. It is assumed that in the center of a black hole, the curvature of space-time becomes infinite, i.e., that space and time come "to an end." This end must remain hidden to every external observer, however, because the "naked" singularity always lies on the other side of the event horizon, over which no light can penetrate to the outside. A black hole can be observed only indirectly, namely, by means of the gravitational force of attraction that it exerts on its environment. A person approaching a Schwarzschild radius would instantly fall into the black hole (according to the person's reference system), but an observer on earth would see the same person for an infinite period of time just in front of the Schwarzschild radius; from her perspective, the person would never cross this boundary. If time dilatation becomes infinite, as it does on the event horizon of a black hole, then a microsecond for one is infinite time for another.[261]

According to the time symmetry of the theory of relativity, there must also be a phenomenon that demonstrates a directly opposite behavior of time, i.e., infinitely dense matter in a singularity that explodes into a cascade of light. In physics, however, such "white holes" are generally thought to be improbable. Due to their untenable physical consequences, Roger Penrose simply excluded them by using a hypothesis called "cosmic censorship." Something similar also applies to so-called time travel into the past; physical laws, at least according to Hawking, appear to favor a cosmic "Chronology Protection Agency,"[262] which does not permit such things to happen.[263]

One should distinguish between the "end" of time in the singularity of a black hole and a possible end singularity of the entire universe. Currently, nothing definitive can be said about the latter, for what one can expect for the distant future of our expanding universe is critically dependent upon the mean density of matter. Up until now, however, the density of the universe has not been determined in any precise way.

If the density is so low that gravity cannot curb the expansion, then the universe will continue to expand. In this case, we are living in an open universe that is becoming infinitely larger and larger. If enough mass exists, however, so that its gravitation stops the expansion and ultimately causes the universe to collapse, then we live in a closed, finite universe.

The third possibility has a special appeal: The mass density of the universe could possess precisely that critical level above which it would collapse and below which it would expand forever. In this case, the expansion velocity of the universe would become slower and slower without ever reaching the zero point. In this case, we would also live in an open universe. This third model is called the Einstein–de Sitter universe.

Until now, however, knowledge regarding the density of matter points to an open universe in accordance with the first model. This also applies when one takes into account the so-called dark matter, which is still "missing," at least when judging by observations of the movements in the accumulations of galaxies.[264] As long as no precise data exist on the density of the universe, the question about the age of the universe also cannot be answered with any precision. Yet we know that, in a universe with a higher density of matter, the expansion velocity is slowed down more considerably by a stronger gravitational force than it is in a universe with a lower density. Therefore, with an expansion velocity known at a specified time, a universe having a higher density of matter must be younger than one having a lower density of matter.

The three scenarios described here presume that the so-called cosmological constant has a value of zero. More recent studies, on the contrary, assert that this constant has a value that is different from zero. If this is correct, it indicates that the universe, possibly driven by the energy in the vacuum itself, is increasing its expansion velocity. Surely, in this area, many more discussions of new theories are likely to ensue.

A Quantum Fluctuation as the Beginning of Everything? On Quantum Cosmology

One cannot go beyond the singularities solely by using the general theory of relativity. Because, to a certain extent, the very large encounters the very small in the singularities, it seems necessary to try to explain the singularities by uniting the relativistic theory of gravity with quantum mechanics. Even if this unification has not yet been accomplished, work with its prerequisites has led to sensational hypotheses and suggestions. The alternatives of either an infinitely existing universe or a beginning singularity that cannot be explained scientifically appear to be surmountable within the framework of the indeterminacy of quantum physics, since here, spontaneous events can occur without a causal connection in the classical sense. Hawking, in particular, has been working on the development of a singularity-free model for the universe. According to Hawking, a theory that unites quantum mechanics and gravity must understand quantum theory as the "sum over histories"[265] and, according to the theory of relativity, gravitational fields as the curvature of space-time. Proceeding from these conditions, his solution reads: imaginary time[266]—a time that, with increasing proximity to the beginning, becomes increasingly spacelike and thus ultimately loses its beginning. Within the framework of the uncertainty of quantum physics, Hawking lets the three dimensions of space, along with the imaginary time, form a universe that has neither boundaries nor edges and, yet, is self-contained—a finite space-time without border, comparable to the surface of the earth, only richer by some dimensions. In this case, space-time would have "always" existed, and every physical event could be explained by laws:

There would be no singularities at which the laws of science broke down and no edge of space-time at which one would have to appeal to God or some new law to set the boundary conditions for space-time. One could say: "The boundary condition of the universe is that it has no boundary." The universe would be completely self-contained and not affected by anything outside itself. It would neither be created nor destroyed. It would just BE.[267]

In models of this type, time is therefore not activated by some type of cause, but rather, it turns itself on, so to speak—an elegant yet speculative theory. Nevertheless, the thought that the universe began with an accidental event on the quantum level, a quantum fluctuation, has become a frequent component of current cosmological theories. Processes in which particles suddenly develop in a vacuum and immediately disappear again are constantly occurring in scientific laboratories. That the entire universe itself could have begun in this manner sounds quite fantastic. There are signs, however, that point in this direction. Thus, there are good reasons to assume that the discussion of cosmological theories that explain the genesis of the universe by a quantum fluctuation will continue.

In some cases, the results, premises, and problems of these theories have been related to theological themes, such as *creatio ex nihilo* and cosmological eschatology.[268] Here, a number of ideas are awaiting theological reflection and reception. Generally, it may be said that theories of this type do not necessarily lead to atheism; instead, they cause what we may call "adeism," that is, a refutation of deism rather than of theism.[269] Hawking emphasizes the challenges with which cosmological models based on quantum fluctuation models confront theology. In the same breath that he closes the door on uncritical theistic explanations of the world, he also opens a window here and there for a larger perspective: "Even if science may possibly be able to explain the problem of how the universe began, it cannot answer the question: Why does the universe make the effort to exist?"[270] And: "What is it that breathes fire into equations and makes for them a universe to describe?"[271]

Viewed from a theological perspective, these thoughts bring up the question of how to talk about God. When God is discussed exclusively in connection with the boundary conditions of the universe, it is difficult to reach beyond an image of God of the type that was found in Newton, for example. According to the legacy of Newton, which in this respect is unfortunate, a God who is linked only to the current boundaries of scientific knowledge will sooner or later inevitably be reduced to a constantly retreating "God of the gaps." Theology certainly does not shut itself off from questions of "a God on the border of the known," but it is just as interested in a "God in the center of the known." While physicists who reflect upon God deal mostly with such boundary questions and thus often presuppose a deistic or an abstract theistic concept of God, theologians tend to be more involved "at the center" of world events, reflecting upon the relation of God in, with, and under things that are happening. To be sure, this difference is not an excuse for avoiding the dialogue about the boundary conditions of the universe, but it can nevertheless explain some of the difficulties of communication that repeatedly threaten to disrupt the discussion.

One of the most easily recognizable difficulties of cosmology is that its insights cannot be verified with absolute certainty by means of experiments. This, in turn, contributes to the extremely hypothetical character of cosmological models, which can therefore also be interpreted very differently, depending on one's viewpoint. For example, if one considers the Big Bang to be the absolute starting point, one can define a universal time using the homogeneity and isotropy of the cosmic background radiation.[272] Although we do not know anything about the behavior of such a universal time within Planck time, such a definition would practically satisfy the requirements of physical time measurement. Thus, both absolute time and, in a certain way, an "ether"—in the form of background radiation—would exist again, although the latter would not be a medium, but rather a reference point for the measurement of time and velocity. The question, though, of whether there is actually only one single timescale in the universe has not yet been answered definitively.[273]

This rather pragmatic interpretation is contradicted by a critical interpretation that, like Hawking, adds quantum physics to the relativistic gravitational theory, but draws other conclusions by basically questioning the continuity of temporality. Against the backdrop of the successive limitation of the concept of time from one level of physical theory to another, this interpretation argues for a collapse of the dynamic concept on the level of quantum gravity.[274] In Newton, time was still an absolute, infinite continuum; the special theory of relativity problematized universal simultaneity, the general theory of relativity focused on boundaries for the expansion of time by means of singularities, and quantum theory showed the impossibility of exact access to the measurement of time. Finally, the integration of quantum and space-time theories at and "prior to" the Planck time point to a collapse of the time concept as such. Instead of an entity of universal significance, time in this interpretation is only a local, internal concept.

According to the assumption that the most comprehensive theory always contains the more special ones as a limiting case, it follows: If this critical interpretation applies, the collapse of the dynamic conception in quantum cosmology must be of greater fundamental significance than the evolutionary models for explaining the world. Then the collapse of the dynamic concept in quantum gravity is "not just a detail at some irrelevant scale, because it affects, or should affect, the concepts of space and time as they are used at *all* levels."[275]

Repeatedly, experiments have been designed with the aim of circumventing the problem of time. The physicist Julian Barbour provides an example in this direction.[276] In 1999, he introduced his theory of a timeless quantum cosmology. He maintains that he has been successful in uniting Einstein's theories of relativity, which deny the existence of a universally valid time, with quantum mechanics, which appears to require such a time. According to Barbour, there is no time. In his eyes, recognizing this represents a revolution in our understanding of the universe. What we consider to be time and movement is illusion. The only things that exist are timeless moments. Barbour considers the notion of a timeline or a time arrow to be unnecessary. Instead, he speaks of "time capsules."[277] Such time capsules describe all static formations that generate the impression that a process has occurred. Both the brain seen in its entirety and the earth in its entirety are time capsules. The time capsules can be hidden inside of one another like Russian dolls. In deliberate allusion to the Greek philosopher, the world, which is made of these special moments, is called Platonia. The name is meant to mirror the mathematical perfection and the timeless landscape. Platonia is the arena that, according to Barbour, replaces space and time. Platonia and the quantum-theoretical wave function, as Barbour understands it, form the universe. The philosophy or theology that appears to result from this concept expresses itself in a worship of the "now" or in a pantheistic worldview.[278] In Barbour, once again that which has already been addressed several times becomes evident, namely, how short, in many respects, the distance is between mathematics and theology: "It seems that the greatest engine of cultural change—the scientific world-view—rests on a mathematical foundation that, in many respects, is ultimately religious."[279]

What has been presented in this section indeed deals with ideas that lie within the sphere of what currently constitutes the boundary of cosmological research and no doubt contains speculative elements. Nevertheless, it is clear that the universe does not have a precisely defined time if one wishes to unite the general theory of relativity with quantum physics. Thus, the possibility "that the evolutionary presentation [of space and time in cosmology] is one of limited validity, and not the most fundamental one"[280] cannot

just be discarded and must be considered when searching for dynamic relational models for time and eternity. Time would then be something secondary that does not belong to the fundamental laws of the universe and something that more or less had come into being by accident.[281] Also, theories
about the nonexistence of time will surely be further discussed in the future.
If one is successful in finding a theory of everything, the so-called TOE, this
theory will probably be timeless (and spaceless) from the beginning. If time
is then derived as emergent from such a theory, time would have to be irreversible from the start. Such a concept of time would be in harmony with
thermodynamics, which we will consider in the next section.

Thermodynamics and Chaos Research

The theories considered so far have one thing in common, namely, the
reversibility of time. None could prove that time has a direction. In the example of the twin traveling through space, the conclusion that the home-
bound twin is older and not younger, is, in a strict sense, not a consequence
of the theory of relativity—the latter verifies only the different lengths of
the time intervals—but rather a conclusion based on what experience teach-
es us. Events in the atomic area are reversible. If we could see atomic
processes in a film, we would not be in the position to decide whether this
film is being wound forwards or backwards. Up to now, there are only very
rare and indirect observations of a nonreversible and thus time-asymmetri-
cal disintegration in the case of an elementary particle named *kaon*.[282] In
any case, the irreversibility of time on the macroscopic level cannot simply
be derived from this.

In the End: Heat Death? Entropy and the Arrow of Time

Can thermodynamics provide us with the desired proof of an irreversible direction of time? To answer this question, I will turn directly to the
Second Law of Thermodynamics, which was first formulated by Rudolf
Clausius during the second half of the nineteenth century and now exists in
various formulations. For the purposes of this study, I will use the following
wording: In an isolated system, entropy never decreases; in the case of reversible processes, it remains constant; and, in the case of irreversible
processes, it continually increases.

While an *open system* can exchange energy and matter with its environment, a *closed system* exchanges only energy with its environment. A theoretical idealization of the closed system that is often used successfully is the
isolated system, in which neither matter nor energy is exchanged. *Entropy*

denotes the measure of disorder in a system. In everyday life, we experience entropy in many ways: Hot coffee cools off at room temperature; it has not yet been observed that milk poured into coffee spontaneously separates out again after dispersing, although according to the laws of classical mechanics, this must be possible. These observations create enigmas. How can it be that coffee and milk follow a temporal sense of direction although the laws that determine the behavior of coffee and milk molecules are time-symmetric?[283]

But it is not only the domestic coffee table that obeys the Second Law; even our solar system continually complies with it. The sun is slowly burning its nuclear energy; it will radiate light and warmth until its collapse in approximately five billion years, and thus, with every photon emitted, it increases entropy in the universe. Applied to the universe as a whole, the theorem of ever-increasing entropy therefore means that the order in the universe is moving toward decay. In this context, one frequently speaks of the inevitable heat death of the universe. This does not mean that the universe is being destroyed by heat. Nor does it mean directly that the heat is disappearing and extreme cold will rule. What is "dying" is the exchange of energy, so that ultimately there will no longer be a gradient between different levels of energy. Heat death thus signifies complete heat equalization (thermal equilibrium) and maximum disorder. A state has been reached where time has ceased to flow. This is why thermal balance is also called a "time peak" [*Zeitgipfel*][284] At the time peak, an isolated system is cut off from a possible future because it can no longer change. It also no longer has access to its past, for the development cannot be directed backwards by the decrease in entropy. For the first time, something like a historical dimension becomes visible in physics itself.[285] The irreversibility in thermodynamics invites one to rethink the relationship of being and becoming. For Newton it was reasonable to understand the universe as a pattern of eternally existing elements. Thermodynamics, on the contrary, urges one to understand becoming as the basic structure of the universe.

Because of the insights in thermodynamics, a modification of the concept of the universe was called for. The view of the universe as a perfect machine as found in Newtonian physics is no longer tenable. The conception of a uniform and, in principle, infinite universe was replaced by the concept of the universe as a heat engine that ultimately destroys itself: no longer an eternal machine, but, rather, a programmed apocalypse.

Here, one may feel compelled to object. How can the Second Law claim absolute validity when, at the same time, we can so often observe an increase in order and a development of higher complexity? Is there not an irreconcilable conflict between thermodynamics and the principle of evolution?

There are several possible answers to this question: First, when order increases at a certain place in a system, we are dealing with a local decrease in entropy that has no effect on the increase in entropy in a system as a whole. Second, under certain conditions, Poincaré's Theorem allows the notion of reverse entropy—i.e., increase in order—for, according to Henri Poincaré, every isolated system eventually returns to its initial state; it is cyclical. The period of such a cycle is unimaginably long, to be sure, but finite. Thus, on the condition of a sufficiently long period of time, a "resurrection" from cosmic heat death is theoretically possible. A third answer has been formulated by the "Brussels School," led by Ilya Prigogine.[286] They have shown that, far from equilibrium, so-called dissipative structures[287] make developmental leaps.

This can be understood as follows: Systems that are not in thermodynamic equilibrium develop toward a final state in which all change ceases. This targeted end-point is called an "attractor." For systems that are located near equilibrium, this development is linear, i.e., with direct proportionality of forces and effects. For systems that are far from thermodynamic equilibrium, this development is nonlinear and precisely these systems can be used to explain the apparently impossible increase in order. The overwhelming majority of everyday life processes consists of such open systems that exchange energy and matter with other systems and that are located far from equilibrium. If these systems are sufficiently far from the state of equilibrium, they can branch out at a critical so-called bifurcation point. Their development becomes unstable, and they "leap" into another state that can be quite well ordered and display new shapes and properties. In this way, diverse patterns with a large number of bifurcation points can be created. These complex processes, which can interact and lead to complicated structures, are called self-organization or autopoiesis.[288] Such developmental leaps to a higher order occur without violating the Second Law of Thermodynamics.

Viewed as an open system far from equilibrium, the universe is therefore not on a straight path to heat death. It is instead encountering bifurcation points continually on its path and thus also the possibility of spontaneous self-organization of galaxies as well as cells. Because these processes are irreversible, time appears to have a direction. It remains a question of interpretation whether this means that the development of entropy and the time arrow can be regarded as identical.[289] Nevertheless, it seems that the key to understanding the time arrow lies in the stability properties of complex systems. Within the framework of chaos research, remarkable results have been achieved in this regard.

Dance Instead of March—Chaos Research

For many people, the term *chaos theory*[290] may immediately bring to mind the well-known butterfly in Brazil, whose wing flapping may cause a hurricane in Texas.[291] This butterfly effect illustrates two basic characteristics of chaos theory, namely, determined initial conditions and developments that are not predictable over the long term.

For understanding chaos theory, it is important to distinguish between indeterminism and unpredictability. Chaotic systems are mathematically determined in their initial conditions but are so extremely sensitive to disturbances that long-term prognoses are impossible. They are determined, but unpredictable—a fact that is shown clearly in the poor accuracy of long-term weather forecasts. Even an infinite number of weather stations that could produce incessant data would not be able to extend the forecast horizon significantly. In complex, nonlinear systems, almost identical initial conditions can lead to very different developments, although no basic deterministic laws are invalidated. One therefore must speak of a deterministic chaos. In this, neither determinism nor chance reigns in solitary majesty; instead, the world appears as an open structure of order, marked by an interaction of the two principles.[292] In this interaction, the causes seeming most insignificant can produce the most significant effects. Chaos occurs when a regular bifurcation, i.e., a periodic split into 2, 4, 8, 16 . . . branches, exceeds the limitation of a continuum in the form of a bifurcation cascade.[293] The behavior of chaotic systems is dependent upon two types of "attractors," namely, the deterministic ones, whose courses are foreseeable (fixed point, limit cycle, and torus), and the nondeterministic, so-called strange attractors, which have a highly differentiated and complex spatial structure. It must be emphasized that the chaos is not "total," because the bifurcations have a regular flow. This is determined by a universally valid constant, the so-called Feigenbaum number $\delta = 4.669201$. The mathematics of chaos theory is based on fractal geometry, which was developed particularly by Benoît Mandelbrot.[294] Chaos itself, and likewise the transition from order to chaos, are thus by no means without rules, so that chaos is significantly more ordered than may have been initially assumed.

Chaos research deals with the description of system developments. Its findings have frequently been linked to process-philosophical thought.[295] Primarily because of this affinity, there has been a great temptation to attribute an explanatory potential to chaos theory that exceeds its capacity.[296] Numerous branches of science—from psychology to economics and biology—have attempted to understand processes by using chaos theory.[297] In this context, the understanding of chaos may be more metaphorical than ontological, i.e., the processes in question exhibit a behavior that is similar to that described by chaos theory, without following this theory in a strict sense. In medicine, it is claimed that chaos theory has led to true intellectual progress in the understanding of adaptive systems (systems that react flexibly to changes in the environment). Concepts that are oriented toward holistic medicine are familiar with the description of health as a delicate balance between order and chaos. An excess of order leads to sclerotic changes; too much disorder leads to disintegration. However, critical voices believe that chaos theory fails when it comes to describing the actual evolutionary creative processes.[298]

Whatever the case may be, the understanding of life as a dissipative structure has contributed to the liberation of scientific knowledge from mechanistic reduction. Thus, chaos research can help us understand, for example, the fact that a person's EEG exhibits a chaotic progression during normal thought processes but is regular during an epileptic seizure. Similarly, a healthy heart does not beat in a mechanically uniform manner; it pumps the blood through the body in a chaotic rhythm: A healthy heart dances; a dying one marches.[299]

Chaos research attempts to account for the complexity of natural forms. Using fractal geometry, it draws conclusions from the fact that Euclidian geometry can be applied only to idealized, simple forms, while nature is constructed in a much more complicated fashion: Mountains are not cones and clouds are not balls; the coastlines of islands do not form circles and the courses of rivers do not form straight lines.[300] Chaos theory makes clear that the "dogma" of the strong causality of deterministic systems, which successfully contributed to the knowledge of the world and the control of nature for a long time, actually applies only to a small portion of what is otherwise a highly complex, nonlinear natural order. With regard to the extremely sensitive evolutionary processes that make up the majority of life's processes, one can speak only of a weak causality.

The understanding of complexity is one of the greatest challenges that confronts science; in the eyes of some, it is even *the* challenge.[301] In a certain sense, we see here the counterbalance to the efforts of physics to find a theory of everything. While one is basically dealing with a reductionist attempt in the "Theory of Everything" because it seeks to reduce the complicated to a single principle, complexity research requires more of a holistic perspective because it deals with such multilayered concepts as life, consciousness, and intelligence.[302] The goal of the TOE is to reduce the many into one; complexity research attempts to understand the emergence of the many.

According to one definition (but not the only possible one), "Complexity is the study of the behaviour of macroscopic collections of such units that are endowed with the potential to evolve in time."[303] Complex systems can still be described with deterministic equations, but the more chaotic a system is, the less it can be compressed algorithmically.

Regarding time, chaotic systems are distinguished from classically deterministic systems primarily to the extent that they permit no reconstruction of the initial situation, while in classical systems, the past can in principle be reconstructed. Irreversibility and the focus on process have led to the development of new theories of time in the context of chaos research. For example, Prigogine speaks of an internal time of a system that should, among other things, permit one to speak of a duration of the present.[304] Instability (chaos), probability, and irreversibility clearly show that the universe is not as (time) symmetric as the fundamental equations lead one to assume. Prigogine maintains, "a second time occurs that is not connected to the individual molecules or the individual persons, but rather to the relationships between the molecules or persons."[305] Some of Prigogine's theses have been disputed. Nevertheless, it appears that there is a solid basis for the conclusion that, in the current state of affairs, a relational concept of time comes the closest to being an accurate description of reality.

According to Friedrich Cramer, the world does not exist; instead, it occurs, and thus, like Prigogine, he contrasts being and becoming.[306] Despite an impressively precise measurement of time within the framework of the Newtonian paradigm, this nevertheless remains closely tied to the question of being. Cramer believes that becoming, the emergence of the new, cannot be comprehended by using Newton's cosmos, which is reversible and, in principle, static. While Newtonian science asks only how the world functions, the science of dynamic systems is primarily interested in how the new comes into being.[307] In this context, Cramer introduces a double structure of time by distinguishing between reversible time t_r and irreversible time t_i. Reversible time applies to periodic, cyclically structured systems, such as clocks, atoms, planetary systems, seasons of the year, menstrual cycles, division of cells, timetables, and rituals. All evolutionary processes belong to irreversible time, be they the Big Bang, volcanism, birth and death, ideas, dreams, or art.[308] Thus, regular, relatively stable processes are characterized by reversible time, whereas unrepeatable processes, including the construction and the destruction of structures, belong to irreversible time. Graphically, t_r would be depicted as a circle, and t_i as an arrow. Nevertheless, it can be easily seen that in reality, the two types of time cannot be sharply separated from each other; instead, they form a helical model of time. Cyclical processes are not so stable that they constantly follow a circular line; rather, every cyclical process can experience disturbances that can lead to the collapse of the entire system. Cramer sees the best description for transitions between t_r and t_i in the model of the strange attractor. According to this, cyclical movement in a system eventually leads to a discontinuity in the system and in the time mode.[309] This, in turn, leads to transitions that follow the rules of deterministic chaos. Thus, the two types of time can be related to each other mathematically by using universal constants. While the cyclical movement is dependent upon π, the chaotic transition obeys the Feigenbaum constant δ. The two times t_r and t_i cooperate and are mutually dependent upon each other. Cramer thinks that this twofold structure of time is applicable to all time systems. The reductionist concept of time in classical physics would therefore be overcome, and the cosmos could be described as an open process that cannot predict its own future.[310]

Cramer does not conceive of transitions between t_r and t_i as being symmetrical. He sees t_r as the basis for all structures. If t_i is bent back into itself and thus forced into reversibility, it becomes structure and thus space. Time and space are therefore seen as two aspects of one and the same existence. Cramer illustrates his theory of time with the image of the time tree.[311] In its limbs and branches, the time tree unifies different times and relationships of t_r and t_i. In contrast to this dynamic conception, the traditional model of a uniform flow of time in classical physics seems far removed from reality.[312] What became clear already in the first chapters is confirmed again here: A polarization of cyclical and linear time leads to a flawed description of reality. Both biblical and systematic theological studies, as well as the development of natural scientific theories, suggest this conclusion.

While the classical image pretends that uniformity is the signature tune of existence, dynamic models, such as that of the time tree, deal seriously with the observation that living systems in their development pass through a series of bifurcation cascades in which uniformity is not ruled out but is included as a special case. Not uniformity, but complexity and transformation, is the basic tenor of a cosmos understood in this way.[313] Time does not really march; it prefers to dance.

Summarizing Reflections

Review

It is of fundamental importance for a physical concept of time that time can be comprehended meaningfully only in conjunction with the existence of matter (that is not infinitely dense). Time concepts are of key importance in all physical theories that deal with dynamic phenomena. Timelessness does not exist within physics, for a physical event must always be defined both in space and time. During the course of the development depicted, time changes its status within the formulation of physical theory. Whereas in Newton and Leibniz, time is a necessary explanatory component without a substantial role, in Prigogine and Cramer, it comes close to being an operational entity. Theoreticians such as J. Barbour, on the contrary, do not think that time exists.

In Newton, space and time are the permanent stage for the cosmic drama. Visible to everyone and in absolute symmetry, every plank is arranged precisely and every position of the actors can be determined objectively. Although it is the scene for the most diverse plays, the stage remains basically untouched by what happens on it. Its solidity is unquestionable; God is its guarantor. Thus the task of the physicist is merely to explain the action of the drama. This point of view dominated two and a half centuries with singular majesty—and for good reason: Its practical applicability in the sphere of daily life gave it an indestructible vitality. Its defects became obvious only when physicists began to deal with the very small, the very large, and the very fast.

Thus the theories of relativity showed that the difference between the stage and the play is an artificial one. Space and time are just as much a part of the drama as are the actors, who are somewhat comparable to the atoms of matter. Scientific research can therefore not limit itself to the behavior of atoms, i.e., to the performing of the actors. It must be able to describe the actors, the drama, the stage, and the audience, as well as their interaction.[314] The special theory of relativity robbed the concept of a universally valid "now" of its validity. It replaced the one absolute time with particular times dependent on motion [*Eigenzeiten*], which can be determined precisely and compared to one another. In the theory of relativity, the issue is less one of relativization than it is one of relation. Not only do the different particular times [*Eigenzeiten*] relate to one another, but space and time also establish a close connection. Time lost even more sovereignty as a result of the general theory of relativity. In this theory, Einstein succeeded in linking time, space, matter, and energy, including gravity. The absolute, true, and mathematical time reappeared as curved space-time.

Quantum physics was even more iconoclastic with regard to the absoluteness of time because it caused its ability to be measured to disappear in the fog of the uncertainty relation. It touched the boundaries of logic and language and essentially called into question the meaning of the concepts "objective" and "subjective." Mathematical undecidability and nonlocality in the quantum regime attest to the fact that we can never have complete information and thus can never have complete control over the reality in which we participate unless there are hidden parameters, yet to be discovered, that once again ensure, on a deeper level, a complete determinacy of nature. In the meantime, it has been proved that simple theories of hidden parameters, as Einstein imagined them, do not describe reality.

Within the framework of thermodynamics, the irreversibility of the increase in entropy was interpreted as proof for the existence of a time arrow; yet, the assumption of a universally valid time arrow presupposes that the universe as a whole can be understood as an isolated system. Here, a dilemma is revealed. In thermodynamics, the thought of a strict time arrow is linked to the idea of the universe as an isolated system, while the emergence of complex structures presupposes open systems far from equilibrium. The strict irreversibility of time that is intended in thermodynamics therefore appears to be modified by chaos research. Instead of speaking of a universal time arrow, one now talks more often of the "multiplicity of time."[315] Rigid static behavior is not the signature of the world, but rather dynamic chaos that can create highly flexible and richly nuanced orders.

Theories of both entropy and self-organization appear to lend themselves to an ideologizing interpretation of entropic disintegration, on the one hand, and creative chaos, on the other. But just as one must be warned against a careless application of quantum theory in areas foreign to physics, one should also be careful when using thermodynamics and chaos theory. Accordingly, the applicability of chaos theory in no way signifies the end of determinism, but rather supports a more complex understanding of it than is found in classical physics. Chaotic processes are deterministic, though they are not predictable. Their openness therefore should not be mistaken for indeterminacy, since the development always follows the attractor acting immanently in the system. Openness to the future based on unpredictability does not therefore essentially cancel the determination by the initial conditions, even if the initial conditions of a chaotically developing system cannot be reconstructed. Nevertheless, the key concepts of nonlinearity, instability, and fluctuations[316] have had a lasting influence on the understanding of nature and time. Twentieth-century natural science has attacked the strict causality principle on the basis of both its premises (in the form of the quantum theory) and its conclusions (in the form of chaos theory).[317]

To speak again metaphorically: Newtonian time is just as barren and lifeless as an empty theater stage. Measured by the multi-temporality that was discussed in chapter 2, it has about as much life in it as a cloister's ossuary. Comparatively, Einstein appears to have exchanged the hard stage floorboards for a trampoline that is constantly in motion. Finally, Heisenberg also doused this trampoline with liquid nitrogen and completed the scene by installing a strobe light: Lightning-like illumination shows instantaneous images of a nebulous drama. The static idea of a cosmology with an infinitely uniform flow of time by no means corresponds to this scenario, which is represented more adequately by the image of a dance, as we repeatedly encountered in the world of the hymns in chapter 1.

From depictions such as these, the layperson easily gets the impression that physics falls apart into diverse theories. Yet this is not the case. A theory is accepted only when it disposes of or subsumes another or contains it as a limiting case. In light of this presupposition, the attractive goal of physical theory formulation is the TOE, the "theory of everything." The struggles to unite all forces into one uniform theory continue. The difficulty of linking deterministic theories, such as the general theory of relativity with the statistical quantum theory, is obvious.

The direction in which the search for unification goes is dependent upon a hierarchy of valid theories, as well as upon space and time. It is well known that in his unification attempts, Einstein mistakenly presumed that field theory was more fundamental than quantum theory. This decision can be interpreted as a decision for the priority of space over time. At least Carl Friedrich von Weizsäcker saw it in this way:

In my opinion, hidden behind [Einstein's] "objectivism" is the unconscious preliminary decision of so many physicists that space ontologically precedes time, i.e., that time is a kind of space, a fourth dimension. Conversely, the decision for the priority of quantum theory contains, in turn, an unconscious preliminary decision for the philosophical priority of time, since probability signifies the temporal mode of futurity.[318]

Thus, says von Weizsäcker, quantum theory distinguishes itself at an important point from Plato's philosophy. While there is nothing actually new in the Platonic world, the concept of probability lies at the center of quantum mechanics. Precisely by this means, it builds upon a time structure[319] and makes possible a renaissance of the Aristotelian notion of possibility. Thus it has a constructively tense relationship with a theology for which the primacy of the possible before the real is the major focus.[320]

If von Weizsäcker is correct, we are dealing here with a twofold motion: on the one hand, the "degrading" of absolute time into curved space-time, and, on the other hand, the quantum-theoretical "elevation" of time, through which objective statements within the framework of probability become a function of time. This development is further intensified by "the primacy of time and change"[321] in chaos theory. A shifting of emphasis, from the category of law to the category of event, has thus resulted, which, speaking from a theological perspective, is also of extreme interest.[322]

The development of natural scientific theories depicted here also touches upon the question of truth. The theories of relativity and especially quantum theory have vigorously shaken the foundations of scientific rigor. Deciding what is objective truth and what is not proved to be more complicated than previously anticipated, although this reservation is far removed from the assertion that it is actually impossible to decide what truth is. Within certain references, rigorous criteria for truth are (still) valid. Complementarity and indeterminacy indeed point to the boundaries of possible knowledge, but the fruit of all striving for knowledge still lies more in the finding than in the fabrication of truth. In his 1954 Nobel lecture entitled "Statistical Interpretation of Quantum Mechanics," physicist Max Born described the normative implications of the situation created by quantum physics as follows:

I believe that ideas such as absolute certitude, absolute exactness, final truth, etc. are figments of the imagination which should not be admissible in any field of science. On the other hand, any assertion of probability is either right or wrong from the standpoint of the theory on which it is based. This *loosening of thinking* seems to me to be the greatest blessing which modern science has given to us. For the belief in a single truth and in being the possessor thereof is the root cause of all evil in the world.[323]

It is not the truth per se that has been lost. Instead, the simplistic, closed-minded perception of truth has been lost. What has been gained in its place is a complex, open-minded truth.

Results and Outlook

What have we learned from this chapter? Was it much ado about nothing? Are the gains from understanding physical theories proportional to the effort involved? Is it not generally true that, within the context of the interdisciplinary dialogue, science speaks and theology more or less silently listens? Is it only theology that benefits from natural scientific knowledge, or could natural science also learn from insights gained by theology?

The answers lie on two levels. First, it is the task of theology to stay informed, because, like philosophy, it is an academic subject that deals with life as a whole. Precisely because it makes statements about life in general, it must also keep nonphilosophical and nontheological knowledge in mind in order to gain insights that satisfy both intellect and intuition. Seen from this perspective, theology is by nature interdisciplinary. Although a theologian can be criticized for being ignorant of relevant natural scientific facts, this does not apply conversely in exactly the same way to natural scientists with regard to theological insights.[324] In this sense, the natural sciences may in fact have reasons to indulge in some self-satisfaction. Theological considerations may indeed do more harm than good in natural scientific research. Insights gained by theologians can nevertheless also make important contributions to the understanding of natural scientific data and theses. The relative self-sufficiency of the natural sciences means that they cannot easily integrate external knowledge, even if this happens over and over again. Newton did it and it occurs today as well.[325] Keeping alive the knowledge of their own limitations thus remains an important task of the natural sciences.

Second, the focal point of the exchange is the struggle for language. Precisely in the area of language, the boundaries between science and theology are much less explicit than is often assumed (see pp. 155–59). With regard to language, I completely agree with the physicist and theologian Robert J. Russell when he views theology and natural science "as the designations for two fields which, to some limited but irreducible degree, already include something of the discoveries, histories, visions, and commitments of one another, both intentionally and inadvertently."[326]

Both natural science and theology tell "stories of the *world*,"[327] but the stories have been formed differently. While the paradigm of natural scientific knowledge is empirical observation, theological knowledge must make use of the attitude that Nicholas Lash has called "prayerfulness."[328] On the one hand, the two modes of behavior differ completely from each other: "To put it very simply: there is a difference between listening to a waterfall and listening to another person, and in the natural scientist's world there are only waterfalls."[329] On the other hand, the two attitudes meet, without relinquishing their respective identities, beyond the antitheses of the modern project in "new possibilities of 'pupilage.'"[330] Now, in the light of twentieth-century physics, the difference between persons and waterfalls does not appear to be as radical as Lash seems to imagine. One cannot go back behind the critical questioning of the classical subject-object dichotomy, as it becomes clear especially with the reference to the role of the observer in the measuring processes of quantum physics. However, this does not at all mean that the gate to irrationality has been opened. Instead, more flexibility and more inclusiveness are made possible, which places demands on the rationality of the scientist that are at least as high as those required by the classical ideal of dichotomy.

Neither in the natural sciences nor in theology can one ignore the facts that, despite their relative difference, subject and object also constantly permeate each other and that theoretical knowledge and practical knowledge interact. Natural scientific discoveries tend to create their own ideologies, and in terms of their consequences, they strongly call for ethical reflection. Theological knowledge, by contrast, pushes toward the building of relationships between the content of faith, the worldview, and the organization of life. Because of these dynamics inherent to their disciplines, natural scientists and theologians are equally challenged to enter into a fruitful dialogue.

Luther said, *Nihil divinitatis, ubi non fides*[331] (No divinity where there is no faith), and thus expressed the necessity of a practical, existential dimension of theological reflection. Such talk must seem highly suspicious to a scientific attitude that reckons with an unproblematic subject-object distinction. Whenever one takes seriously the subject-object relationship as it has been problematized precisely in physics, however, new opportunities open up for thinking in relationships and for integrating diverse dimensions of knowledge, without lowering the level of rationality of the scientific undertaking. Following Luther's words, where there is no faith there is no divinity, I wish to define the general viewpoint that results from these considerations with the words *Nihil veritatis, ubi non relationes* (No truth where there are no relations). Wherever relations move to center stage, human beings are conceived as participants, as co-players in a nature that is viewed as an event, so that one can overcome both an exclusively anthropocentric understanding of the world and a static conception of nature. From this perspective, a mutual enrichment of theology and natural science is not only desirable, but even likely to happen.

Third, in the dialogue with theology, the natural sciences can also deepen their understanding of themselves. From the example of physical theories of time, it became clear how theological reflections have acted as godparents in the development of theories and how physics, for its part, has also influenced theology. In numerous cases, an unshakable belief in the unity and harmony of nature has driven scientific research. This certainly applies to Einstein. His struggle with quantum theory is also evidence of how natural scientific thinking is related to transcendental experience and religiosity. Later portrayals of Einstein as a kind of sacred genius and high priest of natural science emphasize this dimension. Even in Newton, there was doubtless an interaction between theology and natural science, which continued in the work of his successors. The scientist and science journalist Margaret Wertheim, who vigorously emphasized the religious undertones in physics, considers it quite possible that precisely his personal experiences with the supernatural—and not least, his preoccupation with alchemy—brought Newton along his successful path. In a mechanistically shaped time, Newton dared to pursue the notion of an invisible and mysterious heavenly power that ultimately took him via the law of gravity to the formulation of the laws of motion.[332] The enthusiasm for the clear structure of Newtonian science finally spread to many other scientists, who began to search for corresponding, uniform structures in completely different fields of knowledge.[333] As later in the cases of Darwin and Einstein, as well as in the wake of quantum physics and chaos research, this results in a relatively strong formation of paradigms that attain significance and influence far beyond the original field. The prevailing theory at any given time can influence the hermeneutics of research processes of the most diverse branches of science; it can attain religious or quasi-religious status; it can become the pattern for the development of corresponding societal models. Science can become religion. The factors and processes that become effective in such developments require critical reflection. For this, natural sciences are also dependent upon theological expertise.

Wertheim believes that, to date, the agenda of physics has been filled with religious values. In the relevant literature, it is not unusual to proceed from parallels between the concept of the laws of nature and a monotheistic concept of God. In the words of the mathematician and physicist John Barrow:

The fact that such a unification [of all the laws of nature into a simple and single representation] is even sought tells us something important about our expectations regarding the Universe. These we must have derived from an amalgam of our previous experience of the world and our inherited beliefs about its ultimate Nature and significance. Our monotheistic traditions reinforce the assumption that the Universe is at root a unity, that it is not governed by different legislation in different places, neither the residue of some clash of Titans wrestling to impose their arbitrary wills upon the Nature of things, nor the compromise of some cosmic committee.[334]

Similarly, Wertheim recognizes a religious motif in the search for the TOE, the uniform theory of the natural forces: "The longing for one all-encompassing cosmic law is, I suggest, the scientific legacy of more than three millennia of faith in one all-encompassing principle known as God."[335] It appears to be no accident that the idea of the unification of all forces was fed by a series of deeply religious men, such as the Jesuit priest Rudjer Boskovič (1711–1787) and the member of the small Christian Sandemanian sect, Michael Faraday (1791–1867). In view of the fact that the dream of the "world formula" preoccupies not only numerous clever minds, but also requires significant material resources in the form of particle accelerators, it seems justified to listen to Wertheim's critical questions concerning the real driving force behind this research.[336] Is it an essentially hierarchically fixed image of the world that makes us believe that physics can explain God to us by discovering a unified theory? Do such high-reaching, quasi-religious ambitions distract us from more urgent problems, the solutions of which could actually improve the world? There must also be a discussion in and with physics about the kind of societal and ethical responsibility required. Due to a common history and to the common tasks of the present, theology is an indispensable interlocutor in this discussion.[337]

Finally, what does physics contribute to the topic of "time"? It tells us that time is that which one measures with clocks. It also tells us that one second does not simply make up 1/86,400 of a day, but rather, 9,192,631,770 oscillations of a special caesium atom. It shows that time measurement functions even if we do not have a uniform theory and cannot say anything definitive about the beginning and the end of time. And, eventually, it also shows that the understanding of time has a fruitful history in the center of the formulation of scientific theory. More recent theories signal an openness in the understanding of what is generally called time. An adequate understanding of time cannot be satisfied with the analysis of individual elements; it must include structures and relations, being and becoming. It must also reckon with the fact that genuinely new things are possible. This openness encourages interpretations that go far beyond physics.

Have the expectations in this chapter thus been fulfilled? No, if we expected a definition package that needs "only" to be applied theologically. Yes, if we sought confirmation that time is a relational and multiple phenomenon. Yes, also, if we considered the fact that in physics, one is dealing with a description of functions that cannot be transferred directly to other areas.

In this third chapter of our study, it has been shown repeatedly that scientific theories and theological models do not exist in isolation from each other. The understanding of the theories of relativity in contrast to the absolute time in Newton is especially significant for the assessment of theological concepts of time. Newton's concept of absoluteness included theological assumptions, and Einstein was not the only one to be troubled by the consequences of quantum physics with regard to worldview and the understanding of God. For this reason, Dilthey's distinction between explanatory natural sciences, on the one hand, and the arts and humanities that are concerned with understanding, on the other hand, proves to be untenable.

The idea of the openness of time is meaningful from a theological perspective. Precisely at this point, however, physics has difficulties; discussion of an open future does not fall into its domain. This discussion belongs to the "central area from which we ourselves shape reality," which, however, "constitutes the infinitely remote singularity for the scientific language that indeed means something decisive for the ordering within the finite, but which can never be attained."[338] In this sense, physics suffers from an eschatological deficit. It *must* do so if it wishes to remain true to its nature.

At the end of this third chapter, the path to an adequate understanding of the concept of "time" therefore still appears to be a long way off.[339] Neither Newton nor Einstein could explain time definitively. Quantum physics and chaos theory add greater meaning to the concepts of relation, dynamics, and openness without providing us with clear definitions. For better or for worse, we must reconcile ourselves to the fact that physics knows a great deal, but certainly not everything, about the phenomenon "time" that is so familiar to everyone, and yet so foreign.

The fourth chapter will consider the extent to which scientific development can be received theologically. For this, the illumination of the basic theoretical concepts of time in their proper contexts has created a necessary foundation. We shall see the extent to which such gains in knowledge can be attained for theology.

[4]

Aspects of a Theology of Time

More Precise Definitions

This study began with the narration of time as is found in Church hymns, and it then turned to the clarification of concepts of time in theology and the natural sciences. Even if the narration generally precedes the explanation, both are very closely related,[1] since both articulate and reflect experience. This final chapter aims to reexamine the summary of insights gained from our narration and explanation and to further develop some of these aspects. In this process, our reflections will concentrate on the doctrine of the Trinity and on eschatology. The motive for this selection is my recognition that the concepts that emerged as the central concepts for a theology of time are best expressed within these two areas of theology.

In order to preserve the greatest possible openness, until now I have made only minimal use of definitions. Now, however, because we are dealing with the content of theological symbol systems, more precise definitions are needed. First, I wish to reexamine the concepts of statics, dynamics, and relation, which are so important for this study.

Statics and Dynamics

In the third chapter of this study, it became clear that, in scientific models, the emphasis shifted from a static to a dynamic description of the world. In the present context, I wish to remind the reader that a static understanding of the world is not the same thing as immobility. Rather, the static worldview proceeds from a uniform mechanical motion; it understands the world to be a machine. Its motion can basically be ignored, because, due to its uniformity, it is irrelevant which time period is excised from the continuum and placed under the microscope. Time is symmetrical and reversible.

For a dynamic worldview, on the other hand, it is common to consider the asymmetry and irreversibility of time. A dynamic concept of time can express negative and positive acceleration, and it is focused on a sequence of moving states that cannot be predicted over the long term. As part of the dynamic view, I also include the attempt to bestow the same ontological status to relations among things as to the things themselves. Within the framework of a dynamic conception, the world's own evolution and history becomes important. Here, one finds a worldview that approximates Christian theology, which would be inconceivable without the dynamics of creation–covenant–incarnation–eschatology. The concept of "dynamics," however, must not be so constricted that the linear, consecutive arrangement of different elements represents the only possibility. We would then be unable to get beyond Cullmann's model, which was criticized on pp. 86–89. Dynamics looks upon the static block-time understanding of time ("spatialized" time) and the irreversible understanding of the time arrow ("flowing" time) as adjacent models.[2] It attempts to articulate being and becoming equally. Thus, it is in harmony with a theology that wishes to relate both categories to God, that wishes to speak of both the God of the philosophers and the God of Abraham, Sara and Hagar, of Isaac and Rebecca, of Jacob, Rachel and Leah, and of Jesus Christ. This basic understanding speaks neither of a God of pure being, which leads to deism, nor of a God that is exclusively thought to be evolving, which would dissolve everything into processes. It speaks instead of a God of being and becoming. In the words of John Polkinghorne: "Such a God can be both the God whose reason underlies the marvellous rational transparency of the physical world, open to human inquiry, and also the God who is not condemned merely to contemplating or guaranteeing that world's regularity, but who is also able to exercise his will within it."[3]

This also presupposes a dynamic understanding of perfection. Change does not decrease the degree of perfection, and absolute perfection is not the same as frozen eminence.[4]

It is therefore necessary to leave behind an antithetical understanding of statics and dynamics.[5] The two concepts do indeed play an important role as distinguishing criteria; however, for an adequate description of reality, their antithetical application proves to be inadequate. In order to arrive at genuine relationality, one needs more than distinctions.

Before I address the concept of relationality in more detail, I shall return again to the three differentiating models that were discussed in chapter 2. I criticized the theological model centered on the quantitative difference of time and eternity because, among other things, it is more a combination of belief in progress and a popular understanding of Newton's notion of absolute time than it is an interpretation of biblical views of time. A linear time arrow model that is based on the Christ event as the center of time, as described by Cullmann, is static in the sense of a uniform mechanical movement, despite the apparent dynamism of the arrow. It became clear already in the second chapter that such a concept is not communicative, it cannot act to create relationships, and it does not create a relationship to the Other. Furthermore, it now becomes clear that it also represents an inappropriate oversimplification from a scientific viewpoint. It represents a naïve conception, for it does not at all discuss questions about a beginning and end of time—i.e., the questions of singularities—and because it specifies a demarcation line, as the center of time, to which all points of the timeline relate. In view of the model of the light cone (cf. pp. 145–49), this linear description denies the existence of spacelike events, since it considers a common causality of all events. It thereby also denies the finite nature of the speed of light, since the spacelike events disappear only when the light cone is completely opened, that is, when the speed of light is infinite.[6] The quantitative model therefore does not do justice to the complexity of spacetime. The fact that the conception of time inherent in the quantitative model roughly coincides with general human experience is no reason to disregard this criticism. To be sure, the idea of the fully opened light cone functions in everyday life; but in light of the knowledge gained in chapter 3, Russell's remark, that one is nevertheless dealing with an artificial product, is easy to understand:

Thus the concept of the present as demarcating the past from the future is an artifact, an *anthropomorphic simplification* abstracted from the objective complexity of spacetime. In reality, there is no present, only an infinite set of lightcones, events and worldlines, a checkerboard of variously overlapping causal and acausal regimes, crisscrossing endlessly throughout spacetime.[7]

For this reason, it is certainly correct to continue searching for multi-temporal[8] models. At the same time, this is an indirect confirmation of the eschatological model of differentiation, because this model was the only one of the three models considered that works concretely with multi-temporality when distinguishing old and new time. Here then, one is not dealing with the construction of a time arrow that emanates from a center of time, but rather, above all, with the question of the presence of the end of time in the midst of time. It is the attempt to speak of time as relationship creating, relational, and dynamic.

The ontological model of differentiation largely avoids the criticism of modern physics because its center—the contrast of time and eternity—is not relevant to science. The problematization of past, future, and present in Augustine nevertheless gives this model of differentiation a greater proximity to modern physics than the quantitative model possesses. The three times of Augustine—the present of the past, the present of the present, and the present of the future—have more in common with the light cone grid than with Cullmann's straight line.

A Relational Understanding of Time

If, during the course of this study, the search for relationality has moved more and more to the center, this should not imply that there has never been a relational understanding of time in the history of theology. In *Space, Time and Incarnation*, Thomas F. Torrance has indicated that both relational and static models have figured in the world of theological concepts. He looks at parts of the history of theology from the point of view of these two competing concepts of space and time: the so-called container model, which goes back to Aristotle, and the more Platonic, relational model.[9] Torrance himself prefers the relational model. While patristic and Reformed[10] theology proceeded from a relational concept of space, Lutheran theology received the container model, allied itself with the Newtonian understanding of space, time, and God, and thus burdened all of modern Protestant theology with numerous problems that led, above all, to deism and the dualism of space–matter, God–World, and spirit–nature. According to Torrance, this development resulted in objectivist, rigid, and closed theological frameworks.[11]

Following the definitive collapse of the container model in the wake of the theories of relativity, Torrance sees the alternative in the conceptual integration of ontological and dynamic starting points. On the one hand, as the transcendent Creator, God does not have a spatial or temporal relationship to the world. On the other hand, because the creation has a relationship as object to God, who is its preserver, God cannot be imagined without space and time as the relation continuum. Space and time are the medium of the presence and the action of God.[12] For this reason, God does not dissolve into space and time, but rather space and time, as created forms of rationality, are to be strictly distinguished from the eternal rationality of God.[13] Here, Torrance allies himself with the Barthian tradition, but he also recognizes the difficulty of this model, namely, that God ultimately remains completely incomprehensible. In other words, ultimately the distinction within simultaneous relatedness does not overcome dualism. By presupposing an asymmetry of relation, he attempts to avoid dualism as well as the absorption of God by space and time: ". . . we must think of God's relation to the world in terms of an infinite differential, but we must think of the world's relation to God in terms of a created necessity in which its contingence is not negated."[14]

According to Torrance, this notion of the relationality of God allows for a concept of God as being free of all necessity, without God thereby being rendered inaccessible to all knowledge. God is not limited by space and time, but space and time are certainly a reality in God's relationship to the world; the relationship of the world to God, however, is always bound to space and time.

Is Torrance successful with this model of relatedness and simultaneous differentiation? It remains doubtful, particularly when Torrance reverts back to the concepts of horizontal and vertical and speaks of the penetration of the horizontal space-time dimensions by the vertical spiritual dimension.[15] Torrance remains too closely tied to Barthian thinking to be able to develop a more radical relational approach at this point. He outlines three ways of understanding the Incarnation, which should do justice to both the divine and human frames of reference and simultaneously coordinate them without mixing them: 1) the Patristic line, as expressed in the creeds of Nicaea and Chalcedon; 2) the analogy of topological language used by physicists in order to express difficult elastic connections between geometric and dynamic aspects and between mechanical aspects and those describing an organism; and 3) the possibility offered by Goedel's Theorem to comprehend the openness or incompleteness of a formal system as the constitutive nature of things. That, according to the latter, every formal system is open at the top and closed at the bottom, means, for theology, the openness of human thought towards God (upwards) and the coordination of theological thought with ordinary thinking and empirical knowledge at the base (downwards).[16] These attempts at harmonization are considerable, even though they remain tied to a dualistic, upward-downward thinking and a narrow exclusivity. For, according to Torrance, without the Incarnation, the conceptions of God and the world lose their meaning.[17]

I consider it to be problematic that, in Torrance, two images overlap, that is, a) the notion of two axes, namely, the horizontal space-time axis of the reality of creation, and the axis of the spirit or incarnation representing the eternal reality that comes from above and is vertical to it;[18] and b) the notion of a coordinate system whose two axes express the divine and human, the eternal and temporal, the invisible and visible, and the spiritual and material relationships.[19] While the supposedly Barthian-inspired model *a* accentuates the discontinuity and inequality of the two axes, model *b* more nearly expresses the correlation and equal reality of the two coordinates. The discontinuity model standing in the foreground appears to prevent Torrance from completely exhausting the potential of *b*. By using model *b* and a formulation by Torrance himself, however, one can add a fourth way of understanding to the three ways just mentioned, namely, one that describes the meshing of the vertical and horizontal dimensionality in the Incarnation. I am thus assuming that, as Torrance says, in transcendent relationship to God, Jesus Christ generates "His own distinctive and continuous 'space-time track.'"[20] The only way to recognize God the Father is by following this space-time track.[21] I believe that this space-time line can be mathematically illustrated using the coordinate model. For this, I use the complex numerical level. The horizontal axis gives the real numerical values, and the vertical axis, the imaginary. In this coordinate system, a given complex number $z = a + bi$ corresponds to a given point with the coordinates (a,b).[22] This number can be represented by the vector from the origin (o) up to the marked point (a,b). This vector z has as its absolute value $|z| = \sqrt{a^2 + b^2}$; $|z|$ is always a real, positive number. By using different calculation operations with imaginary numbers, it becomes clear how real and imaginary parts interact, complete each other, and, as a total entity, represent a highly real meaning. Understood as a vector in the plane of complex numbers, the conception of an incarnational space-time line that has a transcendent relationship to God thus results in real, conceivable meaning. This model could be added to Torrance's three. It would have the advantage of overcoming the dualism of top-bottom. It would not first speak of relation and then—like Torrance—again move discontinuity into the foreground; it would instead actually make relation the focal point.

This model would therefore do justice to the thought of differentness and simultaneous relation: Imaginary[23] and real axes are just as clearly different as imaginary parts and real parts of a complex number, but, jointly, they nevertheless form a real unit (in the form of a vector). This model would furthermore have the advantage of being able to express dynamism, because one can compute with complex numbers in a way that generates real numbers and causes complex numbers to look like real (if $b = o$) or imaginary ($a = o$) ones. Complexity occurs, so to speak, "in, with, and under" real and imaginary elements. The complex plane allows the presentation of all combinations of complex, imaginary, and real numbers on a single relational level (imaginary numbers lie on the vertical axis, and real ones on the horizontal). It seems to me that this model is thereby able to overcome the narrow christological exclusivity that one finds in Torrance. The numbers that are "only" real do not fall outside of the system, that is, an understanding of God and the world that does not take the incarnational space-time line into consideration need not necessarily be declared meaningless from the outset, as happens in Torrance's view. The elements that are only real remain a part of the complex plane; they just have different distances from the incarnational vector.

Overall, as a model for understanding the spatial-temporal Incarnation of God in Jesus Christ, the complex plane therefore means three things. It permits the depiction of relationality within preserved alterity, it expresses dynamism, and it enables an inclusive interpretation of the Incarnation.[24] In this regard, it fulfills the requirements that, according to the findings of the previous chapters, must be placed on an adequate understanding of time.

At this point, the relationship of *relativity* and *relationality* should also be defined more precisely. There is a correlation between the two that must be differentiated in more detail. The statement that something is relative always implies relativity in relation to something else. The absoluteness of that "something else" is not presupposed; it can itself be relative. According to this, relativity always presupposes some type of relation and therefore carries its own relationality. When the absolute, which is conceivable without relation, was called into question, the possibility of a new paradigm opened up. Out of the deficiency of the loss of the absolute was born the virtue of relationality. The classical priority of substance over relation gave way to a new paradigm, which is more concerned with relationships and correlations than with nature and essence as such. In other words, relationships become more important than differences, without the existence of differences or the necessity of differentiation thereby being called into question. Both—differences and relationships—should be kept in focus. While traditionally definitions—and thus differentiations—of substance were the hallmark of scientific activity, it is now time to make relationality a priority. This in no way means a reduction in rationality. It instead means an increase, since the recognition that even rationality exists only in relatedness, only as conditional and not absolute rationality, enhances the claims on scientific precision and honesty.

The shift in emphasis from substance to relation therefore does not represent a simplification, but, rather, a complication and increase of these requirements. Whereas substance-thinking proceeds from a clear subject-object distinction, relationality attempts to describe processes and dynamic interactions. Out of the supposed unproblematic spectator or observer in substance metaphysics, there evolves, within the framework of relational thought, the actor or—to stay with the metaphor that has repeatedly imposed itself upon us since the first chapter—the dancer. Furthermore,

causality and openness, determinism and history, and necessity and possibility are contrasted. While substance-thinking, as orientation toward that
which exists, is more oriented toward the past, relational thinking, as orientation toward that which is possible, is more strongly oriented toward the
future.

The trend away from a static reductionism and toward a relational dynamism was already visible in modern science; it can likewise be observed
in theology.[25] When the shortcomings of an absolute, theistic, static concept of God become obvious,[26] a renewed search must be made for dynamism and relations in the concept of God. Thus, the renaissance of Trinitarian theology in particular elucidates the paradigm shift "from natures to
persons, from substance metaphysics to a metaphysics of relations."[27] This
Trinitarian reflection claims structural significance for all of theology, not
only for a certain specified area. I therefore consider it important to reexamine more recent Trinitarian concepts—now against the backdrop of what
was elaborated in chapter 3—for their usefulness for a theology of time.

Trinitarian Models of Time

In the second chapter, I showed that the strength of Trinitarian models
lies in the possibility of conceiving multi-temporality and relational dynamics between time and eternity. Their weakness, however, consists in the arbitrary assigning of Trinitarian aspects and time-eternity aspects to each other.
The theology of the Trinity is thus quite suitable for referring to the
significance of the *that* of relationality, but the doctrine of the Trinity cannot contribute much to the *how* of a relationality. At this point, the results
of our reflections on the scientific concept of time have also not altered the
conclusion of the second chapter, namely, that a theology of time cannot be
based on a Trinitarian theology without running into problems. There is
neither a good reason to project some type of temporal-theological distinctions into a doctrine of the Trinity nor an appropriate cause to explicate the
time-eternity relationship with a Trinitarian theology.

Nevertheless, the results of the scientific chapter lead me to revisit the
topic of the Trinity. The observation that an absolute understanding of God
has a certain correspondence to the Newtonian worldview raises the question of whether modern physics then requires a relational understanding of
God. Of course, physics does not "require" an understanding of God.
Something more general can be said, however, namely, that the basic characteristics of modern physics are more consistent with a relational under-

standing of God than with an absolute understanding. If the physical theories adequately describe the basic structures of reality, then the statement—that no complete dissimilarity of the basic structures of creation and Creator exists—can be considered theologically rational. If what I found to be essential features in the formation of modern theories of physics agrees with reality, i.e., if 1) a relative concept of time, 2) the problems of distinguishing between subject and object, 3) the dynamics between observer and the observed, as well as 4) the description of the development of dynamic systems far from equilibrium are appropriate descriptions of reality, then an interpretation of the concept of God as a relational fellowship corresponds more closely to this description of reality.

From this starting point, I think it makes sense to present some further concepts of Trinitarian theology that go beyond our treatment in the second chapter and to the understanding of which our findings in the third chapter contribute substantially.[28] These concepts share a tendency to move from the metaphysical notion of a divine substance or nature toward a relationally constituted conception of God. The latter cannot avoid thinking also in the direction of God's temporality.

Unity, Diversity, and Alterity

Both Kevin J. Vanhoozer and Colin Gunton formulate their Trinitarian reflections within the problem field of unity and diversity. Both are concerned with conceiving of relationality and alterity. In the background is their concern that neither modernism nor postmodernism has succeeded in actually affirming alterity. Where modernism constantly tries to constrict the Other into uniform, objectivizing correspondence, postmodernism negates the Other by its refusal to differentiate, so that even here, the final result is equalization. Relativism without differentiation cannot provide a solution. The counterpart, also called "foundationalism," is a misstep inasmuch as this position—in a kind of intellectual Pelagianism—thinks that it can establish a universally valid, eternal truth exclusively through the efforts of human rational activities.[29] Vanhoozer wants to make the doctrine of the Trinity useful for a theology of religion by attempting to show that an identity of God that is understood to be Trinitarian enables both exclusivistic, as well as pluralistic and inclusivistic, thinking. If the Trinity is made the transcendent condition of interreligious dialogue, then, Vanhoozer says, there is no danger of reducing the Other to the "same."[30] Gavin D'Costa thinks similarly when—following, among others, Lévinas and Derrida—he attempts to create an open eschatological and Trinitarian inclusivism. With the aid of this, he thinks that it is possible to have a theology that does not subject other religions to a leveling process or push them into a negative alterity.[31]

Vanhoozer bases his concept of identity on Ricoeur's distinction of Idem-Identity (*mêmeté*/sameness) and Ipse-Identity (*ipséité*/selfhood).[32] The Idem-Identity corresponds to the God of the philosophers, a perennially identical God who, according to the Greek model, reduces the alterity of the Other in an ontology without narrativity. The ipse-identical God, by contrast, is the God of Abraham, Isaac, and Jacob, who, in faithfulness, proves to be the same over the course of time. Identity thus conceived aims at a relationship to an Other. It is identity that must be understood narratively. The biblical stories ascribe to God a "dynamic identity." This has significance for God's relationship to time and eternity, for "it is the narrative figuration of the economic Trinity—that is, the story of the temporal missions of Jesus and the Spirit—that alone configures God's eternity."[33] Here, the unity of God is not understood as a presupposition, but is rather derived from the Trinitarian self-manifestation of God in history. Ontology is secondary to narration.[34] While Idem-Identity only has room for God's unity, the focus of Ipse-Identity includes also the Trinity. This makes it possible to express both difference and relation in interreligious dialogue.

Just as enthusiastically, Gunton describes the potential of the doctrine of the Trinity to formulate an appropriate theology of creation:

It is the trinitarian formulation of a doctrine of creation that allows God to be God, the world to be the world, distinct beings and yet personally related by personal mediation as creator and creation. . . . [T]he plurality in unity of the triune revelation enables us to do justice to the diversity, richness, and openness of the world without denying its unity in relativist versions of pluralism. It is that vision that trinitarian theology has to offer the fragmented modern world.[35]

Trinity does not merely mean that three persons enter into relationships with one another, but rather that the persons mutually constitute one another within the relationships. A distinction between being and relating is possible only in theoretical thinking. Viewed ontologically, there is no difference. Being and relating are "part of the one ontological dynamic."[36]

Under the motto "relation and relativity," Gunton attempts to form a bridge between Trinitarian theology and modern science.[37] He argues to the effect that the key Trinitarian concepts of freedom, energy, and relation have a certain similarity to their scientific counterparts. With this argument, he surely goes much further than most theologians and scientists would be willing to go:

Indeed, what I want to suggest is that some modern scientific theories look as though they are the result of a process almost of intellectual evolution, from static theories owing more to Greek than to Christian influences to a dynamism reflecting the more eschatological emphasis of a doctrine that pays due attention to the role of the Holy Spirit.[38]

Even if the development from statics to dynamics is scientifically verifiable, as chapter 3 shows, one cannot automatically draw a line from here all the way to eschatology. If, in spite of this fact, such is the case in Gunton, then this points less to a good understanding of scientific theories than to theological appropriation or overestimation of such theories. Gunton's manner of argumentation is reminiscent of Newton. Thus, as in Newton, absolute God and absolute space and absolute time corresponded to one another, in Gunton dynamic Trinity and a universe that is understood as "a perichoresis of interrelated dynamic systems"[39] belong together. It even seems to him that the development of modern field theories have led "inexorably to the conceptual echo of trinitarian theology in relativity theory and its developments."[40] Despite enthusiasm for dynamics and relationality, one must still expressly emphasize the distinction between scientific and theological theory formation because this distinction is important for guaranteeing the understanding of theories in their respective contexts and protecting each from mutual appropriation. Gunton's assumption, that Trinitarian theology could have contributed to the development of the concepts that aided modern science in discovering the relationality, contingency, and dynamism of the universe,[41] appears rather naïve to me, in view of chapter 3. I do share his viewpoint, however, that it is a task of theology to ask questions that go beyond science.

The mutually constituting persons of the Trinity, dynamics and relationality in the universe and in God—to be sure, these notions are inspiring. Nevertheless, something essential has been omitted. If the essence of the Trinitarian God is love, then how can relation be conceived without autonomy? If God is transcendent, then how can God's identity be used as a model for interreligious dialogue or for a theology of nature? Is it not precisely God's alterity that is again violated in such a project? Is not the appropriate *frui* of the relationship with God replaced by an *uti* that is subject to human categories? Regardless of how stimulating Trinitarian reflections may appear to be within the context of the weaknesses of modernism and postmodernism and in view of the formulation of modern physical theories, it should always remain clear that we are dealing here with an inspiring analogy in the broadest sense and not with an identification of one with the other.

Order, Chaos, and Relationality

According to Gunton, the doctrine of the Trinity was developed "to show that God's being is not motionless, impassible eternity but a personal *taxis* of dynamic and free relations."[42] That this is more wishful thinking than fact is shown not least of all by Elizabeth Johnson's discussion of Trinitarian theology. Johnson also develops her doctrine of the Trinity in the light of the concept of relation. Her rhetorical question—"Not an isolated, static, ruling monarch but a relational, dynamic, tripersonal mystery of love—who would not opt for the latter?"[43]—outlines her Trinitarian theological approach. With regard to the traditional Trinitarian frameworks, she criticizes the use of exclusively male images, which tend to place men and the role of God on the same level and to put women in the role of dependent and sinful humanity. She also takes issue with the notion of a hierarchical structure of the Trinity whose sole goal is to define who proceeds from whom, who gives what to whom, and who receives what. As an alternative, Johnson chooses the approach for which I have also opted in this study: She does not proceed from definitions, but rather from relationality. For this reason, she distances herself from the attempt to base a doctrine of the Trinity on a definition of what constitutes a person.[44] Instead, she develops her thoughts from a relational model of mutual giving and receiving, in order to bring the equality, the mutuality, and the reciprocal dynamism of the Trinitarian relationships into the discussion.[45]

Two Trinitarian understandings of God oppose each other: a Trinitarian God understood as the guarantor of order who establishes what is to be, and a Trinitarian God who is experienced as the guarantor of life who liberates what is bound, so that a life in community is possible in the presence of diversity. The ontological priority of relation to substance implies that relationality, and not a solitary ego, is the heart of all reality.[46] There is no absolute divine person, but only the three relative persons. God is not a monolithic, undifferentiated block, but rather a living mystery of relationship who has turned to the world. The divine secret is not monarchy, but rather community; not an absolute ruler, but rather a threefold *koinonia*.[47] Here it becomes clear how theological reflection is linked to the criticism of social order in Church and society. A social order that is modeled on monarchy must look quite different than one that is oriented toward a divine communion of persons that is constituted in free loving relationships. Even if a warning here against projections in one direction or the other is appropriate, it can hardly be denied that an interaction exists between the conception of God's nature and the understanding of the natural and social orders.[48] The reflections on Newton and Leibniz already showed this (see pp. 125–40). Johnson legitimizes Trinitarian thinking by claiming that it emerged from the historical experience of salvation. Trinitarian thought is more than speculative philosophy; Johnson says that it is, instead, synthesized experience of salvation that is expressed in this "symbol of holy mystery." Thus, the doctrine of the Trinity is indeed a legitimate concept, although a secondary one.[49]

When Johnson says that the fear of chaos, among other things, is hidden behind the defense of a static, hierarchically structured concept of the Trinity,[50] she thereby addresses a thought that deserves to be further developed against the backdrop of chaos research. Such a static concept of God is used to legitimize and maintain order and to keep at bay all chaos that is felt to be threatening. This fear of chaos is a symptom for the fact that chaos is not understood correctly, however. As shown on pp. 169–72, chaos is an ambivalent concept that certainly contains disorder, but it also is not free of ordering structures and it contains thoroughly creative aspects. This means that the supposed dualism of order and chaos must, at the very least, be radically revised. In the context of the discussion of weak causality, it became clear that only a minority of processes can be explained using strong determinism, while for the overwhelming majority of life processes, it is precisely chaotic behavior that is the norm. If some type of correspondence between Creator and creation can be assumed, then it is more reasonable to link chaotic dynamism to God's nature than it is to link God to a static order. Then it may also be more than pure accident that both the depiction of chaos research (pp. 169–72) and Johnson's Trinitarian model end with the same metaphor. It is the metaphor that already appeared in the first chapter of this study, namely, the metaphor of the dance. As an image of the Trinity, Johnson draws a triple helix engaged in a *perichoretic* dance, as an expression of apparent chaotic and, nevertheless, highly disciplined movement and complexity.[51] The dance is creative: "The circular dynamism within God spirals inward, outward, forward toward the coming of a world into existence, not out of necessity but out of the free exuberance of overflowing friendship."[52]

Proceeding from these reflections, I believe we should reassess the traditional talk of God as the highest *simplicitas*. I see a promising alternative in the possibility of taking up the stimuli of complexity research and pursuing the question of what happens when we instead speak of God as the highest *complexitas*. Naturally, one of the responsibilities of theology is to examine critically how, for example, the concepts of monotheism, natural laws, strivings for unity, and the concepts of order affect one another and then show the consequences that result from this. If, in light of this background, we again consider how scientific authors deal with the concept of God, then our impression is confirmed that their concepts of God often stay very close to Newton's level of theological sophistication. They tend to fall short of taking into account the current state of theological knowledge and discourse.

Time, Eternity, and the Trinity

Dance presupposes time, but Johnson does not particularly deal with this. Robert W. Jenson, on the other hand, considers the doctrine of the Trinity also on the basis of time. His starting point is that the biblical story that deals with God and ourselves is true with respect to God and for God.[53] Like Vanhoozer, he wants to understand God's nature as narrative,[54] which means that, in God, there must also be room for surprise and genuinely new things. From this, Jenson then concludes that God's eternity cannot be merely the absence of time, but, rather, that eternity must be for God something like what time is for us.[55] In this conclusion, the description of what is meant by eternity remains open and general: "it only denotes whatever it is on which a particular spiritual community relies to join the poles of time, to knit future and past into a coherent fabric."[56] According to this, eternity is what holds past, present, and future together—i.e., it is what constitutes coherence. Eternity thus becomes the principle of meaning: the supposition of an Archimedean point whose appearance can vary considerably, however. There are therefore a multitude of eternities. The Christian interpretation of eternity is based on the Trinitarian God whose hallmark is life: "'God' simply as such denotes *what happens between* Jesus and the one he calls 'Father' and the Father's Spirit in whom Jesus turns to him. . . . 'God,' simply as such, denotes a life, as the Eastern tradition has put it, a complex of *'energeia.'*"[57]

This life of God surrounds time, thus it must appear correct when Jenson concludes that "Time . . . is the *accommodation* God makes in his living and moving eternity, for others than himself."[58]

Jenson also specifies a direction of time in God. While the Father appears as the "from where" of divine events, the Spirit represents the "to where" of divine life. For the Son, God's "specious present"[59] remains. Jenson pays particular attention to the Spirit as the power of the future. He sees a close correlation between the Holy Spirit, the narrative structure of God's nature, and the freedom in God that makes what is still to come into more than a mere consequence of what has already happened: "The Spirit is God as his and our future rushing upon us, he is the eschatological reality of God, the Power as which God is the active Goal of all things. . . ."[60]

Jenson does not draw parallels to science at this point. However, his description of eternity as diverse and his depicting God's eternity as alive and mobile, while simultaneously adhering to Karl Barth's talk of eternity as "pure duration," are interesting. The definition of time as the home that God creates in divine eternity for that which is different from God goes beyond the three differentiating models of time and eternity that are outlined in chapter 2. It does not allow time to dissolve into space, even if it is very close to spatial categories. It is also consistent with the biblical description of the nature of God as love, if love is understood as that which, in its essence, receives the Other. The link of eschatology to the role of the Spirit of bringing otherness and novelty to the Father and the Son is also interesting.[61] At the same time, this connection elucidates, once again, the insurmountable difficulty of all attempts to link a dynamic and relational time-eternity understanding to the differentiation of the Trinitarian persons. If Dalferth allocated the eschatological perspective to the Son,[62] then Jenson is just as certain of his position when he links eschatology to the Spirit. While the role of the Son remains diffuse in Jenson, in Ted Peters, it is the Spirit that has a very weak profile. Peter's Trinity instead resembles a duality that is held together by the Spirit as a connecting link,[63] a difficulty that Peters shares with all approaches that allocate to the Spirit the role of the unifier within the Trinity.

One cannot avoid the impression that all of these Trinitarian models include a relatively large portion of arbitrary speculation. The problems shown on p. 109 have not yet been solved. In what is now a broader perspective, we can see that a Trinitarian understanding of God certainly corresponds to the paradigm that prefers relationality and thus also has a fixed place within the framework of a study that deals with a relational theology of time in the perspective of modern science; yet, it may not be able to explain such a theology. The attempt to develop the most precise Trinitarian models possible, in order to use them to explain the relationship of God, time, and eternity, proves not to be the most fruitful path.

Nevertheless, the explicit articulation of a Trinitarian concept of God can make an important contribution to the dialogue between science and theology by offering a beneficial contrast to the one-dimensionality of the Newtonian concept of God. The newly awakened interest in Trinitarian theology also clearly shows what may appear to be self-evident to theologians, but what is not at all so familiar to many scientists and laypersons, namely: Not only does science change and advance in knowledge; theology does the same thing. At the beginning of his book *God and the New Physics*, Paul Davies supports the opinion that science offers a more certain path to God than does religion; and Stephen Hawking concludes *A Brief History of Time* with the remark that, if we discover a complete theory, "then we would know the mind of God." In both books, God remains even more abstract than in Newton. The question of what kind of God they more or less explicitly identify with a world formula remains basically unanswered. This lack of sophistication vis-à-vis theological complexity is perplexing. A certain amount of specialized scientific knowledge is expected of theologians who deal with science, and rightly so. However, this demand evidently does not apply in reverse—as these two examples show—yet it should. A dialogue that is to succeed will have to consciously take into consideration the entire scope of competence of all dialogue partners.

Trinitarian thought can make an important contribution to both inter-disciplinary discussions and a theology of time, but its potential alone does not suffice for constructing a theology of time. Rather, even after considering the findings from chapter 3, our impression from chapter 2 remains, namely, that eschatology is the theological place where the most can be said about a relational theology of time. Eschatology allows reflection upon time as multi-temporality or a complexity of times—indeed, it even demands such reflection.

Eschatology as the Key to a Relational Understanding of Time

If, at the end of the previous section, there was reason to complain about arbitrary speculation, then here arises the question of whether the area of eschatology does not provide an even more slippery slope. Can eschatology be more than speculation? It could hardly be more than this if it were concerned only with providing calculations of future events. However, eschatology is instead concerned with the question: "What may we hope?" It is certainly not thereby automatically relieved of the suspicion of mere speculation, and it continues to be fraught with difficulties; but this question makes clear that eschatology cannot be circumvented if one wishes to gain a good understanding of existence, time, and the cosmos.

Ferment or Finale—The Role of Eschatology in Theology

In the words of Catherine Keller, eschatology is a "clumsy nineteenth century term."[64] If this is true, then can it really be meaningful to make it the key concept for a relational understanding of time? A few comments on the concept of eschatology, though in no way exhaustive, thus appear necessary before we can proceed.[65]

As Sigurd Hjelde[66] has shown, there has never been a clear definition of eschatology. A certain ambiguity has accompanied it from its beginnings and "must . . . be recognized as the historically and principally given framework."[67] Traditionally, questions regarding the reign of God, death and res-urrection, God's judgment, and eternal life belong to eschatology. Nevertheless, the arrangement and formulation of topics have changed over the course of time. The history of the term *eschatology* is relatively short. Its predecessor was the expression *de novissimis*, which was first introduced into dogmatics by Johann Gerhard (1582–1637). Since about 1800, the term *eschatology* has appeared as a "slight Germanization of a Latin-Greek original."[68] Beginning around 1840, it has become an established concept.[69] To be sure, the topics belonging to eschatology, or to the "Last Things," also existed before the term was coined, and they probably had a stronger presence in popular piety than in established theology. At least the detailed treatment of these topics in classical hymns, which we observed in chapter 1, seems to confirm this possibility.[70] Thus, the modern concept of eschatology is based on the terminology of early Lutheran dogmatics, which, for its part, probably adopted the term *novissima* from the late medieval tradition of meditative-devotional piety.[71] In Catholic writing, the term *eschatology* did not become generally established until the twentieth century.[72] With regard to its contents, the development of eschatology was different in Catholicism than within Protestant and Eastern Orthodox theologies.[73]

The twentieth century experienced numerous eschatological awakenings. From a "short and perfectly harmless chapter entitled 'Eschatology'" added "at the conclusion of Christian Dogmatics,"[74] there emerged a crucial theological concept. Hans Urs von Balthasar spoke of eschatology as the "weather corner" [*Wetterwinkel*] in the theology of our time: "From it arise those thunderstorms which fruitfully threaten the entire land of theology: hail damage or refreshment."[75] Folke Holmström saw in eschatology a "motto" for a radical theological reorientation that contributed to the liberation of Christian theology from the "oppressive clutches" of the "worldview of the Enlightenment."[76] The last century witnessed a "continuous eschatological upswing"[77] or even an erupting "eschatological hectic," "following the long slumber of the nineteenth century."[78] In retrospect, the eschatological eruption may not appear as abrupt as it seemed several decades ago. Carl Heinz Ratschow suggests a greater continuity when he summarizes the systematic-theological development of eschatology with the words: "Subliminally, understood by only a few, that which almost inundates the twentieth century announces itself in the nineteenth century, namely, the recognition of the eschatological conditioning of the Christian faith as a whole."[79] We find an echo of the words of the early Barth—"If Christianity be not altogether thoroughgoing eschatology, there remains in it no relationship whatever with *Christ*"[80]—in Moltmann's *Theology of Hope*: "From first to last, and not merely in the epilogue, Christianity is eschatology, is hope, forward

looking and forward moving, and therefore also revolutionizing and transforming the present. The eschatological is not one element *of* Christianity,
but it is the medium of Christian faith as such . . ."[81]

Whether a cliché or not, the history of the degradation and elevation of
eschatology appears to be accurate at least in broad terms.[82] Eschatology
went from being an appendage of dogmatics to being a characteristic feature of theology. This development also radiated into areas that, at first
glance, have nothing to do with eschatology. Thus, for example, Dalferth
remarks that the rejection of theism and its antithesis, atheism, as once conceived by the philosophy of the Enlightenment, as well as the christological
orientation of current Trinitarian theology, are both by-products of the eschatological reorientation of theology in the twentieth century.[83] Given all
the diversity of twentieth-century eschatological approaches, the least common denominator in the concept may be that eschatology is not an appendix, but a central topic, of Christian theology. This reevaluation, however,
has also increased the ambiguity of the term *eschatology* to the point of linguistic confusion and a loss of distinct meaning.[84]

If eschatology is here claimed to be the core of a theology of time, then
this is, to some extent, in harmony with a development that marked the
twentieth century. At this point, however, a further distinction must be
made. Precisely because the eschatological reorientation is in no way uniform, the main directions of this development should be outlined briefly, so
that, against this background, the focus of this study can be shown more
clearly.

Eschatology can be understood as the doctrine of the *eschata*, the "Last
Things," that is, as the doctrine of the events at the end of time. The "Last
Things" would then be primarily understood as the great finale, as the
chronological "Last Things." However, another interpretation should also
not be rejected. The *eschata* are "Last Things" also in the sense of matters of
ultimate validity and decisive importance. At least on the individual level,
this results in an interaction between the *eschata* and the *realia* of the here
and now. On the one hand, according to traditional teaching, one's actual
lifestyle has consequences for the expected end, for judgment, and for the
anticipated resurrection. On the other hand, the prospect of these "Last
Things" leads to normative consequences for present-day life. Thus, a conception of time based on eschatology does indeed correspond to the findings of our examination of biblical understandings of time (see pp. 64–81).
In both cases, the primary concern is not a quantitative conception of time,
whose task it is to specify tempos and dates; rather, we find a concept of
time that cannot be separated from the contents of time. The concern is not
with time as such but, rather, with time *for* something.

The eschatological renaissance of the twentieth century was prepared and introduced by works of Johannes Weiß, Franz Overbeck, and Albert Schweitzer. These theologians were essentially concerned with showing the eschatological character of Jesus' teachings and, thus, its discrepancy to the situation of the waning nineteenth century. Barth took up the challenge inherent in this by attempting to place all of theology under an eschatological perspective. Paul Tillich also set an important course with his 1927 lecture entitled "Eschatology and History,"[85] in which he turned attention away from the *eschata* and toward the *eschaton*. His primary concern is no longer with the chronologically "Last Things," but rather with the Last in the sense of the ultimate and deepest meaning of everything. This eschatology receives a primarily existential interpretation. Tillich speaks of the *eschaton* as the "transcendent meaning of events."[86]

If such an understanding is primarily oriented toward the individual, then this is at the cost of the temporal and the cosmological aspects of eschatology. In this case, the interest in the transcendent meaning of an actual event forces into the background the question of the individual end, as well as the question about the end of heaven, earth, and the universe. Even more, it obscures the question of how the doctrines of the final judgment and the creation of a new heaven and a new earth can be consistent at all with the cosmological theories of an infinite expansion, a big crunch, or a cosmic heat death.

Following the turn away from the *eschata* to the *eschaton*, theological attention shifted from the *eschaton* to the *eschatos;* after the concentration on "Last Things" (chronological understanding) and the Last (existential understanding), the Last One (christological understanding) became the focus of reflections, i.e., Christology—and thus essentially all of Christian theology—took on a distinct eschatological character. This all-encompassing presence of eschatology calls for urgent attention, but, at the same time, it also makes it difficult to identify what eschatology actually is.[87] One gets the impression that discussion now is less about "eschatology" than about the characteristic of all theology as being (also) "eschatological." Thus the adjective also escapes a clear definition. Its significance appears to lie somewhere between a primarily existential conceptual definition—the eschatological is at any moment equally near and equally far—and an indication of temporality and finality.

Gerhard Sauter structures the variety of meanings of eschatology in three ways, namely, first, eschatology as the doctrine of the (temporally) "Last Things" in the shape of the final part of Christian dogmatics; second, as the articulation of conceptions of the future and expectations regarding the future; and, third, "no longer as the finale, but rather as the ferment of theology," as a radical eschatology.[88] The second form of eschatology readily takes the form of a theology of history, which declares what is seen as the will of God to be the desirable end goal of history. Sauter does not believe that eternity is thereby moved into time.[89] In looking back at chapter 1, however, we are reminded that in some modern hymns we find precisely this tendency to incorporate eternity into time; however, there, this occurred less from the point of view of universal history than from the perspective of individual experiences.[90] Using the example of the United States, both Sauter and Moltmann mention how a historical-theological eschatological interpretation of the reign of God as the final stage that is to be realized can shape a political mission in dramatic ways.[91] The third form of eschatology blocks the path to any millenaristic theology of history by emphasizing that God, as the one who is coming, cannot be derived from the world or from history. Eschatology thus conceived is linked to a special understanding of time as "an incomparably intense perception of the present," for "every moment in time also runs aground, so to speak, in eternity."[92] Here, time is not a continuum that will at some time be replaced by eternity or will merge into it; here, eternity is also not something absolutely different from time, but rather—in the words of Sauter—it "*befalls* us as that which limits us."[93]

In comparison to this, the first form, the eschatology of "Last Things," appears to separate time and eternity strictly from each other. It corresponds most closely to the model of the ontological distinction of time and eternity.[94] This type of eschatology can give hope and comfort, but it can also prevent one from acting by deferring to eternity. It can appear threatening or senseless, but it seldom leads to social or political activism. On the contrary, it may well encourage escapism. The second form presupposes a chronological understanding of time and goes hand in hand with the quantitative differentiation model of time and eternity.[95] It contains an appeal to realize, as far as possible, the reign of God through personal, social, or political efforts, which has brought much good to humanity even though the goal was never achieved. Cullmann's image of the ascending line applies extremely well to all sorts of more or less ambiguous programs for improving the ills of the world, regardless of whether it is Cultural Protestantism, an inner-worldly thousand-year empire, ecclesiastical chiliasm, political imperialism, or something else. The understanding of time in the third type of eschatology, in comparison, corresponds most closely to what I have called the eschatological difference of time and eternity.[96] It emphasizes the relatedness, and even interaction, of time and eternity. It proceeds from God's alterity and simultaneously presupposes contact between time and eternity. For this reason, it reckons with the breakthrough of eternity into time and that this breakthrough does something of significance with time. Precisely because of this interactive aspect, however, it is also subject to a certain lack of clarity and risks overextending the term *eschatology* to the point of total inexplicability.

A New Creation or a Hibernating Universe?
Eschatology and Science

Despite the much described eschatological revival during the twentieth century and its accompanying flood of books, articles, and essays, it appears that the relationship of eschatology and science has hardly been a topic of discussion until now. Bibliographies at the end of encyclopedia articles or in monographs allow us to conclude that, whenever eschatology has sought dialogue partners outside of its traditional field, it has generally turned to philosophy, occasionally to social ethics, and in some cases even to ecology, but hardly ever to the traditional natural sciences.[97] It seems curious how, in one book after another, theologians can speak rather objectively of the end or consummation of the world without ever seriously asking what the future of the universe is likely to look like from the scientific perspective.[98] The book edited by John Polkinghorne and Michael Welker entitled *The End of the World and the Ends of God—Science and Theology on Eschatology*[99] sparks the hope, however, that this will change in the future.

It is certainly true that eschatology "does not examine the general future possibilities of history,"[100] but it also cannot completely circumvent this topic. A strict division between the Christian future and the future of the world would make things far too simple for theology. An eschatology without cosmology becomes "a Gnostic myth of redemption,"[101] Moltmann says—and subsequently outlines a cosmic eschatology that then no longer takes seriously the issue of cosmology itself. For him, at some points, cosmos seems to be synonymous with nature as we encounter it on our planet. Even if the inclusion of nature and his attempt at "synchronization of historical time and natural time"[102] already represent a correction to one-sidedly anthropocentric approaches, Moltmann's eschatology remains nevertheless earth-centered. A clear terminological distinction among earth, world, cosmos, and universe is absent in Moltmann, though he is not alone in this regard. It appears to be taken for granted that the end of human history is the end of the world. This creates the impression that there is not the slightest possibility for the existence of extraterrestrial forms of life and civilization.

Eschatology and scientific questions show points of contact first and foremost in the area of cosmology. In this regard, it is not only modern cosmological theories that have significance for the understanding of theological eschatology. Much more fundamental is the fact that theology still does not pay enough attention to the paradigm shift from the closed cosmos of antiquity and the Middle Ages to the open universe of modern times.[103] From this development emerges a basic question addressed to eschatology. In the face of the immensity of the universe, is eschatology not simply an anthropological particularism that has grown immeasurably? From a cosmological perspective, much in eschatology appears to be an absurd exaggeration of the significance of this earth, which actually is "just a tiny part of an overwhelmingly hostile universe."[104] Both Steven Weinberg and Jacques Monod knew how to formulate this cosmological challenge in a suggestive manner: "The more the universe seems comprehensible, the more it also seems pointless,"[105] Weinberg says, and then continues: "The effort to understand the universe is one of the very few things that lifts human life a little above the level of farce, and gives it some of the grace of tragedy."[106] Monod's words are even more disillusioning. In his opinion, humans must finally awaken from their age-old dreams and recognize their complete desolation, their radical alienation; the ancient covenant is in pieces; we need to recognize that we are alone in the unfeeling immensity of the universe, out of which we emerged only by chance.[107] Even if these conclusions drawn from cosmological theories are highly debatable scientifically, they nevertheless help us to understand how unnatural, indeed, and even how presumptuous, the postulate of a valid eschatology can seem from the cosmological perspective.[108]

Is it possible at all to speak of something resembling a scientific eschatology? In fact, there are examples for eschatological models that have been developed by scientists on the basis of cosmological theories.[109] Yet one must add that these models are controversial among physicists, which does not exclude the fact that schemes of this type create a certain amount of public sensation and exercise some influence on human thinking. The reason for discussing the following schemes is therefore not their degree of scientific seriousness, but rather their claim to be able to replace theological eschatology with physics.

The physicist Frank J. Tipler has repeatedly discussed this topic and, through his book, *Physics of Immortality*, has become widely known to the general public. In this book he proclaimed his intention, which seemed suspect to many physicists and theologians alike, to establish theology as a branch of physics: "Either theology is pure nonsense, a subject with no content, or else theology must ultimately become a branch of physics."[110] Freeman J. Dyson thinks along the same lines. He would like to accelerate the arrival of the day when eschatology—defined by him as the study of the end of the universe—is not only a branch of theology, but also a respectable scientific discipline.[111] The quintessence of his theory of the end of the universe is that there is no end: Under the condition of validity of the presuppositions specified by Dyson, life and the communication of information can continue forever.[112]

Tipler claims that the probability of the existence of God, of human free will, and of eternal life after death can be proven by pure physics alone. The Omega Point Theory provides him with the proof that God exists. It says that in the present, in the past, and in the future—and here he really speaks of the distant future, for it is assumed that the universe, despite its existence of approximately fifteen billion years, is still in a very early stage of its history—there must be an omnipotent, omniscient, and omnipresent person who is immanent and changeable in space and time, as well as transcendent and unchangeable, and who will "have a 'pointlike' structure in the ultimate future."[113] The universe exists only when the omega point also exists in this universe, as the structure of the limiting condition that determines reality. Even if Tipler does not intend to equate the Omega Point Theory with Christianity, but rather to show that it harmonizes with the basic ideas of virtually all religions, he frequently refers to the theology of Pannenberg.[114] A Christology does not result directly from the omega point model, but it also does not contradict it; however, it "depends on some unlikely possibilities in quantum cosmology."[115] Eternal life is not based on the immortality of the soul; it is instead the result of a resurrection. The preservation of identity is not achieved by means of physical continuity, but instead by the most far-reaching correspondence in pattern. Resurrection is "an exact replica of ourselves . . . being simulated in the computer minds of the far future."[116] The next stage of intelligent life will be information-processing machines—the extinction of humankind is *a logically necessary consequence of eternal progress*"[117]—and, in the distant future, a computer capacity will be available that enables the perfect simulation (emulation) of all possible variants of the world and, thus, of the entire visible universe of all times.[118] The resurrection of the dead will occur "when the computer capability of the universe is so large that the amount of capacity required to store all possible human simulations is an insignificant fraction of the entire capacity."[119] Thus, the physics of immortality is not really concerned with "immortality" as such, but rather with the spontaneous reconstruction in the form of emulations—as if, "in the last moment," someone would build a super computer that images all human beings as a holograph program.

In contrast to Tipler, Dyson speaks neither of resurrection nor of eternal life. By using quantitative arguments, he wishes to demonstrate that life and intelligence can survive without limitations and that the communication of information is possible in spite of constantly increasing intergalactic distances. He is conscious of the fact that he mixes "science" and "science fiction" in his reflections, but he does not consider this particularly problematic, as long as the science is precise and the fiction is plausible.[120]

If consciousness is linked to the substance of molecules, then life will stop as soon as the necessary supply of free energy is consumed. If, on the other hand, as Dyson assumes, consciousness depends merely upon the structure of the molecules, then life can seek all kinds of practical embodiments, such as an interstellar black cloud or a sentient computer.[121] Dyson sees the most probable form of future life in just such a cloud-type collection of dust particles, which, as carriers of positive and negative charges, organize themselves and communicate among themselves by using electromagnetic forces. The greatest problem with this lies in the fact that, in this case, the waste heat generated by the metabolism of life cannot be radiated away into space quickly enough. Dyson's solution to this difficulty is hibernation: The metabolism occurs periodically, so that, during constant radiation of waste heat, active phases alternate with phases without metabolism.[122] In this way, an unlimited survival is possible with finite energy, and subjective time is infinite.[123] In principle, Dyson says, even in an ever-expanding universe, infinite communication of information at finite expenditures of energy is possible.[124] As he further states, in fact, the amount of energy that the sun radiates in eight hours is already sufficient to keep alive indefinitely a society with the degree of complexity that characterizes current human development. The energy supply of an entire galaxy would be able to supply a society with a 10^{24} greater degree of complexity.[125] Even if Dyson stresses that, despite the 137 equations he lists, he is unable to present an ultimate mathematical proof for these claims, he is optimistic and extremely satisfied with his results: "I have found a universe growing without limit in richness and complexity, a universe of life surviving forever and making itself known to its neighbors across unimaginable gulfs of space and time."[126] Thus, he says, science offers a solid foundation for a philosophy of hope.[127]

The evident thematic commonalities cannot hide the fact that theological and scientific eschatologies are considerably different in several respects. The task of theological eschatology is not limited to describing future conditions. From the very beginning, theological eschatology has not been merely descriptive; rather, it has also constantly had an appellative character that aimed to influence human conduct by offering an interpretation and orientation for life. In this way, it distinguishes itself from cosmological theories, which do not draw any moral conclusions from the description of different end-time or future scenarios.[128] The "Last Things" of cosmology are then last things primarily in the chronological sense; they are the finale, but hardly ferment. The last things of theology, by contrast, have an indisputable ambiguity of temporal and meaning-related finality; thus, they are more ferment than finale. The tension between the "already" and the "not-yet" that is constitutive for theological eschatology is lacking in scientific eschatology.

The difference in the respective subject matters of scientific eschatology and biblical eschatology is also striking. While in the one field the chief concern is with the human attempt—in the case of Tipler, with the help of an evolving God—to live eternally, in the other, one speaks primarily of God's initiative. That which is theologically conceived as an act of God with creation is, according to scientific understanding, a self-induced "hibernation." The former contains a cosmology,[129] and the latter aims to explore usable opportunities, thus making eschatology a question of technology.

Furthermore, there is an obvious difference in the eschatological objective. Biblical eschatology is concerned less with the end of the world than with the end of evil. It climaxes in a new society, in the New Jerusalem that comes down from heaven adorned as a bride (Rev. 21:2). Life as computer emulation or in a cosmic dust cloud, on the contrary, basically seems to have to manage without the perspective of the victory over evil and the realization of new social complexity. Scientific concepts culminate instead in an exhaustive accumulation of information. The goal of biblical eschatology is a city; the goal of scientific eschatology is a computer.

In both cases, the question of what it means to be a person really becomes a burning issue. Whereas biblical eschatology hardly problematizes the identity and quality of personal existence within and beyond life, scientific eschatology can assert that a living person and his or her computer simulation are one and the same.[130] This also leads to different understandings of resurrection. For Tipler, resurrection means the exact replica of ourselves, whereas, viewed theologically, as Colin Gunton remarks, "[t]he resurrection is not a doctrine of replication, but of transformation."[131] The conception of life that is still somehow "human," but that, as a computer simulation or a cosmic dust cloud no longer has anything to do with the human being as a biological species, seems paradoxical. Anthropocentrism would finally have been overcome—but what would then replace anthropology?

What remains unclear in both concepts is the relationship between universal and local eschatology. The limitations of the biblical worldview result in a competition between statements with universal claims and those that relate only to this world. Furthermore, the uncertainty of cosmological theories in relation to the end of this universe leaves open the question of whether survival by means of information accumulation is a local or a universal phenomenon. Just as uncertain is whether or not the different scenar-

ios are to be conceived as intrinsic to history. Disregarding the fact that the
proposals of Tipler and Dyson necessarily contain much speculation, from
the perspective of Christian eschatology, primarily three weaknesses are evident.[132] First, there are theological reductions that ultimately make the distinction between God and universe impossible.[133] Also, Christology is missing altogether. Second, there is an anthropological reduction caused by an
equating of life with information transmission or information production.
Humans are one-sidedly defined in light of their rationality: "In the end,
reason will sway emotion."[134] The future perspective of endless information
processing in cosmic dust clouds is not easily compatible with the eschatological question: "What may we hope?" Third, one can also speak of a temporal reduction, because the openness of the future is basically sacrificed to
a determinism. John Polkinghorne is rigorous in his criticism at this point.
He describes physical eschatology as a cosmic Tower of Babel and sees in it
the most extreme *reductio ad absurdum* of an exclusively evolutionary optimism.[135]

The accomplishment of scientific eschatologies of this type consists in
their illumination of the question of how survival or resurrection can be
possible if the end of the universe means maximum entropy and thermal
equilibrium, infinite expansion or a Big Crunch possibly followed by a new
Big Bang. The fact that they are able to conceive only of different types of
hibernation models, but not of models of divine re-creation, is intrinsic to
the undertaking itself. There cannot be any scientific justification for theological eschatology precisely because it would be a contradiction in itself to
treat aspects of eschatology, such as the resurrection of the dead and the
New Creation, which by definition are rooted in divine initiative, as if they
were a preprogrammed aspect of evolution. Not all language can be sub-
sumed within scientific or philosophical language, but obvious contradictions should also not remain undiscussed.

Past, Present, Future, and Advent—Modes of Time in Light of Theological Eschatology

The preconception of the unity of time has been philosophically so predominant that the difference in the three modes of time—past, present, and
future—can be considered "the unsolved and constantly suppressed problem in the conception of time within metaphysics."[136] In theology, the trinity of the time modes has understandably stimulated a connection to the
doctrine of the Trinity. On pp. 98–101, I showed how Dalferth relates the
Father as the timeless ground of everything, the Spirit as multi-temporal
companion of everyone, and the Son as temporal mediator of salvation to
one another. This addresses the three modes of time only indirectly. In his

book, *Negative Theologie der Zeit*, philosopher Michael Theunissen chooses a more direct path. He proceeds from the bold supposition that, when speaking of the trinity of faith, love, and hope, Paul was thinking of the divine Trinity. Theunissen then connects faith, as something that grows out of the experience of fidelity, with the Father. Hope, which looks into the future, belongs with the Son, as the one who is coming. Love, as the foundation, is contemporized through the Spirit. Thus, Theunissen arrives at the combinations of past/faith/Father, future/hope/Son, and present/love/Spirit. It is interesting that, in this way, because it belongs to love as the greatest of the three, the present takes a prominent position in Theunissen. He also views the present as the "place" in which eternity is most readily understandable.[137] A philosophical justification for the primacy of the present is provided by the thought that only the present exists, whereas the past no longer exists, and the future does not-yet exist. Nevertheless, the question then arises whether the present, as the infinitesimal point between past and future, exists at all. Theunissen's emphasis on the present is worth noting, because many contemporary theologians tend to favor the future.[138]

The question then arises, which mode of time should have priority, the present or the future? Georg Picht suggested a thoughtful solution by linking the three modalities of necessity, reality, and possibility to the three modes of time. When the past is linked to necessity, the future to possibility, and the present to reality, then the present must be understood as something other than a "nothing" between past and future. It is given a prominent position instead: "Past and future are related to (a possible) present; necessity and possibility, to (possible) reality."[139] It is therefore impossible to describe the present merely as a point on a line. It must instead be understood relationally, because "The present-ness *within a communication network* constitutes reality. Outside of the multidimensionality of the reference system in which reality appears to us, the word 'present' has no possible meaning."[140]

This understanding of the present is consistent with the concept of the light cone network. Time is both the relation of the many and the unity of the whole. It is "a multidimensional, open structure with mobile parameters" and, as such, "the universal horizon of the phenomenality of phenomena as such."[141] This temporal structure that is held together by the present as the mode of reality is transcended, however, by the possibility of that which can be true,[142] so that all human thought moves within the difference of two forms of one and the same time that are not reducible to each other.[143] Whenever the question of possibility is asked, we get in touch with the future. Even if the present as reference point is constitutive, an understanding of time that takes seriously the modality of possibility cannot, for this reason, be bent back onto an eternal present. One can conclude from this that an appropriate understanding of time has, so to speak, two centers—present and future—and therefore must always be interested in openness.

In his account of the background of eschatological thought in the twentieth century, Ratschow identifies "a deep restructuring in the understanding of time" as the main motif.[144] This restructuring, which already began during the Age of Enlightenment, went in the direction of an orientation toward the future and took shape in a belief in progress that was influential in virtually all areas of life: "Development becomes the key that fits all locks."[145] Wherever the enthusiasm for progress grew, tradition—and therefore even the past—lost its importance. The present also forfeited some of its significance by falling victim to the search for usable development opportunities for the future. This process was closely tied to the upswing in science and technology.

The elaboration of the primacy of the future is quite visible in Western philosophy during the twentieth century. Heidegger, Bloch, and Whitehead are only three of the philosophers who also strongly influenced the eschatological thinking of Pannenberg and Moltmann.[146]

Amidst all the enthusiasm about the future, an important distinction in the concept of the future should not be neglected. On the one hand, future can be understood as that which results from the past and the present—thus, as an extrapolation from that which exists, that is, a prediction that can be more or less reliable. This idea forms the basis for the belief in progress. If the future were not that which is set free from existing possibilities and which can also be optimized by skillful exploitation of precisely these possibilities, then the striving for progress and world improvement would be without meaning. On the other hand, future can be understood as that which comes towards me "from what is ahead." Time flows, then, as imagined by Augustine: from the future, through the unextended present, into the past.[147] An understanding of time defined in such a manner is particularly suitable for expressing the future's own trait of unpredictability. While purely deterministic thinking must hold to the first-mentioned understanding (that of becoming), a more fatalistically oriented feel for life can take refuge in the second understanding (that of coming), unless it wishes to understand the future as the advent of the faithful God, as Moltmann does.[148]

Since these two conceptions of the future point in precisely opposite directions, they seem at first to be irreconcilable. Which of the two variants is then the more appropriate? It looks as if the first concept of the future is favored strongly by a world marked by technology and feasibility: What comes is the result of more or less well-used, actual possibilities. At first glance, the recognition that this does not exhaust what future means recedes to the background. The saying "Man proposes, God disposes" seems to be reversed: "Man disposes, God proposes"—and what God proposes plays no role. Understanding "what is ahead" is then more a matter of futurology than of eschatology.[149] The more successful the structuring of the future is, the less interesting are the "Last Things"; the more tangible the heaven on earth, the more superfluous the new heaven. It often goes unnoticed that this tangible success has at least some of its roots precisely in that which it ultimately rejects, namely, in a life style and a world order that is oriented toward an eschatological goal.

This description is incomplete, however, as long as it refrains from asking how the problems related to the unforeseen and the far removed future are dealt with in the framework of futurology. The question arises: Where does an understanding of the future that is shaped by science and technology place the unpredictable if it excludes a future coming "from what is ahead"? This thought leads back to chaos theory as the attempt to accommodate the unforeseeable within the time that flows forward by turning the unforseeable into a question of greater complexity. In this, Augustine ultimately appears to be wrong about the direction of the flow of time from the future to the past; for what is fascinating about chaos theory in this respect is that it sees the unforeseeable coming not from the future, but essentially from the past. What happens in the process of self-organization is deterministic, but unforeseeable.[150] Thus, chaos theory seems to neutralize the view that it is possible to distinguish between two types of future: futurist becoming that emerges from the past, and adventist coming that approaches from the future. Where general experience sees causality resulting from freedom, the theory of self-organization points in the opposite direction: Freedom can be explained by causality. Again, it becomes clear how quickly a model of linear time that is preoccupied with the directions of the flow of time reaches its limits. From the perspective of chaos research, the distinction between a future dependent upon the past and a future reliant upon what is ahead proves to be a questionable construction. For understanding the unforeseen, the direction of time need not be reversed. The "new," that which results from a weak causality or the indeterminate—here the terms overlap[151]—need not come from a direction other than that which is predictable or that which is determined by strong causality.

The distinction between futurist and adventist future becomes obsolete if it cannot be liberated from its ties to spatial-directional thinking. A theological distinction between future and advent that is content to let the future proceed in direct causality, more or less determined, from the past, but expecting the advent, determined solely by divine causality, to come from

the future, cannot be reconciled with the insights of modern science. Such a
model tends to restrict the concept of future. The future then appears as a
reservoir of possibilities that are successively exhausted, something which
ultimately must lead to a reduction of evolutionary possibilities and complexity, unless God is viewed as the force that continually refills this reservoir with new possibilities. This understanding of God, however, would approximate a "god of the gaps" concept and lead to more problems than
solutions. Here, scientific theories suggest a different understanding: Future
does not mean a reduction of possibilities, but, instead, an increase in possibilities and complexity. The dead end of linear conceptions of time can be
avoided only by thinking of time in terms of openness toward the future.
The possible conclusion, on which science and theology can agree, is in this
case: "Time is, in a privileged sense, future."[152]

The theological distinction between futurist and adventist future is
therefore pointless if it is tied to a one-sidedly linear understanding of time.
The difference between advent and future cannot be qualified by using different directions of time. Within the framework of a relational understanding of time, however, this differentiation remains relevant. Here, dependence upon the past and dependence upon the future, or determinism and
indeterminism, are no longer contrasted in order to correlate future and determinism, on the one hand, and advent and indeterminism, on the other.
Development that is dependent upon the past is not identical to deterministic development, and events that are dependent upon the future are not
identical to indeterministic events. Indeterminism belongs to the whole of
development. It does not compete with "normal" regularities; it occurs
within the framework of the given. The adventist future no longer has to be
conceived of as a competing indeterminism; it can just as well represent an
emerging indeterminism.[153]

A relational understanding of time accentuates the adventist future as
the mode of eschatological time, since, more than the futurist future, the
adventist future guarantees the openness of the two time centers—present
and future; and it presupposes plurality and interaction. Departing from
here, attention is drawn to the category of the new, which breaks through
and makes old that which exists.

See, everything has become new![154]—
The Category of the New

It was shown (see pp. 93–97) that the central idea of the eschatological
difference between time and eternity lies in the category of the "new." It is
only the "new" that makes the "old" old. The category of the "new" is
linked to the privileged position of the future and to the differentiation

within the concept of the future. Essentially, the "new" is a relational concept. Even if the "new" that breaks through is something radically different from that which becomes old due to this breakthrough, it is nevertheless unrecognizable as something new unless it is related to the "old."

Before I discuss the theological significance of the category of the "new," I would like to remind the reader that the concept "new" in human consciousness is indubitably filled with affective values. The values attached to the new tend to be quite ambivalent. A simple example: On the one hand, we are easily attracted by the new; who would reject the most recent computer model as a gift? On the other hand, we also surround the old with an aura of luxury, especially when it finds its way into the display window of an antique shop. When the main concern is the utility value of an object, we prefer the new. If the primary concern is aesthetic value, then the old is frequently preferred. If the category of relevance is added, then this results in combinations that can have significant consequences. When useful, new, and relevant—as counterparts to old, aesthetic, and irrelevant—form a coalition, there are consequences for the future. The future then risks being understood unilaterally as the future in the futurist sense. Its adventist character is suppressed. If theology is relegated to the sphere of aesthetics, of the old and the irrelevant, and becomes something that is dragged along from the past, then it loses its eschatological character, namely, the dimension that addresses the "new" as advent.

Restricting the concept of the new to an extrapolatively understood future robs the new of half of its nature, namely, the dimension of surprise. A new that does not at least bear the possibility of surprise is not new. Surprise thus makes clear the limits of a future understood only in an extrapolative manner. Without surprise, the future is nothing other than an extended past. It then dissolves in a confirmation of existing conditions, for better or for worse. What it lacks is the dynamics brought about by the surprisingly new. Another power must therefore be added to extrapolation, namely, what we may call "intropolation," that is, the readiness to accept the surprisingly new.[155] Here, the "new" is also a judgment of the "old." It belongs to the characteristics of Christian theology, especially to eschatology, that coming is placed before becoming, thereby profoundly provoking the (extrapolative) future by means of the (intropolative) advent. It is "the eternal newness, according to which the eternal God is always his own future,"[156] that makes this possible. This, again, is linked to the fact that God should be understood as love: "God and love never grow old. Their being is and remains one that is coming."[157]

How then are "new" and "old" held together? What does the continuity between the "old" and the "new" look like in eschatology? Moltmann speaks, on the one hand, of an analogy between things past and things to come, whereby the "new" is always more than the "old."[158] I understand this in the sense that nothing remains of the old, but the structure stays intact so that recognition is possible. On the other hand, he also says that nothing dies; instead, everything is brought back in another form,[159] which means that, in this case, the old material is reutilized and possibly fashioned into a completely new structure. Moltmann does not really explain the difference between these two possibilities of understanding old and new. Nevertheless, the difference is significant, as a simple example shows. If I say that I have got myself a new dress, then the primary association is probably that this new thing does not contain any material from my old dress. In this case, the continuity consists in the fact that one is dealing with something that can be identified as a dress. It lies thus in the analogy of the dress. The new dress is not, in this sense, an extrapolation of the "old"; instead, its newness can be understood as more adventist than futurist. It could be, though, that I am very skillful with a needle and thread and that I completely transform the old dress. I could make it shorter or longer, replace the worn collar, dye it, and trim it with piping in the latest color. Does the renovated object thereby become a new dress or only a dress that is like new? Because I have proceeded here according to the motto "make do and mend" [aus alt mach neu] and have thus extrapolated, as far as material and structure are concerned, it is more nearly a futurist than an adventist dress. I could take all of the seams out of the old dress, however, and possibly make a pair of trousers out of the material. Then I would have brought back the old material in a new form. But would it be a new dress? The new structure of the trousers hardly allows one to recognize the structure of the old dress.

Because Moltmann is so concerned with the physicality of the New Creation, he comes into conflict with his own preference of the adventist "new." For how new is the New Creation really, if it is essentially a renovation of the "old?"[160] It would then more likely be the future of the existing creation, but not its advent. If one wishes to imagine the adventist "new," then it would be reasonable to seek the continuity less in the material itself than in the structure. This viewpoint is consistent with the biblical findings, and it also does not contradict a cosmology that must contend with the instability of matter. The new Jerusalem, which is already present with God, relativizes the "old." This relativizing, however, can be imagined as a relationing, so that "the old cosmos [is] rendered historical by the new cosmos and vice versa,"[161] Future and advent belong together, without being reduced to each other. This issue leads us further into the problems of destruction and transformation.

Everything old has passed away[162]—On the Understanding of Annihilation and Transformation

The relationship between the old creation and the new heaven and new earth is traditionally described in two conceptual models. The differences between these models are expressed most clearly with the terms *annihilation* [*annihilatio*] and *transformation* [*transformatio*].[163] The annihilation tradition was expressed most succinctly in Lutheran orthodoxy, while the transformation tradition is part of the Catholic, the Reformed, and—as the doctrine of the deification of the world—the Eastern Orthodox traditions. The idea of annihilation stresses that everything is dependent upon God's action. It accentuates the difference between creation and Creator, and thus also the discontinuity between the old and the new creation. The conception of transformation, on the other hand, emphasizes precisely the continuity between old and new creation and the nearness or indwelling of God in creation. The first conceptual model elucidates the radicality of the "new." In it, the new creation is advent and only advent. The second model accentuates the link between old and new. It somehow tries to bring future and advent together. In the first case, both the form and matter of the old creation is destroyed; in the second case, by means of a change in form, matter instead appears to be consummated and glorified, which could make it easier to avoid a worldless and bodiless anthropocentrism.[164]

Until now, continuity and discontinuity appear to be irreconcilable opposites. However, the application of the three differentiating models developed in chapter 2 leads us further in this case as well. An ontological distinction between continuity and discontinuity results in the following: In light of the human horizon, human beings are dependent upon the thought of continuity. Because, for human beings, identity is tied to continuity, people seek continuity even into the *eschaton*. This leads, on the one hand, to an eschatology that is basically oriented toward the individual; and, on the other hand, it restricts the sovereignty of God, because continuity on the human side "forces" God, so to speak, to orient divine judgment exclusively toward human behavior. In the ontological model of differentiation, this continuity on the human side then stands in contrast to the discontinuity on the side of God. This, in turn, guarantees God complete freedom. God is the wholly Other; but, for human beings, God risks becoming the absolute Other to whom no relation is possible. The quantitative model of differentiation, on the contrary, largely ignores discontinuity. It builds instead upon continuity. By means of extrapolation, time is lengthened into infinite future. The reign of God grows out of history. Finally, the eschatological model of differentiation concentrates on the dynamic relation of continuity and discontinuity. Discontinuity is expressed in the attempt to take alterity seriously. Before the reign of God is given expressive forms that can be received by human beings, it is initially always that which breaks through, that which breaks off, and that which breaks in. Continuity is expressed in the persistent attempt to conceive of the discontinuous at least in terms of a solid confirmation that—even in the face of the most extreme discontinuity (death)—a relation of human/world/God is possible.[165]

Here, however, we have reached the limits of what can be clearly stated. Knowing about the radicality of discontinuity, we are unable to speak of discontinuity without images of continuity. The two stand next to each other, yet they are impossible to harmonize. Hymns seem to have the capacity of expressing this. For example, Paul Gerhardt finds beautiful images for both aspects. In the following text, he speaks clearly of the discontinuity in the *annihilatio mundi:*

> The human being,
> what has it been?
> In one hour
> it is destroyed, as soon as
> the tiny breath of death blows into it.
> Everything must collapse and fall,
> heaven and earth must become,
> what they were before their creation[166]

In another hymn, he talks eloquently about the opposite. In the face of the summer splendor of nature and the flower garden, he presupposes heavenly continuity:

> The mother hen parades her little chicks,
> the stork builds and inhabits his house . . .
> The indefatigable swarm of bees flies hither and yon, . . .
> The wheat grows vigorously;
> both young and old rejoice in this . . .
> Oh, I think, how beautiful you are
> and you give us so much pleasure here . . .
> What great pleasure, what bright light
> will well be in the Garden of Christ![167]

What the poetry of the hymns exemplifies also applies to rational discourse: The two concepts of continuity and discontinuity should not be locked away in a closed system.[168] The unresolved tension between them provides eschatological movement and openness.

. . . what we will be[169]—The Question of the "Preserved Identity"

In chapter 2, I objected to the notion of the immortality of the soul. Although I oppose such generalizing labeling, this means that my position should be classified with what is generally called the "total death theory." In the background of my theory of death as "neither less nor more than death" was the thought that the radicality of the Christ event prohibits an escape through the back door.[170] Resurrection presupposes death; life beyond death cannot be achieved by avoiding death. It also appears to be rationally and scientifically difficult to substantiate the notion of a soul that flies away from the body at the moment of death.

Nevertheless, a notion that does not consider the immortality of the soul is also fraught with difficulties. The main problem that remained unsolved (see pp. 115–16) is the problem of "preserved identity": If death is understood as radical discontinuity and a complete end, how can continuity and a new beginning still be conceived? How can one then speak of identity and individuality? Precisely this problem is therefore also addressed by critics of the total-death concept.[171] There are basically two possible alternatives: First, it would be conceivable that God simply recreates the identities of the dead; or, one could imagine that identity is preserved by living on in the memory of God. While the first possibility is linked to the intricate question of why God would be forced to choose the path of the identical second creation, the second alternative appears to be able to find greater spontaneous acceptance in the computer age. If the "memory" of an electronic computer is already able to store an unimaginable amount of the most diverse data and visually reproduce them upon command, why then should the memory of God be unable to store the identities of countless human beings and embody them again physically in some form?

Theodor Mahlmann, who argues for the immortality of the soul, rejects both the theory of God's memory and the theory of the new creation. He finds the solution of living on in the memory of God unsatisfactory primarily because it is a survival in the memory of an Other.[172] I will return to this argument shortly. First, however, we must ask: What can be said from the perspective of a theology of time with regard to the question of preserved identity?

First, the anthropological perspective is inescapably tied to our temporal existence. *From the human perspective*, we are unable to see death as anything other than the end, which no part of a person can circumvent. Second, over the course of this study, it has repeatedly been shown that a chronological-linear understanding represents at best a partial understanding of what time is. This means that it would be a bottleneck that, from the very outset, would necessarily lead to false results if one wanted to base theological reflections about death and resurrection on a purely chronological-linear understanding of time. That the idea of a preserved identity cannot simply and exclusively be tied to the continuity of time is, according to this view, an important insight. Precisely this happens in the notion of the immortality of the soul, however. Circumscribing death with the words "to step out of time" [att gå ur tiden], which is customary in Swedish, proves to be an appropriate reference to discontinuity. From the human perspective of our dependence upon time, death must be described as non-relationality,[173] as well as complete deprivation, and thus also as deprivation of the self. The person who has died is deprived of her self. What she will be, she cannot make; she can only receive it. And, thus, as my third point, I return to Mahlmann's feeling of unease about the possibility of preserving identity in the memory of *an Other* (in this case, in the memory of God). In contrast to Mahlmann, I see the great advantage of this model precisely in this relationship to an Other, since, here, one finally takes relationality and alterity seriously. Mahlmann, on the other hand, makes the possibility of eternal life dependent "upon a human existence—independent of another person's knowledge, but self-known—that continues beyond the person's death,"[174] an existence that is also continuously bound to a timeline. Due to its fixation on self-known existence, this eschatological model remains anthropocentrically restricted from the very outset and thus leaves little room for cosmic dimensions.

In contrast, I would propose to understand eschatology as a hope that is precisely not hope in oneself. The preserved identity does not lie in a static conservation of one's own sameness along an infinite timeline, but is rather found in relation to the Other—or, to use Ricoeur's terminology again, when the immortality of the soul is made the precondition for eternal life, it seems to me that preserved identity is understood in the sense of *mêmeté*, of Idem-Identity, while the understanding that I am proposing goes more in the direction of *ipséité*, selfhood or Ipse-Identity.[175] I do not see this selfhood as being constituted primarily through self-conservation, but rather through self-reception, that is, through receiving one's self. Only in this way is it completely possible to come to oneself and to find oneself; and, indeed, eternal life then presumably has to do with finding more than one's self. Identity thus becomes a question of relation. If death and eternal life are described as that through which one's life or self finds itself eternally,[176] then the basic assertion that God is love is violated, for love is inconceivable without alterity, without a dynamic giving and receiving. Without surrender and letting go of oneself, selfhood is impossible. Thus, the key to preserved identity does not lie in the self-knowledge of human existence as an infinite finding-of-oneself; rather, it is found in the relation, in the receiving of oneself from an Other.[177] This must then always imply a coming-to-the-Other and a coming-together. What Theunissen claims to be the relationship of self and faith also applies to the eschatological self: It would be a "*communicative* genesis of selfhood."[178]

In this context, I would like to question the self-evidence with which individual self-preservation is so frequently declared as the highest good. Does the concentration on the identity of the self in the form of an autonomous individualism not more closely reflect a particular, Western tradition than it does global reality? Does it not say more about the power of the Enlightenment than about the totality of the biblical evidence? This is not to be a plea for the opposite and an assertion of the dissolution of identity. My concern is rather with changing the rank order: The consummation of an ego is not the preeminent goal, but, rather, the healing of relations. This change in order has consequences for the shaping of theology, life, and the world. An example used by Keller may illustrate this. She talks about mothers in El Salvador whose foremost wish is not the resurrection of their murdered children but the realization of those qualities and opportunities of life for which their sons and daughters had fought: healed relationships rather than perpetuation of individual life.[179]

I believe that the basic error in a position such as Mahlmann's lies in an inadequate theology of time. Because Mahlmann assumes—evidently without reflecting upon it—a constant timeline, and understands eternity as infinite time,[180] he ends up with "bad infinity," with an endlessly extended sequence of ages. Due to this understanding of time, the difference between identity and continuity escapes him, at least partially. His problem is not in fact that of preserved identity, but, rather, of preserved continuity. These two, however, coincide only when a linear model of time is presupposed. In a relational model of time, the question of continuity recedes, giving way to the question of identity constituted by relation, which, in turn, is coupled with the question of what a person actually is.[181]

The "Already" and the "Not-Yet": Eschatological Disruption of Linear Chronology

In chapter 2 (see pp. 64–81), it became clear that the tension between the "already" and the "not-yet" is constitutive for the New Testament understanding of time. The reign of God has already dawned, but it has not yet been realized. According to Paul, a person who has been baptized has already been dead and buried with Christ, so that he or she can live a new life; however, according to 1 John, what we will be has not yet been revealed.[182]

But how can something not yet exist and yet already exist? Is this not a paradox that one simply has to accept, unless, for the sake of intellectual honesty, one merely rejects it altogether?

One way out would be to declare that this dilemma is only an apparent contradiction. Ratschow chooses this solution when he presents the view that the paradoxical relation of the "already" and the "not-yet" has in fact nothing to do with temporal categories. In his opinion, the issue instead concerns the relationship of hiddenness and clarity.[183] Ratschow thus attempts to circumvent aspects of time by making eschatology a question of hiddenness and unveiled emergence. This combination is distinguished from the concepts of promise and fulfillment inasmuch as that which is promised actually already exists. The End Time has dawned, but is hidden. The obvious strength of this approach consists in detemporalizing the problems by elevating them beyond a merely linear understanding of time without thus succumbing to an existential reduction, that is, an exclusive focus on the moment of individual existence. Furthermore, this also takes into account the insight that time cannot simply be abstracted, but instead has to be seen as "time for something." The weakness of this approach, however, is its fading out of history and history's significance. The hidden God, whose unveiled emergence must be awaited, seems to be a God who has largely been removed from history. It is also difficult to see how an "already" and a "not-yet" understood in this way can become relevant for shaping the world. If everything already exists and simply awaits its unveiling, then what could I still contribute, except perhaps the longing for my own death? With regard to a theology of time, Ratschow does not quite live up to the standards that he himself previously set.[184]

Moltmann's eschatological concept in *The Coming of God* offers an alternative to this "unhistoricalness" in Ratschow. Without getting entangled in either individual eschatology or universal-historical eschatology, Moltmann sees in the coming God a possibility for conceiving both, i.e., of not having to sacrifice either earth for heaven or heaven for earth.[185] History does not become universal history; instead, it becomes a place of struggle and of messianic hope. For this reason, he also cannot—as Ratschow does—dismiss chiliasm as an idea that misses the basic concept of Christian eschatological thought.[186] Properly understood, chiliasm does both: It conceives of and anticipates crises of an apocalyptic nature, and it calls for responsibility for the world. Moltmann therefore also rejects the notion of a "final Big Bang" and speaks instead of a chiliastic eschatology of transition. This model has strengths in that it mercilessly criticizes various types of millenarianism by claiming responsibility for the world, precisely in the face of the *eschaton*, and by overcoming individualistic salvation by means of social physicality.[187]

Eschatological existence can be structured as a comprehensive exercise in multi-perspective vision. Conceived individually, the breakthrough of the *eschaton* means a reorganization of one's lifetime. Justification can be understood as the breakthrough of the "already" into the present circumstances of life. The process that is referred to as sanctification then corresponds to the "not-yet." Thus, the *kairos* of the breakthrough stands in relation to the *chronos* of continual development. The point at which the "already" and the "not-yet" touch each other appears to be characterized by an indeterminacy that is similar to quantum physics. A fixation of the "already" means inexactness with respect to the "not-yet," and a concentration on the "not-yet" obscures the view of the "already." The multi-temporality of the Spirit that was addressed by Dalferth is useful here as the factor that integrates the proper times into a common history. This multi-temporality would then correspond to what the theories of relativity accomplish in physics: Determination and comparison of the motion-dependent proper times, and the combining of time, space, matter, and energy via gravitation.

In addition to this, one should consider whether the Spirit can also be assigned an anti-entropic function. The Spirit could be understood as a force that counteracts the relentless increase in entropy.[188] The role of faith in the tension between the "already" and the "not-yet" could be further examined with ideas from chaos research. In a combination of determinacy and unforeseeability, a higher level of complexity is reached by a self-organizing "build-up." The emergence of faith can be understood similarly as the interaction and cooperation of that which is given and that which realizes itself: a self-organizing "build-up" to a higher level of complexity. This model permits an understanding of how faith can be described both as a gift and as one's own "accomplishment." It also explains why faith refers to two different things: the unique event of coming to faith—the "already" of faith, and the unending need for further growth—the "not-yet" of faith. The opposition of realized and future-oriented eschatology therefore turns out to be only apparent.

The role of the "already" and the "not-yet" can thus build bridges between the given and the unforeseen, between pure determinism and unforeseeable development, between freedom and causality. In this way, path and goal are held together—something that scientific eschatology is unable to accomplish. The dynamic nature of the "already" and the "not-yet" also holds together ethics and expectation, struggle and hope. This dynamic relation is the quintessence of Christian eschatology. It can be reconciled with findings from the field of natural science, but it cannot be derived from them.

In this regard, the absence of a fixed time–eternity relation in more recent hymns, which we observed in the first chapter, is certainly desirable from a theological standpoint. It can be interpreted as an eschatological interruption of linear chronology by means of which new ways of conceiving relationality are opened up.

The Possibility and Urgency of a Theology of Time

In this final section, I would like to consider the possibility of a theology of time by summarizing the findings of this study. Since reflections on a theology of time fittingly take a central place in Moltmann's book entitled *The Coming of God,* and since Moltmann also signals a certain alertness with respect to scientific theories, I believe that this book can enrich basic considerations of the possibility of a theology of time. The following critical appreciation of Moltmann's theology of time presumes familiarity with the theories of physics that were presented in chapter 3.

Finally, I will emphasize the urgency for a relational understanding of time by using some biblical-theological examples. Such an understanding of time invites one to reflect further, in directions that lead beyond the dialogue between theology and science.

Is a Theology of Time Possible?

After all of our considerations, the question of whether a theology of time is even possible is still justified. Already in chapter 1, it became clear that neither time nor eternity is a unified concept. They are related to each other in a variety of ways and linked to metaphorical meanings. The second chapter confirmed this impression. In the examination of "Time in the Bible" (pp. 64–81), it became apparent that, for a successful study, we would have to define what cannot be defined clearly on the basis of biblical material alone. The chapter on science was able to contribute important insights, for example, on the relativity of time, but it could not offer clear ideas that need "only" be applied in theology. How should a conclusive theology of time be constructed on the basis of such an ambiguous starting point?

By using Moltmann's eschatology, I will show the basic problems with which a theology of time must struggle. To this end, I will analyze the content of a theology of time as it is found in *The Coming of God.* I am not primarily concerned with specific problems in Moltmann's approach. Rather, from the inconsistencies of his concept, I conclude that a sound theology of time is not possible as a closed thought structure, but only as an open one.

According to Moltmann, time starts with the beginning of creation, namely, in the form of future, from which the present originates.[189] As in

Augustine, time is therefore oriented from the future toward the past. It is characterized as irreversible. This time arrow can evidently be distinguished in its direction from the time arrow that belongs to thermodynamics (see pp. 166–68), which is oriented from the past toward the future. Although Moltmann refers to the Second Law of Thermodynamics, he does not make this difference a topic of discussion.[190] His reception of scientific concepts seems somewhat strange when he says: "Reversible time is a kind of timeless time, for this form of time is itself timeless, like Newton's absolute time."[191] As shown in chapter 3, reversible time is not "timeless" at all; reversibility of time does not mean that $t = 0$, but rather that $+t$ and $-t$ yield the same result. Furthermore, the meaning of the relation of space and time (see pp. 140–49) to each other does not appear to be taken seriously when Moltmann asserts that creation begins in time and will be consummated in space.[192] Whereas the space of creation is simultaneously outside and inside God,[193] time remains without a direct relation to God. A type of eternity does, in fact, stand in relation to time, but time does not of itself have a relation to eternity; temporality reflects instead the absence of God.[194] The "source" of time is not eternity; instead, the future—understood as advent, not as future[195]—is the transcendental possibility of time per se and the unity of time.[196]

In contrast, in another passage, Moltmann says that, at the moment of origin, time emerged from eternity.[197] Temporal creation is an open system (cf. pp. 166–72). The "essence" of its time is future, but the "constituting category" of this time is the present. Precisely where the difference between the essence and source of time and its constitutive category lies remains incomprehensible. Thus, the primacy of the future and the primacy of the present seem to compete with each other. Moltmann needs the primacy of the future for establishing the eschatological "time arrow" and the primacy of the present for anchoring eternity in existence. Because future and past are categories of nonexistence—the future is not yet and the past is no longer—only the present remains as the category of existence and of eternity in time. The "now" of the present "is 'the event of eternity in Being.'"[198] Moltmann can also say of the *Sabbath*, however, that it is "the dynamic presence of eternity in time"[199] and that, in the sabbatical rhythm, time is regenerated out of the presence of eternity. In the rhythm of the Sabbath, "interruptions of 'time's flow,' earthly creation—human beings, animals and the earth—vibrate in the cosmic liturgy of eternity."[200] How this is compatible with temporality as the reflection of God's absence remains a mystery. Then again, Moltmann emphasizes that the unity of eternity and time does not lie in an eternal present, but instead in the creative Word of God,[201] which, in turn, is not necessarily consistent with the statement that the simultaneity of the (remembered) past and the (anticipated) future is contemporized eternity or the image of eternity.[202]

Eternity is not timelessness, but rather the fullness of time.[203] Moltmann gives the impression that eternity consists of several different eternities; namely, the absolute eternity of God, which is to be understood as universal simultaneity, and at least three relative eternities: the relative eternity of the new creation,[204] the relative eternity of the simultaneity of past and future in the present, and the relative eternity in creative acts effected by human remembering and anticipating.[205] At least in its first form, relative eternity participates in the absolute eternity of God.[206] The relative eternity of the new creation also means "the aeonic time, the time filled with eternity, the eternal time."[207] According to Moltmann, it corresponds to the eternity of God in that it is reversible, symmetrical, infinite, and, in that respect, timeless.[208] This correspondence, however, is actually a contradiction, because eternity has just been described not as timelessness, but as the fullness of time. In fact, relative eternity/eonic time appears to be an unfortunate and homeless hybrid: On the one hand, it is a part of absolute eternity; but, on the other hand, it is one side of the two-part structure of time (infinite cycle of time and transitory time arrow).

For Moltmann, the eschatological moment is simultaneously the final moment; in it, time is transformed into eternity.[209] This happens via the eschatological self-unlimiting of God. Then, there is neither death nor time—which, strangely enough, does not signify the end of time, however, since the eternity that then breaks through is presented as relative eternity. As eonic time presented as the cycle of time, as reversible time, it is the image of God's eternity: "In the aeonic cycles of time, creaturely life unremittingly regenerates itself from the omnipresent source of life, from God." [210] Does this mean that eternity is in fact only infinite time? What is the precise difference between absolute eternity and relative eternity? There is no clear answer. Instead, according to Moltmann, the irreversible time of history is fulfilled "in the cyclical movements of life's eternal joy."[211] Due to the indwelling of God in this new, eternal creation, "a mutual perichoresis between eternity and time also comes into existence."[212]

It is remarkable that reversible time appears to be superior to irreversible time. In the realm of nature, it is just the opposite. The inability of physical equations to express irreversible time has certainly been considered a defect (see pp. 166–72). For Moltmann, on the other hand, the reversion of irreversible time is an expression of universal salvation, the restoration of all things, which also includes the return of all times. All times are therefore brought back together with all things, so that they can be transformed and transfigured. "The unfurled times of history will be rolled up like a scroll, as

Revelation 5 intimates."[213] Apart from the fact that in Rev. 5 the issue is the opening of the scroll sealed with seven seals, it seems that Moltmann is in fact less concerned with the reversion—the rewinding—than with a revisioning—an examination from very precise points of view—or, as he says elsewhere, with the new creation of all things.[214]

Despite its unquestionable merits, Moltmann's eschatological work disappoints the reader precisely in the area where the interest of this study lies, namely, in the formulation of a theology of time that also deals constructively with scientific concepts. Moltmann certainly gives the impression of having considered physical theories, but he uses them guided by spontaneous association rather than by hermeneutical insights. His explanations of time and eternity remain difficult to comprehend because they are fraught with contradictions and a lack of clarity; many good ingredients form a mixture that is difficult to digest. It may be that, if there had been more thorough kneading, a smoother composition would have emerged. As it is, individual ingredients can be easily identified: Theunissen's *Negative Theologie der Zeit* and Picht's *Zeit und die Modalitäten*, the Thomistic notion of *aevum*, the Jewish Sabbath tradition and the teaching of *zimzum*,[215] Greek philosophy, some process philosophy, and Orthodox theology. To use another metaphor: Here, many valuable pearls are gleaming, but they do not become a necklace. Is this an indication that a theology of time in the form of a beautiful pearl necklace is, in fact, an impossibility?

An explanation for the weakness in Moltmann's theology of time (and for the difficulties of any theology of time) is provided in a reversion to Sauter's eschatological typology.[216] Sauter divided the eschatological approaches into three major groups according to their respective emphases, namely, the "Last Things," universal history, and the coming God. I have shown that this division corresponds quite well to the division into the ontological, the quantitative, and the eschatological differences of time and eternity. In my opinion, however, Moltmann's thought does not fit within any one of these categories; instead, he moves in and among several of them simultaneously. On the one hand, he moves the end, the cosmic *shekina* of God, the restoration, the new earth and the new heaven into the focus of his eschatology. On the other hand, he deals with history—yet not as a universal history—within the framework of a theology of struggle and of messianic hope. Previously I emphasized this as one of the strengths of Moltmann's eschatology. At this point it nevertheless becomes clear that it is precisely this strength that makes his theology of time so problematic. Namely, it appears to force him to mix the conceptual worlds of ontological, quantitative, and eschatological accounts of time and eternity, which leads to the lack of clarity that has been described. If one strives for the greatest conceptual clarity possible, then it is reasonable to select one of the three models. During the course of this study, it has become evident that many arguments spoke in favor of the eschatological model. First, this model impressed us with its power to overcome the dualism of time and eternity. Second, it implied the possibility of speaking reasonably of the temporal openness of God. Thus, the nearness of the reign of God and the fullness of time could be conceived of as a unity with simultaneous differentiation, which ultimately would contribute to the comprehensibility of the "already" and the "not-yet." Third, it corresponded in a most promising way to the scientific theories that speak of dynamic development and complexity. Without thereby making theology dependent upon scientific theories or "exploiting" physical theories theologically, a hermeneutics that rests on the self-evidence of the discussion and the desire for contact leads here to an enhanced understanding.

More than once, it has become clear that the attempt to express dynamism and to describe the transcendent God as the coming God (and the God who has already come) breaks through the framework of traditionally objectifying conceptuality and seeks other forms of expression. Already Moltmann's *God in Creation* concludes with the metaphor of dance. This metaphor reappears in *The Coming of God*.[217]

Metaphors go beyond rational thought in their appeal to intuitive understanding, but they always remain subject to the critique of lacking conceptual clarity. What Moltmann does is narrate eschatological history. For this reason, a criticism of his work that applies only the method of logical conceptual analysis to this narration is not adequate.[218] Ricoeur's theory seems once again confirmed: Time must be narrated. It cannot be confined within a simple, unambiguous concept.

If it is possible to draw a conclusion from this, then it is as follows: Because time cannot be abstracted, but occurs instead as lived time, it cannot be captured theologically in a fixed system. It can be talked about only under the auspices of dynamism and relationality.

The Relation to the "Other" as the *conditio sine qua non* of a Theology of Time

Beginning with the first chapter of this study, it has become increasingly clear that an abstraction of time is not possible. There is no such thing as one single generally valid concept of time. One can view time as a convention or a construction and consider it an aid for structuring and organizing life, but one can come close to it only as lived time and narrated time. From the anthropological perspective, time is "life-time" and, just so, the medium of relationships: relationships to living things and nonliving things, to one's self, and to God.

A chronological-linear concept of time alone does not do justice to these facts. Visualized through the image of the infinite straight line, it cannot even render comprehensible the irreversibility of time that is firmly anchored in experience. Time is more than can be expressed in a geometrical figure, regardless of whether the figure is a straight line, a circle, or even a spiral. Theological reflection has repeatedly shown that an open understanding of time marked by the "already" and the "not-yet" is indispensable. From scientific observations, I was also able to conclude that, for an adequate understanding of time, a consideration of the respective proper times of systems is essential. The significance of proper time is not exhausted by marking an individual extension on a universal timeline. In a broader sense, the meaning of proper time includes also internal time, as can be observed in biological, political, and economic systems.[219]

I consider it important and productive to bring a concept of time that is broadened by this perspective into the discussion with interpretations of time that tend to be accepted uncritically by sheer force of habit. As an example, we shall take a look at Eccles. 3:1–15. Is it not precisely this internal time, in its relation to external time, that actually explains the significance of the words of Ecclesiastes—"For everything there is a season, and a time for every matter under heaven"?[220] The text would be banal if it dealt merely with chronological-linear time, with an infinite conveyor belt on which birthing and dying, weeping and dancing, war and peace are transported like small parcels. However, a look at some commentaries on this passage indicates that the interpretation that claims that Ecclesiastes is giving prominence to a temporal determinism is presented as the only reasonable one. Even if the views are somewhat divided with respect to details, general agreement prevails regarding the emphasis on the fateful character of time. The commentators formally indulge in determinism: Everything happens according to a fixed plan; "every single *fact* is determined";[221] every event happens beyond human control;[222] God's acts overpower and overshadow all human actions;[223] all actions are predetermined, and every human activity is therefore useless;[224] only one and the same thing is repeated over and over;[225] we are dealing with the helplessness of human beings vis-à-vis the time that is determined by God, whereby the twenty-eight uses of the word *time* ($^c\bar{e}t$) elicit a feeling of fatalism;[226] indeed, we are dealing with the "emphasis on the absolute dependence of all earthly things, with a strong emphasis on the exclusiveness of God."[227] It is striking to me how securely these deterministic glasses fit on the noses of the commentators. An opening of the closed concept of time in the direction of internal time and multi-temporality is not considered. Yet, it need not necessarily be the "music of the unamendable"[228] that is found in these verses; it can just as well be the roundelay of multi-temporality.

In addition to the version of closed determinism, there is also that of open relationality. The latter could be argued more or less as follows: It makes complete sense to speak of an internal time of the processes named in the pericope; and it also makes sense to conceive of "eternity" ('ôlām) not as the antithesis of human time, but instead as God's "proper time," which is related to the other times but does not merge into them. In this pericope, Ecclesiastes does not make a dualistic contrast of time and eternity. The text speaks of God's (proper) time with which God has accomplished everything in a perfect way. It is the gift and mystery of life that God has laid God's own (form of) time—namely, eternity—into everything. God's proper time is included in this relational structure, but it assumes a unique position in this structure. Thus, an understanding of God's relationship to time that automatically ascribes to God one and the same relation to all times is also overcome.[229] From this viewpoint, one can speak of human discernment in relation to time, as well as of the dependence of world time on God's proper time (v. 11); and the overarching dynamic nature of these proper times can be expressed—the relativizing of present and future, the possibility of still being able to do something with that which has already hardened into a necessity (v. 15). Thus, a relational understanding of time contributes to elucidating those parts of this pericope that several commentators have referred to as *crux interpretum*.

"Everything has its time, and everything has its internal dynamic" would then be a more appropriate paraphrase of the words from Ecclesiastes than, for example, Paul Gerhardt's formulation: "Everything has its time, but God's love is eternal."[230] Paul Gerhardt is evidently not the only one who presupposes the notion of limited intervals of time on a line that is contrasted to God's eternity. Rather, it once again seems reasonable to suspect that, in much of theology, there is still the uncritical assumption that God is at home in Newton's time. This attitude is actually understandable, since Newtonian mechanics functions perfectly in the realm of our everyday life. Consequently, what is known and what has proved itself to work is universalized and also carried over into conceptions of God. Understandable, but nevertheless careless. It is much more astute to recognize the illusory in the assumption of universal time and, subsequently, also to consider theological approaches critically. Especially eschatological reflections on classical themes, such as judgment and the intermediate state, seem to assume that God measures with Newton's time and that the only category available to God is the category of "determinism." Here, insights from the natural sciences can sharpen our consciousness of the fact that the alternative does not mean either strict determinism or complete relativism, either rigorous rationalism in keeping with the Enlightenment outlook or the all-encompassing arbitrariness of an extreme postmodernism.

This train of thought also opens up the possibility of understanding eternity indeed as temporal, but nevertheless as incommensurate with chronological time. There is something process-like in eternity,[231] This is expressed not only in a passage like John 14:2f., but also in the announcement of the reign of God (Mark 1:15). Nearness means unavailability and not-yet-present. However, it also means presence as that which is coming and, thus, as an interruption of linear chronology.

From this perspective, a solution to the dilemma posed on pp. 82–97 offers itself: Can God be temporal and still be God? Can God really be God without being temporal? We can now see that this way of asking is confined to a static-dualistic way of thinking and therefore juggles with false alternatives. A relational conception of time, by contrast, assumes the temporal openness of God,[232] which is qualified eschatologically. In this sense, one can speak of the "constitution of our time through God's selection from divine time"[233] and also of eternity as the internal ground that enables temporal life.[234]

A good theology of time does not confine itself to discussing amounts of time or the antithesis of time and eternity. It instead considers an increase in complexity that occurs "in, with, and under" nonlinear interactions. Only in this way can it approach an adequate understanding of time, which acknowledges that time is not encountered as something abstract, but rather as lived time and life time.

A relational understanding of time has consequences for the understanding of life and the world. Relational thinking, for example, does not tolerate the leveling of differences.[235] It opposes the obliteration of the dissimilarity of proper times and rhythms. And it does not tolerate a flattening of time into the simple infinity of a super-continuity or a total synchronicity in which everything is available nonstop. In a relational understanding of time, time is conceived as "time for," which always stands in relation to an Other. The primary communicative form that corresponds to this understanding is not information, but, rather, communication. This also results in an alertness to how and where time is utilized as a means of power.[236] In a relational understanding of time, time is not merely that which rules over us or that relentless power of transitoriness against which we struggle; rather, it is seen as the time in which, with which, and under which we live and structure life and the world.[237]

The eschatologically qualified relationality of time also has consequences for understanding the future. In this perspective, future becomes
comprehensible as a relational structure consisting of future and advent. Resulting from this is the fact that futurist striving for world improvement and
the adventist composure in the expectation of a consummation lying beyond the immanently possible complement each other. Eschatology is not
speculation about the grand finale, but rather, above all, the ferment of
hope. In this capacity, it certainly does not eliminate the finale, but it is not
fixated on it. Eschatology is primarily the expression for the relationality of
old and new, of future and advent, of identity and alterity.

For dealing with time, this means that we certainly need our chronome-
ters, which help us to divide up and organize time. However, just as urgent-
ly, we need the experiences of forgetting time; we need time periods in
which measurable time plays no role. These are often precisely the experiences that offer what affects human life on the deepest level. At least two
types of languages are prerequisite for an optimal understanding of time:
the formal language of mathematics, in which we can present calculations
with positive, negative, squared, and imaginary time, and the language of
narrative, which unites phenomenological and cosmological time[238] and is a
superior means of expression for relationality. Even the physics of complex
systems can no longer survive without narrative—if Prigogine is right: "In
connection with irreversibility, we reach a description of physics that brings
a narrative element into play on all levels."[239] At least in this regard, narrated time and time in both theology and science are closer to each other than
often presumed. A possible story of time that recurred repeatedly over the
course of the study is the narration of time as a dance.[240] Its strength lies in
its ability to thematize the relationships of process and rhythm, space and
time, the unique and the recurrent, detail and generality, individuality and
sociality, idea and action, and the like. This flexibility and openness is simultaneously also its weakness. It need not necessarily be a liturgical dance
of joy in God, as hymns and theological literature so gladly assume. It can
just as well be the Nietzschean dance of the self-glorification of the
strong.[241]

After everything that has emerged from the reflections in the four chapters of this study, we still have the ongoing task, first, of narrating good and
appropriate stories of time. In hindsight, it is clear that, in this respect,
hymns are guardians of rich treasures. Their narrations on time and eternity
offer a diversity that highlights contrasts, so that the Church which sings
"any and everything" has experiences that are manifold to the point of being conflicting. Expressing the whole range of the diversity of these experiences, in turn, corresponds very well with the realities of life. In this sense,

the hymns of the Church open up a wider spectrum than many theological models can provide. Although they are superior to theology in this regard, the hymns also need supplementation by means of theological reflection. The example of the reduction of eternity to the area of the immanent, which is found in more recent hymns, reminds us of the urgency of theological questions. If, as was clear in the example of death understood as the end, the irrelevance of eternity ultimately destroys time,[242] then we must ask: What does it mean for the individual, and for Church and society, if eternity as the Other of time loses all authority for the structuring of life? How could we today motivate and express the necessity for a perspective of eternity? How, for example, is an ethic with a perspective on eternity different from one without any relationship to eternity?

Second, in light of the starting points selected in this study, further reflections in different directions are not only possible—they are highly desirable. The reflections concerning a theology of time that I have presented go beyond the dialogue with the natural sciences in their urge for relationship to the Other. Let me conclude by suggesting a few further questions for which a relational understanding of time could be valuable. On the basis of reflections on time and death in the second chapter, it would be fruitful to examine different notions of reincarnation with respect to their understandings of time. A continuation of reflection in the direction of the mystical experience of time would also be appealing.

The obvious popularity of the topic of time—seen in the number of publications on the subject—surely also results from the fact that time is a difficult aspect in the contemporary structuring of life. Many problems of the modern age have been diagnosed and addressed as a "time sickness" [*Zeitkrankheit*].[243] For this reason, I consider it promising to reflect upon a relational theology of time not only within the context of the natural sciences, but also in dialogue with other disciplines, such as psychology, sociology, and economics.

> *Non vacant tempora nec otiose volvuntur per sensus nostros:*
> *faciunt in animo mira opera.*
> The times are not empty, nor do they roll idly through our senses:
> They work remarkable things in the mind.[244]

Notes

Introduction

1. On theological hermeneutics, see Jeanrond, *Theological Hermeneutics.*

2. For an overview of correlational theology, its methods, development, and reception, see Jeanrond, "Correlational Theology."

3. Ibid., 137.

4. Isabelle Stengers, in her book *D'une science à l'autre. Des concepts nomades* (Paris: Seuil, 1987), speaks of nomadic concepts ("concepts nomades"), according to Bühler and Karakash, *Science et foi font système*, 38.

5. I am indebted to my colleague Vítor Westhelle for the focus on this dimension of relativity.

6. Tracy, *Plurality and Ambiguity*, 20f.

7. Jeanrond, "Correlational Theology," 142.

Chapter 1

1. Paul Ricoeur, *Time and Narrative,* vol. 1, 3 and 52. Narrative is also meaningful only to the extent that it follows the characteristics of temporal existence. It is interesting that the telling of stories and the measuring of time have a concrete common history, since "aus dem Kalender gingen . . . erzählerische und poetische Traditionen hervor: angefangen von lateinischen Kalenderversen und altirischer Poesie über die 'Contes' des Mittelalters bis zu den volkstümlichen Kalendern der Neuzeit und den Kalendergeschichten Grimmelshausens, Hebels, Brechts" (the calendar produced . . . narrative and poetic traditions: beginning with Latin calendar verses and Old Irish poetry about the "Counts" of the Middle Ages and culminating in the traditional calendars of modern times and the calendar stories of Grimmelshausen, Hebel, Brecht) (Maier, "Eine Zeit in der Zeit?" 115).

2. Ricoeur, *Time and Narrative*, vol. 3, 241.

3. Ibid., vol. 2, 158.

4. Ibid., vol. 3, 169.

5. Ibid., 173. See also Ricoeur, *Från text till handling,* esp. pp. 29–98 and 205–35 (summary of the central ideas in Ricoeur, *Time and Narrative*, vol. 3).

6. Ibid., 210f.

7. Streib ("Erzählte Zeit," 181), along with Johann Baptist Metz, wishes to characterize the Christian church as a "Erinnerungs- und Erzählgemeinschaft" (community of memory and narrative), in which humans are supposed to become "Subjekte der Geschichte" (subjects of history). Along with Ricoeur, he ascertains that identity is dependent upon narrative. Without narrative, identity gets lost in time. Ibid., 189.

8. Frere, "Introduction," *Hymns Ancient and Modern*, ix.

9. According to Robin A. Leaver in "The Theological Character of Music in Worship," in Leaver, Litton, and Young, eds., *Duty and Delight* (47–64), 51 (who is citing P. W. Hoon, *The Integrity of Worship: Ecumenical and Pastoral Studies in Liturgical Theology* [Nashville: Abingdon Press, 1971]).

10. Ellingsen, *Skjult som vind i treets krone*, 7 (Foreword by Åge Haavik), and 9.

11. According to Fred Kaan and Brian Wren, hymnwriting has a double function and task, namely, the collection of past—lived—experiences and the search for formulations for future—not-yet-lived—experiences. Those formulations survive that correspond to vital and lived experience. Leaver, Litton, and Young, eds., *Duty and Delight*, 222.

12. *The Australian Hymn Book*, Editor's Preface, xiii.

13. Ibid., xii.

14. *Evangelisches Gesangbuch*, 7.

15. *Sing Alleluia*, Foreword, vi.

16. Hereafter abbreviated as *EG*. The official edition of *the Evangelische Gesangbuch* for the Protestant Church in the Rhineland, the Protestant Church of Westphalia, and the Lippian Church, in conjunction with the Reformed Church (Synod of Reformed Churches in Bavaria and Northwest Germany), appeared in 1996; it is also used in the Protestant Church in the Grand Duchy of Luxembourg. The main portion (Hymns 1–535) is identical in both editions (the provisional one from 1995 and the final one from 1996), whereas in the regional church portion, about forty hymns from the 1995 edition were deleted, and at least fifty new hymns were included. A considerable portion of these are psalms, canons, and liturgical songs containing few indications of time. Wherever songs from the 1995 regional church portion are found in the 1996 edition under a different number, this number is specified in parentheses, e.g., *EG* 630(631). Texts that are found only in the 1995 edition are signified by the remark "not included in *EG1996*."

17. Hereafter abbreviated as *GL*.

18. Hereafter abbreviated as *Sv ps*. Its predecessor, *Den Svenska Psalmboken* from 1937, is hereafter abbreviated as *Svps1937*.

19. Hereafter abbreviated as *Ps90*.

20. Hereafter abbreviated as *AHB*.

21. Hereafter abbreviated as *SA*.

22. These and the following figures correspond to the status as of 1995.

23. According to the Foreword from 1986, nos. 1–325 are obligatory for the Svenska kyrkan (Church of Sweden, Lutheran), the Adventistsamfundet (Seventh-day Adventist Church in Sweden), the Evangeliska Fosterlands-Stiftelsen (Swedish Evangelical Mission; movement within the Church of Sweden), the Fribaptistsamfundet (Free Baptist Church), the Frälsningsarmén (Salvation Army), the Helgelseförbundet (Holiness Union Mission), the Katolska kyrkan i Sverige (Catholic Church in Sweden), the Liberala Katolska kyrkan (Liberal Catholic Church), the Metodistkyrkan (Methodist Church), the Pingströrelsen (Pentecostal Movement), the Svenska Alliansmissionen (Swedish Alliance Mission), the Svenska Baptistsamfundet (The Baptist Union of Sweden), the Svenska Frälsningsarmén (Swedish Salvation Army), the Svenska Missionsförbundet (now: Svenska Missionskyrkan, The Mission Covenant Church of Sweden), and the Örebromissionen (Örebro Mission). Since 1997, the Free Baptist Church, the Holiness Union Mission, and the Örebro Mission

have together formed the Nybygget kristen samverkan (in English: Interact; affiliated with the European Evangelical Alliance).

24. Archbishop Gunnar Weman in the Foreword to *Psalmer i 90-talet* (my translation).

25. Thirty texts were written in the 1990s, twenty-three in the 1980s, twenty-four in the 1970s, eight in the 1960s, and three in the 1940s. Nineteen are biblical texts, and sixteen are undated (data partly according to year of translation).

26. The Uniting Church is a merger of The Congregational Union of Australia, The Methodist Church of Australia, and The Presbyterian Church of Australia.

27. Also belonging to these expressions are *noch, bald, einmal, schon; än(nu), alltjämt, snart, en gång, redan; yet, still*. These words occur both as fillers (as such, however, they can be emphasized by placement within the sentence or by the melody) and as independent, stressed meaning. Not infrequently, they appear in conjunction with other time-indicating expressions, which is why they have been included to some degree in the qualitative analysis despite being omitted from the quantitative analysis.

28. It would be tempting to examine the relationship between text and melody with respect to the question of time. Melody as the passage of time certainly does not describe time itself, but, through its direction, it could strengthen, emphasize, weaken, or even contradict the expressions of time in the text. The agreement between text and melody with respect to expressions of time (e.g., as it is realized in *Sv ps* 490) is diverse. A discussion of these correlations, however, would go well beyond the framework of this study.

29. The hymns numbered 1–535, 550–691.

30. For the summarizing comparison, see the following table:

	Number of Hymns	Number of Examined Passages Containing Time Indications	Number of Hymns Containing Time Indications	Average Number of Passages Per Hymn Containing Time Indications
EG	677	885	452	1.31
GL	917	579	264	0.63
Sv ps	700	1128	550	1.61
Ps90	123	166	85	1.35
AHB*	624 (45)	782 (44)	437 (29)	1.25 (0.98)
SA	105	142	77	1.35
Total	3146	3682	1865	

* The figures in parentheses refer to the figures for the hymns of the Catholic supplement that are contained in the total numbers.

31. Meditations/prayers are not included in these calculations, since they have no comparable stanza organization.

32. Summarizing table:

	Number of Hymns Containing Time Indications	Number of Time Indications in the Final Stanzas of These Hymns	Occurrence of Time Indications in the Final Stanzas of Hymns Containing Indications of Time, in %	% of all Time Indications Found in Final Stanzas
EG	452	203	44.91	22.94
GL	264	96	36.36	16.58
Sv ps	550	281	51.09	24.91
Ps90	85	54	63.53	32.53
AHB	437	238	54.46	30.43
SA	77	41	53.25	28.87

33. For example, *EG* 119,5 (= *GL* 230,5), text by Bartholomäus Gesius (1601), based on *Coelos ascendit hodie* from the sixteenth century.

34. *GL* 550,6, text *Jesu dulcis memoria* (twelfth century), translated by Friedrich Dörr in 1969.

35. Text by Lorenz Lorenzen (1700).

36. *Tid* (time) occurs fifty times (four of these times as *framtid* [future]); *evig* (eternal) and *evighet* (eternity), etc., occur 103 times; *tid* (time) occurs in combination with *evighet* (eternity); and *evig(a) tid(er)* (eternal time[s]) occurs nineteen times.

37. *Dag* (day) and/or *natt* (night) appear approximately seventy times, while *morgon* (morning) and/or *afton* (evening) appear only twelve times.

38. *Tid* (time) occurs thirteen times, and *framtid* (future) occurs once; *evig* (eternal) occurs six times, and *evighet* (eternity) occurs eight times.

39. *Eternal, everlasting, endless/unending, eternity* appear eighty-three times; *ever/evermore* appear seventy-one times; and *age, time, future* appear thirty-six times.

40. This is found a total of 104 times, with *day* clearly dominating (ca. fifty times); *today* occurs eleven times.

41. A total of twenty-two times; *day* is also the dominant term here (ten times); *today* occurs five times.

42. Eternity terminology in the broad sense appears ten times; in the strict sense, it occurs only three times (*eternal* twice and *everlasting* once).

43. In contrast to *EG, Sv ps,* and *GL, AHB* and *SA* are not organized according to the church year. *SA* cannot be divided according to the festivals of the church year. The study of *AHB*, on the other hand, could be based on the list entitled, "Hymns for the Church's Year," which was printed in the index section on p. li.

44. The categories "Passion" in the *EG* and "Fastan" (Lent) in *Sv ps* correspond to each other. The corresponding categories in the *AHB* are "Lent," "Passiontide," "Palm Sunday," and "Good Friday."

45. In *GL*, this includes Ascension Day.

46. Various categories are found in the individual hymnals: "Tod und Vollendung" (death and consummation) (*GL*), "Sterben und ewiges Leben" (dying and eternal life), "Bestattung" (burial) (*EG*), "All Saints' Day and All Souls' Day"(*AHB*), "Himlen" (heaven) (*Sv ps*), "Livets gåva och gräns" (the gift and limitation of life) (*Sv ps* and *Ps90*), and "Sjukdom, lidande och död" (illness, suffering, and death) (*Ps90*).

47. The first figure in the parentheses refers to the number of passages in the *EG;* the second to that in the *GL*.

48. Of the thirty hymns dealing with the topic *Loben und Danken* (Giving Praise and Thanks) (nos. 316–340 and 640–644), only two texts were written during the twentieth century. Five of the twenty-four hymns in the group dealing with *Sterben und ewiges Leben* (dying and eternal life) (516–535 and 688–691) come from the twentieth century. For the *modern* topic of *Angst und Vertrauen* (fear and trust), which did not exist as such in the predecessor of the *EG*, the *Evangelisches Kirchengesangbuch* (the Protestant Hymnal), which contains twenty-four hymns, the figure is higher; here, the text of nine hymns originated after 1900. Of twenty-seven Easter hymns (99–118 and 571–577), seven have texts from the twentieth century.

49. The *Sv ps* gives several translation and/or revision dates for many hymns, which makes an age determination of the time terminology very difficult. In the *AHB*, a certain inaccuracy cannot be avoided, since it specifies biographical data of the authors rather than the years in which the texts were written. With this qualification, the following distribution of *AHB* hymn texts containing time terminology has been determined: 40.5 percent

from the nineteenth century, 33.8 percent from the twentieth century, 21.6 percent from the eighteenth century, 2.7 percent from the seventeenth century, and 1.4 percent from the sixteenth century. As a comparison, we have taken the age distribution of texts from two subject areas: In "God: In Creation, Providence, and Redemption" (nos. 1–120), 34.7 percent came from the twentieth century; 31.4 percent from the nineteenth century; 22.3 percent from the eighteenth century; 10.7 percent from the seventeenth century; and 0.8 percent from the sixteenth century. In The Church: Its Life and Witness" (nos. 342–402), 41.0 percent originated during the nineteenth century, 29.5 percent during the eighteenth century; 19.7 percent during the twentieth century, and 9.8 percent during the seventeenth century. Here, therefore, we find no significant deviations to derive peculiarities for the age distribution of time terminology.

50. A total of only five times.

51. To my knowledge, this appears only once, namely, in *GL* 706,3. The text *Te Deum* (fourth century) was translated by Romano Guardini in 1950.

52. In a total of ca. 640 examined passages containing eternity terminology

53. See *GL* 137,2, text based on *Dies est laetitiae* (ca. 1320), translated by Maria L. Thurmair in 1969; *EG* 359,6, text by Kurt Müller-Osten (1941); *EG* 393,11, text by Gerhard Tersteegen (1738); *EG* 630(631),4, text by Matthias Jorissen (1793).

54. *GL* 706,4, text *Te Deum* (fourth century), translated by Romano Guardini in 1950.

55. Seventy-six times. The plural forms occur primarily in a set phrase: "i evigheter(na)s evighet" (in the eternity of eternity[ies]).

56. Among these: *evighetens värld* (world of eternity), *vår* (spring), *tröst* (comfort), *ljus* (light), *sommar* (summer), *nya liv* (new life), *sköna dag* (beautiful day), *brunnar* (fountains), *ro* (rest), *frid* (peace), *land* (land).

57. *Tid(er)*, thirty-two times.

58. *Liv(et)*, twenty-one times.

59. *Ljus* and *väl*, nine times each; *frid*, seven times; and *fred*, twice.

60. The word *(sabbats)ro*, six times, and *(sabbats)vila,* four times (Sabbath [rest]); *nåd* (grace), three times; *fröjder* (joys), four times; *nöd* (need), three times; and *död* (death), three times.

61. *Fader*, four times; *konung*, twice; *den Gode, makt och ära, härlighet, barmhärtighet, råd, lag, förbund, tron, kors.*

62. The term *(lov)sång*, three times; *halleluja, jubel, glädje, tröst, rikedom, frukt, ordet.*

63. *Försoning, paradis, boning*, three times; *sällhet, sommarskrud, högtidssal.*

64. *Nu, dag, morgon, vår, nyår, gudstjänstår.*

65. *Tjänst, mål, grund, men.*

66. *Sv ps* 368,1.4: "Blås på mig skaparvind, eviga andedräkt . . ."; text by Anders Frostenson (1969), based on Edwin Hatch (1835–89).

67. *Sv ps* 228,2: ". . . Kring helga nattvardsbordet . . . möter han de sina, en evig kärleks tolk . . ."; text by Göran Widmark (1945), revised.

68. Two occurrences each of *i evigheters evighet* (in an eternity of eternities) and *från evighet till evighet* (from eternity to eternity).

69. *Dag, kärlek, himmel, källa, vår.*

70. ". . . i evig enlighet med Guds kalender" (*Ps90* 883,2, text by Gulli Lundström-Michanek [1949]).

71. *Eternal life* or *life eternal.*

72. *SA* 13,1: ". . . I trust in your eternal name, beyond all changes still the same . . . ," text by Donald Hughes (1911–67); *SA* 74,5: ". . . the everlasting Name . . . ," text by Timothy Dudley-Smith (1926–) based on Psalm 91(90).

73. *SA* 60,3: ". . . for ever by your victory is God's eternal love proclaimed . . . ," text by Alan Gaunt (1935); *SA* 89,3: ". . . His vict'ry over death is th'eternal sign of God's love for us . . . ," text by Mimi Farra (1975).

74. *SA* 40,3: ". . . everlasting Son of God . . . ," text by Christopher Idle (1938–); *SA* 50,1: ". . . the sound and sight of heaven's everlasting feast," text by Erik Routley (1917–82); *SA* 11,2: ". . . the eternal purpose which their Father shall fulfil . . . ," text by Norman Elliott (1893–1973), revised.

75. *For ay* is also included in this figure (four times).

76. One hundred times.

77. Twice.

78. Nine times.

79. Once.

80. Forty-four times.

81. Seventeen times.

82. Twenty-three times.

83. In *AHB* and *SA*, the first figure given in the last two columns refers each time to eternity terminology in the strict (literal) sense, and the second figure refers to eternity terminology in the broad sense.

84. Compound and derivative nouns, such as *Morgenglanz* (morning glory), *Stündlein* (a short while), *aftonstund* (evening hour), and *födslotimma* (hour of birth) have been included here.

85. Cf. *GL* 263,1, text based on Albert Curtz (1659) (Psalm 19).

86. These exceptions include *AHB* 102,6, text by James P. McAuley (1917–76); *Sv ps* 413, text by Svein Ellingsen (1975) and Britt G. Hallqvist (1978); *EG* 490,1, text by Karl Albrecht Höppl (1958), based on the English lyrics "The day thou gavest, Lord, is ended" by John F. Ellerton (1870). In more recent hymns, night can also be portrayed positively as the time of rest and peace, in contrast to the stress of daytime, e.g., *Ps90* 858, text by Sigurbjörn Einarsson (1980), Swedish by Jonas Jonson (1992).

87. Here, all compound nouns, such as, *summertime, winter storm*, etc., have been included.

88. *Summer* is found six times, *winter* once, and *spring* once.

89. A total of about ten times.

90. In *Sv ps*, in five out of ninety places where seasons are mentioned, and in *Ps90*, in three out of twenty-seven places.

91. Approximately twice as frequently as in *Sv ps*.

92. The following table (data in percent of all time indications) provides an overview of the frequency of everyday terminology and seasonal terminology in pure or combined forms:

	Pure Form	Pure and Combined Form
EG	36	59
GL	25	41
Sv ps	46	83
Ps90	54	93
AHB	42	60
SA	61	64

93. The future is his domain (*EG* 395,3, text by Klaus Peter Hertzsch [1989]).

94. *AHB* 48,2, text by Katharina von Schlegel (1697–?), translated and revised by Jane Laurie Borthwick (1813–97).

95. Cf. *AHB* 52,3: "With grateful hearts the past we own; / the future, all to us un-

known, / we to your guardian care commit, / and peaceful leave before your feet," text by Philip Doddridge (1702–51).

AHB 512,7 should also be understood in this sense: "I know not what the future hath / of marvel or surprise, / assured alone that life and death / his mercy underlies," text by John Greenleaf Whittier (1807–92).

96. *AHB* 494,1 (*Sv ps* 275,1, text by John Henry Newman [1833], revised by Berndt David Assarson [1922] and Torsten Fogelqvist [1937]).

97. "Guide our hearts, that we treat not lightly / Thy punishments, but endeavor on earth / to remain devoted in light of your future. / Praise the Lord!" (*EG* 447,9).

98. The *AHB* contains several passages from the eighteenth and nineteenth centuries (eighteenth century: 52,3; 473,3; 483,3; nineteenth century: 124,5, 499,3; 512,7; 522,4). 499,3 in particular reflects the ambivalence of surrendering and grasping a future that is felt to be ambivalent: "Though the cause of evil prosper, / yet the truth alone is strong; / though her portion be the scaffold / and upon the throne be wrong— / yet that scaffold sways the future, / and, behind the dim unknown, / God still stands within the shadow / keeping watch above his own"; text revised by James Russell Lowell (1819–91).

99. This is reflected by the fact that *Zukunft* (future) occurs more frequently in the 123 hymns that are contained in the *Ps90* than in the 677 hymns of the *EG,* and just as often as in the 624 hymns of the *AHB.*

100. *Svps1937* 5,3, text by Gustaf Ållon (1694): "Lord, be the strength of the faithful / and offer help to your Anointed One. / Save your people and support your church, / which is your inheritance and your property. / Let them here be content in you / and be elevated for eternal time."

101. *Sv ps* 8,3: "Lord, be the strength of the faithful / further justice in our land. / Save your people and support your church, / take our future in your hand. / Give us peace here in time, / embrace us in your peace at last."

102. *Anointed One* probably refers to the king as the highest official responsible for administering justice (cf. Ps. 28:8 and Ronnås, *Våra gemensamma psalmer,* 13), which may well have inspired Britt G. Hallqvist's version.

103. Frykman indeed wrote *Min framtidsdag*—which he himself describes as the best of a large number of hymns that he wrote—during a time that, for him personally, was fraught with conflicts (Ronnås, ibid., 219). Nevertheless, these individual troubles do not endanger the collective future, but are rather relativized by the safety of heaven.

104. *Sv ps* 302,1: "My future day is bright and long, / it lasts beyond the constraints of time / there I shall blissfully behold God and the Lamb / and there will be no more sorrow and affliction," text by Nils Frykman, revised. Frykman's confidence is based on the everlasting inheritance stored up in heaven, the attainment of which is prepared by the earthly time of testing (302,2). Here, future is basically synonymous with heaven.

105. "I stand before you with empty hands, o Lord; . . . /my fate is death, have you no other blessings? / Are you the God who promises me the future? / I want to believe, oh, please come to me," *GL* 621,1 (= *EG* 382,1, where the last line reads: "Ich möchte glauben, komm du mir entgegen" (I want to believe, oh, come to me); text by Lothar Zenetti (1974), based on the Dutch "Ik sta voor U" by Huub Oosterhuis (1969).

106. *Sei unsre Zukunft* (*GL* 764,40, Litany of God's Presence; text by Huub Oosterhuis, translated by Lothar Zenetti).

107. *Für unsere Kinder sei du die Zukunft* (*GL* 764,70, Litany of God's Presence; text by Huub Oosterhuis, translated by Lothar Zenetti).

108. "God's Word is like light in the night; / it has brought hope and [the] future,"*EG* 587(591), text by Hans-Hermann Bittger (1978). Cf. also the Easter hymn *Sv ps* 155,1: ". . .

Hoppet är framtid, nu är livet, vår möjlighet" (Hope is the future, / now is life, our possibility), text by Göran Bexell (1971).

109. *Sv ps* 435,2: ". . . där barn i dag får lida / och leva utan framtid / i slum och ökensand," text by Svein Ellingsen (1977) and Britt G. Hallqvist (1980).

110. *Sv ps* 602,1: ". . . så länge ögon ännu lyser av hopp och framtidstro . . . ," text by Per Harling (1980).

111. *Sv ps* 602,4: "Så länge barnen vågar hoppas på ett framtidsland. . . ."

112. *EG* 212,2: "Bange vor der unbekannten Zukunft / legen wir dies Kind in deine Arme. / Du willst taufen. Das gibt uns Gewißheit" (Fearful of the unknown future / we place this child into your arms. / You wish to baptize. That gives us certainty), text by Jürgen Henkys (1982), based on the Norwegian *Fylt av glede over livets under* by Svein Ellingsen (1971, 1973). Cf. also the Swedish translation of this hymn by Britt G. Hallqvist (1977) in *Sv ps* 383,2.

113. Ellingsen worked on the text of this hymn during a time of grief over the accidental death of his young daughter, while at the same time experiencing expectant joy at the upcoming birth of a new child (Nivenius, *Psalmer och människor*, 70).

114. *EG* 212,5: "Unsre Zeit kommt bald an ihre Grenze, / aber deine Taufversprechen bleiben . . ." (Our time will soon reach its limits, / but your baptismal promises last forever . . .). Cf. *Sv ps* 383,5.

115. *SA* 18,2.5, text by Brian Wren (1936–).

116. *Ps90* 817,2: "Heaven on earth, here we may live, . . . / Practice, children, living in the Spirit, / dare today to taste God's future!"; text by Jonas Jonson (1978).

117. *Sv ps* 398,1–3: "We are setting an example, an example of justice, the meal is shared by all. / We taste the future that the poor hope for, the time when the walls will fall," text by Jonas Jonson (1980).

118. *Ps90* 831,1.2.4: "At this table humankind has gathered, / hope turned toward the One who will come. / A threatened hope that is kept alive by longing. / Only one world. / In this bread is the sign for our future. / It will be distributed and sufficient for all of us. . . . / At this table, heaven meets earth. . . . A liberated people can anticipate peace. Only one world," text by Jonas Jonson (1985, 1993).

119. For example, *AHB* 48,2, text by Katharina von Schlegel (1697–?), translated by Jane L. Borthwick (1813–97), revised; *AHB* 52,3, text by Philip Doddridge (1702–51). This observation can also be verified from another perspective. By using catechetical material from the seventeenth century, Aurelius shows that the notion of divine Providence (*providentia dei*, consisting of God's *praescientia* and God's *cura*) was the natural horizon for thought and understanding at that time (*Luther i Sverige*, 26–31).

120. "Have confidence in the new paths, / on which God has sent us! / Godself comes to greet us. / The future is God's land. / Whoever sets out on the path can hope / in time and eternity. / The gates stand open. / The land is bright and large," *EG* 395,3, text by Klaus Peter Hertzsch (1989). The contents of this hymn includes significant parallels to *Sv ps* 90: "Blott i det öppna har du en möjlighet . . . vänd mot Guds framtid . . . ," text by Britt G. Hallqvist (1972), based on Johannes Kierkegaard (1971).

121. *Ps90* 885,2.3.4: "As yet hope is a burning spark . . . / The dream and the hope take root in our hearts . . . / The future is alive: a future for the earth! / Hopelessness wanes, and day follows the night," text by Svein Ellingsen (1991), translated by Jan Arvid Hellström (1991).

122. *Sv ps* 637,1: "Once in the morning of time, the earth will be new, / the air will be cleansed and the seabed visible . . . ," text by Göran Bexell (1972).

123. "Today He again opens the gate," *GL* 134,4 (= *EG* 27,6), text by Nikolaus Herman (1560).

124. *EG* 47,1–4, text based on a Bohemian Christmas carol from 1844.

125. *EG* 36,2, text by Paul Gerhardt (1653).

126. *GL* 134,4 (= *EG* 27,6), text by Nikolaus Herman (1560).

127. *AHB* 228,7, text possibly by John F. Wade (ca. 1711–86); *EG* 45,4, text by Friedrich H. Ranke (1823, 1826); *Sv ps* 122, text by Eva Norberg (1974, 1984).

128. *AHB* 238,1, text by John Mason Neale (1818–66), revised.

129. *AHB* 238,2–3: ". . . he has opened the heavenly door, . . . now you need not fear the grave . . ."; cf. also *EG* 36,3–5, text by Paul Gerhardt (1653).

130. *EG* 50, tune by Volker Gwinner (1970).

131. "Today the world is reverberating with joy. / You, however, are lying in a poor stable. / Your verdict was issued long ago, your cross has already been erected for you. / *Kyrie eleison*," *EG* 50,2.

132. ". . . No one prevents your misery. / The grave yawns before your manger . . . ," *EG* 50,3.

133. ". . . we also remember your suffering, / which we caused you on this late night / by our sin . . . ," *EG* 50,1.

134. "Today, the world is rich with song. / But no one places you on a soft bed / and soothingly sings you to sleep. / We heap our punishment upon you. / Kyrie eleison," *EG* 50,4.

135. "If one day we are resurrected with you / and see you face-to-face, / only then does our heart without bitterness / open wide to song. / Hosanna," *EG* 50,5.

136. *AHB* 280,1, anonymous text (1708) based on *Surrexit Christus hodie*. Cf. *EG* 577(564), 1.4, text by Emil Schaller (1972), based on "Christ the Lord is ris'n today" by Charles Wesley (1741).

137. *EG* 109,1, text by Kaspar Stolzhagen (1591).

138. *Sv ps* 149,1, text by Johann Franck (1653), Gustaf Ållon (1694), and Anders Frostenson (1978).

139. *Sv ps* 151,1, text by Jane E. Leeson (1807–82) and Britt G. Hallqvist (1984), based on a Latin sequence (ca. 1100).

140. *GL* 225,1 (= *EG* 106,1), text by Nikolaus Herman (1560); cf. also *AHB* 283,3.4, text based on "Christ lag in Todesbanden" by Martin Luther (1483–1546), translated by Richard Massie (1800–1887), revised; *AHB* 285,1, text by Edmund Spenser (1552?–99); *AHB* 289,2, text by Isaac Watts (1674–1748), revised.

141. *EG* 100,3 (= *GL* 223,3), text by Cyriakus Spangenberg (1568), based on *Resurrexit Dominus* (fourteenth century).

142. *SA* 56,1–3, text based on an aboriginal song of the Torres Strait Islands.

143. E.g., *EG* 42,1 (Christmas): "Dies ist der Tag, den Gott gemacht, sein werd in aller Welt gedacht . . ." (This is the day that the Lord has made, to be celebrated throughout the entire world . . .), text by Christian F. Gellert (1757); *GL* 220,1 (Easter): "Das ist der Tag, den Gott gemacht . . ." (this is the day that the Lord has made . . .), text by Heinrich Bone (1851); *AHB* 289,1–2 (Easter): "This is the day the Lord has made; he calls the hours his own; . . . Today he rose and left the dead, . . . today the saints his triumphs spread, and all his wonders tell," text by Isaac Watts (1674–1748), revised. In our context, it is interesting that the Swedish *Psaltaren i ny översättning* (1995) translates Ps. 118:24: "Detta är dagen då Herren grep in" (this is the day on which the Lord intervened).

144. For example, *Sv ps* 142: "Skåda, skåda nu här alla, se hur Jesus plågad är . . ." (Look, look here, everyone, and see how Jesus is being tormented), text by Johann Qvirsfeld (1682), revised several times; *EG* 85: "O Haupt voll Blut und Wunden, voll Schmerz und voller Hohn . . ."(Oh, head covered with blood and wounds, full of pain and scorn), text by Paul Gerhardt (1656), based on the *Salve caput cruentatum* by Arnulf of Louvain (before 1250).

145. *AHB* 544,1.2.4, text by Timothy Rees (1874–1939), revised.

146. *AHB* 274,2.3, text by Valerie M. Dunn (1932–), revised.

147. *SA* 94,2, text by Robin Mann (1949–).

148. *SA* 94,3.

149. *AHB* 411,2, text by Judith Beatrice O'Neill (1930–).

150. *Sv ps* 385,3: "Saved with Noah out of his ark / from the stormy seas onto vernal land / raised with Moses from the river / we celebrate with newborn hope," text by Fred Kaan (1968), Swedish by Britt G. Hallqvist (1977 and 1982).

151. *Sv ps* 383,5: "Beyond the boundaries of time, live evermore / the words of your promise in the baptismal waters. The light of the baptism remains when life is extinguished," text by Svein Ellingsen (1971), Swedish by Britt G. Hallqvist (1977). The German translation of this stanza by Jürgen Henkys (1982) reads: "Unsre Zeit kommt bald an ihre Grenze, / aber deine Taufversprechen bleiben. / Wir verlöschen. Deine Kerze leuchtet" (Our time soon comes to an end, / but your baptism promises remain, / We are extinguished. Your candle burns), *EG* 212,5.

152. *Ps90* 829,1.2.4, text (from the Philippines) by Francisco F. Feliciano (1941–); Swedish by Anders Salomonsson (undated). Cf. also the English paraphrase of this text in *SA* 30.

153. See pp. 28–32 above, *Ps90* 831.

154. Cf. here *Sv ps* 398,1–3, which was also cited on pp. 28–32.

155. *Sv ps* 74,3: "You who passes through time and space / with the bread of life / Christ, give us / this bread for every day," text by Olov Hartman (1968).

156. *Sv ps* 392,2: "Here is the manger—I fall to the ground and worship . . . / Oh, Sacrament that prepares us in grace / to see God, the Eternal One, on earth," text by Elis Erlandsson (1935).

157. *Sv ps* 396,2: "No more distance, no estrangement / and time is permeated by God's *today,* / You and I are companions with Abraham. / God is one of us at this table," text by Anders Frostenson (1974), based on Robert J. Stamps (1971).

158. "Until, after this time, I praise and love you in eternity," *EG* 325,10, text by Paul Gerhardt (1653).

159. "Only one breath separates time from eternity," *GL* 791, from a meditation commemorating the dead.

160. E.g., *Sv ps* 655,5 and 660,5, where it appears each time in set phrases: "nu och alltid och i evigheternas evighet" (Honor be to the Father and the Son and the Holy Spirit, / now and forever, and in the eternity of eternities); texts based on Pss. 24 and 47.

161. *EG* 359,6: ". . . freu dich . . . Kirche, allezeiten . . . sein Volk in Ewigkeiten" (Rejoice . . . Church, always . . . his people in eternities), text by Kurt Müller-Osten (1941); *EG* 393,11: ". . . wir gehn durch Jesu Leiten hin in die Ewigkeiten . . ." (. . . we are led by the guidance of Jesus into the eternities), text by Gerhard Tersteegen (1738); *EG* 630(631),4: ". . . wird der Herr dich selber leiten bis in die Ewigkeiten" (. . . the Lord himself will lead you into the eternities), text by Matthias Jorissen (1793).

162. *GL* 257,10 (= *EG* 331,10) has "zu allen Zeiten" [for all times]; *Sv ps* 1,8 has "genom alla evigheter" (through all eternities). Both texts refer to Ignaz Franz (ca. 1770); translated into Swedish by Olov Hartman (1980). According to *Svps1937* 603b, the Latin text of this passage reads: "Et laudamus nomen tuum in saeculum et in saeculum saeculi." Luther's version from 1529 (*EG* 191) says at this point, "Täglich, Herr Gott, wir loben dich und ehrn dein' Namen stetiglich" (Daily, Lord, we praise you and honor your name always). Cf. here also *Sv ps* 247,2 (text by J. O. Wallin [1816], revised): ". . . Det är för andra tider han lönen åt dig spar" (he is saving your reward for other times), whereby "other times" probably means eternity.

163. Cullmann's theory that "Eternity is endless time, or better said, that which we call 'time' is *nothing more* (my emphasis) than a God-limited portion of this same endless divine period of time" [*Ewigkeit unendliche Zeit ist, oder besser gesagt, daß das, was wir 'Zeit' nennen, nichts anderes (meine Hervorhebung) ist, als ein von Gott begrenztes Stück dieser gleichen unendlichen Zeitdauer Gottes*], Cullmann, *Christus und die Zeit*, 69, cannot be verified in the findings of the hymns.

164. *Sv ps* 314,4, text by Natanael Beskow (1886), revised; *Sv ps* 321,4, text by Magnus B. Landstad (1861) and J. A. Eklund (1910); *eviga tider* (eternal times) occurs here both times in contrast to *strider(nas dal)* (valley of conflicts); *(in)till evig tid* or *för evig tid* (until or for eternity) occurs much more frequently, though almost exclusively in older hymns. In at least two cases, *till evig tid* in hymns from the nineteenth century was changed to *för evig tid* in a revision in the 1980s. This could be a shift of emphasis from a formal usage of the meaning of *always* to a more content-oriented way of thinking.

165. E.g., *AHB* 84,1, text by Horatius Bonar (1808–89); *AHB* 354,6, text by Jean-Baptiste de Santeüil (1630–97), translated by Henry Williams Baker (1821–77); *AHB* 422,6, text by Thomas Aquinas (1227–74), translated by John Mason Neale (1818–66), revised. One can also speak of "endless ages" as an equivalent, e.g., *AHB* 279,6, text by Fulbert of Chartres (before 1028), translated by Robert Campbell (1814–68). These expressions do not occur in *SA*.

166. A difference between the Swedish and English usages must be noted here. While *Sv ps* often has *(in)till* or *för evig tid*, the *AHB* speaks of God's glory "while eternal ages run." In *AHB*, these passages are found entirely in nineteenth-century hymns or revisions of hymns, and always in a doxological context.

167. *Sv ps* 376,1, speaks immanently of a proclamation of the grace of God to a future young generation (text by Samuel Gabrielsson [1929]). The new worlds, creations, and times in *Sv ps* 285,2 appear to be meant above all transcendentally (text by Britt G. Hallqvist [1970], based on Frederick W. Faber [1814–63]). In *Sv ps* 623,4, there is a clearly time-transcendent meaning: here one speaks of the re-creation of life in death for future times and worlds (text by Aurelius Prudentius Clemens [ca. 400] and Olov Hartman [1979]).

168. Twenty-six hymns from *Sv ps* that follow this pattern were arranged according to their times of origin. The results were: three hymns from the sixteenth century, five from the seventeenth century, three from the eighteenth century, eleven from the nineteenth century, and four from the twentieth century (from 1914, 1915, 1927, and 1971). The nineteenth century thus dominates here, which does not necessarily mean that the time-eternity perspective is typical for this time period. Here, one may simply be dealing with a stylistic feature of Johan Olof Wallin, who wrote seven of the eleven hymn texts.

169. *GL* 901,5: "Wir glauben dir und deinem Wort, das leitet uns zum Frieden dort aus dieser Zeit Beschwerden" (We believe in you and in your Word, which leads us there to peace away from this time of tribulation), text by Heinrich Bone (1847), revised version by Friedrich Kienecker (1973).

170. *Sv ps* 566,6, text by J. O. Wallin (1816) and Anders Frostenson (1979).

171. *Sv ps* 615,6: ". . . en liten tid . . . så kommer hemmets frid . . . i evighetens ro" (just a little while longer and then the peace of home will come in the rest of eternity), text by Gerhard Tersteegen (1738); Swedish (1741); Britt G. Hallqvist (1983); *Sv ps* 624,6: ". . . då är jag i hamn, jag skådar mitt hemlands stränder . . ." (then, I am in the harbor, viewing the beaches of my native land), text by Johannes Johnson (before 1915), Oscar R. Hallberg, and Oscar Mannström (1920). For the wandering and home motifs, cf. Selander, *O hur saligt att få vandra*, 103–33, particularly 130ff.

172. *Sv ps* 63,8: "Och tidens kval fick sammanhang med evighetens tröst . . ." (And the torment of time became connected to the solace of eternity), text by J. O. Wallin (1816).

173. *EG* 148,7: "Mit Gott wir werden halten das ewig Abendmahl, die Speis wird nicht veralten . . . wir werden . . . trinken zugleich mit Gott" (We will celebrate eternal communion with God; the food will not get old . . . we will . . . drink at the same time with God), text by Johann Walter (1552).

174. *Sv ps* 616,3: "O klarhet som fördriver all tidens dunkelhet, o härlighet, som bliver min lott i evighet! . . ." (Oh, clarity, which drives out all darkness of time; oh, splendor, which will be my lot in eternity), text by J. O. Wallin (1814) and Anders Frostenson (1978). Cf. also *Sv ps* 324,2, text by Johann Walter (1552), revised in 1604, 1911, and 1978; as well as *Sv ps* 11,6: "När en gång alla tidens höljen falla, . . . och evighetens klara klockor kalla min frälsta ande till dess sabbatsro . . ." (When all coverings of time are dropped and the clear bells of eternity call my redeemed soul to its Sabbath rest), text by Carl Boberg (1885), revised (1984).

175. *GL* 870,2.3, text by Franz Johannes Weinrich (1938).

176. *AHB* 621,5, text by James Quinn (1919–); *EG* 148,1, text by Johann Walter (1552) (Swedish *Sv ps* 324); *EG* 450 (= *GL* 668,1), text by Christian Knorr von Rosenroth (1654, 1684), partly based on Martin Opitz (1634).

177. Cf. here, for example, *GL* 518,6: "Stärk unsre Hoffnung in der Zeit, daß uns aufleuchte die Ewigkeit" (Strengthen our hope in this time so that eternity becomes our light), text by Maria L. Thurmair (1962).

178. *Sv ps* 314, text by Natanael Beskow (1886), revised; *Sv ps* 321,3–4, text by Magnus B. Landstad (1861) and J. A. Eklund (1910); *Sv ps* 638, text by Henry Williams Baker (nineteenth century) and Britt G. Hallqvist (1977).

179. *Sv ps* 262,4, text by Nils Frykman (1877), revised; *Sv ps* 305,5, text by J. O. Wallin (1818); *EG* 503,9–11, text by Paul Gerhardt (1653); cf. also the Swedish version of this hymn, *Sv ps* 200,5–6.

180. "One day says to the other, / my life is a journey / toward the great eternity. / Oh, eternity, so beautiful, / make my heart accustomed to you, / my home is not in this time," *EG* 481,5, text by Gerhard Tersteegen (1745). Cf. also *EG* 683,2, text by Paul Kaestner (1921) (not included in *EG1996*); *EG* 152,4, text by Philipp F. Hiller (1767); *EG* 148,9, text from Dresden (1557); *GL* 568, text by Maria L. Thurmair (1951, 1973); *GL* 656,1 (= *EG* 690,1 not included in *EG1996*), text by Georg Thurmair (1935, 1938); *GL* 897,2, text from *Sursum Corda* (1874), revised version by Friedrich Kienecker (1973); *AHB* 147,5, text by Charles Wesley (1707–88).

181. *Sv ps* 469,2, text by J. O. Wallin (1819); *Sv ps* 322,1–5, text by Lina Sandell-Berg (1868); *Sv ps* 635,5, text by Edmund Gripenhielm (1694), J. O. Wallin (1816), and Britt G. Hallqvist (1983); *AHB* 582,2, text by Richard Connolly (1927–); *EG* 521,1–2 (= *GL* 659), text from Nuremberg (ca. 1555).

182. *GL* 565,1: "Komm, Herr Jesus, komm zur Erde . . . , daß die Zeit beendet werde und die Ewigkeit anbricht . . ." (Come, Lord Jesus, come to earth . . . , so that time will end and eternity will begin . . .), text by Georg Thurmair (1939). *EG* 114,10, text by Lorenz Lorenzen (1700); *EG* 458, text by Erasmus Alber (1537); *EG* 344,3, text by Martin Luther (1539); *Sv ps* 421,5, text by Edvard Evers (1914).

183. *Sv ps* 634,2: "The walls of space will collapse from the resounding tone of the last trumpets. All of time will become a single *now*, because the clock(s) of time will stop," text by Olov Hartman (1978), based on multiple revisions of the *Dies irae* from the thirteenth century. Cf. also *EG* 332,4, text by Georg Geßner (1795); *Sv ps* 627,4: "Dagen kommer, Kristi dag, då tid blir till evighet . . ." (The day is coming, Christ's Day, when time becomes eternity), text by Svein Ellingsen (1977), Swedish by Britt G. Hallqvist (1978).

184. "Go into the confusion of these times, / Ray of eternity; / Show the warriors the

location, path, / and goal of the City of God," *EG* 600,4, text by Otto Riethmüller (1932); not included in *EG1996*.

185. *Sv ps* 34,1–2: ". . . Stilla inom tidens gränser evighetens sol går opp . . . Kristus kom, och dagen tändes full av sanning och av nåd . . ." (Quietly within the boundaries of time, the sun of eternity rises . . . Christ came, and the day was ignited with truth and grace . . .), text by J. O. Wallin (1818).

186. *Sv ps* 601,2–3: ". . . Han fyller vår dag med det eviga nu som är och som var och förbliver . . . Han ger oss uppståndelsens morgon" (He fills our day with the eternal *now*, which is and was and remains . . . He gives us the morning of the Resurrection), text by Anders Frostenson (1961).

187. *Sv ps* 258,7: "O kärlek, som är / det eviga livet i växlingen här" (Oh love that is eternal life amidst the change here), text by Nicolai Frederik Severin Grundtvig (1824) and Emil Liedgren (1935), revised in 1937.

188. *Sv ps* 520,2: ". . . o Gud, din tröst, . . . som kommer då ingen vet och fyller ett fattigt intet till randen med evighet" (Oh, God, your solace that comes when no one knows and fills a poor nothing to the rim with eternity), text by Viola Renvall (1933); *Sv ps* 303,2: ". . . Vad ingen sett, vad ingen hört, det har Han in i tiden fört" (That which no one has seen or heard, He has introduced into time), text by Bo Setterlind (1972); *EG* 582(572),4: "Ewigkeit, / in die Zeit / leuchte hell hinein, / daß uns werde klein das Kleine / und das Große groß erscheine, / selge Ewigkeit, / selge Ewigkeit" (Eternity / shine brightly / into time, / so that the insignificant appears small to us / and the important seems large, / blessed eternity, / blessed eternity), text by Marie Schmalenbach (ca. 1876).

189. The formulation "von Ewigkeit zu Ewigkeit" (from eternity to eternity) may actually be understood in this sense. This meaning is suggested, for example, by Ps. 118 in *EG* 294,1 (= *GL* 269): ". . . seine Gnad und Güte währen / von Ewigkeit zu Ewigkeit. / Du, Gottes Volk, sollst es verkünden: / . . . er will sich selbst mit uns verbünden / und wird uns tragen durch die Zeit" (. . . his goodness and mercy last / from eternity to eternity. / You, people of God, shall proclaim it: / . . . he will ally himself with us / and carry us through time), text by Ambrosius Lobwasser (1565, 1573).

190. *Sv ps* 311,1: "Jag skall gråtande kasta mig ner / på en kust som jag aldrig har sett. / . . . i ett land som är nytt och är före all tid . . ." (In tears, I will prostrate myself on a shore that I have never seen before . . . in a land that is new and before all time), text by Anders Frostenson (1970, 1980). Cf. also *Sv ps* 338,2.4: The inner Trinitarian community is the origin of everything, and it is also the goal of everyone who is on the way to a day that no one has ever seen; text by Anders Frostenson (1970).

191. "You, creator of all beings. / You, the ruler of all time, / the week that has been, / returns home to eternity," *EG* 485,1, text by Otto Riethmüller (1934), based on *Deus, creator omnium* by Ambrose of Milan (386). *GL* 249,4 (= *EG* 579[566],4, text by Maria L. Thurmair [1941, 1946]): ". . . Da schreitet Christus durch die Zeit / in seiner Kirche Pilgerkleid . . ." (. . . Christ strides through time / in the pilgrim's clothing of his church . . .) could also be understood in this sense.

192. *SA* 69,6 and 95,6 contain a traditional image of eternity; here, one is dealing with timeless, or eternal, heavenly joy. In *SA* 32,1, eternal life is spoken of in a context having to do with overcoming current difficulties.

193. For reflections on this-worldliness, cf. also *Ps90* 843,2; 849,2; 850,1; and 852,5.

194. *Ps90* 821,2: "Jesus, help us to find time . . . In our haste, create peace," text by Seppo Suokunnas (1984), Swedish by Catharina Östman (1985).

195. *SA* 49,4, text by Melchizedek M. Solis (1966).

196. *Ps90* 896 and 897, text by Svein Ellingsen (1976 and 1973); *SA* 25, text by Robin Mann (1949–).

197. *SA* 50,1, text by Erik Routley (1917–82). *AHB* 547,1, where one prays for justice and peace for this world, points in the same direction: "O day of God, draw nigh / . . . come with your timeless judgment now / to match our present hour," text by Robert B. Young Scott (1899–).

198. *Ps90* 884 and 885, text by Svein Ellingsen (1977 and 1991), Swedish by Jan Arvid Hellström (1992 and 1991). On the concept of the "eighth day" (cf. *Ps90* 885,3) that follows the week of creation, which is already found in the Letter of Barnabas ca. 130 C.E., Stinissen remarks that the "eighth day" was the "sacrament" of eternal life for Basil the Great (ca. 330–379) (*Evigheten mitt i tiden*, 180).

199. "Remember that each second is a small moment of eternity with God, and if you hear birds singing all the day long, then you are hearing heaven's own sounds . . . remember that justice and peace in our own age should reflect the law of the Love of God. Thus, live [in] God's now," *Ps90* 863,2–3, text by Tore Littmarck (undated).

200. *Ps90* 862,4, text by Ingela Forsman (1993).

201. "Heaven on earth, here we may live, love, and give, supported by joy . . . Practice living in the Spirit, children, heaven is here, eternal in time!" (*Ps90* 817,2–3, text by Jonas Jonson [1978]).

202. Cf. Karl Barth, *The Epistle to the Romans*, Foreword to the 2nd ed.

203. "To Him belongs space and time, eternity is also his," *EG* 408,1, text by Arno Pötzsch (1934, 1949). Cf. also *EG* 533,3, by the same author: "Wir sind von Gott umgeben / auch hier in Raum und Zeit / und werden in ihm leben / und sein in Ewigkeit" (We are surrounded by God, also here in space and time / and will live in Him / and [be] his in eternity), text from 1941. For the expression "Welt und Zeit" (world and time), cf. *EG* 167,4, text by Theo Schmid (1957); and *EG* 313,3, text by Jürgen Henkys (1975, 1977), based on the Dutch "Jezus die langs het water lie" by Ad den Besten (1961).

204. An exception is found in *AHB* 68,5: ". . . dwellers all in time and space: praise him . . . ," text by Henry F. Lyte (1793–1847), based on Ps. 103:20ff.

205. *Rymd* (outer space) is more likely combined here with *jord* (earth) (819,3; 852,1; 803,1); *rum* (space, room) is used two times to characterize the inner region of human beings (810,3; 897,5).

206. Nine of twenty-three examined passages in which *rymd* occurred were written by Olov Hartman; Anders Frostenson was the author in four instances.

207. Such an expansion of perspective can be observed by comparing *Sv ps* 350,1, with *Svps1937* 50,1; *Sv ps* 351,1, with *Svps1937* 86,1; and *Sv ps* 575,4, with *Svps1937* 369,5.

208. For example, *Ps90* 823,3; 810,3; 897,5; an exception: 826,1–2.

209. "God, our origin, Lord of Space, / you created out of unlimited power / the matter in which fire moves. / You kindled the glow of the stars . . . / You yourself are flame, God, you are / the love that burns in Christ. / It keeps watch when the course of thought / moves through the universe, the element. / Lead us past an atomic night / awaken hope," *EG* 431,1.2, text by Walter Schulz and Jürgen Henkys (1982, 1984), based on George Utech (1964, 1969).

210. *AHB* 112,1.3, text by Catherine Bonnell Arnott (1927–).

211. *AHB* 567,1, text by Stewart Cross (1928–).

212. A Trinitarian-doxological interpretation is obvious in *AHB* 107,4; the first three stanzas of the hymn are dedicated to the Father, the Son, and the Holy Spirit; text by Fred Kaan (1929–).

213. *AHB* 102,1, text by James P. McAuley (1917–76). In *SA* 84,1, the Son is also called the "Lord of time and space"; text by Basil E. Bridge (1927–).

214. *SA* 18,2.3.5, text by Brian Wren (1936–).

215. *Sv ps* 641,2: "Jerusalem är staden högt ovan rum och tid, / med sällhet över alla mått och översinnlig frid . . . ," text by Staffan Larsson (1963).

216. "[V]ere Ierusalem est illa civitas, cuius pax iugis est, summa iucunditas . . ." The same word—*iugis*—occurs again at a different place in the same hymn, namely: "et iuges gratias de donis gratie beata referet plebs tibi, Domine," which corresponds to *Sv ps* 641,5: ". . . dig prisar då ett lyckligt folk för tid och evighet" (you will be praised then for time and eternity by a joyous people). Latin text based on *Hymns* 381.

217. *Sv ps* 634,3: "Då finns ej tid, då finns ej rum, / då finns blott räkenskapen . . . (Then there will be no time, no space; there will only be [the day of] reckoning); 1978 revision. The Latin text (based on *Svps1937* 609) makes no mention of space and time at the corresponding place (stanzas 7 and 8). The only reference that could have perhaps inspired Hartman to speak of the non-existence of space and time is found in the first stanza: "Dies irae, dies illa Solvet saeclum in favilla. . . ." In this context, however, it seems to me that *saeclum* should be translated as *world* rather than *time*, as was customary in Late and Middle Latin. Correspondingly, the wording of the English version (*Hymns* 302, text by William J. Irons [1848]) says: "Heav'n and earth in ashes burning."

218. *Sv ps* 634,1.2 (cf. above, pp. 37–41).

219. The most closely related lines with respect to content are "Mors stupebit et natura Cum resurget creatura Iudicanti responsura."

220. *Sv ps* 623,4: ". . . Så nyskapas livet i döden / för tider och världar som kommer" (Thus, life, in death, will be recreated for ages and worlds to come), text based on Aurelius Prudentius Clemens (ca. 400).

221. *Sv ps* 335,4: "We believe that God is more than the world and space and time, the first and the last of all that exists. When the world collapses, he is our life." An indication that Hartman consciously reflected on time is found in some lines from one of Hartman's letters (1972) to A. Frostenson. This letter mentions a hymn entitled "Som fåglar" (Like Birds), which was not contained in *Sv ps* and *Ps90*: "As you noticed, the hymn 'Like Birds' deals with time, too. And it is true: There is no abstract time (chronometric time) in the New Testament. Time is creation, and the tenses are burst. I picked up the returning of moments from Augustine, by the way, a prayer from the *Confessiones* that has accompanied me for many years: 'tua est dies,' as it says there, 'et tua nox est: ad nutum tuum momenta transvolant'—and there are also the birds and the flight." Belfrage, *Guds kärlek är som stranden*, 88.

222. ". . . die Welt bereitet nach unbegriffnem Plan, . . . der hinter Zeit und Maßen, davor der Geist erschrickt, gebahnt die schönen Straßen . . . zur ewgen Gegenwart, da die vollkommne Klarheit sich allen offenbart," *EG* 646,5–6, text (1927, 1930) (not included in *EG1996*).

223. "You Who hold time in your hands," *GL* 157,1 (= *EG* 64,1), text by Jochen Klepper (1938).

224. *AHB* 540,1: "Father eternal, ruler of creation, / Spirit of life, which moved ere form was made . . . ," text by Laurence Housman (1865–1959); *AHB* 513,1: "Eternal Ruler of the ceaseless round / of circling planets singing on their way . . . ," text by John White Chadwick (1840–1904); *AHB* 332,1–3, text by Charles Wesley (1707–88).

225. *Sv ps* 436,1, text by Anders Frostenson (1960).

226. "The sunrise, with its light, had not yet appeared; / and behold, the Light that shines eternally had already arisen. / The sun was not yet awake, / then the uncreated Sun awakened and rose full of power," *GL* 226,2, text by Paul Gerhardt (1653).

227. "Wie du warst vor aller Zeit, so bleibst du in Ewigkeit," *GL* 257,1 (= *EG* 331,1), text by Ignaz Franz (ca. 1770); Latin text based on *Svps1937* 603b.

228. *GL* 257,9 (= *EG* 331,9). The Latin text here says: "et rege eos, Et extolle illos usque in aeternum"; therefore, the aspect of time is a product of the translation. Similarly, *GL* 279,2, text by Friedrich Dörr (1969). Christ also leads through time: "Du Hirt, von Gott gesandt, um sicher durch die Zeiten das Volk des Herrn zu leiten" (You, shepherd, sent by God to lead the people of God safely through the ages), *GL* 538,5, text by Friedrich Dörr (1954, 1971).

229. *Sv ps* 330,1, text by J. O. Wallin (1811). Cf. also *Sv ps* 503,2: ". . . Du skapat natt och dag, / själv oföränderlig / när allt förändrar sig . . . " (You created night and day, your-self unchanging, when everything is changing), text by Anders Frostenson (1980), based on Samuel Columbus (1674).

230. *Sv ps* 330,2.

231. *Sv ps* 330,5: "He is capable of doing at all times all things alone."

232. "Vor ihm steht die Welt unwandelbar, da seine Hand sie hält," *EG* 620,1 (see 623,1, where it says, however: "vor ihm steht die Welt unwandelbar, da er sie hält" [before him, the world stands unchangeable, since he holds it]), text by Matthias Jorissen (1793). Jorissen's Psalm hymns became very important in reformed churches.

233. *EG* 620,2–4 (623,2–4, text slightly changed).

234. *Sv ps* 64,3, text by Johan Ludvig Runeberg (1857).

235. *SA* 13,3, text by Donald Hughes (1911–67).

236. *SA* 13,1 (referring to the eternal name of God), text by Donald Hughes (1911–67). Thus, also *AHB* 153,1: "This, this is the God we adore; / our faithful, unchangeable friend . . . ," text by Joseph Hart (1712–68).

237. *EG* 610(615),3, text based on Matthias Jorissen (1798). Also similarly in *Sv ps* 570,2: ". . . I urtids dagar Fadern på oss tänkte, / och till en Frälsare sin Son han skänkte . . ." (At the beginnings of time, the Father thought of us and gave us his Son as a savior), text by Johann E. Schmidt (1714), Carl Jonas E. Hasselberg (1927), revised.

238. *Sv ps* 342,5: "Innan vi var födda / visste Gud vårt namn . . ." (Before we were born, God knew our name), text by Anders Frostenson (1960). A special kind of fore-knowledge concerns Mary, "Christi Mutter, auserkoren vor der Zeit aus deinem Rat" (Mother of Christ, chosen before time from your counsel), *GL* 873,2, text by Melchior Lu-dolf Herold (1803), new version by Friedrich Kienecker (1973).

239. *Sv ps* 486,1: "O Gud, du som de världar ser / varom vi ännu inget vet" (O God, you who sees the worlds of which we as yet know nothing), text by John Ellerton (1826–93), Anders Frostenson (1978).

240. *AHB* 65,2, text by Reginald Heber (1783–1826), revised.

241. *AHB* 7,1, text based on a medieval Jewish doxology, by Max Landsberg (1845–1928) and Newton Mann (1836–1926). Cf. also *AHB* 89,1: "God of eternity, Lord of the ages, / Father and Spirit and Saviour of men! / Thine is the glory of time's numbered pages; thine is the power to revive us again," text by Ernest Northcroft Merrington (1876–1953).

242. *AHB* 343,5, text based on a Latin hymn from the seventh or eighth century; En-glish by John Mason Neale (1818–66), revised. Cf. also *AHB* 5,3: "Holy, holy, we adore you / one in power, in nature one; / God the Father, God the Spirit, / God the co-eternal Son," text based on a Russian church hymn, English by John Brownlie (1857–1925), revised.

243. "There we will finally receive answers to all of our questions. We shall look into God's mystery, and, following loneliness and death, we shall live in communion with him beyond time and space," *Sv ps* 638,2, text by Henry Williams Baker (1821–77), Swedish by Britt G. Hallqvist (1977). Similarly, *Sv ps* 635,6: ". . . så att jag kan nalkas dig / och lovsjun-ga dig i friden / i ditt rike bortom tiden" (so that I may come close to you and sing praises to you in peace in your realm beyond time), text revised by Britt G. Hallqvist (1983) (cf.

Wallin's version of the hymn in *Svps1937* 590,7, where it says at the place cited here: "och ditt namn där evigt ära" (and there eternally honor your name). In *Sv ps* 570,6, time appears as the subject, which is extremely rare: "Fördolda tid . . . / När för du mig min Frälsare till möte, när når min själ sin vila i hans sköte / och smakar evighetens frid, fördolda tid?" (Hidden time. . . when will you lead me to meet my Savior, when will my soul reach its resting place in his bosom and taste the peace of eternity, oh hidden time?), text by Johann E. Schmidt (1714) and Carl Jonas E. Hasselberg (1927), revised.

244. *GL* 469, text by Erhard Quack (1965).

245. *Sv ps* 392,2: ". . . O, sakrament, som oss i nåd bereder / att Gud, den evige, på jorden se," text by Elis Erlandsson (1935).

246. *EG* 225,2, text by Friedrich Walz (1964).

247. *Sv ps* 174,3: ". . . dolt som vatten under jorden, dolt som vind i trädets krona . . . ," text based on the Norwegian hymn "Herre, når din time kommer" by Svein Ellingsen (1976), translated by Olle Nivenius (1980).

248. *Sv ps* 174,4.

249. Thus, Ellingsen himself describes *Sv ps* 174 as a summary of what he is attempting to communicate through all his texts, namely, "en levendegjøring av håpets dimensjon i vår kristne tro" (bringing to life the dimension of hope in our Christian faith), Ellingsen, *Skjult som vind I treets krone*, 54.

250. *AHB* 540,5: "How shall we love thee, holy, hidden Being, / if we love not the world which thou hast made?"; text by Laurence Housman (1865–1959).

251. "You who hold the time in your hands, Lord . . . / A person's day and works are transitory: / You alone will remain. / Only God's year lasts forever and forever, / Therefore, turn every day towards you, . . . / You alone are called the Eternal One / and [you alone] know the beginning, the end and the middle / in the passing of our times: / continue to be merciful to us . . . ," *EG* 64,1.3.6 (= *GL* 157), text by Jochen Klepper (1938). Cf. also *GL* 293,3: "Es steht in deinen Händen die Zeit und Lebensfrist" (Time and the duration of life are in your hands), text by Caspar Ulenberg (1582), based on Ps. 31, revised in 1971; and *EG* 199,5: "Gott steht am Anbeginn, / und er wird alles enden. / In seinen starken Händen / liegt Ursprung, Ziel und Sinn" [God stands at the beginning, / and he will end all / In his strong hands / lie the origin, the goal, and the meaning], text by Markus Jenny (1970), based on the Dutch "God heeft het eerste woord" by Jan Wit (1965).

252. "From his radiance and light / he enters into your night: / And all that frightens you / shall be destroyed," *EG* 379,4 (= *GL* 290,4), text by Jochen Klepper (1938).

253. *EG* 515,9: ". . . Sei gepriesen, du öffnest uns die Zukunft! . . ." (Be praised, you are opening up the future to us!), text based on the Italian hymn to the sun by Francis of Assisi (1225).

254. *Sv ps* 27,3 (= *Psgo* 866): ". . . du, . . . som är evig; som är nu," text by Kerstin Anér (1946).

255. *Psgo* 810,1–3, text by Tomas Boström (1992).

256. *EG* 631(632),5, text by Jürgen Henkys (1979), based on the Dutch "Zalige ure!" by Dirk R. Camphuysen (1624). The text of the stanza quoted here is a free translation by Henkys.

257. *AHB* 107,4: "He shall for ever reign, / ruler of time and space, / God in the midst of men, / seen in the human face . . . ," text by Fred Kaan (1929–).

258. Cf. the already quoted *EG* 225,2: "Wir haben sein Versprechen: Er nimmt sich für uns Zeit" (We have his promise: He will take time for us), text by Friedrich Walz (1964).

259. *Sv ps* 342,3: ". . . Gud har tid att lyssna . . ." (God has time to listen), text by Anders Frostenson (1960). That one is speaking here of hearing the twittering of birds is of little significance. Cf. also *Sv ps* 499,2–5, text by Anders Frostenson (1965, 1981), which is

concerned with making sure of God's presence amidst the hustle and bustle of everyday life, the noise of traffic, the stress, and work: "Här din vingård ligger, här vi dig kan se" (Here lies your vineyard, here we can see you).

260. *Sv ps* 255,1–2: "Everyone is in a hurry, no one has time . . . God, however, has time. Eternity, indeed, time to quietly listen," text by Britt G. Hallqvist (1958).

261. *Ps90* 867,3, text by Ylva Eggehorn (1986). The hymn contains allusions to Gen. 32:22–32.

262. *AHB* 46,6, text by Isaac Watts (1719); corresponds to *Sv ps* 195,6.

263. *SA* 65,4, text by Pat Lewis (1938–); cf. also in the second stanza, the dynamics of the expression "clowns of creation in the circus of God."

264. The Word proceeds from the Father and yet remains eternally at home: ". . . geht zu der Welten Abendzeit, das Werk zu tun, das uns befreit" (goes to the evening of the time of the world to do the work that liberates us), *EG* 223,1, text by Otto Riethmüller (1932, 1934), based on a Corpus Christi hymn by Thomas Aquinas from 1263, 1264. Latin text: "Verbum supernum prodiens, nec Patris linquens dexteram, ad opus suum exiens venit ad vitae vesperam," *Hymns* 261.

265. *EG* 74,1, text by Johann Gottfried Herder (before 1800), revised (after 1817). This is an epiphany hymn that speaks of Jesus as the "Morgenstern" (morning star).

266. *GL* 781,1, text taken from a meditation to Jesus Christ.

267. *EG* 184,1 (= *GL* 276,1), text by Rudolf Alexander Schröder (1937).

268. *EG* 674(683),1, text by Fritz Enderlin (1949, 1952) based on the hymn *Splendor paternae gloriae* by Ambrose of Milan (before 386). The Latin text, according to *Hymns* 2, says nothing of time in this stanza. Instead, it speaks of ". . . de luce lucem proferens, lux lucis, et fons luminis. . . ."

269. *GL* 830,1, text by Leisentritt (1567).

270. "A virgin bore him, / who was her own creator, / God before all time began. / And the infant that she nurses, / has filled all eternities / with his radiance," *GL* 137,2, text based on *Dies est laetitiae* (ca.1320), translated by Maria L. Thurmair (1969). Cf. *Sv ps* 431,3: "Maria i sitt sköte bar / Guds Son som före världen var" (Mary carried in her womb the Son of God who existed before the world began), text by Martin Luther (1524), Swedish (1567), Anders Frostenson (1977).

271. *AHB* 127,1, text from 1446, translated by John Mason Neale (1818–66), among others.

272. *AHB* 38,1, text by Isaac Watts (1674–1748); *AHB* 36,2; *AHB* 5,3: "God the Father, God the Spirit, God the co-eternal Son," text based on a Russian church hymn, translated by John Brownlie (1857–1925), revised.

273. Cf. here the text of *AHB* 203,1.5, which is based on Ps. 72: "Hail to the Lord's anointed, great David's greater Son; hail, in the time appointed, his reign on earth begun! . . . The tide of time shall never his covenant remove . . . ," text by James Montgomery (1771–1854).

274. *GL* 706,3, text from *Te Deum* (fourth century), translated by Romano Guardini (1950). Latin text cited according to *Svps1937* 603b. In *EG* 331,6 (=*GL* 257,6), this passage reads, "Du, des Vaters ewger Sohn" (You, the eternal Son of the Father), and in *Sv ps* 1,5, "evigt född av Faderns vilja" (eternally borne by the will of the Father).

275. *AHB* 226,4, text by Charles Coffin (1676–1749), translated by James R. Woodford (1820–85); *AHB* 163,2, text by Matthew Bridges (1800–1894) and Godfrey Thring (1823–1903). Cf. also *Sv ps* 350,1 (cf. *EG* 67): "Vår Herre Krist var Sonen / hos Gud i evighet, / den älskade, fördolde / och alltings hemlighet" (Our Lord Christ was the Son with God in eternity, the beloved, the hidden and the secret of everything), text by Elisabeth Cruciger (Kreuziger) (1524), and Olov Hartman (1978).

276. *AHB* 190,1.2: "Christ, our King before creation, Son, who shared the Father's plan . . . Lord of life and Lord of history . . . ," text by Ivor H. Jones (1934–).

277. *AHB* 163,6, text by Matthew Bridges (1800–1894) and Godfrey Thring (1823–1903).

278. *AHB* 249,2, text based on the *Pange, lingua* by Venantius Fortunatus (ca. 600); English by John Mason Neale (1818–1866), revised. The translation is faithful to the Latin text: "quando venit ergo sacri plenitudo temporis, / missus est ab arce Patris Natus, orbis conditor, / atque ventre virginali carne factus prodiit," *Hymns* 107.

279. *EG* 409,4 (= *GL* 297,4), text by Walter Schulz (1962, 1970).

280. *EG* 67,2, text by Elisabeth Cruciger (Kreuziger) (1524). Cf. *AHB* 227,2, text by Charles Wesley (1707–88), revised.

281. *Sv ps* 127,2, text by Johann C. H. Holzschuher (1829), Swedish (1859).

282. *Sv ps* 175,2, text by J. O. Wallin (1812) and Olov Hartman (1978).

283. *Ps90* 842,2: "Oxen och åsnan samlas kring krubban i skapelsens timmar" (The ox and the donkey gather around the manger at the hours of creation), text by Göran Bexell (1972).

284. "Christ has appeared. / Look, the time of salvation began . . . ," *GL* 147,3, text by Maria L. Thurmair (1971).

285. "That which no one had ever seen and no one ever heard, he brought into time," *Sv ps* 303,2, text by Bo Setterlind (1972). Cf. also *AHB* 214,1: "When God almighty came to be one of us, masking the glory of his golden train, dozens of plain things shared the experience, and they will never be the same again . . . ," text by Michael E. Hewlett (1916–).

286. *Sv ps* 175,8, text by J. O. Wallin (1812) and Olov Hartman (1978).

287. "He who travels through the world and time, / calls not, as one yells at the market. / He addresses the heart, today . . . ," *EG* 313,3, text by Jürgen Henkys (1975, 1977) based on the Dutch "Jezus die langs het water liep" by Ad den Besten (1961).

288. "So that strangers become friends, / you come as a human being in our age . . . / . . . you walk as a brother about the land . . . ," *EG* 667(674),1.2, text by Rolf Schweizer (1982).

289. *GL* 249,4 (=*EG* 579[566],4), text by Maria L. Thurmair (1941, 1946).

290. *SA* 61,2, text by Fred Pratt Green (1903–). Cf. also *AHB* 244,1–5, text by Laurence Housman (1865–1959).

291. *Sv ps* 108,2, text by J. Erik Nyström (1893), revised.

292. *Sv ps* 348,1.2: "Kristus, konung som hör hemma / hos vår Gud till evig tid, / du fick mänsklig kropp och stämma . . . Av en ringa jordisk moder, / Herre, du dig födas lät / . . . döljande ditt majestät" (Christ, King, who is at home with our God until eternal time, you received a human body and a human voice . . . You allowed yourself to be born of a humble, earthly mother . . . concealing your majesty), text by Johan Åström (1814) and Britt G. Hallqvist (1983). Åström's text, according to *Svps1937* 36,1, is not as clear as Hallqvist's revision: "Kriste, som ditt ursprung leder Evigt från din Faders sköt Och, från himlen stigen neder, Dig i jordisk skepnad slöt . . ." (Christ, you whose origins come eternally from your Father's lap, and you who came down from heaven to shroud yourself in earthly form . . .).

293. *GL* 565,1, text by Georg Thurmair (1939); *Sv ps* 318, text by Nils Frykman (1889), revised; *Sv ps* 319,1, text by J. O. Wallin (1816) and Britt G. Hallqvist (1981); *Sv ps* 627,4, text by Svein Ellingsen (1977) and Britt G. Hallqvist (1978).

294. *AHB* 205,4, text by Julia Ward Howe (1819–1910) et al. Cf. also *Sv ps* 490, text by John Brownlie (1907) and Anders Frostenson (1984).

295. *Sv ps* 35,3, text by Frans Mikael Franzén (1812), revised.

296. *EG* 184,4 (= *GL* 276,4): ". . . und kommt am Tag, vorherbestimmt, da alle Welt ihr Urteil nimmt" (. . . and it is coming on the day that is predetermined for the entire world to be judged), text by Rudolf Alexander Schröder (1937).

297. *Sv ps* 490,3: "Hans stora dag, låt oss med bön / och tro påskynda den" (His great day, let us hasten it with prayer and faith), text by John Brownlie (1907) and Anders Frostenson (1984). Cf. also *Sv ps* 609,3: "Advent är väntan på Kristus: Kom Herre, kom hit i tid" (Advent is waiting for Christ: Come, Lord, come here in time), text by Margareta Melin (1969).

298. *Sv ps* 425,3.5.7, text by Lars Thunberg (1968).

299. *SA* 92,2, text by Malcolm Stewart (1967).

300. *Psqo* 905,1.4, text by Eyvind Skeie (1981); Swedish by Jonas Jonson (1993).

301. *GL* 564,1, text from 1973; cf. *EG* 81,7, text by Johann Heermann (1630).

302. *GL* 811,3, text: *Kyrie eleison*, revised version, Osnabrück (undated).

303. *Psqo* 849,1, text by Jan Arvid Hellström (1990).

304. *Sv ps* 21,2, text by Britt G. Hallqvist (1974); *Sv ps* 463,4, text by Ylva Eggehorn (1970); *Sv ps* 591,1–4, text by Brian Wren (1975); Swedish by Anders Frostenson (1984).

305. *Sv ps* 352,5, text by Anders Frostenson (1970, 1984).

306. *AHB* 176,3: "A man there stands at God's right hand, / divine, yet human still; / that grand, heroic, peerless soul / death sought in vain to kill. / All power is his: supreme he rules / all realms of time and space . . . ," text by Somerset C. Lowry (1855–1932), revised. *Sv ps* 600,4: "O sårade kropp / som aldrig kan dö . . ." (Oh, wounded body that can never die), text by Anders Frostenson (1968, 1979).

307. *SA* 69,1: "O changeless Christ, for ever new . . . ," text by Timothy Dudley-Smith (1926–); *AHB* 153,1: ". . . our faithful, unchangeable friend . . . ," text by Joseph Hart (1712–68); *Sv ps* 417,4: "Du är oss evigt ny och dock dig lik" (You are eternally new to us and yet remain the same), text by Sigrid (Siri) Dahlquist (1923), revised; *Sv ps* 471,2, text by Olof Arbman (1927), revised.

308. *AHB* 204,1.2, text by George MacDonald (1824–1905).

309. *Sv ps* 407,1, text by Ernst G. Woltersdorf (1752) and Britt G. Hallqvist (1984); *Sv ps* 39,1, text by Anders Frostenson (1935), revised.

310. *EG* 119,2 (= *GL* 230,2; cf. also *Sv ps* 158,1), text by Bartholomäus Gesius (1601), based on *Coelos ascendit hodie* (sixteenth century).

311. *SA* 18,3, text by Brian Wren (1936–).

312. *GL* 704,1, text based on *Christe, qui lux es et dies* (sixth century), translated by Friedrich Dörr (1969).

313. *Sv ps* 40,6, text by Anders Frostenson (1936).

314. *Sv ps* 100,3, text by Lina Sandell-Berg (1872), revised.

315. *Sv ps* 469,5, text by J. O. Wallin (1819).

316. *AHB* 390,3, text by Joseph A. Robinson (1858–1933), revised.

317. *AHB* 595,3.6, text by John Greally (1934–).

318. *AHB* 214, text by Michael E. Hewlett (1916–).

319. *SA* 92,3, text by Malcolm Stewart (1967).

320. *AHB* 183, text by Sydney Carter (1915–).

321. "Supreme Comforter within Time," *GL* 244,3, text based on *Veni sancte spiritus* (thirteenth century), translated by Maria L. Thurmair and Markus Jenny (1971). Time is not mentioned at the corresponding place in the Latin text, *Hymns* 184: "consolator optime."

322. *Sv ps* 367,1, text by Anders Frostenson (1976); *Sv ps* 286,1, text by J. A. Eklund (1934), revised; *Sv ps* 436,2, text by Anders Frostenson (1960); *AHB* 319,1, text by Cecil Frances Alexander (1818–95).

323. *AHB* 230,3: Christ was filled "with the eternal Spirit's power," text by Charles Wesley (1707–88).

324. *AHB* 592,6: "To the everlasting Father and the Son who reigns on high, with the Holy Ghost proceeding forth from each eternally . . . ," text based on *Pange, lingua* by Thomas Aquinas (1227–74), translated by Edward Caswall (1814–78). Latin text at the corresponding place: "Genitori Genitoque . . . procedenti ab utroque compar sit laudatio," *Hymns* 260.

325. *AHB* 325,7: "Come, Spirit, show us Father, Son, / with whom for ever you are one," text by Tom Colvin and people from Ghana (1965). *EG* 127,5: "Wie mit dem Vater und dem Sohn du eins bist . . . im ewgen Liebesbunde" (As with the Father and the Son, you are one . . . in an eternal bond of love), text by Ambrosius Blarer (ca. 1533/34).

326. *AHB* 320,1–4, text by Edwin Hatch (1835–89), revised. Swedish translation in *Sv ps* 368,1–4, text by Anders Frostenson (1969).

327. *Sv ps* 403,5, text by Laurentius Jonae Gestritius (1619), Jesper Svedberg (1694), and Anders Frostenson (1978).

328. *Sv ps* 522,3, text by Jonas Jonson (1984).

329. *AHB* 323,3: ". . . Holy Spirit, ever binding / age to age, and soul to soul, / in a fellowship unending . . . ," text by Timothy Rees (1874–1939).

330. *EG* 127,6, text by Ambrosius Blarer (ca. 1533/34).

331. *EG* 133,13, text by Paul Gerhardt (1653).

332. "It passes swiftly. We hold nothing in [our] hands," *EG* 491,1 (= *GL* 702,1), text by Christa Weiss and Kurt Rommel (1965).

333. ". . . As a stream begins to run / and does not stop flowing, / so our time flows away," *EG* 528,2 (= *GL* 657,2), text by Michael Franck (1652). *AHB* 46,5: "Time, like an ever-rolling stream, / bears all its sons away: / they fly forgotten as a dream / dies at the opening day," text by Isaac Watts (1674–1748), based on Ps. 90; cf. the translation of this hymn in *Sv ps* 195. *Sv ps* 83,4: "När öden och tider väller / som strömmande vattendrag . . ." [when fates and times pour forth like flowing watercourses], text by Karl-Gustaf Hildebrand (1936, 1983); *Ps90* 888,2: ". . . alla är vi ett, / färdas samman på tidens flod . . ." (we are all one, and we travel together on the stream of time), text by John Nilsson (1968).

334. *EG* 530,1, text by Ämilie Juliane von Schwarzburg-Rudolstadt (1686, 1688).

335. *Sv ps* 369,6, text by Edvard Evers (1914) and Britt G. Hallqvist (1983); *EG* 527,8–9, text by Andreas Gryphius (1650).

336. *Sv ps* 622,3 ". . . du vet med vilken skräck vi ser vårt timglas sandkorn falla ner . . ." (you know the terror with which we watch the sands fall through our hourglass), text by Nicolai Frederik Severin Grundtvig (1845) and Sven Christer Swahn (1979).

337. Cf. *GL* 897,2: "im Glauben soll ich streben aus der Zeit zur Ewigkeit" (in faith, I should strive to leave time and enter into eternity), text from *Sursum corda* (1874), new version by Friedrich Kienecker (1973); *Sv ps* 262,2 and 302,1–5, text by Nils Frykman (1877, 1883), revised.

338. *EG* 378,5: ". . . Deine Zeit und alle Zeit stehn in Gottes Händen" (Your time and all of time are in God's hands), text by Rudolf Alexander Schröder (1936, 1939).

339. *AHB* 66,2: "Chance and change are busy ever, man decays, and ages move; but his mercy waneth never," text by John Bowring (1792–1872); cf. also *AHB* 265,1.5, text by John Bowring, revised; *EG* 564(551),2, text by Arno Pötzsch (1947). On the constancy of the church, see *Sv ps* 163,1, text by Lars Thunberg (1983), based on Samuel Gabrielsson (1929).

340. *Ps90* 821,2–3, text by Seppo Suokunnas (1984), Swedish by Catharina Östman (1985); *Ps90* 874, text by Britt G. Hallqvist (undated); *Sv ps* 255,1, text by Britt G. Hallqvist (1958); *Sv ps* 264,2, text by Ylva Eggehorn (1970).

341. *EG* 136, 2, text by Philipp Spitta (1827, 1833); *EG* 298,2, text by Samuel Gottlieb Bürde (1787); *EG* 344,5, text by Martin Luther (1539).

342. *Sv ps* 561,3, text by J. O. Wallin (1819), revised. *AHB* 484,5, text by Charles Wesley (1707–88); *AHB* 520,1, text by Frances Ridley Havergal (1836–9). Cf. also *GL* 788,4: The text is a meditation of thanks at year's end.

343. *EG* 441,5 (= *GL* 557), text by Johannes Zwick (1545).

344. For example, *EG* 151,4.8, text by Lorenz Lorenzen (1700).

345. Long before we were born, you looked upon us! / "They are the ones who stand waiting before the gates of life. / Make room for them . . . ," *EG* 646,2, text by Rudolf Alexander Schröder (1927, 1930) (not included in *EG1996*). Cf. also *GL* 554,5 (=*EG* 70,5): ". . . du hast mich ewig vor der Welt in deinem Sohn geliebet . . ." (you loved me eternally in your Son before the world began), text by Philipp Nicolai (1599).

346. *Sv ps* 376,2: "Allt klarare skall varje tid förstå ditt helga ord . . ." (each age will understand your Holy Word evermore clearly), text by Samuel Gabrielsson (1929); *AHB* 335, text by George Rawson (1807–89), revised; *Ps90* 819,3–4, text by Tore Littmarck (1992).

347. *Sv ps* 535,1–2, text by Frans Mikael Franzén (1812, 1816); *Sv ps* 81,3, text by Lina Sandell-Berg (1872); *EG* 145,1.6, text by Johann Walter (1561).

348. *Sv ps* 585,1.4, text by Annie L. Coghill (1854) and Sigrid (Siri) Dahlquist (1913), revised; *Sv ps* 364,8, text by an unknown Swedish author (1694), Olov Hartman (1978). The admonition to use time properly appears to be an important concern during the nineteenth century.

349. *Sv ps* 182,6, text by Karl Laurids Aastrup (1960), Britt G. Hallqvist (1973); *EG* 363,3.5, text by Georg Grünwald (1530); *AHB* 566,5, text by Fred Kaan (1929–).

350. *Ps90* 853,3, text by Eyvind Skeie (1970), Swedish by Jonas Jonson (1988). According to *GL* 888, one should also pay attention to saints as signs of the times; text by Friedrich Kienecker (1973).

351. *Sv ps* 524,3, text by Maj Bylock (1983).

352. *Ps90* 863,1–3, text by Tore Littmarck (undated).

353. *Ps90* 871,4, text by Jonas Jonson (1990), based on Fred Kaan's "Christ is alive."

354. *Ps90* 890,6, text by Fred Kaan and Britt G. Hallqvist (1983); *Ps90* 891,3, text by Olov Hartman (undated); *Ps90* 895,3, text by Jonas Jonson (1992, 1993). Cf. also pp. 37–41 above.

355. *GL* 661,2, text by Melchior Ludolf Herold (1808); *AHB* 621,3–4, text by James Quinn (1919–).

356. "In us circles the life / that God has given us, / it circles as the dying and becoming of this earth," *EG* 670,1 (not included in *EG1996*).

357. *EG* 671(678),2, text by Peter Spangenberg (1989).

358. *EG* 432,1, text by Eckart Bücken (1982).

359. *EG* 426,3, text by Walter Schulz (1963, 1987).

360. *Sv ps* 572,4: ". . . Korta minuter känslan åtnjuter vad vi i sanning dock äga all tid," text by Carl Olof Rosenius (1847).

361. "Already you are the one that you will one day be: condemned and pardoned, dead and resurrected," *Sv ps* 87,4, text by Anders Frostenson (1963). An expression of realized eschatology of the more traditional type is found in *AHB* 473,4 in the exposition of the thought that "whate'er we hope, by faith we have, / future and past are present now," *AHB* 473,3, text by Charles Wesley (1707–88).

362. *EG* 153,5, text by Kurt Marti (1971). Cf. also *Sv ps* 559,2, text by Anders Frostenson (1960); *Sv ps* 580,4, text by J. A. Eklund (1910); *Sv ps* 548,1–3, text by Elis Erlandsson (1936).

363. *Sv ps* 173,3, text by Svein Ellingsen (1971) and Britt G. Hallqvist (1978). *Sv ps*

363,5, text by Johann Franck (1653) and Petrus Brask (1690); the expression "att gå ur tiden" (to leave time) has been added here by Britt G. Hallqvist (1983) as a replacement for "när en ände sker på mitt elände" (when the end of my misery comes), see *Svps1937* 137,8; here, "elände" can also have the older meaning of "banishment, exile," cf. Selander, *O hur saligt att få vandra*, 107. In *Sv ps* 519,3, the expression "jag blir ur tiden tagen" (I am being taken from time) was also inserted by Britt G. Hallqvist (1983) or Lars Lindman (1981) into the original text by J. O. Wallin (1818); here, as a replacement for "Snart är . . . min själ ifrån mig tagen" (soon my soul will be taken from me), see *Svps1937* 403,7.

364. "We want to live and assert ourselves. / But we risk your freedom. / We want the world to arrange itself according to our will. / Self-righteously, we build the tower of time," *EG* 360,3, text by Christa Weiss (1965). This hymn inspired A. Frostenson to write the text of *Sv ps* 289 (Belfrage, *Guds kärlek är som stranden*, 7f.). *Sv ps* 289, in turn, became known in German translation as "Herr, deine Liebe ist wie Gras und Ufer" (Lord, your love is like grass and seashore) and was then included, as number 663, in the final version of the *EG*.

365. "Let your grace, O Lord, prevail over the law; / release us from yesterday and tomorrow," *EG* 360,5.

366. Augustine held that the "present, should it always be present, and never pass into time past, would no longer be time, but indeed eternity." *Confessiones* XI.14.17.

367. For definitions of these concepts, see pp. 15–17.

368. These faces can be experienced as completely negative. Cf. Benktson, who, in his book on the problems of time, distinguishes four faces of time in the novels of Swedish writer Lars Gyllensten, namely, elapsing time, empty time marked by ennui, destructive time, and unavailable time. *Samtidighetens mirakel*, 45–81.

369. 140–44. Gronemeyer discusses in detail the thesis that Western civilization has developed out of terror of death and excessive fear of failure. Its response to the fear of death is the attempt to safeguard the individual lifespan to the maximum degree possible; it confronts the fear of failure with the attempt to outwit time by a terrific acceleration of life's tempo.

370. "Mit der Zukunft, jedenfalls mit jener, die ihren Namen zu Recht trägt, weil sie das, was ungemacht und ungeplant auf uns 'zukommt', enthält, hat sich 'homo accelerandus' gründlich überworfen. Er hat dem unberechenbaren und unvorhersehbaren Noch-Nicht einen Gestellungsbefehl erteilt: die Zukunft hat in der Gegenwart zu erscheinen," ibid., 144.

371. Cf. Boethius, *De consolatione Philosophiae* IV.4. Punishment means that the evil person can be freed of his or her malice; something just (thus, good) is thereby granted to the evil one, thus lessening the tragedy. Such a notion is conclusive only if one presupposes an indisputable primacy of eternity over all temporality.

372. Thus also Gronemeyer, *Das Leben als letzte Gelegenheit*, 147ff.

Chapter 2

1. Ratschow, *Anmerkungen zur theologischen Auffassung des Zeitproblems* (Remarks Concerning the Theological Conception of the Problem of Time).

2. Ratschow, ibid., 362, sees rudimentary demonic conceptions in linguistic expressions such as time eats, gnaws, acts, heals. Also, the Greek god Chronos "devoured" his children.

3. Ratschow understands Kant's philosophy of time as related to the "Dämon der Vergänglichkeit und dem Schicksal des Wandels" (demon of transitoriness and the destiny of change"), ibid., 362f.

4. ". . . [der Mensch] entwindet sich dem Schrecken der Zeit und springt auf der via negationis hinüber zum Unvergänglichen, Unwandelbaren und Unveränderlichen," ibid., 363.

5. Ibid., 363.

6. Ibid., 368.

7. Ibid., 371.

8. Ibid., 374.

9. "Zwischen unseren Tagen, den Tagen der Urzeit und dem Tage Jahwes ist eine grundsätzliche Verbindung eben im Tag-Sein," ibid., 375. At this point, Ratschow also mentions that the three-tiered past, present, and future is distinguished from the two-tiered Hebrew thinking, which is expressed in the conceptuality of day and night and also in the inflection of the verb in only two tenses. When it has to do with the appropriation of salvation, Ratschow sees in the biblical concept not simply a temporal forward movement, but rather a movement that is similar to the pattern "one step back and two steps forwards": Looking back at the act of salvation becomes the reception of the coming God (386).

10. ". . . [d]er moderne Mensch ist insofern modern, als er von der Empfindung lebt, daß er keine Zeit hat," ibid., 377. Ratschow asks himself here if, instead of speaking of having no time, we should perhaps speak more clearly of having no eternity; but, unfortunately, he does not follow this trail, which I would consider very productive. Cf. Jackelén, "Förlorad evighet som orsak till kronisk tidsbrist?" (Lost eternity as the reason for chronic lack of time?).

11. "[D]er ganz und gar verschlossene Mensch." Ratschow, *Anmerkungen zur theologischen Auffassung des Zeitproblems*, 378.

12. ". . . läßt sich weder auswalzen zur Dauer noch aneinanderketten zur Unendlichkeit. . . . Was hier Ewigkeit heißen kann, geht nicht Dauer oder Kürze dieser Zeit an, sondern die Tiefe ihrer Ermöglichung," ibid., 380.

13. *Anchor Bible Dictionary* (New York: Doubleday, 1992) lists neither *time* nor *eternity* and has no cross-references at the pertinent spots. *Begriffslexikon zum Neuen Testament,* ed. L. Coenen, E. Beyreuther and Hans Bietenhard (Wuppertal: Rolf Brockhaus, 1970), references the key words *eternity* and *time.* In the *Theologische Realenzyklopädie,* vol. x (1982), 696, references to *resurrection* and *life* are found under *eternal life,* and *eternity* has cross-references to *eschatology, God,* and *time. Neues Handbuch theologischer Grundbegriffe,* 4 vols., ed. Peter Eicher (Munich: Kösel, 1984–85), lists neither *time* nor *eternity;* only in the new expanded edition (vol. 5 [1991], same editor, place, and publisher) is there a substantial article under the key word *time/eternity* (pp. 300–326).

14. ". . . von Haus aus keine Neigungen zu Abstraktionen hat." Herrmann, *Die neue Physik,* 97. Cf. also Ebeling, *Zeit und Wort,* 364: Time in the Old Testament is "stets konkrete Zeit" (always concrete time).

15. German: "gefüllte Zeit" (time as containing events). Von Rad, *Theologie des Alten Testaments,* ii.109; *Old Testament Theology,* 100.

16. ". . . das Geschehen ist nicht ohne seine Zeit, und die Zeit nicht ohne ein Geschehen denkbar." Ibid.

17. Delling, "Zeit und Endzeit," 22 and 25. Also Muilenburg, "The Biblical View of Time," 236.

18. In the OT, ʿōlām designates the most distant past and, above all, the most distant future. In the Psalms, one finds a doxological usage (as in the hymns examined in chapter 1). The term possibly develops in an eschatological direction; cf. Preuß, "ʿōlām." ʿēt stands for *moment, occasion, period of time,* and *time.* In the *Septuagint,* the term is usually translated as *kairos,* which corresponds to its primary meaning—the definite/right time for

something; cf. Kronholm, "ʿēt." Wilch, *Time and Event*, provides an in-depth study. According to Wilch, in contrast to other OT expressions for time, ʿēt marks not only the aspect of temporal relation, but also "the occasion itself," by giving a specific event "a definite, singular place in time" (167ff.).

19. Compare to this also Barr, *Biblical Words for Time*. Barr considers a lexical method of word study inappropriate for biblical theology (12). A specific biblical concept of time cannot be developed in this way because "the lexical stock of neither Hebrew nor New Testament Greek is laid out in a plan or pattern which corresponds with the distinctiveness of biblical thought" (160); linguistically, then, neither the Old Testament nor the New Testament permits the postulate of biblical uniqueness. Due to the lack of explicit statements about time and eternity in the Bible, which does not really permit the development of a philosophical-theological concept of time, Barr cautions one not to try to extrapolate such a concept of time from the words that have been used (131f.), particularly with respect to Cullmann. At the very least, the syntactical context must also be constantly kept in mind. An understanding of time can be built only on the "statements" and not on the "words" of the Bible (147). At this point, I basically agree with Barr, but (as suggested in chapter 1) I would replace "statements" with "narratives."

20. Cf. Ps 76:5; Deut. 33:15; Ps. 89:37f.

21. Ebeling, *Zeit und Wort*, 364. Cf., e.g., Ps. 90:2; Isa. 43:10, 44:6.

22. On this, see also Kessler, "Das Sabbatgebot," who refers to the tension existing in the biblical canon, namely, that in creation the Sabbath is presented as a universal model, yet it is commanded exclusively of Israel.

23. Cf. also to the explanation of the Sabbath of creation in Link, *Schöpfung*, 384ff.

24. Clifford, *Creation Accounts*, 83.

25. Levine, "The Jews in Time and Space," 2.

26. Ibid., 3. It is worth noting that Levine bestows precisely upon the *cyclical* character of time the function to conserve and strengthen identity.

27. Ibid., 4. From the perspective of Christianity, Levine's thesis would have to be modified so that it is valid for certain periods, for example, the era of the Crusades or the Baroque period with its intoxication with space; in the case of the European West, however, a development away from a spatial connection toward a gradual relativization of the significance of space, and, finally, to a massive dominance of time can also be demonstrated. Cf. in this regard Smith, *To Take Place*, esp. 114ff. Smith notes the development of an increasing trend toward temporalization brought about by the cultivation of the Church year.

28. Levine, "The Jews in Time and Space," 10.

29. Von Rad, *Theologie des Alten Testaments*, II.112; trans., 103. In this context, von Rad also cites Ps. 118:24, which, as I have shown above on pp. 32–37, also plays a role in Church hymns, particularly in Christmas and Easter hymns.

30. ". . . vehemente[n] Erlebnis der Gleichzeitigkeit der göttlichen Heilstaten." Ibid., II.114 trans., 105.

31. ". . . die Bedeutung dieser Umprägungen als Leistungen eines ganz eigenständigen Welt- und Daseinsverständnisses wohl kaum überschätzen." Ibid., II.113 trans., 104.

32. Ibid., II.116 trans., 106.

33. Ibid., II.118 and II.121–29 trans., 108 and 112–19.

34. ". . . garstiger Graben." In relation to the neighboring religions of the ancient orient, von Rad asserts: "Keine dieser Religionen hat die Dimension der Geschichte so erfaßt wie Israel!" (Not one of them [these religions] understood the dimension of history in the way that Israel did.) Ibid., II.119f. trans., 110. One must ask whether, here, in this claim of uniqueness, underlying value concepts—which are not being accounted for—are not also

playing a role. Von Rad's account of the epochal, unique, and inestimable nature of Israel's conceptions of time does not appear to be completely free of a triumphalistic undertone. By using non-biblical writings, Albrektson shows that the antithesis (which can also be found in Mowinckel, Noth, Vriezen, etc.) of Israel's God as the god of history and the surrounding gods as nature gods is untenable and that the belief in historical events as divine acts, which reveal anger or goodwill, is part of a common legacy in the Near East. The exaggerated emphasis on historical events as the principal medium of revelation must therefore be modified to the effect that divine revelation through the word is to be regarded as something specific to Israelite thinking (Albrektson, *History and the Gods*, 11ff. and 120ff.). Whitrow also believes that the claim of the uniqueness of Hebrew historical thought must be revised by a positive reevaluation of Sumerian, Babylonian, and Persian (Zoroastrian) influences (*Time in History*, 53f.). Instead, he attaches the linear concept of history—no less exclusive, as it appears—to the New Testament, in particular to the unique event of the crucifixion. "This essentially historical view of time, with its particular emphasis on the non-repeatability of events, is the very essence of Christianity" (57).

35. According to Otto, one can easily find at least a dozen words in Egyptian that correspond to our term *time* and thus mark different aspects of this concept ("Zeitvorstellungen und Zeitrechnung im Alten Orient," 744).

36. Morenz, *Ägyptische Religion*, 83; *Egyptian Religion*, 79. Cf. also Whitrow, *Time in History*, 21–36: "Time at the Dawn of History" (prehistory of Egypt, the Sumerian and Babylonian Kingdoms, and Iran).

37. Morenz, *Ägyptische Religion*, 79; trans., 76.

38. ". . . nicht oder jedenfalls nicht nur als absolute und quantitative Größe gegenüber, sondern gibt ihr Relation und damit Qualität," ibid., 80; trans., 76.

39. "Zeit wird Gefäß für eine erfüllte Gegenwart," Hornung, *Geist der Pharaonenzeit*, 75. Cf. here also the pictorial depiction of time as an endless, two-strand rope that is being unwound out of the mouth of the divinity: Time emerges from hidden, divine depths; it unfolds into an ordered and structured continuum and falls back into the depths from which it came (70).

40. "Die Jahre sind in seiner Hand," Pap Berlin 3049 XIII 2, cited here according to Morenz, *Ägyptische Religion*, 79; trans., 66.

41. "Der du die Zeit in Händen hast," *EG* 64,1 [= *GL* 157,1], text from 1938.

42. Morenz, *Ägyptische Religion*, 84; trans., 80.

43. ". . . jeder hat seine Nahrung, und seine Lebenszeit ist berechnet." From Amenophis IV's (Akhenaton) "Hymn to the Sun," ca. 1370–1352 B.C.E., in which it is also said of Re: "Du bist die Lebenszeit selbst, man lebt durch dich" (you are life [time] itself, one lives through you), which is cited here according to the sources collected by Eliade, *Geschichte der religiösen Ideen*, vol. 4, 37ff.; *From Primitives to Zen*, 179. Even if the religious movement of Akhenaton remains a parenthesis in Egyptian history and thus lacks general validity, it may well be justified to cite the "Hymn to the Sun" in this context due to the commonalities with Ps. 104.

44. Otto, *Zeitvorstellungen und Zeitrechnung*, 749. Otto's belief that a concept of time is partially shaped by the spatial conception of the world can hardly be repudiated. But his assumption that, in the case of Egypt, the geographical shape of the country affected the understanding of time appears to be more speculative. On the Egyptian perspective, cf. also Assmann, "Das Doppelgesicht der Zeit." Colpe offers interesting comparative material in *Die Zeit in drei asiatischen Hochkulturen*.

45. Gese, *Geschichtliches Denken*, 127–45.

46. Ibid., 142–44.

47. Rochberg-Halton and Vanderkam, "Calendars," 816f.

48. Ibid., 810–17.

49. Schmid, who starts with the two modes of thinking, namely, the concept of world order and that of historical development, also emphasizes, in contrast to von Rad, "daß Israel auf weite Strecken von Geschichte nicht sehr viel anders gesprochen hat als seine Nachbarn" (that Israel did not talk very differently from its neighbors throughout broad stretches of history). *Das alttestamentliche Verständnis*, 14. He criticizes the idea of a primal revelation of God in history that was postulated by von Rad; in his opinion, the processing of experience in history instead takes place, as in Egypt and Mesopotamia, by means of a relative and immediate integration into the correlations of the world order (16). Von Rad's (mis)understanding of history as the exclusive category of revelation had consequences: He made "Geschichte . . . zum Fundamentalbegriff einer spezifisch biblisch-theologischen Hermeneutik" (history . . . a fundamental concept of a specifically biblical-theological hermeneutics), so that an overall systematic-theological plan based on the concept "revelation as history" was made possible (Pannenberg). Schmid, *Das alttestamentliche Verständnis*, 10. Cf. also Pannenberg, *Das Wirklichkeitsverständnis der Bibel*. Here, Pannenberg supports the theory that the biblical understanding of reality—as history that has a basic pattern of promise and fulfillment—stands not only in contrast to archaic-mythic cultic thinking, on the one hand, and the cosmic understanding of reality, on the other, but also overcomes both by incorporating them. According to Schmid, there is no such thing as *the* Old Testament understanding of history. History is also not a major topic in the OT; the concern is rather the maintenance of a good world order. Israel nonetheless did not develop an ideologically rigid concept of order, but instead a belief in God that, both in keeping with and contrary to historical experience, held fast to the divine intention to save. This, according to Schmid, is Israel's accomplishment (20f.).

In connection with his criticism of the American Biblical Theology Movement, Perdue goes back far beyond von Rad when he says that, influenced by the Enlightenment, Old Testament scholarship was in the grips of historical categories (*The Collapse of History*). He sees this expressed in von Rad's unquestioned assumption of the superiority of the historical over the mythical. (Such a notion is also found, for example, in Würthwein, "Chaos und Schöpfung.") According to Perdue, the postulation that Israel was unique because of its idea of a god revealed in history, while other cultures were bound by their concepts of God to nature and myth, proved to be a dead end, since the anchoring of revelation in theological uniqueness and the presumption that the historical is superior to the mythical is untenable in two ways: First, non-Israelite cultures also believed in divine action in history (39; cf. also Albrektson, *History and the Gods*, n. 34); and, second, the Israelites also held the notion that God was in nature (40).

50. Von Rad is silent here about the cyclical dimension (*Theologie des Alten Testaments*, II.III; trans., 102). Instead of this, he sees in Gen. 8:22 a typical expression for the older Israel's understanding of time: non-eschatological, a stringing together of ages of various contents (although it deals *expressis verbis* with a constant return of a merely two-part time sequence) based on a natural rhythm.

51. Against this backdrop, von Rad's juxtaposition of event and history is surprising: "Diese Erkenntnis, daß sich Israel nicht auf einem Ereignis gründete, sondern daß ihm ein langer Weg, d.h. eine Geschichte voraufging, bedeutet einen epochalen Schritt" (This realisation—that Israel was not founded upon one single event, but there was a long road, that is to say, a history which led up to her formation—is an epoch-making step). *Theologie des Alten Testaments*, II.116; trans., 106. In addition to the knowledge of history, the events of establishing this and other covenants are likely to have played a significant role in the founding of Israel.

52. ". . noch nicht die eigentliche sündenvergebende Gnade . . . , sondern ein Gnaden-

willen, . . . der in dem wandellosen Bestand der Ordnungen der Natur wirkt und erkennbar wird." Von Rad, *Das erste Buch Mose*, 92; *Genesis: A Commentary*, 123.

53. Ibid., 134. Von Rad's tendency to harbor underlying value judgments that prefer a linear to a cyclical concept of time and the historical to the natural is also evident here: "Die durch Gottes Wort gefestigten *natürlichen* Ordnungen sichern ja nur geheimnisvoll dienend eine Welt, in der dann zu seiner Zeit Gottes *geschichtliches* Heilshandeln einsetzen wird" (The *natural* orders that were established by God's Word only safeguard, in a myste- rious way, a world in which God's *historical* acts of salvation will begin in God's good time). Von Rad, *Das erste Buch Mose*, 101. It seems to me that the basic error lies in his jux- taposition. Von Rad starts with an antithesis rather than with a parallelism or merging, which, among other things, results in an instrumentalization of nature and a forfeiting of its history. Westermann more appropriately emphasizes that in the Yahwist account, pre- cisely here, in the Flood narrative, with its climax in Gen. 8:20–22, the world is granted its own life.

54. ". . . das kosmische Geschehen in zeitlicher Erstreckung als Ganzheit gesehen." Westermann, *Genesis*, 613; trans., *Genesis 1–11*, 457.

55. Rendtorff, "Genesis 8,21," 195ff. Also here, it seems reasonable to suspect an under- lying value hierarchy that is more concerned about collecting the most evidence possible for the superior uniqueness of belief in Yahweh than about tracking down the commonali- ties and parallels that may have evolved organically.

56. Eichrodt, "Heilserfahrung und Zeitverständnis," 105.

57. Westermann also shares this opinion (*Genesis*, 614; trans., 458). In his commentary to Gen. 8:22, he understands God's acts of blessing as being effective in the rhythms set here, whereas he sees God's redemptive work being effective in contingent events. This ap- proach allows a parallelism that seems to be more productive than the antithetical, under- lying hierarchical train of thought in von Rad. (Cf. with this also Westermann's account of the Old Testament experience of time in Westermann, "Erfahrung der Zeit.") The prob- lem with von Rad's thinking in this context can also be elucidated by using an example from Cullmann, who reasons in similar ways about the New Testament: The reception of the Old Testament into the New, he says, means that Christian belief is belief in a salvation history, which means "daß der christliche Glaube wie der jüdische sich von allen antiken Religionen der Umwelt gerade durch diese heilsgeschichtliche Ausrichtung unterscheidet" (that Christian faith, like Jewish faith, was distinguished from all other religions of this time by this salvation-historical orientation). Cullmann, *Heil als Geschichte*, 7; trans., *Sal- vation in History*, 25.

58. Gorman, *The Ideology of Ritual*, 227.

59. In this context, one can also discuss the relationship of the past, the present, and the future in Hebrew thought. In opposition to the theories of Marsh (a melting together of present, past, and future in realistic time), Boman (argues with the temporal bi-polarity of the Hebrew language; the ability of the Israelites to consider past, present, and future as a totality has essentially to do with their psychological uniqueness; this predestined them to become the people of revelation; cf. Boman, *Das hebräische Denken*), and Ratschow (the two-tiered concept of Old Testament time compared to our three-tiered concept, see n. 9 above), Eichrodt stresses (in "Heilserfahrung und Zeitverständnis") the awareness of the future that is expressed in explicit admonitions (Deut. 6:7, etc.), the emphasis on genealo- gies (in P) as the expression of the consciousness of linear time, the consciousness of epochs in the Deuteronomistic corpus, the juxtaposition of present and past in view of the future in prophetic proclamation, and the marking of "today" as the time of decision. Thus, Eichrodt prefers to account for the Hebrew understanding of time (as a three-tiered concept) neither as something coming from a special psychologically determined sense of

time or from a different type of understanding of reality, but rather from the experience of salvation, from the "Begegnung mit dem Gott, der die Zeit der Aufrichtung seiner Herrschaft dienstbar macht" (encounter with the God who uses time for the purpose of establishing divine rule), 125. In this way, he moves the question of the Old Testament concept of time beyond the cyclical-linear categorization and makes it dependent upon the category of salvation history.

60. See also Herrmann, *Zeit und Geschichte*, 101.

61. ". . . Umwandlung kosmischer religiöser Strukturen in Ereignisse der Heilsgeschichte," Eliade, *Geschichte der religiösen Ideen*, vol. 1, 170; trans., 179.

62. ". . . daß die Hebräer als erste die Bedeutung der Geschichte als Epiphanie Gottes entdeckten." Ibid., 326. With respect to the interpretation of history in the Deuteronomistic corpus, Ringgren remarks that this interpretation is certainly not without parallels outside of Israel, but that it nevertheless forms the earliest consistently developed philosophy of history in antiquity. *Israelitische Religion*, 101.

63. According to Eliade, in pre-Christian times, an understanding of time as salvation history also matured in other places. Thus he gives the example of a cosmogony from the Iranian region that already presupposes an eschatology and a soteriology (Zurvanism). *Geschichte der religiösen Ideen*, vol. 2, 265–70; trans., 309–13.

64. Eliade, *Geschichte der religiösen Ideen*, vol. 1, 326.

65. Eliade shows the occurrence of both perspectives within one tradition using the example of the exodus tradition. Ibid., 382f.

66. Cf. Herrmann, *Zeit und Geschichte*, 110.

67. Cf. this also to Eliade's theory of the "eternal return," which speaks of a continuity between Christian eschatology and the archaic pattern of the periodic regeneration of history, between the drama of the Church year and the superseding of concrete, historical time by the repetition of archetypal (cosmogonic) acts. The fact that in Judaism and Christianity the regular regeneration of creation is replaced by a single future new creation *in illo tempore*, which puts a definite end to history, exhibits what is still basically an anti-historical perspective. Eliade, *The Myth of the Eternal Return*, esp. 111–30.

68. "Alle Jahre wieder," *EG* 556,1, text by Wilhelm Hey (1837) (not included in *EG1996*).

69. These reflections basically agree with Eichrodt, *Theologie des Alten Testaments*, 256–63, 286–94.

70. Gowan, *Eschatology in the Old Testament*, 2f.

71. Ibid., 127f.

72. Ibid., 126.

73. It appears that the Greeks, starting from the philosophical question of eternal being, may have been the first to address the issue of time *philosophically*. The priorities thus established are expressed in the fact that Greek culture made no basic contributions with respect to the measurement of time and the creation of calendars (above all, in comparison to Egypt and Babylonia). Wendorff, *Zeit und Kultur*, 53–68.

74. In distinction to Heraclitus's conviction that constant becoming and change make up the essence of the world.

75. Delling, *Zeit und Endzeit*, 13.

76. Plato, *Timaios* 37D.

77. ". . . die Zeit gewissermaßen einfangen durch kreislaufartige Wiederholungen von Prozessen, die unvermeidliche zeitliche Bewegung erlauben, aber ein, Ausufern' durch Ausbrechen in eine lineare Unendlichkeit . . . verhindern." Wendorff, *Zeit und Kultur*, 56. Cf. to the following also the discussion of time in classical antiquity in Whitrow, *Time in History*, 37–70.

78. "Zeit zyklisch [zu] zähmen." Wendorff, *Zeit und Kultur*, 56.

79. Ibid., 60–63. Wendorff draws attention to the fact that "rhythm" means not only "flowing," but also primarily a halting and firm limitation of movement.

80. ". . . Gegenwartsbezogenheit, ja Gegenwartsfreudigkeit," ibid., 55.

81. ". . . mit einer besonders starken Ausprägung des Raumbewußtseins, das mit dem linearen, zukunftsgerichteten Zeitbewußtsein rivalisiert," ibid.

82. Muilenburg, "The Biblical View of Time," 230.

83. Ibid., 231.

84. Ibid.

85. Ibid.

86. Ibid., 239.

87. Such skepticism is developed and substantiated by Barr using the example of the popular claim of a cyclical concept of time among the Greeks (*Biblical Words for Time*, 137ff.). Cf. in this regard also Cancik, "Die Rechtfertigung Gottes." Cancik calls the contrasting of the spatial-static thinking among the Greeks to the dynamic-linear ideas in Hebrew thought an uncritical "Fortentwicklung des nietzscheanischen Griechenbildes" (die ewige Wiederkehr des Gleichen) (further development of Nietzsche's image of the Greeks [the eternal return of the same]), 262–65, 284f.

88. ". . . einer transzendentalen Grundhaltung, in der der Mensch—von seiner Angst umgetrieben—sich dem Anspruch des Augenblicks versagt" (Anz, "Christlicher Glaube," 535). Cf. also 531ff. to this train of thought. The contradiction that can be presumed here—between the joyfulness in the present that is found in Greek thought, which was just mentioned, and the evasion of the moment—is somewhat misleading, because *Augenblick* here in Anz does not simply mean moment, but should rather be understood, in terms of an existential interpretation, as the situation of decision.

89. This study (Delling, *Das Zeitverständnis des Neuen Testaments*) is discredited by the fact that Delling applies a pattern of thought to his analysis that aims to show the uniqueness and superiority of New Testament thought, first vis-à-vis the Old Testament and Jewish thinking and second vis-à-vis the Greek environment. The book's argument is saturated with racist ideology (64, 70f., 94, etc.). The "conclusions" in the final chapter (149ff.) can be read only with feelings of great uneasiness: The New Testament understanding of time manages to overcome both the defective Greek concept of time, which recognizes time's powerfulness over life and history, but then collapses (154), and the Jewish sense of time shaped by apocalypticism, which is said to be, for example, unclear, muddled, confused (153), egotistic (155), irreligious and bound by eschatological expectation hostile to God (157), unclean in thought (158), and religiously degenerate (160). Against this backdrop, the consequence can then be the following logical somersault: "Das biblische Zeitverständnis—wir dürfen es biblisch nennen insofern, als es im Alten Testament schon von ferne in Kleinem vorgedeutet ist—steht so im Gegensatz sowohl zum griechischen wie zum jüdischen Zeitempfinden" (The biblical understanding of time—we may call it biblical inasmuch as it is already partially foreshadowed from afar in the Old Testament—contrasts both the Greek and the Jewish sense of time), 155. In this, one can see not only a depressing testimony to a certain period of time, but also an indication of what ideology, philosophy, and worldview can do to scientific research. In 1970 Delling summarized his findings in refined form in the essay entitled "Die Gegebenheit 'Zeit' im Neuen Testament" (The Phenomenon of "Time" in the New Testament), to which I will refer in the following discussion. If in 1940 the primary concern was to demonstrate the New Testament's discontinuity with everything Jewish, then, in 1970, the continuity between the OT and the NT is emphasized. The essay from 1970 does not mention the study published in 1940.

90. Delling, *Zeit und Endzeit*.

91. "Die Zeit läuft zunächst auf das Christusereignis zu. Dieses ist schlechthin die Sinnmitte, die Sachmitte der Zeit." Ibid., 28. Cf. Cullmann, *Christus und die Zeit*, 84–94, 117–59; trans., *Christ and Time*, 81–93, 121–74.

92. Gal. 4:4: the fullness of time *(to plērōma tou chronou); cf.* Mark 1:15.

93. "Das Heilshandeln Gottes ist eines in Vergangenheit, Gegenwart und Zukunft, in Vorwegnahme, Erfüllung und Vollendung." Delling, *Zeit und Endzeit,* 31.

94. E.g., Rom. 6:3ff.

95. ". . . Zeit 'nach Christus' im chronologischen Sinn, sondern Christuszeit, Zeit, die vom gekreuzigten und erhöhten Christus her bestimmt ist." Delling, *Zeit und Endzeit,* 38.

96. ". . . ein sachbegründetes Zugleich," ibid., 49.

97. ". . . in der Auseinandersetzung zwischen Ichwillen und heiligem Geist," ibid., 42.

98. Ibid., 44f.

99. Ibid., 46. Cf. Werner, *Die Entstehung des christlichen Dogmas.* Even Lohse stresses that the delay of the *parousia* probably led to a more conscious shaping and an increasing significance of apocalyptic ideas, but not to a crisis. The effectiveness of the Spirit made the presence of salvation conscious, and by means of Baptism as incorporation into the eschatological people of God, hope in the future was kept alive. Simultaneously, deliberations about the time of the *parousia* became increasingly unimportant (Lohse, *Grundriß der neutestamentlichen Theologie,* 60f.).

100. Delling, *Zeit und Endzeit,* 52; Cullmann, *Christus und die Zeit,* 69; trans., 62, etc.

101. Delling, *Zeit und Endzeit,* 54.

102. Ibid., 55.

103. Ibid., 56.

104. The word *aiōn* occurs more than 100 times and *aiōnios* 70 times; *kairos* 84 times; *chronos* 54 times; and *hōra* 106 times. From *Exegetisches Wörterbuch zum Neuen Testament,* ed. Horst Balz and Gerhard Schneider (Stuttgart et al.: Kohlhammer, 1980–83); *Exegetical Dictionary of the New Testament,* 3 vols., ed. Horst Balz and Gerhard Schneider (Grand Rapids: Eerdmans, 1991).

105. Whether or not the plural usage actually presupposes the knowledge of ages and periods of time whose endless chain constitutes eternity, as Sasse ("*aiōn, aiōnios,*" 199) maintains, I, along with Barr (*Biblical Words for Time,* 64f.), dare to doubt. Plural usage of *aiōn* does not necessarily mean that a cessation of time or timelessness is inconceivable.

106. Cf. on this Sasse, "*aiōn, aiōnios.*"

107. In Gnosticism, eons appear, on the one hand, as periods of time and an echelon of worlds in both the earthly and divine spheres; on the other hand, they also appear as beings produced by the externalization of divine attributes. From the overflow or outpouring fullness *(plēroma)* of God arises a class of heavenly beings having different traits and authorities. On its return to the world of light, the soul must pass through a series of eons and, in the process, chase off the ruling powers in each eon. Cf. on this Rudolph, *Die Gnosis,* esp. 76–98 and 186–221, and trans., *Gnosis,* as well as Walker, *Gnosticism: Its History and Influence,* esp. 35–71.

108. See also pp. 86–89.

109. Cf. on this Barr's criticism of Cullmann, whose theory he faults precisely because of the false opposition of *aiōn* and *kairos* (Barr, *Biblical Words for Time,* 47–81, 157). On Cullmann's response to Barr, see Cullmann, *Christus und die Zeit,* 26f.; trans., 14ff.

110. See Barr, *Biblical Words for Time,* 20ff., which includes, as proof, comparisons of Mark 1:15 to Gal. 4:4, Acts 3:20, and Acts 3:21, as well as of 1 Pet. 1:5 to 1 Pet. 1:20 and Jude 18.

111. Linnemann, "Zeitansage und Zeitvorstellung."

112. Cullmann also thinks (too) simply that the juxtaposition of present and future

statements is no problem, since, as he says, Jesus sees God's reign being realized in his person. *Heil als Geschichte*, 175; trans., *Salvation in History*, 195.

113. ". . . als Zeit-zu, Sein bei, als Gegenwart," Linnemann, "Zeitansage und Zeitvorstellung," 260.

114. Ibid., 261.

115. ". . . fand den Begriff [der *basileia tou theou*] vor in einem Vorstellungsrahmen, der den vulgären uneigentlichen Zeitbegriff impliziert und bezog ihn auf ein Zeitverständnis, das Zeit ursprünglicher erfaßt als Zeit zu," ibid., 262.

116. ". . . als Drehweiche, welche das Gleis der traditionellen jüdischen Eschatologie mit der Bahn der Zeitansage Jesu verbindet," ibid.

117. Fuchs, "Christus das Ende der Geschichte."

118. Ibid., 84n10. Cullmann, on the other hand, accuses Fuchs of dissolving time in existentialist manner by reducing temporality and historicity to the specific situation of decision (*Heil als Geschichte*, 27; trans., 45). Jesus, as he says, is not in fact the end of all salvation history: "Die Endzeit ist im Gegenteil ganz und gar heilsgeschichtlich verstanden, da jede ihrer Perioden, so kurz sie auch sei, als solche ihre Eigenbedeutung hat und von der anderen unterschieden ist" (The end time is, on the contrary, understood as belonging to salvation history, since each of its periods, short as they may be, has its own significance and is distinguished from others), ibid., 208; trans., 230. What seem here to be diametrically opposing standpoints, however, are not in fact so far apart: Fuchs still speaks of Jesus' time or Jesus' cross as a moment or a time between the ages (Fuchs, "Christus das Ende der Geschichte," 91f., as well as Fuchs, "Das Zeitverständnis Jesu," 366f.); and Cullmann admits that, despite the continuation of salvation history, something did in fact come to an end in the Christ event: "Die Heilsgeschichte selbst geht, allerdings nur noch als Entfaltung des Christusgeschehens, weiter, aber die durch Ereignis und Deutung gebotene Offenbarung über den göttlichen Plan, nach dem sich die Heilsgeschichte entwickelt hat und weiter bis zum Ende entwickeln wird, ist abgeschlossen" (Salvation history itself continues, but only as an unfolding of the Christ event. However, the revelation of the divine plan presented through event and interpretation, according to which salvation history has developed and will continue to develop up to the end, is concluded), Cullmann, *Heil als Geschichte*, 270; trans., 294.

119. Fuchs, "Christus das Ende der Geschichte," 91.

120. ". . . chronologisch unmögliche Zeit," Fuchs, "Das Zeitverständnis Jesu," 366.

121. "Jesus nimmt seine Zeit als Gegenwart vor Gottes Kommen so in Anspruch, daß er sie jeder andern Zeit entgegenstellt," ibid., 367.

122. Ibid., 347.

123. Ibid., 374ff.

124. "Sein Wort *war* dann *Zeit-wort*, nichts sonst," ibid., 367.

125. "Die Zukunft bestimmt die Gegenwart, aber in einer Weise, daß das in der Zukunft Vollendete in der Gegenwart anteilhaft erfahren werden kann." Gnilka, *Das Evangelium nach Markus*, 29.

126. Ibid., 30

127. Schulz, *Die Stunde der Botschaft*, 9–46, esp. 45.

128. Cf. Bornkamm, "Enderwartung und Kirche."

129. ". . . offenbar im Stande der noch zweideutigen Niedrigkeit," ibid., 31.

130. Schulz sees the *Una sancta apostolica* as the decisive precondition for understanding Luke's two-volume work (*Die Stunde der Botschaft*, 255–75).

131. Opinions differ regarding the number of periods in salvation history. Schulz speaks at one point of three phases or epochs (*Die Stunde der Botschaft*, 275f.), then, however, of two continual stages (284), while Bovon expressly emphasizes that one is dealing

not with three, but rather with two, periods of salvation history (*Das Evangelium nach Lukas*, 26).

132. Lazarus and the rich man (Luke 16:19ff.); the criminal on the cross (Luke 23:43).

133. Schulz, *Die Stunde der Botschaft*, 275f., 284f. Cf. on this also Conzelmann, *Die Mitte der Zeit*, as well as Cullmann's comment on Conzelmann in Cullmann, *Heil als Geschichte*, 28f.; trans., 45f.

134. "Sein eschatologisches Glaubensbekenntnis ist der einmalige und unerhörte Protest gegen die Vergleichgültigung und Entleerung der Gegenwart, die durch Jesu Kommen als eschatologische qualifiziert ist." Schulz, *Die Stunde der Botschaft*, 354.

135. "Die eschatologische Krisis ist also im *Glauben* schon entschieden." Lohse, *Grundriß der neutestamentlichen Theologie*, 137. Cf. also Kümmel, *Die Theologie des Neuen Testaments*, 290f.; trans., *The Theology of the New Testament*, 327f.

136. On John's eschatology, see also Frey, *Die johanneische Eschatologie*.

137. Lohse, *Grundriß der neutestamentlichen Theologie*, 109ff. Cf. also Stuhlmacher, "Erwägungen zum Problem von Gegenwart und Zukunft": The formative division of eschatology into series of assertions about the present and the future is reconciled in a doxological outline that is to be understood primarily in light of the thought of God's proleptic advent in Christ.

138. Gal. 4:4.

139. Thus, Stendahl, "The Apostle Paul and the Introspective Conscience of the West," 86f.

140. ". . . grundlegend die Gegenwart als die Zeit des beginnenden endzeitlichen Heilshandelns Gottes." Kümmel, *Die Theologie des Neuen Testaments*, 126; trans. 144.

141. Rom. 6:3f.

142. Gal. 5:21; 1 Cor. 15:50.

143. 1 Cor. 15:23; 1 Thess. 2:19, etc.

144. 1 Cor. 1:7; 2 Thess. 1:7.

145. Rom. 8:18f.

146. Kümmel, *Die Theologie des Neuen Testaments*, 129f., trans., 143f.; 210ff., trans., 235ff.

147. 2 Cor. 4:16b; Rom. 12:2. In the tension between the "already fulfilled" and the "not yet consummated," Cullmann (*Heil als Geschichte*, 181f.; trans., 190f.) sees primarily a temporal dialectic, while Fuchs ("Christus das Ende der Geschichte," 85 and 93f.) is of the opinion that one is dealing here with more than mere temporality. He suggests that one must begin at a deeper level, precisely with the disempowering of history, with what Bultmann called "Entweltlichung" (stripping of worldliness). Fuchs appears to understand Cullmann's temporality purely quantitatively, and he desires to refute and revise it by a qualitative definition. Under this condition, his criticism is justified. It seems to me, however, that Cullmann himself leaves the domain of mere temporality when he says: "That is the path of all salvation history: *universalism as its goal, concentration as the means of its realization*" [Das ist der Weg aller Heilsgeschichte: *Universalismus als Ziel, Konzentration als Mittel zu seiner Verwirklichung*] (*Heil als Geschichte*, 285; trans., 310). For this reason, at this point, I again consider the contrast of the two positions less a matter of theological conditioning than an expression of a varying and unclear use of time terminology.

148. 1 Thess. 4:16f.; 1 Cor. 15:44, 52; Rom. 8:19, 23; 13:11; Phil. 3:21.

149. Phil. 1:23.

150. 2 Cor. 5:1ff.

151. On this train of thought, cf. Kümmel, *Die Theologie des Neuen Testaments*, 211ff.; trans., 235 ff.

152. Lohse, *Grundriß der neutestamentlichen Theologie*, 158.

153. Ibid., 158f.

154. "Die Fülle der apokalyptischen Bilder ist vom christologischen Bekenntnis um-klammert. Damit aber haben die apokalyptischen Stoffe eine Bindung an die Geschichte erfahren, die ihren Charakter grundlegend verändert, so daß sie nunmehr dazu dienen, die Universalität des Christusgeschehens zu veranschaulichen." Ibid., 160.

155. I agree with Fagg (*The Becoming of Time*, 10, 156f.) that, when speaking of time, it is not always possible to avoid spatial expressions. When they are used, however, they should always be used with care.

156. Even if, e.g., Cullmann changes his linear representation, found in *Christ and Time,* into a concept of time as a wavy line—with reference to the charming Portuguese proverb brought to his attention by Yves Congar, "God writes straight, but with crooked lines" [Gott schreibt geradeaus, aber in Wellenlinien] (Cullmann, *Heil als Geschichte*, 107; trans., 125; cf. also ix; trans., 14. When translated from the French, however, the proverb says: "Even on crooked lines, God writes straight")—and believes that by doing so he has enabled a connection between God's plan of salvation and historical contingency, his mod-el is characterized by a profoundly inadequate spatialization of time.

157. See above, pp. 37–41.

158. Cf., e.g., Aquinas, *Summa Theologiae*, 1a.10.1–5, and Schleiermacher, *Der christliche Glaube*, 267ff., § 52; *The Christian Faith*, 203ff. Aquinas gives two marks of eter-nity: Everything existing in eternity is without end *(interminabilis);* eternity itself exists as a simultaneous whole *(tota simul).* God is identical with God's own eternity. Of course, in the truest sense *(vere et proprie),* God alone is eternal; but God grants certain things a share in divine immutability and, thus, in divine eternity. This, however, does not eliminate the fundamental difference between time and eternity. Eternity is and remains the measure of being itself, whereas time is the correct measure for change and motion. Between time and eternity lies the *aevum*, which, unlike time, does not have a before and after, but can be ac-companied by it, whereas eternity has no before and after and cannot exist together with such qualities. Schleiermacher understands the eternity of God to be "the absolutely time-less causality of God, which conditions not only all that is temporal, but time itself as well" (203) [die mit allem Zeitlichen auch die Zeit selbst bedingende schlechthin zeitlose Ursächlichkeit Gottes (312)]. In contrast to time, eternity is pure timelessness. So that this timelessness does not remain a completely empty concept, Schleiermacher links it to the notion of divine omnipotence and permits an analogous link in the relationship between causal and finite being and that which is thereby caused.

159. The early Karl Barth is frequently mentioned as a classic representative of such a position. In the foreword to the 2nd ed. of *The Epistle to the Romans*, Barth says openly that, if he has a system of inner dialectics, then it "is limited to a recognition of what Kierkegaard called the 'infinite, qualitative distinction' between time and eternity." He is hereby less concerned, however, with a conceptual dialectic than with the distinction of two related spheres: "The relation of *this* God to *this* human being and the relation of *this* human being to *this* God is, for me, the subject of the Bible and the sum of philosophy in one" [Die Beziehung *dieses* Gottes zu *diesem* Menschen, die Beziehung *dieses* Menschen zu *diesem* Gott ist für mich das Thema der Bibel und die Summe der Philosophie in Einem], ibid. Although designated as a system, strangely enough, the concepts of time and eternity do not occur a single time as key words in the index. The book deals more with the dis-tinction between, rather than the separation of, the spheres of heaven/earth, God/human, invisible/invisible. That Barth was concerned not only with the negative but also with the positive meaning of the distinction is frequently overlooked by the criticism that accuses Barth of a metaphysical or ontological dualism (on this, see the work by Ola Sigurdson on the reception of Barth in Sweden, Sigurdson, *Karl Barth*, e.g., 46ff., 53f., 70, 284, etc.).

Thus, in his interpretation of Romans 8:22–25, Barth speaks not only of difference, but also of relatedness: "But we know that every created temporal thing . . . bears its eternal existence in itself as unborn, eternal Future, and seeks to give it that birth which can never take place in time. . . . Therefore, it is precisely our not-knowing what God knows that is our temporal knowledge about God" (310) [Wir wissen, daß alles Geschaffene, alles was in der Zeit ist . . . sein ewiges Sein als ewige Zukunft ungeboren in sich trägt, gebären möchte und—in der Zeit nie gebären wird. . . . Und gerade das Nicht-Wissen dessen, was Gott weiß, ist das Wissen *von Gott*, . . . das Wissen der Ewigkeit, mit dem wir in der Zeit sind], Barth, *Der Römerbrief*, 294. "How could the Truth be God, if it were for us but one possibility among others? How could we be saved by it, if it did not with compelling power urge us to hazard the leap into eternity, to dare to think what God thinks, to think freely, to think anew, and to think wholly?" (313–14) [Wie könnte sie (die Wahrheit) unsre Errettung sein, wenn sie nicht in jedem Augenblick der Zeit der übermächtige Zwang wäre, den Sprung in die Ewigkeit zu wagen: den Gedanken Gottes selbst zu denken, frei zu denken, ganz zu denken?], 297. In light of these sentences, the path to the Barth of the *Church Dogmatics*, who can speak of eternity as the source and original form of time (Barth, *Die Kirchliche Dogmatik*, vol. III.1, 72f.; trans., 67f.) and of pre-, supra-, and post-temporality as God's eternity (Barth, *Die Kirchliche Dogmatik*, vol. II.1, 720; trans., 638), is not as far as generally assumed.

160. "Wenn wir Gott einen lebendigen Gott nennen, behaupten wir, daß er Zeitlichkeit und damit eine Beziehung zu den Modi der Zeit in sich begreift." Tillich, *Systematische Theologie*, 315; *Systematic Theology*, vol. 1 (Chicago, University of Chicago Press, 1951), 274.

161. ". . . de[n] Gottesgedanke[n] aus seiner babylonischen Gefangenschaft eines abstrakten Gegensatzes zum Zeitbegriff zu befreien" (Dalferth, "Gott und Zeit," 10, referring to Barth, *Die Kirchliche Dogmatik*, vol. II.1, 689; trans., 611). On this, see also Keith Ward, *Religion and Creation* (Oxford: Clarendon, 1987), 256–84, who criticizes the notion of God's timelessness and substantiates this criticism on the basis of a dynamic understanding of time: "God is temporal, though God transcends the physical space-time system of this universe" (293).

162. Dalferth, "Gott und Zeit," 10–12.

163. Larson, *Times of the Trinity.*

164. Helm, *Eternal God.*

165. Leftow, *Time and Eternity.*

166. Padgett, *God, Eternity, and the Nature of Time.*

167. On the religious-philosophical dimension of this question, see, e.g., also Helm, *Eternal God,* and Stump and Kretzmann, "Eternity," as well as Swinburne, *Time and Space,* and Swinburne, *The Coherence of Theism;* cf. also Boethius, *Philosophiae consolatio* v.6. 3ff., Boethius, *The Theological Tractates, De trinitate,* chap. 4, and Anselm, *Proslogion,* esp. chap. 21.

168. Dalferth, "Gott und Zeit," 13f.

169. ". . . folgt keineswegs, daß es eine universale Zeitstruktur gibt, in der alle kausalen Ereignisabläufe in eindeutiger und irreversibler Ordnung lokalisiert sind," ibid., 16.

170. One should note that Dalferth ascribes the term *ontological* a meaning that is different from the one used below in 2.3.1.3. In my opinion, Dalferth could just as well have spoken of protological as of ontological.

171. ". . . die ontologische Zeitdifferenz zwischen Ewigkeit und Zeit [and] die eschatologische Zeitdifferenz zwischen Alter und Neuer Zeit," Dalferth, "Gott und Zeit," 18.

172. ". . . im Lichte dessen, was noch nicht ist, aber unaufhaltsam kommen wird," ibid., 19.

173. ". . . freiwillige eschatologische Wechsel zur Neuen Zeit," ibid., 21.

174. ". . . Entschärfung des grundsätzlichen Gegensatzes zwischen Alter und Neuer Zeit zu einem Epochennacheinander im Kontinuum einer angeblichen Weltgeschichte," ibid., 22.

175. ". . . entstammt nicht der christlichen Grunderfahrung, aber sie dominiert die Haupttradition theologischer Zeitreflexion seit der Alten Kirche," ibid.

176. Ibid., 23.

177. Ibid., 27–32.

178. Leftow, *Time and Eternity.*

179. ". . . die Art dieser Bezogenheit als Gottes alles neu machende und neu qualifizierende Nähe theologisch zur Geltung zu bringen." Dalferth, "Gott und Zeit," 29.

180. "Um den selbstverschuldeten Orientierungsverlust des Gottesgedankens zu korrigieren, ist vielmehr eine Neubestimmung des Ewigkeitsgedankens notwendig," ibid.

181. The first edition was published in 1946.

182. Cullmann, *Christus und die Zeit,* 19f.; trans., 9.

183. Ibid., 24ff.; trans., 12ff.

184. ". . . daß das Neue Testament, da es nur von Gottes Heilshandeln spricht und nirgends über sein ewiges Sein reflektiert, die philosophische, qualitative Unterscheidung zwischen Zeit und Ewigkeit nicht macht und daß es folglich nur eine lineare Zeit kennt," ibid., 22.

185. ". . . so unphilosophisch wie möglich," ibid., 71; trans., 64.

186. Cullmann himself does not use the term *quantitative;* in this context, however, the term is justified, both because of Cullmann's formal comparison of the Greek qualitative distinction between time and eternity and his description of the infinite timeline.

187. ". . . die Grundvoraussetzungen aller neutestamentlichen Theologie," Cullmann, *Christus und die Zeit,* 41; trans., 26.

188. ". . . das Heil gebunden an ein *fortlaufendes*, Vergangenheit, Gegenwart und Zukunft umfassendes Zeitgeschehen, Offenbarung und Heil erfolgen auf einer ansteigenden Zeitlinie," ibid., 45; trans., 32.

189. ". . . die Bezogenheit aller Punkte dieser Heilslinie auf die eine *geschichtliche Tatsache* der Mitte . . . : Tod und Auferstehung Jesu Christi," ibid., 46; trans., 32–33.

190. Ibid., 34. Nevertheless, as Hans Maier noted, it belongs "to the irony of history that the calendar that places Christ at the center of time should finally be accepted precisely in the Age of Enlightenment—that is, in an age that, in many areas, was beginning to liberate itself from Christian traditions" [zur Ironie der Geschichte, daß sich jene Zeitrechnung, die Christus in die Mitte der Zeit rückte, just in der Zeit der Aufklärung endgültig durchsetzte—in einer Zeit also, die sich in vielen Bereichen von christlichen Überlieferungen loszulösen begann], *Eine Zeit in der Zeit?,* 119.

191. See on this Maier, *Eine Zeit in der Zeit?,* 111.

192. ". . . daß die—nur als Attribut Gottes mögliche—Ewigkeit unendliche Zeit ist, oder besser gesagt, daß das, was wir 'Zeit' nennen, nichts anderes ist, als ein von Gott begrenztes Stück dieser gleichen unendlichen Zeitdauer Gottes," Cullmann, *Christus und die Zeit,* 69; trans., 62.

193. Ibid., 70; trans., 63.

194. ". . . Ewigkeit nur als ins Unendliche verlängerte Zeit [erscheint]," ibid., 72; trans., 65.

195. Ibid., 70; trans., 63.

196. Ibid., 75; trans., 69.

197. ". . . bedeutet nichts anderes, als daß er, der Ewige, über die ganze Zeitlinie in ihrer unendlichen Ausdehnung verfügt . . . ," ibid., 77; trans., 72.

198. Ibid., 73f.; trans., 66f.

199. ". . . nichts anderes als Vorwegnahme des Endes in der Gegenwart," ibid., 78; trans., 72.

200. Ibid.

201. "Es handelt sich also nicht um ein Mitherrschen des Gläubigen über die Zeit," ibid., 80; trans., 76.

202. Cullmann's concept of time is a good example of what Michael Welker calls "the *totalization and unification* of time" ("God's Eternity, God's Temporality, and Trinitarian Theology," *Theology Today* 55 [H. 3]: 321). In agreement with Welker and Dalferth, I find it more appropriate to start with multi-temporality.

203. Cullmann, *Christus und die Zeit*, 61; trans., 52.

204. Ibid., 59f.; trans., 49f.

205. Ibid., 45; trans., 32.

206. Ibid., 75; trans., 69.

207. Ibid., 19; trans., 9.

208. Cullmann, *Heil als Geschichte*, 107; trans., 120; see also the foreword, esp. viii–ix. Against the backdrop of a more or less statically conceived dogmatics, Cullmann's models signify considerable dynamism. They remain, however, removed from nature and closed to the dialectic of repetition and uniqueness. Cf. in this regard the attempt, from an Asian perspective, to express both direction and regularity in the model of history as ascending spiral, without pitting history and nature against each other in the process (Koyama, "Wird Gott vom Monsunregen naß?").

209. Cullmann, *Christus und die Zeit*, 69; trans., 62; 75, trans., 69.

210. "Wir müssen also alle solche Erklärungen als unangemessen verwerfen, welche nur die Schranken der Zeit, nicht die Zeit selbst, für Gott aufheben und welche den Begriff der Ewigkeit aus dem der Zeitlichkeit, dessen Gegenteil er doch ist, durch Entschränkung bilden wollen." Schleiermacher, *Der christliche Glaube*, 269f. (§ 52,2); trans., *The Christian Faith*.

211. Cullmann, *Christus und die Zeit*, 19; trans., 13.

212. ". . . das Mittel ist, dessen Gott sich bedient, um sein Gnadenwirken zu offenbaren," ibid., 60; trans., 51.

213. The critical reception of *Christus und die Zeit* did not always pay due attention to the problems linked to Cullmann's concept of time. Bultmann ("Heilsgeschichte und Geschichte"), e.g., questions Cullmann's use of the concepts *history, revelation, faith, salvation, world, sin, justification*, etc., and complains that the Christian philosophy of history that Cullmann outlines is "nothing other than Jewish apocalyptic speculation that has been modified merely by shifting the 'center' backwards" [nichts anderes als die jüdisch-apokalyptische Spekulation, modifiziert nur dadurch, daß sich die "Mitte" nach rückwärts verschoben hat]—mixed with a shot of gnosticism. Finally, Bultmann disapproves of Cullmann's lack of awareness of problems related to the temporality of eschatological being (= the life of the believer in faith); but, at this point, he does not criticize the crux of Cullmann's concept of time.

214. ". . . er hat die Zeit in die Seele verlegt, um die Seele aus ihrer Veräußerlichung und Zerstreuung in die Welt heimzuholen," Quispel, "Zeit und Geschichte," 133; similar also, Duchrow, "Der sogenannte psychologische Zeitbegriff," 279.

215. See, e.g., the detailed study by Flasch (*Was ist Zeit?*) on the eleventh book of the *Confessions*.

216. Manzke, *Ewigkeit und Zeitlichkeit*, 259–365; on the question of relationality, see 261, 336, and 349ff. (eternity as a relational attribute of God). In his chapter on the Augustinian doctrine of time, Manzke draws from *De immortalitate animae*, *De musica*, the two

early interpretations of Genesis, *Confessiones*, and *De Genesi ad litteram*. Thus, his analysis has the broadest foundation of all of the interpretations of Augustine discussed here.

217. "... der sogenannte psychologische Zeitbegriff Augustins," Duchrow, "Der sogenannte psychologische Zeitbegriff," 280f.

218. Ibid., 284.

219. "... nicht unschuldig an der Entwicklung zur neuzeitlichen Diastase von Subjekt und einer vom Geist verlassenen Welt," ibid., 288.

220. Dalferth, "Gott und Zeit," 29.

221. "... daß das Pathos des Fortschritts eine Säkularisierung urchristlicher Vorstellungen ist," Quispel, "Zeit und Geschichte," 118.

222. Ibid., 131.

223. "... die Urwörter der jüdisch-christlichen Eschatologie," ibid., 140.

224. Ibid., 134.

225. Augustine, *Confessiones* XI.11.13 (*semper stantis aeternitatis*).

226. *Confessiones* XI.11.13.

227. *Confessiones* XI.11.13: "nullum vero tempus totum esse praesens . . . et omne praeteritum ac futurum ab eo, quod semper est praesens, creari et excurrere."

228. *Confessiones* XI.11.13 (*esse inconparabilem*).

229. *Confessiones* XI.4.17.

230. Manzke, *Ewigkeit und Zeitlichkeit*, 326.

231. *Confessiones* XI.20.26: "tempora 'sunt' tria, praesens de praeteritis, praesens de praesentibus, praesens de futuris."

232. *Confessiones* XI.20.26: "Sunt enim haec in anima tria quaedam et alibi ea non video, praesens de praeteritis memoria, praesens de praesentibus contuitus, praesens de futuris expectatio."

233. *Confessiones* XI.23.30: "Video igitur tempus quandam esse distentionem."

234. *Confessiones* XI.26.33: "Inde mihi visum est nihil esse aliud tempus quam distentionem: sed cuius rei, nescio, et mirum, si non ipsius animi" (That is why I have come to think that time is simply a distension. But of what is it a distension? I do not know, but it would be surprising if it is not that of the mind itself), trans., *Saint Augustine, Confessions*, 240.

235. *Confessiones* XI.13,1.5.

236. *Confessiones* XI.24.31: "Non est ergo tempus corporis motus."

237. *Confessiones* XI.29.39.

238. *Confessiones* XI.28.38.

239. *Confessiones* XI.27.36.

240. *Confessiones* XI.29.39.

241. *Confessiones* XI 29.39: "et tumultuosis varietatibus dilaniantur cogitationes meae, intima viscera animae meae, donec in te confluam purgatus et liquidus igne amoris tui," trans., 244.

242. *Confessiones* XI.28.37. On the concept of *attentio*, see also Manzke, *Ewigkeit und Zeitlichkeit*, 332.

243. *Confessiones* XII.29.40.

244. Manzke, *Ewigkeit und Zeitlichkeit*, 360–62.

245. *Confessiones* IX.10.24.

246. "Der Mensch bleibt für Augustin in seiner Geschichte immer gleich weit von der Ewigkeit Gottes entfernt." Manzke, *Ewigkeit und Zeitlichkeit*, 365; cf. also 347.

247. The lack of relevance ascribed to the shaping of time is also confirmed by a glance at the beginning of time. The doctrine of the seminal reasons, the *rationes seminales*, as Augustine presents them in *De Genesi ad litteram*, suggests that development in time can ac-

tually provide nothing new, since it is merely the realization of that which existed at the beginning; cf. on this Manzke, *Ewigkeit und Zeitlichkeit*, 353f. It should not be forgotten, however, that there is also a kind of de-temporalization that in fact stands in a constructive relationship to the requirements of a concrete shaping of time, namely, the de-temporalization of the mystical experience.

248. Rahner, "Theologische Bemerkungen zum Zeitbegriff," 305; trans., *Theological Investigations*, vol. 11, 291. Johann Baptist Metz also complains about "the refined, routine lack of consciousness vis-à-vis the problem of time" [die eingeschliffene, routinierte Bewußtlosigkeit gegenüber dem Zeitproblem] on the part of theology (*Glaube in Geschichte*, 169). He describes an "evolutionist" understanding of time, whose empty, evolutionarily extended infinity leads to a cult of omnipotent control of destiny, on the one hand, and to a cult of apathy on the other (ibid., 166). Since, to him, eschatology seems to be very weighed down with false alternatives, he desires—as an antidote—to recall an apocalyptic consciousness (ibid., 170–74).

249. Rahner, "Theologische Bemerkungen zum Zeitbegriff," 302f.; trans., 309f.

250. Cf. on this Pröpper, *Erlösungsglaube*, esp. 123–37, 269–73.

251. Rahner, "Theologische Bemerkungen zum Zeitbegriff," 308f.; trans., 294f.

252. ". . . das, worauf der tiefste Wille der Freiheit geht, weil diese Freiheit das Ende des bloß sich Weiterzeitigenden wollen muß, um vollendet zu werden," Rahner, "Theologische Erwägungen," 334; trans., 319.

253. ". . . begehrt nach dem Ende des Unvollendeten, damit Vollendung sei," ibid.; trans., 319–20.

254. ". . . dem einzelnen menschlichen Dasein," Rahner, "Theologische Bemerkungen zum Zeitbegriff," 303; trans., 289.

255. ". . . des Geistes als solchen," ibid., 304; trans., 290.

256. ". . . daß die Zeit des Materiellen im allerletzten nicht die Macht ist, die über die menschliche Geschichte dominiert, vielmehr ein partikuläres und defizientes Moment an der Zeit der personalen Freiheit bleibt," ibid.

257. "Man kann und muß eine Endlichkeit der Zeit der Welt positiv aussagen . . . , insofern und wenn eine unendliche Zeit der Welt ein Material der endlichen Freiheit des auf das Ganze der Welt bezogenen Menschen bedeuten würde, mit dem er grundsätzlich nicht fertig werden würde." Ibid., 316; trans., 302.

258. Ibid., 314: "On a Christian view the history of nature can, in the last analysis be understood only as an element in the history of the free spirit in its dialogue with God who bestows himself with grace," trans., 302 [Die Naturgeschichte kann, letztlich, christlich nur als ein Moment an der Geschichte des freien Geistes im Dialog mit dem sich selbst mitteilenden Gott der Gnade verstanden werden . . .].

259. On the concept of matter or the physical in Rahner, cf. Geister, *Aufhebung zur Eigentlichkeit*, 27ff. Geister distinguishes a three-fold use of "matter" in Rahner: abstract use, in the ontological sense, as the condition of possibility for everything that exists; concrete use, in the popular-scientific sense; and, finally, in a broad sense that encompasses the first two usages. Matter is certainly the condition of possibility for each higher instance, but "considered from the standpoint of human consciousness, matter denotes the lower end of the scale whose upper end marks precisely this human consciousness" (29). Particularly with respect to the natural scientific understanding of the concept of matter, there seems to me to be a lack of problem awareness in Rahner. Consequently, the dualistic-hierarchical impression continues to exist, even when Rahner tries to balance this with the concept of matter as frozen spirit (cf. hereto Rahner, "Die Einheit von Geist und Materie," 203, 205; trans., 184, 186).

260. Rahner, "Theologische Bemerkungen zum Zeitbegriff," 314: The temporality of

the world "should never be understood in a way that leaves no room for the internal time of the personal spirit, with beginning and end" [Die Zeitlichkeit der Welt darf nie so verstanden werden, daß die innere Zeit des personalen Geistes mit Anfang und Ende darin keinen Platz hat].

261. ". . . und diese Negativität ist als Negativität der Zeit des Materiellen diejenige Negativität, die verhindert, daß diese Zeit als solche sich selbst in Endgültigkeit hinein aufhebt und beendet," ibid., 318; trans., 304–5.

262. "Zeit ist offenbar keine Modalität, die in einem univoken Sinn überall gegeben ist, wo sich etwas ereignet, sondern eine Modalität, die sich analog innerlich abwandelt mit der Wirklichkeit, deren Zeit sie ist." Ibid., 319; trans., 305.

263. Ibid., 320; trans., 306.

264. Ibid., 321; trans., 307.

265. Ibid., 322; trans., 308.

266. Ibid., 303f.; trans., 289f.

267. ". . . wirklich das *Zukünftige*, das in einem ganz gewöhnlichen, empirischen Sinn zeitlich noch Ausständige . . . ein je jetzt in der Existenz des einzelnen und seiner je jetzt fallenden Entscheidung sich ereignendes Geschehen," Rahner, "Theologische Prinzipien," 404; trans., 326.

268. ". . . die des prospektiven Entwurfs des Daseins auf die zeitendliche Vollendung," ibid., 416; trans., 335.

269. "Biblische Eschatologie muß immer gelesen werden als Aussage von der Gegenwart als geoffenbarter her auf die echte Zukunft hin, nicht aber als Aussage von einer antizipierten Zukunft her in die Gegenwart hinein. Aus-sage von Gegenwart in Zukunft hinein ist Eschatologie, Ein-sage aus der Zukunft heraus in die Gegenwart ist Apokalyptik" (ibid., 418; trans., 337). Cf. also Geister, *Aufhebung zur Eigentlichkeit*, 61f.

270. Rahner, "Das Leben der Toten," 434f.; trans., 351.

271. Geister, *Aufhebung zur Eigentlichkeit*, 68f., 85.

272. Ibid., 85.

273. "Die eschatologische Vollendung erscheint so wie ein kosmisches Puzzle, dem in jedem menschlichen Sterben ein neues Teil hinzugefügt wird, bis es schließlich—am Ende der Zeit und des Kosmos—ganz fertiggestellt ist." Ibid., 81.

274. For a critical discussion of cosmic eschatology in Rahner, the reader is referred to Geister, *Aufhebung zur Eigentlichkeit*, 89–118.

275. Pannenberg, *Systematische Theologie*, vol. 3, 573, 649, etc.; trans., 532, 602.

276. Ibid., 649; trans., 602.

277. "[D]ie künftig zu offenbarende Wahrheit der Dinge, ihr im Eschaton ans Licht kommendes wahres Wesen, bestimmt ganz allgemein schon ihr gegenwärtiges Dasein," ibid., 651; trans., 605.

278. Ibid., 650; trans., 604.

279. Ibid.

280. ". . . nicht als eine völlig andere Realität," ibid., 652; trans., 605.

281. ". . . aber nur möglich unter der Bedingung einer radikalen Verwandlung," ibid., 653; trans., 607.

282. "Die Auferstehung der Toten und die Erneuerung der Schöpfung stellen sich darum dar als der Akt, durch den Gott dem in seiner Ewigkeit bewahrten Dasein der Geschöpfe durch seinen Geist *die Form des Fürsichseins wiedergibt*." Ibid., 652 (my emphasis); trans., 606.

283. Dalferth, "Gott und Zeit."

284. Dalferth is by no means the only person who does not solve this problem. In *Church Dogmatics* II.1, Barth is also unsuccessful in establishing a connection between the

Trinity and time-eternity relationships (Barth, *Die Kirchliche Dogmatik*, vol. ii.1, 694–722; trans., 608–36). On the one hand, he says: "Daß und inwiefern Gott Zeit hat und selber ist, das muß uns vielmehr gerade an seinem Wesen als der dreieinige Gott deutlich werden" [the fact that God has and is Himself time, and the extent to which this is so, is necessarily made clear to us in His essence as a triune God], 694; trans., 615. On the other hand, despite his talk about the Trinitarian God, he then deals only with Father and Son: As the creator, God has and gives time (695; trans., 616), and as the Son, God is temporal (696; trans., 618). Incarnation then means that, in its power as eternity, eternity became time, i.e., God takes time, God becomes time, God is willingly subjected to time (694; trans., 616). The threeness is then instead discussed as God's (not differentiated in a Trinitarian way) pre-, supra-, and post-temporality; it corresponds to God as God was, is, and will be. Supra-temporality thereby signifies the accompaniment of the duration of time; it is God in time; it is the positive relationship between eternity and time (702; trans., 623), and it is even a merging of time and eternity (703; trans., 624).

Pre-, supra-, and post-temporality are in equal measure God's eternity and therefore the living God (720; trans., 638). Eternity as the time-encompassing element (709; trans., 717) is not a "uniform grey sea" [kein einförmig graues Meer], 721; trans., 639. True eternity contains the potentiality for time: Without itself being time, eternity is "the absolute basis of time, and therefore absolute readiness for it" [als schlechthiniger *Grund* der Zeit zugleich die schlechthinige *Bereitschaft* für sie], 696; trans., 618. Kjetil Hafstad also holds the view that Barth's doctrine of the Trinity determines his understanding of time (Hafstad, *Wort und Geschichte*, 209). He affirms that Barth holds a complicated, though dynamic, conception of the phenomenon of time (283). He repeatedly emphasizes the dynamic nature of the time-eternity relationship in Barth (211f., 214, 221, etc.), without denying, however, the tensions and contradictions in Barth's concept of time (237ff., 254, 283, etc.). Among things that are problematic are the changing meanings of the concepts of "absolute" and "relative" time, as well as the assertion that "new" time is the revelation of what time actually is.

285. Dalferth, "Gott und Zeit," 30–33.

286. Ibid., 30.

287. "Gott ist allen Zeiten in jeder Zeitsequenz nahe," ibid.

288. ". . . [Gottes] Kopräsenz mit der Vielheit der Zeiten erfordert, seine Ewigkeit nicht einfach als endlose Zeitlichkeit, sondern als Einheit von Zeitlosigkeit und Vielzeitigkeit zu denken," ibid.

289. ". . . weil Gott vom konkreten Ereignis seiner zeitlichen Selbstoffenbarung her trinitarisch differenziert als Vater, Sohn und Geist in den Blick kommt, und dementsprechend auch sein Verhältnis zur Zeit trinitarisch differenziert in den Blick zu fassen ist—also je anders im Horizont seines Schöpfungshandelns, seines Rettungshandelns und seines Vollendungshandelns" (ibid., 31).

290. ". . . daß er sich zeitlos zur Zeit bestimmt, d.h. zur zeitlosen Realisierung bestimmter zeitlicher Möglichkeiten," ibid., 32.

291. ". . . seine zeitlose Bereitschaft, seiner Schöpfung Zeit einzuräumen und sich für seine Schöpfung ewig und zeitlich Zeit zu nehmen," ibid.

292. "Das ewig Licht geht da herein, / gibt der Welt ein' neuen Schein; / es leucht' wohl mitten in der Nacht / und uns des Lichtes Kinder macht. Kyrieleis," *EG* 23,4 (= *GL* 130), text by Martin Luther (1524). English translation according to *Lutheran Book of Worship:* "Your coming in the darkest night / Makes us children of the light, / Enabling us in realms divine / Like all your angels bright to shine! Hallelujah!" (48,4).

293. "Gott ist als unterschiedene Einheit von Vater, Geist und Sohn dreifach auf seine Schöpfung bezogen: als zeitloser Grund von allem, als vielzeitiger Begleiter von jedem und

als zeitlicher Vermittler des Heils in der bestimmten Lebens-Zeit Jesu Christi und aller, die an ihn glauben. Seine Ewigkeit ist der Inbegriff dieser Zeit-Verhältnisse und mit keinem als solchem zu identifizieren" (Dalferth, "Gott und Zeit," 33).

294. ". . . Gott gehört nicht einfach zum Jenseits unserer Welt, aber er geht in ihr auch nicht einfach auf und damit in ihren Widersprüchen, Ambivalenzen, Freundlichkeiten und Scheußlichkeiten unter. Er unterscheidet sich vielmehr von ihr, indem er in ihr Unterschiede setzt" (ibid.)

295. ". . . wenn die Wirklichkeit Gottes nicht als unterschiedslose Identität, sondern als in sich differenzierte Einheit zu verstehen ist." Pannenberg, *Systematische Theologie*, vol. 1, 438; *Systematic Theology* vol. 1, 405.

296. "Kraft ihrer trinitarischen Differenzierung umschließt die Ewigkeit Gottes die Zeit der Geschöpfe in ihrer ganzen Ausdehnung, vom Beginn der Schöpfung bis zu ihrer eschatologischen Vollendung," ibid., 439; trans., 405–6. One problem with Pannenberg's doctrine of the Trinity (and not only with this part of his theology) is that he wants to do two things at once. On the one hand, he wishes to derive the Trinity from Christology (Jesus' self-differentiation from the Father); on the other hand, he clings firmly to a philosophical-theistic argument. In order to solve this conflict, it appears that the reference to the eschatological verification is all that remains.

297. Pannenberg, *Systematische Theologie*, vol. 1, 441; trans., 407.

298. This does not prevent Pannenberg, however, from occasionally thinking of time and eternity as opposites, e.g., Pannenberg, *Systematische Theologie*, vol. 3: "Insofar as eternity is in antithesis to time, its relation to time has in fact the form of judgment," 594 [Insofern die Ewigkeit der Zeit entgegengesetzt ist, hat ihr Verhältnis zur Zeit tatsächlich die Form des Gerichts], 640.

299. "Der Gedanke der Ewigkeit, der der Zeit nicht nur entgegengesetzt, sondern zugleich positiv auf sie bezogen ist und sie in ihrer Totalität umfaßt, bildet eine geradezu paradigmatische Veranschaulichung und Konkretisierung der Struktur des wahrhaft Unendlichen, das dem Endlichen nicht nur entgegengesetzt ist, sondern diesen seinen Gegensatz zugleich umgreift. Die Vorstellung einer der Zeit nur entgegengesetzten, zeitlosen Ewigkeit entspricht dagegen dem schlecht Unendlichen, das in seinem Gegensatz zum Endlichen nur als ihm gegenüber anderes bestimmt ist und sich so selber als endlich erweist." Pannenberg, *Systematische Theologie*, vol. 1, 441; trans., 408.

300. Pannenberg, *Systematische Theologie*, vol. 3, 653; trans., 607.

301. Ibid., 639f.; trans., 593f.: The end of the temporal is the gateway to eternity. Judgment is the confrontation of temporal existence with God's eternity; a favorable outcome leads to participation in God's divine eternal life.

302. Pannenberg, *Systematische Theologie*, vol. 3, 487; trans., 449.

303. ". . . weil nur von ihr her dem Zeitlichen jene Ganzheit zuteil werden kann, die die Einheit und Kontinuität des Prozesses der Zeit ermöglicht," Pannenberg, *Systematische Theologie*, vol. 1, 441; trans., 408.

304. Pannenberg, *Systematische Theologie*, vol. 3, 640f.; trans., 594ff.

305. ". . . Anbruch der Ewigkeit Gottes in der Zeit; . . . Ort der Ewigkeit selbst in der Zeit; . . . Ort Gottes in seinem Verhältnis zur Welt," Pannenberg, *Systematische Theologie*, vol. 1, 442, and vol. 3, 641ff.

306. "Gott ist ewig, weil er keine Zukunft außer sich hat, sondern die Zukunft seiner selbst und alles von ihm Verschiedenen ist," Pannenberg, *Systematische Theologie*, vol. 1, 443; trans., 410.

307. ". . . der ewige Gott als absolute Zukunft—in der Gemeinschaft von Vater, Sohn und Geist—der freie Ursprung seiner selbst und seiner Geschöpfe," ibid.

308. Pannenberg, *Systematische Theologie*, vol. 2, 36ff.; trans., 22ff.

309. Ibid., 55, 75, 165.

310. Pannenberg, *Systematische Theologie*, vol. 1, 472f.; trans., 438ff.

311. ". . . das Eschaton als den schöpferischen Ursprung des Weltprozesses überhaupt zu denken," Pannenberg, *Systematische Theologie*, vol. 2, 171; trans., 145.

312. ". . . die eschatologische Zukunft Gottes im Kommen seines Reiches die Perspektive für die Auffassung der Welt im ganzen [bestimmt]," ibid., 172; trans., 146.

313. ". . . nur noch der Anfang dessen, was sich erst am Ende in seiner Vollgestalt und wahren Eigenart herausstellen wird," ibid.

314. Cf. Pannenberg, *Systematische Theologie*, vol. 1, 433ff; trans., 401ff.

315. Ibid., 464; trans., 430.

316. Kuschel, *Geboren vor aller Zeit?*; trans., *Born Before All Time.*

317. Ibid., 637; trans., 491 (liberation theology and feminist theology are in the singular in Kuschel).

318. Ibid., 658; trans., 506.

319. "Einen spekulativen Topos 'Präexistenz Christi' kennt das Neue Testament nicht." Ibid., 637; trans., 491.

320. This interpretation of the findings in the texts is criticized by Pannenberg (*Systematische Theologie*, vol. 2, 413n134; trans., 369). Pannenberg accuses Kuschel of wishing to purge the image of Jesus "of all starting points that lead to the doctrine of the Trinity." If this is true, then in this there is an advantage for my study, for I do not want to begin with Trinity as a dogmatic given, but, rather, I would like to examine the Trinity as an explanatory model for time-eternity relationships.

321. Kuschel, *Geboren vor aller Zeit?*, 638; trans., 492.

322. Here, the assumption of an allusion to the so-called *Credo*-thesis is correct; but the assumption is made without simultaneously pitting salvation history against natural and universal human history.

323. ". . . so fragte man auch jetzt von der Erfahrung des neuschaffenden Gottes (er hatte ja Jesus aus dem Tode befreit) zurück auf den urschaffenden Gott," Kuschel, *Geboren vor aller Zeit?*, 369; trans., 493.

324. ". . . an der Gestalt des geschichtlichen Jesus vorbei," ibid., 640; trans., 493.

325. ". . . das 'Ereignis' Jesus in seiner geschichtlichen Tiefe und universalen Bedeutung verständlich zu machen," ibid.

326. Ibid., 641f.

327. Ibid., 642f.

328. "Hat Gott in Jesus Christus nicht nur einen Teil von sich, sondern sein Wesen definitiv und vorbehaltlos geoffenbart, dann ist Jesus Christus auch—als Geist und im Geist—aller Zeit gegenwärtig, aller Zeit gleichzeitig, aller Zeit gegenüber frei. Nichts anderes ist gesagt, wenn wir das Wort Präexistenz Christi benutzen." Ibid., 644; trans., 495.

329. Pannenberg argues at the corresponding place with a kind of reverse conclusion from the Son back to the eternal Father: "If the relation to the historical person of Jesus of Nazareth in eternity characterizes the identity of God the Father, then we must speak of a preexistence of the Son, who was to be historically manifested in Jesus of Nazareth, even before his earthly birth." [Der Ursprung der Gottessohnschaft Jesu kann also nur in der Ewigkeit Gottes selbst liegen. Das ist der eigentliche, wenn auch in den meisten Fällen erst vage erfaßte Sinn der neutestamentlichen Präexistenzaussagen.] Pannenberg, *Systematische Theologie*, vol. 2, 414, trans., 368. Simply put: If the Father is eternal, then the Son must also be eternal (cf. ibid., 410; trans., 364). Here, Pannenberg basically says less than Kuschel and Jüngel.

330. "Gott kommt zwar von Gott und nur von Gott, er wird von niemandem und

nichts als allein von sich selbst bestimmt; er selbst aber bestimmt sich dazu, nicht ohne den Menschen Gott zu sein. Das ist der Sinn der neutestamentlichen Aussagen von der Präexistenz des mit Jesus identifizierten Sohnes Gottes." Jüngel, *Gott als Geheimnis*, 47; trans., *God as the Mystery of the World*, 37.

331. Ibid., 448; trans., 328.

332. Ibid., 498; trans., 349.

333. Schelkle, *Theologie des Neuen Testaments*, 189.

334. Kuschel, *Geboren vor aller Zeit?*, 645; trans., 497.

335. "Weil in den Geschöpfen der ewige Sohn in Erscheinung tritt, werden sie Gegenstand der Liebe Gottes." Pannenberg, *Systematische Theologie*, vol. 2, 36; trans., 21.

336. Ibid., 38; trans., 22.

337. Pannenberg, *Systematische Theologie*, vol. 3, 673f.; trans., 626f.

338. Pannenberg, *Systematische Theologie*, vol. 1, 480f; trans., 446f.

339. Pannenberg, *Systematische Theologie*, vol. 3, 674; trans., 627.

340. I do not intend to discuss the correctness or adequacy of the theological reception of one (or several?) scientific field concepts in Pannenberg at this point. For a (critical) treatment of the field theory in Pannenberg, see, e.g., Worthing, *God, Creation, and Contemporary Physics*, 120–24.

341. Pannenberg, *Systematische Theologie*, vol. 1, 402f., 414f.; trans., 371, 382f.

342. "Die trinitarischen Personen sind also . . . die Singularitäten des dynamischen Feldes der ewigen Gottheit." Ibid., 464; trans., 430.

343. Ibid., 463; trans., 429.

344. ". . . die Selbstdifferenzierung Gottes in seinem trinitarischen Leben [als] die Selbstunterscheidung des Sohnes vom Vater, die durch Heraustreten aus der Einheit des göttlichen Lebens zur Möglichkeitsbedingung selbständigen geschöpflichen Daseins wird." Pannenberg, *Systematische Theologie*, vol. 2, 75; trans., 58.

345. Pannenberg, *Systematische Theologie*, vol. 3, 13; trans., 1: "In all its forms the activity of the Trinitarian God in creation is an activity of the Father by the Son and the Spirit, an activity of the Son in obedience to the Father, and the glorifying of both in the consummation of their work by the Spirit" [Das Handeln des trinitarischen Gottes in seiner Schöpfung ist in allen seinen Gestalten ein Handeln des Vaters durch Sohn und Geist, ein Handeln des Sohnes im Gehorsam gegen den Vater und die Verherrlichung beider in der Vollendung ihres Werkes durch den Geist].

346. Pannenberg, *Systematische Theologie*, vol. 3, 596; trans., 545.

347. Ibid., 32, trans., 47: ". . . einerseits das Prinzip der schöpferischen Gegenwart des transzendenten Gottes bei seinen Geschöpfen, andererseits umgekehrt Medium der Teilhabe der Geschöpfe am göttlichen Leben—und damit am Leben überhaupt."

348. ". . . positive[n] Bezogensein im Sinne der Gemeinschaft des Unterschiedenen," ibid., 104.

349. Pannenberg, *Systematische Theologie*, vol. 3, 598; trans., 555.

350. Ibid. This notion of Pannenberg's seems to be anthropocentric; the question arises whether there is room here for the whole of creation in all of its diversity.

351. Ibid., 594; trans., 550.

352. Pannenberg, *Systematische Theologie*, vol. 2, 47; trans., 20.

353. Kuschel, *Geboren vor aller Zeit?*, 641; trans., 494.

354. ". . . ungeteilte Gegenwart des Lebens in seiner Ganzheit." Pannenberg, *Systematische Theologie*, vol. 2, 113; trans., 92.

355. Ibid.

356. ". . . als aus der Ewigkeit hervorgegangen und bleibend von ihr umgriffen zu denken," ibid., 114; trans., 92.

357. Ibid., 116; trans., 95. Pannenberg distances himself, however, from the interpretation of this leap as a "fall."

358. Ibid., 117; trans., 95.

359. Ibid., 123; trans., 101.

360. ". . . [d]as Hervorgehen des kontingenten Einzelgeschehens aus dem Möglichkeitsfeld der Zukunft; . . . in der Integration der Ereignisse und Lebensmomente zur Einheit der Gestalt," ibid., 124; trans., 102.

361. ". . . den geschöpflichen Gestalten durch Teilhabe an der Ewigkeit Dauer zu gewähren und sie gegen die aus der Verselbständigung der Geschöpfe folgenden Auflösungstendenzen zu behaupten," ibid.

362. "Der Geist ist also der schöpferische Ursprung des Auferstehungslebens—sowohl bei der Auferstehung Jesu als auch in bezug auf die übrigen Menschen," Pannenberg, *Systematische Theologie*, vol. 3, 669; trans., 622.

363. "Er ist Ursprung des Heils, des neuen und ewigen Lebens, aber auch Organ des Gerichts." Ibid., 670; trans., 623.

364. Ibid., 670–72; trans., 623–25.

365. Pannenberg, *Systematische Theologie*, vol. 2, 114 and 124; trans., 92f. and 102.

366. Ibid., 116, 124; trans., 94, 102.

367. Ibid., 118; trans., 96.

368. Ibid., 121f., 123, 124; trans., 99f., 101, 102.

369. Pannenberg, *Systematische Theologie*, vol. 1, 441ff.; trans., 410ff.

370. Jüngel, *Gott als Geheimnis*, 289ff.; trans., *God as the Mystery*, 213ff.

371. "Das Wesen des Todes ist Verhältnislosigkeit," Jüngel, *Tod*, 171; trans., *Death, the Riddle and the Mystery*, 135.

372. Bauman, *Mortality, Immortality and Other Life Strategies*, 2.

373. Jüngel, "Der Tod als Geheimnis," 340.

374. "Der Drang in die Verhältnislosigkeit, der die Beziehungen abbricht, um das Leben sozusagen als Privatbesitz für sich selbst zu haben, . . . ist der Drang in den Tod. Und der Tod selbst ist das Fazit dieses Dranges in die Verhältnislosigkeit: das Ereignis, in dem auch die letzte Beziehung abbricht, auch das letzte Verhältnis zusammenbricht—die Beziehung, die ich zu mir selbst habe, das Selbstverhältnis." Ibid.

375. Ps. 115:17; Isa. 38:18f.

376. Dan. 12:1–3; 2 Macc. 7:9, 11, 14, 29, 36.

377. I agree here with Jeanrond's thesis that a life-undergirding horizon for the human understanding of death and life is lost if death is interpreted only as a relatively uncomfortable crossover of the soul, separated from the body, to a kind of immortality. An adequate theory of life, and also of eternal life, is impossible without taking seriously the challenge of death in all of its radicality. Jeanrond, *Call and Response*, 50.

378. In this context, Jüngel discusses an understanding of death as the final and real act of human self-realization, exemplified in F. W. J. Schelling's words that human death is "an *essentification* . . . , wherein only the coincidental perishes, but the *essence*, or that which the human person really *is*, is preserved" [eine *Essentification* . . . , worin nur Zufälliges untergeht, aber das *Wesen*, das was eigentlich der Mensch *ist*, bewahrt wird] (cited according to Jüngel). This position is certainly impressive and must be respected by the Christian faith because it does not suppress the hatred of death with the aid of numbing ideas and images, but rather uses them to mock death. An important objection, however, contradicts this: "The understanding of death as the essentification of the person is also deceptive in that human beings *suffer* death" [Das Verständnis des Todes als Essentifikation der Person täuscht darüber hinweg, daß der Mensch den Tod *erleidet*]. Jüngel, "Der Tod als Geheimnis" (1980), 343.

379. "Als Ereignis vollendeter Verhältnislosigkeit ist der Tod das genaue Gegenteil einer Freigabe von so etwas wie einem unzerstörbaren Person-Kern und erst recht das genaue Gegenteil eines sich selbst vollendenden oder essentifizierenden menschlichen Aktes. Im Tod *wird* der Mensch *vernichtet.*" Ibid., 344.

380. For the sake of clarity, it is noted here that, in speaking of the immortality of the soul, I principally mean immortality conceived on the individual level. This should be distinguished from super-individual or pantheistic notions of immortality that occurred, for example, in the idealistic tendencies of Romanticism, which, incidentally, sought to unite numerous notions of immortality with ideas of resurrection (cf. on this Segerbank, *Dödstanken i svensk romantik*). When Schleiermacher speaks of immortality at the end of his second talk, *Über die Religion*, then he does so precisely in a polemic against a fearful concern for one's own individuality and as an appeal to the educated among those despisers of religion "to annihilate their personality and to live in the One and All" [schon hier eure Individualität zu vernichten, und im Einen und Allen zu leben]. Schleiermacher, *Über die Religion*, 95–97; trans., *On Religion*, 100–101.

381. Jüngel says succinctly and conclusively: "there is no immortality of the soul" [eine Unsterblichkeit der Seele gibt es nicht]. Jüngel, *Tod*, 152; trans., 120. Jeanrond warns of the consequences of a dualism of body and soul (*Call and Response*, 55ff.). He criticizes official Roman Catholic theology as it is presented, for example, in the Catechism of the Catholic Church of 1993 (on the doctrine of the separation of the immortal soul from the body at the moment of death, see ibid., nos. 366, 1005, and 1016): "It is sad that the countless warnings by prominent theologians, including Roman Catholic ones, during the last few decades were ignored once again, and an old and fundamentally non-Christian doctrine of death was reaffirmed." Jeanrond, *Call and Response*, 58. The *Evangelische Erwachsenenkatechimus* 1975 (532f.) is also not nearly as clear as Jüngel; it is more concerned with trying to combine the hope of resurrection and the immortality of the soul than it is with trying to contrast death as the end of all human activity with God's action. Stendahl, on the other hand, distances himself from notions of immortality with the argument that this is far too large and, simultaneously, far too small ("Immortality is Too Much and Too Little"). Far too large because it arrogantly glorifies the human being with individual immortality and claims to know more than is useful. Far too small because it is far too egoistic, far too concerned with one's own self, one's own family, or one's own race, thereby forgetting that the New Testament deals with something far greater than the concern about individual identity, namely, with the advent of the reign of God. In his study of the various aspects of the idea of eternal life, Küng does not deal in particular with ideas about the immortality of the soul *(Ewiges Leben?)*. He appears to want to assume a middle position when he says that the human being does indeed die "as a whole, with body and soul, as a psychosomatic unity" [als ganzer, mit Leib und Seele, als psychosomatische Einheit], but he distances himself from a "total death" [Ganztod] (178; trans., *Eternal Life?*, 138). Cf. hereto also the discussion of various concepts of the soul, as well as the reflections on immortality, in Tysk, *Evigt liv*, 81–148. Ratzinger argues for the immortality of the soul, claiming, in his own words, to "rehabilitate an originally Christian concept of the immortality of the soul" [einen originär christlichen Begriff der Unsterblichkeit der Seele rehabilitiert], *Eschatologie*, 137.

382. Cf. Wittgenstein, "Tractatus logico-philosophicus," 6.4312.

383. See above pp. 52–54, n. 363.

384. Bauman, *Mortality, Immortality*, 130.

385. Ibid., 138.

386. Küng points out that, already in 1794, the revolutionary Antoine de Condorcet proclaimed "the abolition or a considerable postponement of death as the long-term goal

of medicine," *Ewiges Leben?*, 21; trans., 8. Ariès speaks in his monumental work *L'homme devant la mort* of a "médicalisation complète de la mort" after 1945 (*L'homme devant la mort*, 577).

387. Baumann, *Mortality, Immortality*, 137, cites Ariès (*L'homme devant la mort*, 580): "La mort a cessé d'être admise comme un phénomène naturel nécessaire. Elle est un échec, un business lost (R. S. Morrison)."

388. Bauman, *Mortality, Immortality*, 141.

389. Cf. ibid., 159f.: ". . . medical practices are surrogate solutions to the existential predicament that allows no solution. They merely avert attention from big things . . . The impotence in the face of the 'biggest of problems' is to be compensated (stifled? masked? shouted down?) by the zealotry and ardour of the agitation about the smaller ones. Hence the hysteria—whether the sniffed dangers come from salmonella-infected chicken, smokers, mad cows, homosexuals, Turks in Germany, Algerians in France, Blacks in England, or Gypsies everywhere." In Bauman's view, in the modern age, smaller problems are used as a diversion from the large existential questions. It is interesting to note that, in Marx, the argument moves in the opposite direction: The eternal questions function as a diversionary tactic that is aimed at preventing work on the solvable and smaller problems of society.

390. Ibid., 164.

391. Ibid., 165f.

392. Gronemeyer, *Das Leben als letzte Gelegenheit*.

393. Bauman, *Mortality, Immortality*, 166.

394. Ibid., 169.

395. Ibid., 187.

396. Ibid., 169.

397. Ibid., 170.

398. Ibid., 174.

399. Ibid., 184 (here with reference to Jean-François Lyotard, *Peregrinations* [New York: Columbia University Press, 1988], 31f.).

400. On the theme of reincarnation, cf. also *Concilium* 1993, no. 5.

401. Bauman, *Mortality, Immortality*, 190.

402. Ibid., 193.

403. Ibid., 188.

404. Ibid., 199.

405. ". . . ist der Eintritt, ist das Ereignis schlechthinniger Verhältnislosigkeit," Jüngel, "Der Tod als Geheimnis" (1980), 340. The relationship that human beings can have to dead people should be distinguished from this non-relationality, because it excludes mutuality.

406. Cf. Jeanrond, *Call and Response*, 60: ". . . as long as we, so to speak, prepare our stamp collection for eternal inspection, as long as we expect to be carried to eternity on the wings of a well-groomed soul, we have missed the point of Jesus's death and resurrection. And most disturbingly, we have missed the point of our own life and death. It is dangerous for our life to speak carelessly about our death."

407. Jüngel, "Der Tod als Geheimnis," 345.

408. ". . . auf jene Grenze, die kein Mensch setzen darf, weil kein Mensch sie aufheben kann," Jüngel, *Tod*, 171; trans., 136.

409. ". . . die Begrenzung des Menschen allein durch Gott, der da, wo wir schlechthin ohnmächtig sind, seine Macht nicht mißbraucht," ibid.

410. Jeanrond, *Call and Response*, 53.

411. Ibid.

412. Ibid., 60.

413. ". . . als ein[en] neue[n] Anfang aus dem vernichtenden Nichts des Todes," Jüngel, "Der Tod als Geheimnis" (1980), 347.

414. "Die Lebenszeit eines Menschen . . . wird nur dann eigentliche Geschichte, wenn sie verstanden wird als Moment der Geschichte Gottes mit allen Menschen." Jüngel, *Tod*, 149; trans., 118.

415. Lévinas, *Time and the Other*. For an introduction into the thinking of Lévinas, especially in relation to Husserl, Heidegger, Kierkegaard, and Rosenzweig, see Kemp, *Lévinas*.

416. Lévinas, *Time and the Other*, 32.

417. In my opinion, "absolute other" should rather be understood here in the sense of "radical other." Cf. in this respect also Ricoeur's criticism of Lévinas in Ricoeur, *Soi-même comme un autre*, 387–93. Whereas Lévinas stresses the incomprehensibility of the "other," Ricoeur emphasizes the meaning, and consequences, of the communication between "me" and "the other": "Bref, ne faut-il pas qu'une dialogique superpose la relation à la distance prétendument ab-solue entre le moi séparé et l'Autre enseignant?" (391).

418. Lévinas, *Time and the Other*, 32.

419. Ibid., 79.

420. Ibid., 39.

421. Ibid., 57.

422. Ibid., 54, 42, etc.

423. Ibid., 86.

424. Ibid., 81, etc.

425. Ibid., 70ff. (the moment we are no longer able to be able; ibid., 74).

426. Lévinas, *God, Death, and Time*. In comparison to the earlier writing entitled *Time and the Other*, the discussion here is no longer about the absoluteness of the "other."

427. Levinas, *God, Death, and Time*, 106–12.

428. Ibid., 107.

429. Ibid., 110.

430. Ibid.

431. Ibid., 111.

432. Ibid., 112.

433. Ibid., 116.

434. Lévinas, *Time and the Other*, 77, 79.

435. In Lévinas, the transcendent alterity that is opening up time is tied only to the human. He takes his starting point from an otherness based on content, which he calls femininity. Subsequently, he speaks of fatherhood as a category in which freedom arises and time is fulfilled (*Time and the Other*, 84–94). The concepts of femininity, fatherhood, and sonship seem to be problematic, however, since they are easily misunderstood. Their usage obscures, e.g., the criticism of power intended by Lévinas, ibid., 37.

Chapter 3

1. Daly, *Creation and Redemption*, 20.

2. "Wenn anders die Theologie bei ihrem Thema verharren will, hat sie sich nicht mit den verschiedenen philosophischen, naturwissenschaftlichen und geschichtswissenschaftlichen Begriffen von Zeit und Ewigkeit zu befassen . . . ," Schneider, "Die Bedeutung der Begriffe," 284. Schneider likewise shares Cullmann's concept of eternity being an eternally long time (ibid). His limited treatment of the question of time and eternity then also leads to such obviously problematic conclusions as: "Der Tag der Erschaffung des Menschen in der Vergangenheit und der Tag der Wiederkunft Christi in der Zukunft

grenzen unsern Aion auf der Zeitlinie der Ewigkeit ein" (The day of humankind's creation in the past and the day of Christ's return in the future places our aeon on the timeline of eternity), 285. Schneider's example clearly shows that a theology that ignores the scientific discussion of its own epoch and erroneously believes itself to be completely independent of science is in danger of (unconsciously) linking itself to concepts that are shaped by the state of scientific knowledge in the past.

3. The framework of this study does not permit a detailed analysis of possible dialogue concepts. Ted Peters provides a helpful overview from a theological perspective ("Theology and Science: Where Are We?"). (A somewhat expanded version of this article can also be found in Ford, ed., *The Modern Theologians*, 649–68.) Peters outlines eight different ways of relating science and religion to each other: scientism, scientific imperialism, ecclesiastical authoritarianism, scientific creationism, dual-language theory, hypothetical consonance, ethical overlap, and New Age spirituality. Peters himself advocates hypothetical consonance and the model of ethical overlap. Using this palette of possible positions, he then presents the concepts of some of the well-known theologians participating in the dialogue (among others, Philip Hefner, Wolfhart Pannenberg, Arthur Peacocke, John Polkinghorne, and Robert J. Russell). For information on the history of the dialogue and on some systematic deliberations, see also Jackelén, "Vom Erobern des Selbstverständlichen" (On the Conquering of the Self-evident). Cf. also Brooke, *Science and Religion;* Brooke and Cantor, *Reconstructing Nature;* and Toulmin, *The Return to Cosmology*, esp. 217–74.

4. E.g., Haught, *Science and Religion;* Richardson and Wildman, *Religion and Science;* Peters, *Science and Theology;* McGrath, *Science and Religion;* and Southgate, *God, Humanity and the Cosmos.* For discussions on the concept of rationality within the area of the relationship between science and religion/theology, see also Stenmark, *Rationality in Science,* and van Huyssteen, *The Shaping of Rationality.*

5. Cf. Hübner, *Der Dialog zwischen Theologie und Naturwissenschaft,* 20–37.

6. Wertheim, *Pythagoras' Trousers,* 127ff., 145ff.; Brooke, *Science and Religion,* 155ff.

7. For a representative, annotated overview of the literature on the different areas of the dialogue between theology and science prior to 1987, see Hübner, *Der Dialog zwischen Theologie und Naturwissenschaft.*

8. Barbour, "Ways of Relating Science and Theology." He developed his basic theses of the complementarity of scientific and religious language, the parallelism of methods, the necessity of an integrated worldview, and the importance of a theology of nature in relationship to God and human beings in his book *Issues in Science and Religion.* See also Barbour, *Religion and Science.*

9. Torrance's books, *Space, Time and Incarnation* and *Space, Time and Resurrection*, are of particular interest for the subject of this study.

10. Mortensen, "Teologi og naturvidenskab."

11. Cf. in this regard also the hermeneutic reappraisal of the presuppositions, possibilities, and goals of the interdisciplinary dialogue in Bühler and Karakash, *Science et foi font système.*

12. Cf. Altner, *Schöpfungsglaube und Entwicklungsgedanke,* and Hübner, *Theologie und biologische Entwicklungslehre.*

13. For an example, see the account of the evangelical-biblical writings in Hübner, *Der Dialog zwischen Theologie und Naturwissenschaft,* 114–21; however, not all criticism of evolution is biblically motivated. In *Human Image: World Image,* Sherrard provides an example of another approach that denounces "modern science," especially for surrendering all teleological explanations; in this, however, he himself argues from the standpoint of a teleological and spiritual concept of nature as he sees it embodied in "the Platonic-Aristotelian-Christian view."

14. Cf. Peters, *GOD as Trinity.*

15. On this, cf. Clayton, *God and Contemporary Science*, which, proceeding from a panentheistic starting point, examines the relationship of science and theology under the aspect of "divine action."

16. Larson, *Times of the Trinity.*

17. Fagg, *The Becoming of Time.*

18. Achtner, Kunz, and Walter, *Dimensions of Time.*

19. E.g., Achtner, *Physik, Mystik und Christentum;* Predel, *Sakrament der Gegenwart Gottes;* Dinter, *Vom Glauben eines Physikers;* Berg, *Theologie im technologischen Zeitalter;* and Cliqué, *Differenz und Parallelität.* Cf. also Gregersen and van Huyssteen, *Rethinking Theology and Science.*

20. Isaac Newton was born on December 25, 1642, which corresponds to January 4, 1643, of the Gregorian calendar that was introduced into England in the middle of the eighteenth century. For this reason, 1643 is also sometimes given as Newton's year of birth.

21. H. G. Alexander, ed., *The Leibniz-Clarke Correspondence: Together with Extracts from Newton's Principia and Opticks*, 181 (*Opticks*, Query 31). The first English edition of *Opticks* appeared in 1704. The first Latin edition of 1706 (translated by Samuel Clarke) was already expanded by, among other things, Query 31, which is important in this context. The text was revised again for the second English edition of 1717. Quotations from *Opticks* are taken here from the text edition cited by Alexander.

22. Ibid., 182 (*Opticks*, Query 31).

23. 1st edition (1687), 2nd edition (1713), 3rd edition (1726).

24. Newton, *Mathematical Principles of Natural Philosophy*, 9. The Latin text reads: "Tempus absolutum, verum, & mathematicum, in se & natura sua sine relatione ad externum quodvis, æquabiliter fluit, alioque nomine dicitur duratio: Relativum, apparens, & vulgare est sensibilis & externa quævis durationis per motum mensura (seu accurata seu inæquabilis) qua vulgus vice veri temporis utitur; ut hora, dies, mensis, annus." Newton, *Isaac Newton's Philosophiae Naturalis*, 1, 46.

25. Newton, *Mathematical Principles*, 9.

26. Ibid., 9.

27. Ibid., 11.

28. Ibid, 12.

29. Ibid., 17.

30. Ibid. "Upon which account, they do stain the Sacred Writings, who there interpret those words for measur'd quantities. Nor do those less defile the purity of Mathematical and Philosophical truths, who confound real quantities themselves with their relations and vulgar measures."

31. Alexander, ed., *The Leibniz-Clarke Correspondence*, 167 (General Scholium).

32. Ibid., 156 (Scholium on def. 8).

33. Newton, *Mathematical Principles*, 17. Therefore, it is not surprising that the German text has "infinity" translated as "eternity" [*Ewigkeit*].

34. x, y, and z are space coordinates, t is the time coordinate, and v specifies the velocity. An example: It should be determined at which point x' a signal post is located at time t', seen from a train that passes by point x at time t with the constant velocity of v. The solution using the Galilean Transformation is $x' = x - vt$. Here, $t' = t$, since according to the presupposition of absolute time, the time t' of the "observing" signal post is identical to the time t of the "observer" train. From the viewpoint of classical mechanics, only the space coordinates require transformation while the time coordinates do not.

35. Cf. Mainzer, *Zeit—Von der Urzeit zur Computerzeit*, 32–39.

36. Burtt, *The Metaphysical Foundations*, 251.

37. Newton, *Mathematical Principles*, 17: ". . . partly from the forces, which are the causes and effects of the true motions."

38. Cf. Alexander, ed., *The Leibniz-Clarke Correspondence*, 182 (end of Query 31).

39. The close connection between theology and science is also emphasized by Brooke in *Science and Religion*, 7, 12, 18, and 144ff. For a brief description of Newton's works and theological world of ideas, see Petry, "Newton, Isaac," 425ff. For a detailed biography, see Westfall, *Never at Rest;* on Newton's theological studies, see esp. 309–34.

40. For insight into the intellectual climate in England between 1640 and 1700—particularly the "Cambridge Platonists" and their disciples or epigones, the Latitudinarians—see Kroll, Ashcraft, and Zagorin, *Philosophy, Science, and Religion.*

41. Newton, *Mathematical Principles*, 15f. (example of a body in motion on a sailing ship); Burtt, *The Metaphysical Foundations*, 255.

42. Burtt, *The Metaphysical Foundations*, 256f.

43. Ibid., 258.

44. Ibid., 261.

45. In his essay of 1967, which attracted attention at the time, the philosopher and historian Lynn White Jr. made the Christian understanding of nature—in terms of the *dominium terrae*—responsible for the ecological crisis. The reception and criticism of White's thesis stimulated the development of ecological theology; see Hübner, *Der Dialog zwischen Theologie und Naturwissenschaft,* 361ff. On this topic, cf. also Krolzik, *Umweltkrise;* Merchant, *The Death of Nature,* and Bergmann, *Geist, der Natur befreit.*

46. Brooke, *Science and Religion*, 159.

47. Ibid., 7, 144–51, etc.

48. Ibid., 12. Koyré feels some discord with this idea (*From the Closed World*, 1ff.). He maintains that, over the course of the seventeenth century, the conception of the cosmos (the world as a finite, closed, and hierarchically structured totality) was replaced by the idea of an unlimited and even infinite universe determined by the identity of its components and laws, whereby all of these elements were on the same ontological level. As a result, he claimed, a separation between the world of values and the world of facts took place, transcendental goals were replaced by immanent ones, and the emphasis shifted from theory to practice, from the *vita contemplativa* to the *vita activa.*

49. Brooke, *Science and Religion*, 144f.

50. Ibid., 118.

51. Ibid., 160.

52. Westfall, *Never at Rest*, 311ff.; and Petry, "Newton, Isaac," 427.

53. Newton certainly used traditional descriptive titles for Christ over and over in his writings, but "[m]it Christus, dem Erlöser von Sünde und Tod, dem Heilbringer, hat Newton offenbar nichts anfangen können" (evidently Newton did not know what to do with Christ, the Redeemer from sin and death, the Savior), Buchholtz, *Isaac Newton als Theologe*, 53.

54. Brooke, *Science and Religion*, 146.

55. Ibid., 149.

56. Ibid., 137, 19.

57. Burtt, *The Metaphysical Foundations*, 261.

58. Ibid., 262.

59. Ibid., 262f.

60. An example of the attempt to understand Newton in light of his theology can be found in Achtner, *Physik, Mystik und Christentum*, 51–72. Achtner identifies the influence of the Platonizing church fathers, on the one hand, and a biblical theism, on the other hand, as the philosophical and theological background for Newton's natural philosophy.

He makes the Platonic, transcendental image of God responsible for the physical dualism of absolute space and absolute time, relative space and relative time, as well as absolute and relative motion; and he finds biblical theism to be expressed primarily in the General Scholium (*Lat. Scholium Generale*). He quite correctly concludes that the evolution to deism is, above all, to be attributed to Newton's "defective Christology" (61). Achtner's interpretation of a passage in the General Scholium as being an expression of God's constant activity, which completely corresponds to the theological doctrines of the *creatio continua* and the *providentia Dei* (67), is too positive, however. He appears to have let himself be misled by the German translation that he used: "[D]adurch, daß er [Gott] immer und überall ist, bringt er die Zeit und den Raum zum Sein" (Since he [God] is eternal and everywhere, he brings time and space into being), allows an interpretation more in the direction of *creatio continua* than the English or Latin texts. The formulations "by existing always and everywhere, he constitutes duration and space" (Alexander, ed., *The Leibniz-Clarke Correspondence*, 167) and "existendo semper & ubique, durationem & spatium constituit" (Newton, *Isaac Newton's Philosophia Naturalis*, II, 761) allow little room for a dynamic interpretation. The evidence of a possible interpretation of Newton's concepts of space and time in terms of interaction (Achtner, *Physik, Mystik und Christentum*, 67f.) is also not convincing to me. On Newton's theology, cf. also Buchholtz, *Isaac Newton als Theologe*.

61. Alexander, ed., *The Leibniz-Clarke Correspondence*, 166.

62. Ibid., 166: "For God is a relative word, and has a respect to servants; . . ."

63. Ibid., 167.

64. Ibid.

65. Newton, *Isaac Newton's Philosophiae Naturalis*, II, 762: "Omnipræsens est non per virtutem solam, sed etiam per substantiam" ("not virtually only, but also substantially," Alexander, ed., *The Leibniz-Clarke Correspondence*, 168).

66. Alexander, ed., *The Leibniz-Clarke Correspondence*, 168.

67. Ibid., 169. These three divine predicates also appear at the end of Query 31 in *Opticks* within the framework of the assertion that natural philosophy can also promote moral philosophy: "For so far as we can know by natural philosophy what is *the first cause*, what *power He has over us*, and what *benefits we receive from Him*, so far our duty towards Him, as well as that towards one another, will appear to us by the light of nature," ibid., 182f., my emphases.

68. Ibid., 170; for an interpretation of this sentence against the backdrop of the polemic against, among others, Descartes, cf. Koyré, *From the Closed World*, 229ff.

69. Newton, *Opticks* 369.

70. Ibid., 370.

71. Ibid., 400.

72. Ibid., 403.

73. Ibid., 403–4: ". . . it may be also allow'd that God is able to create Particles of Matter of several Sizes and Figures, and in several Proportions to Space, and perhaps of different Densities and Forces, and thereby to vary the Laws of Nature, and make Worlds of several Sorts in several Parts of the Universe."

74. Ibid. Influenced by the criticism of Leibniz, Newton added some sentences in 1717 that make clear that the universe is not to be understood as the body of God, or parts of the universe as parts of God. God is no more the soul of the (parts of the) world than the human soul is part of sensory impressions.

75. Alexander provides an illuminating commentary on Newton's *sensorium* concept. The expression *sensorium Dei* is the result of Newton's "acceptance of the representative theory of perception in its most extreme form." Human *sensoria* are understood as "inter-

nal cinemas" in which images are transmitted by means of sensory nerves. God's perception of world events, on the other hand, must occur more directly. For this reason, Newton declared all space to be the *sensorium Dei* (ibid., xvi). The *sensorium* idea is thus an expression of an image of God that places the omnipresence of the almighty God in the forefront.

76. Such summarizing entails risks. Depending upon the interpretation, very diverse concepts apply. Thus, for example, Achtner, Kunz, and Walter, *Dimensions of Time*, 111, speak of Newton's complete idealization of time, and thereby mean universality, quantification, and symmetry. Leibniz, on the other hand, condemns Clarke and respectively Newton, precisely because of a realization of time (Gerhardt, *Die philosophischen Schriften*, 363), and characterizes his own relative concept of time as being ideal (415).

77. Newton speaks of the sequence of time segments (Newton, *Mathematical Principles*, 16).

78. Thus in his third letter, sec. 4, Gerhardt, *Die philosophischen Schriften*, 363; Alexander, ed., *The Leibniz-Clarke Correspondence*, 25f.

79. Examples of accounts of and commentaries on this correspondence: Alexander, ed., *The Leibniz-Clarke Correspondence*, ix–lv; Koyré, *From the Closed World*, 235–72; Manzke, *Ewigkeit und Zeitlichkeit*, 86–98.

80. In the following discussion, I refer sometimes to the edition by Gerhardt, *Die philosophischen Schriften*, which presents Leibniz's writings in French and Clarke's replies in English, and sometimes to the 1956 Alexander edition, *The Leibniz-Clarke Correspondence*, which has an introduction and commentary by Alexander, and which was based on *A COLLECTION OF PAPERS which passed between the late Learned Mr. LEIBNITZ AND Dr. CLARKE in the years 1715 and 1716 relating to the PRINCIPLES OF NATURAL PHILOSOPHY AND RELIGION With an Appendix, by SAMUEL CLARKE, London, MDCCXVII.* Here, the original French letters of Leibniz were probably translated into English by Clarke himself (Koryé, *From the Closed World*, 300n2). To facilitate the use of various text editions, in addition to citing page numbers, I have also referenced the letter (L or C 1–v). Although in the body of my study I cite all the passages from the Alexander edition, I have included in the footnotes some of the French citations when they have seemed more appropriate.

81. The extent to which Clarke is acting as a direct mouthpiece for Newton (thus Koyré, *From the Closed World*, 300n3) or defending or further developing his own understanding of Newton has not been considered here, for we are not concerned with the person of Newton, but rather with a debate of an issue.

82. Alexander, ed., *The Leibniz-Clarke Correspondence*, 11; cf. Gerhardt, *Die philosophischen Schriften*, 352 L 1: "[p]lusieurs font les ames corporelles, d'autres font Dieu luy même corporel."

83. Gerhardt, *Die philosophischen Schriften*, 352 L I; cf. Alexander, ed., *The Leibniz-Clarke Correspondence*, 12: "the beautiful pre-established order."

84. Alexander, ed., *The Leibniz-Clarke Correspondence*, 13 C I, sec. 3. In his second response, Clarke adds that, while the human soul is present to the images of things, God per se is present to all things without thereby being the soul of the world (*intelligentia mundana*), 21ff., C II, sec. 3ff.

85. Ibid., 14 C I, sec. 4.

86. On the history of space theories in physics, cf. Jammer, *Concepts of Space*.

87. This becomes particularly clear, for example, in Clarke's second response, in which he initially admits that he is concerned not only with the power but also with the wisdom of God as the source of creation; he then, however, continues, "but the wisdom of God consists, in framing originally the perfect and complete idea of a work, . . . by the continu-

al uninterrupted exercise of his *power* and *government.*" Alexander, ed., *The Leibniz-Clarke Correspondence*, 22 C II, sec. 6 and 7 (my emphasis).

88. See, for example, Gerhardt, *Die philosophischen Schriften*, 357f. L II: "La simple production de tout marqueroit bien la *puissance* de Dieu; mais elle ne marqueroit point assés sa *sagesse*" (my emphasis), or Alexander, ed., *The Leibniz-Clarke Correspondence*, 18: "The bare production of every thing, would indeed show the *power* of God; but it would not sufficiently show his *wisdom.*" Cf. also Gerhardt, *Die philosophischen Schriften*, 396, L V sec. 30 and 408, L V sec. 72: ". . . il [Dieu] est determiné par des raisons internes, c'est à dire par sa sagesse," or Alexander, ed., *The Leibniz-Clarke Correspondence*, 64 and 80: ". . . he [God] is determined by internal reasons, that is, by his wisdom."

89. Thus Clarke writes in his third reply (similar to Newton at the end of his General Scholium): "God, being omnipresent, is really present to every thing, essentially and substantially." Alexander, ed., *The Leibniz-Clarke Correspondence*, 33f. C III, sec. 12.

90. Gerhardt, *Die philosophischen Schriften*, 358 L II: "Dieu a tout prevû, il a remedié à tout par avance. Il y a dans ses ouvrages une harmonie, une beauté déja preétablie." Cf. also Alexander, ed., *The Leibniz-Clarke Correspondence*, 18 L II, sec. 8, 26.

91. Gerhardt, *Die philosophischen Schriften,* 364f. L III, sec. 7f.; Alexander, ed., *The Leibniz-Clarke Correspondence*, 25.

92. Ibid., 377f. L IV P.S.: The assertion of a vacuum (just like the atomic theory) means attributing a very imperfect work to God, "c'est violer le grand Principe de la necessité d'une raison suffisante" (378).

93. Alexander, ed., *The Leibniz-Clarke Correspondence*, 23 C II, sec. 10, 25f.

94. Gerhardt, *Die philosophischen Schriften*, 363, L III, sec. 3: "un étre reel absolu"; Alexander, ed., *The Leibniz-Clarke Correspondence*, 25.

95. Gerhardt, *Die philosophischen Schriften*, 363, L III, sec. 4: "Pour moy, j'ay marqué plus d'une fois, que je tenois l'Espace pour quelque chose de purement relatif, comme le Temps; pour un ordre des Coexistences, comme le temps est un odre [sic] de [sic] successions."

96. Cf. Alexander, ed., *The Leibniz-Clarke Correspondence*, xxxiiff.

97. It therefore seems doubtful to me that it is justified to say that "Leibniz den heutigen Standpunkt genial antizipiert hat" [Leibniz brilliantly anticipated the current point of view], as Wild did in "Wie kam die Zeit in die Welt?" (155).

98. Gerhardt, *Die philosophischen Schriften*, 405 L V, sec. 55: "le temps doit coëxister aux creatures." Cf. Alexander, ed., *The Leibniz-Clarke Correspondence*, 75: "whereas time does only coexist with creatures."

99. Gerhardt, *Die philosophischen Schriften*, 374 L IV, sec. 16; 395 L V, sec. 29; and 405 L V, sec. 55; Alexander, ed., *The Leibniz-Clarke Correspondence*, 63f.

100. Alexander, ed., *The Leibniz-Clarke Correspondence,* 31 C III, sec. 3; and 47 C IV, sec. 10.

101. ". . . Medien der Wirksamkeit Gottes in der Welt," *Manzke, Ewigkeit und Zeitlichkeit,* 93, etc.

102. Alexander, ed., *The Leibniz-Clarke Correspondence*, 32 C III, sec. 4.

103. Ibid., 52 C IV, sec. 41.

104. Gerhardt, *Die philosophischen Schriften*, 409, L V, sec. 76: ". . . on confond la volonté avec la puissance de Dieu. Il peut produire tout possible, ou ce qui n'implique point de contradiction; mais il veut produire le meilleur entre les possibles." Cf. Alexander, ed., *The Leibniz-Clarke Correspondence*, 81: "God can produce every thing that is possible, or whatever does not imply a contradiction; but he wills only to produce what is the best among things possible."

105. "Phrases estranges," ibid., 399, L V, sec. 44.; cf. Alexander, ed., *The Leibniz-Clarke Correspondence*, 73.

106. Gerhardt, *Die philosophischen Schriften*, 402f., sec. 49: "l'un [space] est aussi ideal que l'autre [time]."

107. Gerhardt, *Die philosophischen Schriften*, 415, L v, sec. 104: ". . . pour montrer comment l'esprit vient à se former l'idée de l'Espace, sans qu'il faille qu'il y ait un Etre reel et absolu, qui y réponde, hors de l'esprit et hors des rapports. Je ne dis donc point, que l'E-space est un ordre ou situation, mais un ordre des situations. . . . Ainsi c'est quelque chose d'ideal . . ."; Alexander, ed., *The Leibniz-Clarke Correspondence*, 89: ". . . the mind comes to form to itself an idea of space, and yet that there need not be any real and absolute be-ing answering to that idea, distinct from the mind, and from all relations. . . . Space is therefore something [merely] ideal."

108. Gerhardt, *Die philosophischen Schriften*, 415, L v, sec. 106. Gerhardt: "S'il n'y avoit point de creatures, il n'y auroit ny temps ny lieu; et par consequent point d'espace actuel. . . . Ainsi je n'admets point ce qu'on avance icy, que si Dieu seul existoit, il y auroit temps et espace, comme à present. Au lieu qu'alors, à mon avis, ils ne seroient que dans les idées, comme les simples possibilités."

109. Alexander, ed., *The Leibniz-Clarke Correspondence*, 104, C v sec. 45: "And when, according to the analogy of vulgar speech, we say that he exists in all space and in all time; the words mean only that he is omnipresent and eternal, that is, that boundless space and time are necessary consequences of his existence; and not, that space and time are beings distinct from him, and IN which he exists."

110. Thus, for example, von Weizsäcker, *Zeit und Wissen*, 354, Coveney and Highfield, *The Arrow of Time*, 39. Around two hundred years later, John C. Squire (1884–1958) added: "It did not last: the devil howling Ho, / Let Einstein be, restored the status quo" (accord-ing to Coveney and Highfield, *The Arrow of Time*, 68).

111. See pp. 41–44, 65–80.

112. Cf. pp. 37–44.

113. Alexander, ed., *The Leibniz-Clarke Correspondence*, 166f. (General Scholium).

114. Ibid., L v, sec. 72, 80; cf. Gerhardt, *Die philosophischen Schriften*, 408, "determiné par des raisons internes."

115. Jüngel, *Gott als Geheimnis der Welt*, 36–43; trans., *God as the Mystery of the World*, 29–34.

116. One should note in this regard that Newton's concept of God is basically less stat-ic than that of Descartes. Whereas Descartes considers God's unchangeability to be central as the guarantee for the cognition processes within a mechanistic explanation of the world, Newton allows God to exert influence on world events by making God—though in unten-able manner, as would soon be shown—responsible for the stability of the planetary sys-tem, for the "winding of the world's clock," and for occasional corrections.

117. Alexander, ed., *The Leibniz-Clarke Correspondence*, 168 (General Scholium); New-ton, *Isaac Newton's Philosophiae Naturalis*, II, 762: "Deus nihil patitur . . ."

118. Alexander, ed., *The Leibniz-Clarke Correspondence*, xl–lv, offers a summary of the most important positions in the discussion of time and space extending from Leibniz to Kant and also including Mach and Einstein.

119. On this, cf. Manzke, *Ewigkeit und Zeitlichkeit*, 85–160, who presents the develop-mental stages of Kant's theory of time in detail primarily using the *Inaugural Dissertation* from 1770 and the *Kritik der reinen Vernunft* under the title "Die von der Relation zur Ewigkeit 'befreite' Zeit" (Time "Liberated" from the Relation to Eternity).

120. ". . . eine notwendige Vorstellung, die allen Anschauungen zum Grunde liegt," Kant, *Kritik der reinen Vernunft*, B 46; trans., *Critique of Pure Reason*, 86.

121. Manzke, *Ewigkeit und Zeitlichkeit*, 55ff.

122. Alexander, ed., *The Leibniz-Clarke Correspondence*, xlvif.

123. ". . . insgesamt im Gemüte a priori bereit liegen," Kant, *Kritik der reinen Vernunft*, B 34; trans., 73.

124. "a) Die Zeit ist nicht etwas, was für sich selbst bestünde, oder den Dingen als objektive Bestimmung anhinge, mithin übrig bliebe, wenn man von allen subjektiven Bedingungen der Anschauung derselben abstrahiert: denn im ersten Fall würde sie etwas sein, was ohne wirklichen Gegenstand dennoch wirklich wäre. Was aber das zweite betrifft, so könnte sie als eine den Dingen selbst anhangende Bestimmung oder Ordnung nicht vor den Gegenständen als ihre Bedingung vorhergehen . . . b) Die Zeit ist nichts anderes, als die Form des innern Sinnes, d.i. des Anschauens unserer selbst und unsers innern Zustandes. Denn die Zeit kann keine Bestimmung äußerer Erscheinungen sein; . . . dagegen bestimmt sie das Verhältnis der Vorstellungen in unserm innern Zustande. Und, eben weil diese innre Anschauung keine Gestalt gibt, suchen wir auch diesen Mangel durch Analogien zu ersetzen, und stellen die Zeitfolge durch eine ins Unendliche fortgehende Linie vor, in welcher das Mannigfaltige eine Reihe ausmacht, die nur von einer Dimension ist, und schließen aus den Eigenschaften dieser Linie auf alle Eigenschaften der Zeit . . . c) Die Zeit ist die formale Bedingung a priori aller Erscheinungen überhaupt . . . , und zwar die unmittelbare Bedingung der inneren [Erscheinung] (unserer Seelen) und eben dadurch mittelbar auch der äußern Erscheinungen." Ibid., B 49–50; trans., 88–89.

125. ". . . zu der widersprüchlichen 'Idee' der sich absolut setzenden Endlichkeit," Manzke, *Ewigkeit und Zeitlichkeit*, 160.

126. ". . . empirische[r] Realität der Zeit, d.i. objektive Gültigkeit in Ansehung aller Gegenstände, die jemals unsern Sinnen gegeben werden mögen [and, on the other hand, however, also the] transzendentale[r] Idealität der Zeit, nach welcher sie, wenn man von den subjektiven Bedingungen der sinnlichen Anschauung abstrahiert, gar nichts ist, und den Gegenständen an sich selbst . . . weder subsistierend noch inhärierend beigezählt werden kann." Kant, *Kritik der reinen Vernunft*, B 52; trans., 89–90.

127. On the unchangeability of time, cf. ibid., B 183. For a comparison of Kant's and Einstein's concepts of time, see Mittelstaedt, *Philosophische Probleme*, 33–44. Mittelstaedt comes to the conclusion that an actual contradiction does not exist, since Kant's results continue to apply to events within the light cone that is defined by the finite speed of light; events outside of this light cone, for which, according to Einstein, other results apply, cannot be conceived at all using Kant's categories.

128. Einstein, "Physics and Reality," 96.

129. The decisive publication on the special theory of relativity was the article entitled "Zur Elektrodynamik bewegter Körper" in: *Annalen der Physik*, no. 4, vol. 17 (Leipzig, 1905), 891–921. (A few months earlier, he completed a work on the light quantum theory.) The final version of the general theory of relativity likewise appeared in 1916 in the *Annalen der Physik*, vol. 49 (769–822), and was entitled "Die Grundlage der allgemeinen Relativitätstheorie" (The Foundation of the General Theory of Relativity).

130. Only two examples of biographical literature are referenced here. Fölsing provides a comprehensive popular biography in *Albert Einstein—Eine Biographie*, while Pais's book *'Subtle is the Lord . . .'* is a more scientifically oriented description of his life and work. Although references in this study apply only to the German edition of Fölsing, readers might wish to consult the English translation: *Albert Einstein: A Biography*, trans. Ewald Osers (New York: Viking, 1997).

131. Pais, *'Subtle is the Lord . . .'*, 303–6, speaks of Einstein's "canonization." The fame, however, did not lack a certain relativity: What was initially praised as a brilliant achievement fell into disrepute in Germany because of anti-Semitic propaganda. Einstein was certainly aware that such fame was unreliable; this is confirmed by the ironic postscript to his article "My Theory," which was published in the November 28, 1919, issue of the *Times:* "Some of the statements in your paper concerning my life and person owe their

origin to the lively imagination of the writer. Here is yet another application of the principle of relativity for the delectation of the reader: –Today I am described in Germany a 'German savant,' and in England as a 'Swiss Jew.' Should it ever be my fate to be represented as a *bête noire*, I should, on the contrary, become a 'Swiss Jew' for the Germans and a 'German savant' for the English." Einstein, *Mein Weltbild*, 198; trans., *The World as I See It,* 81f.

132. Max Born with whom and with whose wife, Hedwig, Einstein corresponded for many years, commented: "Das Urteil Einsteins über die Quantenmechanik war ein harter Schlag für mich: er lehnte sie ab—zwar ohne eigentliche Begründung, vielmehr unter Berufung auf 'eine innere Stimme'. Diese Ablehnung ... beruht auf einer tiefen philosophischen Meinungsverschiedenheit, die Einstein von der jüngeren Generation trennte, zu der ich mich auch zählte, obwohl ich nur wenige Jahre jünger war als Einstein" (Einstein's verdict of quantum mechanics came as a hard blow to me: he rejected it not for any definite reason, but rather by referring to an "inner voice." This rejection ... was based on a basic difference of philosophical attitude, which separated Einstein from the younger generation to which I felt that I belonged, although I was only a few years younger than Einstein). Einstein and Born, *Briefwechsel 1916–1955*, 130; trans., *The Born-Einstein Letters*, 91; cf. also Heisenberg, *Physics and Beyond* 135f.

133. "Das durch die Entwicklung der Elektrodynamik und Optik erhärtete Gesetz der Konstanz der Lichtgeschwindigkeit im leeren Raum in Verbindung mit der durch Michelsons berühmten Versuch besonders scharf dargetanen Gleichberechtigung aller Inertialsysteme (spezielles Relativitätsprinzip) führten zunächst dazu, daß der Zeitbegriff relativiert werden mußte, indem jedem Inertialsystem seine besondere Zeit gegeben werden mußte. Bei der Entwicklung dieser Idee zeigte es sich, daß früher der Zusammenhang zwischen den unmittelbaren Erlebnissen einerseits, Koordinaten und Zeit andererseits, nicht mit genügender Schärfe überlegt worden war" (The law of the constant velocity of light in empty space, which has been confirmed by the development of electro-dynamics and optics, and the equal legitimacy of all inertial systems [special principle of relativity], which was proved in a particularly incisive manner by Michelson's famous experiment, between then made it necessary, to begin with, that the concept of time should be made relative, each inertial system being given its own special time. As this notion was developed, it became clear that the connection between immediate experience on the one side and co-ordinates and time on the other had hitherto not been thought out with sufficient precision). Einstein, *Mein Weltbild*, 132; trans., 69f.

134. If a light signal is sent out at time t_1 in x_A, reflected in x_B, and then arrives again in x_A at time t_2, then a clock in x_B is synchronous to a clock in x_A if it gives the time $(t_1 + t_2)/2$ for the moment of the signal's reflection in x_B (example according to Mittelstaedt, *Philosophische Probleme*, 23).

135. An inertial system is a system of coordinates that moves uniformly and in a straight line, thus free of rotation or acceleration.

136. Einstein, "Physics and Reality," 68f.

137. Fölsing, *Albert Einstein—Eine Biographie*, 179 and 198ff.; cf. also sec. 8 and 9 in Einstein, "Über die spezielle und die allgemeine Relativitätstheorie," 438–43.

138. ". . . daß die Relativitätstheorie zum großartigen Gedankengebäude Maxwells und Lorentz' eine Art Abschluß geliefert hat, indem sie versucht, die Feldphysik auf alle Erscheinungen, die Gravitation eingeschlossen, auszudehnen," Einstein, *Mein Weltbild*, 131f.; trans., 69.

139. Fölsing, *Albert Einstein—Eine Biographie*, 237 (according to Einstein, *Annalen der Physik* 23 [1907]: 206–8). Epistemologically, Einstein attributes much greater significance to the field equations developed from the theory than to the empirical proofs: "Es ist eigentlich merkwürdig, daß die Menschen meist taub sind gegenüber den stärksten Argu-

menten, während sie stets dazu neigen, Meßgenauigkeiten zu überschätzen" (It is really rather strange that human beings are normally deaf to the strongest arguments, while they are always inclined to overestimate measuring accuracies). From Einstein's letter to Max Born dated May 12, 1952, in Einstein and Born, *Briefwechsel 1916–1955*, 258; trans., 192. Cf. also "§ 14. Der heuristische Wert der Relativitätstheorie," in Einstein, "Über die spezielle und die allgemeine Relativitätstheorie," 452f.

140. The principle of relativity is, however, not Einstein's invention. In mechanics, the so-called Galilean principle of relativity applies ("Wenn die Gesetze der Mechanik in einem bestimmten System gelten, so gelten sie auch für alle andern Systeme, die sich relativ zu jenem gleichförmig bewegen" (If the laws of mechanics are valid in one CS [co-ordinate system], then they are valid in any other CS moving uniformly relative to the first). Einstein and Infeld, *The Evolution of Physics*, 165. In the case of Einstein, however, the principle of relativity was "in den Rang einer fundamentalen Eigenschaft *aller* Naturgesetze emporgehoben" (elevated to the level of a fundamental property of *all* natural laws). Wild, "Wie kam die Zeit in die Welt?," 163.

141. Fölsing, *Albert Einstein—Eine Biographie*, 237f.

142. Ibid., 238ff.

143. Bergmann, "The Space-Time Concept in General Relativity," 150.

144. It should not be forgotten, however, that this boundary moves at a speed of ca. 300,000 km/s. Nevertheless, when one looks into space, space and time merge, since a look into the distance is simultaneously a look into the past. If we were to receive a message today at the speed of light from a civilization located one hundred light years away, then this would link our present time with their past of one hundred years ago. If we immediately sent an answer, then our present time would thereby be "simultaneous" with their future in one hundred years.

145. Wild, "Wie kam die Zeit in die Welt?," 163.

146. Einstein and Infeld, *The Evolution of Physics*, 185.

147. ". . . dessen Ergebnis einem Todesurteil für die Hypothese von dem ruhenden Äthermeer gleichkommt," ibid., 185; trans., 183.

148. ". . . 'enfant terrible' unter den physikalischen Substanzen," ibid., 186; trans., 184.

149. Example: An observer observes an object that moves relative to him/her at the velocity of v_1. Relative to this object, on the other hand, another object moves at the velocity of v_2. This second object then moves for the observer at the velocity of $v_1 + v_2$, which represents no problem for velocities in the everyday sphere. If, however, for example, v_1 and v_2 each amounted to three-fourths of the speed of light c, then this would result in the sum of 1 1/2 c, which, however, would violate the theorem that the speed of light cannot be exceeded.

150. Einstein and Infeld, *The Evolution of Physics*, 198–202. According to $E = mc^2$, mass would then approach infinity.

151. x, y, and z specify the space coordinates, and t the time coordinates, of an event; v stands for velocity.

152. "Ist die Trägheit eines Körpers von seinem Energieinhalt abhängig?," in *Annalen der Physik* 18 (1906): 639–41. Cf. also "E = MC²" and "An Elementary Derivation of the Equivalence of Mass and Energy" from 1946 in Einstein, *Out of My Later Years*, 49–53 and 116–19.

153. "Die Mittel, mit denen die Natur erkannt wird, sind nichts anderes als Teile eben dieser Natur," Mittelstaedt, *Philosophische Probleme*, 31.

154. Ibid., 44.

155. ". . . daß die bisherige Relativitätstheorie in weitgehendem Maße zu verallgemeinern sei, derart, daß die ungerecht scheinende Bevorzugung der gleichförmigen Translation

gegenüber Relativbewegungen anderer Art aus der Theorie verschwindet." Einstein, "Die formale Grundlage der allgemeinen Relativitätstheorie," 74.

156. Cf. "Einiges über die Entstehung der allgemeinen Relativitätstheorie," in Einstein, *Mein Weltbild*, 134–38. Notes on the origin of the original theory of relativity, 101f.

157. Invariance means the fact that every observer, regardless of his or her own movement, always measures the same speed of light.

158. Bergmann, "The Space-Time Concept in General Relativity," 150f. See also ibid., 149f.: "The principal innovation . . . is that in the general theory of relativity the characteristics of space-time geometry are not fixed a priori, as they are in classical physics and in the special theory of relativity, but that many different space-times are possible. True, these space-times . . . obey Einstein's field equations. But different distributions of gravitating matter lead to different space-time geometries."

159. Einstein, "Über die spezielle und die allgemeine Relativitätstheorie," 483–89.

160. On the inapplicability of Euclidian geometry, see "§ 23, "Verhalten von Uhren und Maßstäben auf einem rotierenden Bezugskörper," in ibid., 477–80.

161. Cf. Pais, *'Subtle is the Lord . . . ,'* 210–23.

162. Davies, *About Time*, 96ff.

163. Ibid., 59–67, provides a detailed presentation of this paradox, which is really no paradox.

164. "M. H.! Die Anschauungen über Raum und Zeit, die ich Ihnen entwickeln möchte, sind auf experimentell-physikalischem Boden erwachsen. Darin liegt ihre Stärke. Ihre Tendenz ist eine radikale. Von Stund an sollen Raum für sich und Zeit für sich völlig zu Schatten herabsinken und nur noch eine Art Union der beiden soll Selbständigkeit bewahren." Quotation according to a reproduction of the assembly minutes in Hermann, *Die neue Physik*, 18, and quoted in Pais, *'Subtle is the Lord . . . ,'* 152.

165. Fölsing, *Albert Einstein—Eine Biographie*, 283.

166. "Die Verallgemeinerung der Relativitätstheorie wurde sehr erleichtert durch die Gestalt, welche der speziellen Relativitätstheorie durch Minkowski gegeben wurde, welcher Mathematiker zuerst die formale Gleichwertigkeit der räumlichen Koordinaten und der Zeitkoordinate klar erkannte und für den Aufbau der Theorie nutzbar machte." Einstein, "Die Grundlage der allgemeinen Relitivitätstheory," 284; similarly in Einstein, "Über die spezielle und die allgemeine Relativitätstheorie," sec. 17, 461–63.

167. ". . . vielleicht in den Windeln stecken geblieben," ibid., 463.

168. Einstein, "The Theory of Relativity," 45.

169. "Das durch Vereinigung von Raum und Zeit gebildete vierdimensionale Kontinuum behält nach der speziellen Relativitätstheorie jenen absoluten Charakter, welchen nach der früheren Theorie sowohl der Raum als auch die Zeit—jeder besonders—besaß." Einstein, *Mein Weltbild*, 132; trans., 70. Einstein gave this speech in the spring of 1921 in the palace of the Royal Society of London, ibid., 198.

170. ". . . keine Aussage banaler als die, daß unsere gewohnte Welt ein vierdimensionales zeiträumliches Kontinuum ist," Einstein, "Über die spezielle und die allgemeine Relativitätstheorie," 461.

171. ". . . mathematische Formen an[nehmen], in denen die Zeitkoordinate genau dieselbe Rolle spielt wie die drei räumlichen Koordinaten," ibid., 462.

172. On the following, see Einstein and Infeld, *The Evolution of Physics*, 210–20.

173. "Allerdings können wir, wenn wir wollen, auch im Rahmen der Relativitätstheorie nach wie vor mit der dynamischen Darstellungsweise arbeiten, nur müssen wir dann immer bedenken, daß der Zerlegung in Zeit und Raum keine objektive Bedeutung zukommt, da die Zeit ja für uns nicht mehr absolut ist," ibid., 221.

174. Einstein, "Über die spezielle und die allgemeine Relativitätstheorie," 507.

175. ". . . keine Schnitte mehr gibt, welche das 'Jetzt' objektiv repräsentieren, wird der Begriff des Geschehens und Werdens zwar nicht völlig aufgehoben, aber doch kompliziert," ibid., 529.

176. ". . . das physikalisch Reale als ein vierdimensionales Sein zu denken statt wie bisher als das Werden eines dreidimensionalen Seins," ibid.

177. Cf. Mittelstaedt, *Philosophische Probleme*, 27–30.

178. Einstein, "Über die spezielle und die allgemeine Relativitätstheorie," 532f.

179. "Der hier geschilderte Entwicklungsgang [zur allgemeinen Relativitätstheorie] nimmt den raumzeitlichen Koordinaten jede selbständige Realität. Das Metrisch-Reale ist jetzt erst durch die Verbindung der Raum-Zeit-Koordinaten mit denjenigen mathematischen Größen gegeben, die das Gravitationsfeld beschreiben." Einstein, *Mein Weltbild*, 133; trans., 72; "Über Relativitätstheorie. Eine Londoner Rede," 1921.

180. ". . . dem Raum und der Zeit den letzten Rest physikalischer Gegenständlichkeit," Einstein, "Die Grundlage der allgemeinen Relativitätstheorie," 291.

181. Fagg fears that the use of spatial metaphors for time paralyzes our perception of time and robs time of its unique and dynamic nature (*The Becoming of Time*, 157). He believes that "nature is telling us that a realistic view of the world is much better described, not by the spatialization of time, but by the dynamitization of space." Prigogine also opposes a spatialization of time (*The End of Certainty*, 58f.).

182. Fagg, *The Becoming of Time*, 33.

183. ". . . daß schon im Rahmen der Physik Zeit, Raum und Materie in einem tiefen inneren Strukturzusammenhang stehen," Weidlich, "Zeit und Raum," 72.

184. ". . . von einem (3 + 1)-dimensionalen Kontinuum," Heller, *Grundbegriffe*, 141.

185. Cf. Davies, *About Time*, 188–91. Davies proves mathematically that, even in the case of Minkowski, time is not entirely equated to space dimensions. Time is as distinguished from space dimensions as imaginary numbers are from real figures.

186. In this overcoming of the double Newtonian dualism, Achtner (*Physik, Mystik und Christentum*, 91–95), along with Torrance, sees the basis for a non-dualistic ontology based on the concept of invariance.

187. Thus, Achtner, *Physik, Mystik und Christentum*, 94 (in agreement with Torrance).

188. Thus, e.g., Achtner, *Physik, Mystik und Christentum*, 94, and Ganoczy, *Suche nach Gott*, 211: "Kein Wunder, daß schon der Mythos, mehr aber die Hochreligionen, aber auch die Universalsprache dichterischer Symbolik aus dem Licht eine Manifestation des Göttlichen gemacht haben" (It is no wonder that already the myth, but even more the world religions and also the universal language of poetic symbolism have turned light into a manifestation of the divine).

189. "Raffiniert ist der Herrgott, aber boshaft ist er nicht." Fölsing characterizes this sentence of Einstein as "eines seiner klassischen Aperçus" (one of his classic witty remarks). Fölsing, *Albert Einstein—Eine Biographie*, 579. As a warning against the rash appropriation of this remark for Christian-apologetic purposes, one ought to keep in mind what Einstein as a Jew, who called himself nondenominational (ibid., 90, cf. also Einstein, *Mein Weltbild*, 171; trans., 29f.: "Konfessionelle Traditionen kann ich nur historisch und psychologisch betrachten; ich habe zu ihnen keine andere Beziehung" [Denominational traditions I can only consider historically and psychologically; they have no other significance for me]), said about religion: "Das Schönste, was wir erleben können, ist das Geheimnisvolle. Es ist das Grundgefühl, das an der Wiege von wahrer Kunst und Wissenschaft steht. Wer es nicht kennt und sich nicht mehr wundern, nicht mehr staunen kann, der ist sozusagen tot und sein Auge erloschen. Das Erlebnis des Geheimnisvollen—wenn auch mit Furcht gemischt—hat auch die Religion gezeugt. Das Wissen um die Existenz des für uns Undurchdringlichen, der Manifestationen tiefster Vernunft und leuchtendster Schönheit, die unserer Vernunft nur in ihren primitivsten Formen zugänglich sind, dies Wissen und

Fühlen macht wahre Religiosität aus; in diesem Sinn und nur in diesem gehöre ich zu den tief religiösen Menschen" (The fairest thing that we can experience is the mysterious. It is the fundamental emotion which stands at the cradle of true art and science. He who knows it not, and can no longer wonder, no longer feel amazement, is as good as dead, a snuffed-out candle. It was the experience of mystery—even if mixed with fear—that engendered religion. A knowledge of the existence of something we cannot penetrate, our perceptions of the profoundest reason and the most radiant beauty, which our minds seem to reach only in their most elementary forms;—it is this knowledge and this emotion that constitute the truly religious attitude; in this sense, and in this alone, I am a deeply religious man). Einstein, *Mein Weltbild*, 9f.; trans., 242. Even if Otto's *tremendum et fascinosum* appears to linger on here, Einstein attaches the greatest importance to the distinction between the "religion of fear" [Furcht-Religion] and its further development into "moral religion" [Moral-Religion] from the third (and highest) level of cosmic religiosity (Einstein, ibid., 15–18; trans., 261–67; initially published as an article in 1930). While the first two hold to an anthropomorphic concept of God, cosmic religiosity knows no dogmas and no God, "conceived in man's image" [der nach dem Bild des Menschen gedacht wäre], 16; trans., 264. Unlike Kant, Einstein separates ethics from religion: "Das ethische Verhalten des Menschen ist wirksam auf Mitgefühl, Erziehung und soziale Bindung zu gründen und bedarf keiner religiösen Grundlage. Es stünde traurig um die Menschen, wenn sie durch Furcht vor Strafe und Hoffnung auf Belohnung nach dem Tode gebändigt werden müßten" (A man's ethical behavior should be based effectually on sympathy, education, and social ties; no religious basis is necessary. Man would indeed be in a poor way if he had to be restrained by the fear and punishment and hope of reward after death), 17; trans., 266. Cosmic religiosity is the type of religion that characterizes religious geniuses of all times. Antagonism between this religiosity and science is excluded, for, as Einstein says, "[e]s scheint mir, daß es die wichtigste Funktion der Kunst und der Wissenschaft ist, dies Gefühl [kosmischer Religiosität] unter den Empfänglichen zu erwecken und lebendig zu erhalten" (In my view it is the most important function of art and science to awaken this feeling [of cosmic religiosity] and keep it alive among those who are capable of it), 17; trans., 265. Conversely, cosmic religiosity is "the strongest and noblest incitement to scientific research" [die stärkste und edelste Triebfeder wissenschaftlicher Forschung], 17; trans., 266. When the notion of a personal God and its associated system of reward and punishment is overcome, then nothing stands in the way of nurturing the good, the true, and the beautiful; cf. Einstein, *Out of My Later Years*, 24–30 ("Science and Religion" II, 1941). Understanding the magnitude of the rationality incarnated in existence gives birth to humility; "science not only purifies the religious impulse of the dross of its anthropomorphism but also contributes to a religious spiritualization or our understanding of life" (29). Thus, the path to genuine religiosity is the striving for rational knowledge. In this sense, Einstein can say: "Science without religion is lame, religion without science is blind" (26). There are idealistic, pantheistic, mystical, and in a way, also elitist characteristics that shape Einstein's concept of God, "[t]his firm belief, a belief bound up with deep feeling, in a superior mind that reveals itself in the world of experience" [jene mit tiefem Gefühl verbundene Überzeugung von einer überlegenen Vernunft, die sich in der erfahrbaren Welt offenbart], Einstein, *Mein Weltbild*, 171; trans., 29. As Jammer showed, Spinoza played an important role in Einstein's thinking on religion (*Einstein und die Religion*).

190. ". . . daß ein einem Strahl ausgesetztes Elektron *aus freiem Entschluß* den Augenblick und die Richtung wählt, in der es fortspringen will." Letter to Hedwig and Max Born, April 29, 1924, in Einstein and Born, *Briefwechsel 1916–1955*, 118; trans., 82.

191. "Die Theorie liefert viel, aber dem Geheimnis des Alten bringt sie uns kaum näher. Jedenfalls bin ich überzeugt, daß der nicht würfelt." Letter to Max Born on December 4, 1926, ibid., 129f.; trans., 91. Later Einstein noticed that the "same 'non-dice-playing

God'" caused so much bitter resentment against him, not only among the "quantum theo-reticians," but also among the faithful of the Church of the Atheists." Letter to Max Born, October 12, 1953, ibid., 266f.; trans., 199.

192. At the International Conference of Physicists in Como in September 1927, as well as at the Fifth Solvay Conference in Brussels in October 1927, Bohr presented the so-called Copenhagen interpretation of the quantum theory with the Heisenberg uncertainty prin-ciple. A reprint of the presentation given in Como, which was entitled "The Quantum Postulate and the Recent Development of Atomic Theory," is found in Bohr, *Collected Works*, 113–36. On Bohr's account of his discussions with Einstein, see Bohr, *Atomphysik und menschliche Erkenntnis* (Atomic Physics and Human Knowledge), 32–67. For a popu-lar account of the development of quantum physics, also see Pagels, *Cosmic Code*.

193. Held offers an analysis of the discussion between Bohr and Einstein on an appro-priate understanding of the quantum theory in *Die Bohr-Einstein-Debatte*.

194. Einstein, "The Fundaments of Theoretical Physics," 104.

195. Ibid., 109f.

196. Pais, *'Subtle is the Lord. . . ,'* 455. Experiments by John Bell and Alain Aspect have proven, however, that a deep underlying theory as Einstein conceived it does not exist (Coveney and Highfield, *Frontiers of Complexity*, 174f.).

197. The world of the very large refers to the cosmic perspective, whereas the world of the very small refers to the microscopic sphere. Between the two lies the macroscopic world of our everyday experience. Each region has its own constant: The cosmic has the speed of light (c); the microscopic, Planck's Constant ($h = 6.626176 \times 10^{-34}$ Joule seconds); and the macroscopic, the electric charge (e).

198. Bohr, *Atomteori og naturbeskrivelse*, 11, in Bohr, *Collected Works*, vol. 6, 282.

199. Barbour, *Myths, Models and Paradigms*, 75ff., provides a short description of the problems associated with this process.

200. Bohr in *The Quantum Postulate and the Recent Development of Atomic Theory*, in Bohr, *Collected Works*, vol. 6, 115.

201. Cf. the overview of different interpretations of quantum physics in Russell, "Quantum Physics in Philosophical and Theological Perspective," 348ff. In *The Ghost in the Atom*, Davies and Brown provide a somewhat more detailed and generally intelligible introduction to quantum physics, with an account of different interpretations that are conveyed in the form of discussions with Alain Aspect, John Bell, John Wheeler, and David Bohm, among others.

202. For information on its development, see Heisenberg, "Bemerkungen über die Entstehung der Unbestimmtheitsrelation."

203. Time here is, however, "only an invariable parameter" [nur ein invarianter Para-meter] and not an actual measurement variable; therefore, no conclusions regarding the di-rection of time can be drawn from it. Mainzer, *Zeit—Von der Urzeit zur Computerzeit*, 59.

204. ". . . daß in den tiefen Schichten der Teilchenwellen das Wesen von Raum und Zeit selbst ungenau und nur vage definiert ist," according to Fraser in *Die Zeit*, 301.

205. Mainzer, *Zeit—Von der Urzeit zur Computerzeit*, 62.

206. Cf. Polkinghorne, "The Quantum World." After listing a series of "non-conse-quences of quantum theory" (and criticizing Fritjof Capra, Gary Zukav, and John Wheel-er, among others), Polkinghorne says emphatically: "I believe that the issues that quantum theory raises for theology are best treated in ways that are modest in metaphysical intent, rather than grandiose. We are presented with a picture of the physical world that is neither mechanical nor chaotic, but at once both open and orderly in its character" (341).

207. Russell, "Quantum Physics in Philosophical and Theological Perspective," 369n2.

208. "Ikke desto mindre må vi fra atomteorins nuværende standpunkt betragte selve denne resignation som et væsentligt led i fremskridtet af vor erkendelse." Thus said Bohr in his 1929 lecture entitled "Atomteorien og Grundprincipperne for Naturbeskrivelsen." Bohr, *Atomteori og naturbeskrivelse*, 94; trans., Bohr, *Collected Works*, vol. 6, 249.

209. This formulation is inspired by Bohr's 1929 lecture entitled "Atomteorien og Grundprincipperne for Naturbeskrivelsen," which he ended with the words ". . . at den i fysikken foreliggende, nye situation på så eftertrykkelig måde minder os om den gamle sandhed, at vi såvel er tilskuere som deltagere i tilværelsens store skuespil." Bohr, *Atomteori og naturbeskrivelse*, 96; trans., Bohr, *Collected Works*, vol. 6, 253.

210. Heisenberg, *Ordnung der Wirklichkeit*, 115. Cf. also Toulmin, *The Return to Cosmology*, 237–54 ("Death of the Spectator").

211. From Bohr's presentation to the Convention of Physicists in Como in 1927 entitled *The Quantum Postulate and the Recent Development of Atomic Theory*, in Bohr, *Collected Works*, vol. 6, 114.

212. "Som vi har set, kræver jo enhver iagttagelse et indgreb i fænomenernes forløb, der efter sin art berøver os grundlaget for årsagsbeskrivelsen," Bohr, *Atomteori og naturbeskrivelse*, 94; trans., Bohr, *Collected Works*, vol. 6, 249.

213. Coveney and Highfield, *The Arrow of Time*, 139ff.

214. In *The Undivided Universe*, Bohm and Hiley advocate a view that goes a long way in eliminating the difference between the observer/measurement instrument and the observed object (6). They speak of the "undivided wholeness" of measuring arrangement and object: "Indeed it may be said that the measuring apparatus and that which is observed *participate irreducibly* in each other, so that the ordinary classical and common sense idea of measurement is no longer relevant."

215. The fate of Schrödinger's cat has been repeatedly discussed. Among other things, it has been emphasized that quantum physics cannot be extrapolated indiscriminately into the macroscopic region. See also Audretsch and Mainzer, *Wieviele Leben hat Schrödingers Katze?*

216. Even more sensational conclusions are suggested by, for example, the so-called EPR paradox, which appears to indicate that particles communicate more rapidly with one another than with the speed of light, and by Alain Aspect's experiment that suggests the physical unity of two quantum particles in areas of the universe that are very remote from each other (Coveney and Highfield, *The Arrow of Time*, 136ff.). There have also been experiments that give the impression that under certain conditions, an observer can influence past reality. In any case, however, exact time data are impossible in quantum physics because exactly when an event will occur can never be precisely observed. Davies, *About Time*, 168–77.

217. Grib, "Quantum Cosmology."

218. Cf. Tipler, *The Physics of Immortality*.

219. Grib, "Quantum Cosmology," 180.

220. Ibid., 167f. Grib's reference to the Communist rulers in the former U.S.S.R. who banned scientific work within the field of relativistic cosmology is interesting. According to Grib their motive was that Big Bang theories allowed the conception of a divine creation out of nothing. For this reason, preference was given to the classical cosmological model of the nineteenth century, since its concept of infinity does not leave any place for a creator God (165f.).

221. On this, cf. also Tracy, *Plurality and Ambiguity*, 28–34 and 47ff.

222. ". . . eine Art Lebenserinnerungen in der Form platonischer Dialoge," von Weizsäcker, "Notizen," 11.

223. Heisenberg, *Physics and Beyond*, 138; thus, also Heisenberg himself: Heisenberg,

"The Development of Concepts in Physics of the 20th Century," 449. Cf. also Bohr, *Essays 1958–1962*, 8–16, on the topic of "The Unity of Human Knowledge."

224. Heisenberg, *Physics and Beyond*, 134.

225. Ibid., 135.

226. "Mit dem Geschirrwaschen ist es doch genau wie mit der Sprache. Wir haben schmutziges Spülwasser und schmutzige Küchentücher, und doch gelingt es, damit Teller und Gläser schließlich sauberzumachen. So haben wir in der Sprache unklare Begriffe und eine in ihrem Anwendungsbereich in unbekannter Weise eingeschränkte Logik, und doch gelingt es, damit Klarheit in unser Verständnis der Natur zu bringen." Heisenberg, *Der Teil und das Ganze*, 163f.; *Physics and Beyond*, 137. Yet for Bohr, clarity in the understanding of nature does not mean uncovering the actual essence of the phenomena, but rather, it lies in pursuing—to the greatest extent possible—connections in the diversity of our experiences [men kun om i størst muligt omfang at efterspore sammenhæng i vore erfaringers mangfoldighed]. Bohr, *Atomteori og naturbeskrivelse*, 21.

227. "Jeder Bereich der Wirklichkeit kann schließlich in der Sprache abgebildet werden." Heisenberg, *Ordnung der Wirklichkeit*, 45.

228. ". . . dem Verzicht auf jenes unendlich vielfache Bezogensein der Worte und Begriffe, das in uns erst das Gefühl erweckt, etwas von der unendlichen Fülle der Wirklichkeit verstanden zu haben," ibid., 41.

229. Ibid., 43.

230. Ibid.

231. "Über die letzten Dinge kann man nicht sprechen." Ibid., 45.

232. Published in *Gestalt und Gedanke*, vol. 6, yearbook of the Bayerischen Akademie der schönen Künste (Munich: R. Oldenbourg, 1960), 32–62; cited here according to Heisenberg, "Sprache und Wirklichkeit in der modernen Physik."

233. Heisenberg, ibid., 278.

234. Ibid., 279.

235. Ibid., 284.

236. ". . . daß die Welt nicht 'wirklich' so ist, wie es uns die gewöhnlichen Begriffe glauben machen," ibid., 285.

237. Ibid., 289. The same mode of expression—painting with words—is used by Bohr in *Atomteori og naturbeskrivelse*, 22: ". . . og vi må gøre os klart, at vi efter sagens væsen til syvende og sidst altid er henvist til at udtrykke os gennem et maleri med ord, der benyttes på uanalyseret måde," trans., Bohr, *Collected Works*, vol. 6, 298.

238. "Wir müssen über sie reden, denn sonst können wir unsere Experimente nicht verstehen." Heisenberg, "Sprache und Wirklichkeit in der modernen Physik," 288.

239. Ibid., 290.

240. Ibid., 291f.

241. On the further development of quantum logic, see, for example, Grib, "Quantum Cosmology," 165–84, esp. 175–79 and 182f.

242. Heisenberg, "Sprache und Wirklichkeit in der modernen Physik," 293f.

243. ". . . in der richtigen Weise in der Mitte zwischen dem Begriff der objektiven materiellen Realität auf der einen, dem der nur geistigen und damit subjektiven Wirklichkeit auf der anderen Seite," ibid., 298.

244. Ibid., 301.

245. Heisenberg, "The Development of Concepts," 460.

246. Bohr in a letter to Wolfgang Pauli, May 16, 1947, in Bohr, *Collected Works*, vol. 6, 452.

247. Bohr, *Atomteori og naturbeskrivelse*, 12; trans., Bohr, *Collected Works*, vol. 6, 283.

248. ". . . die uns ein Ideal von Objektivität vor Augen hält, dessen Erreichung, bei je-

dem in sich geschlossenen Anwendungsgebiet der Logik, kaum Grenzen gesetzt sind,"
Bohr, *Collected Works*, vol. 6, 205 (in *Wirkungsquantum and Naturbeschreibung*).

249. Ibid.

250. Bohr, *Atomteori og naturbeskrivelse*, 95; trans., Bohr, *Collected Works*, vol. 6, 250.

251. ". . . daß einerseits die Beschreibung unserer Gedankentätigkeit die Gegenüber-
stellung eines objektiv gegebenen Inhalts und eines betrachtenden Subjekts verlangt,
während andererseits . . . keine strenge Trennung zwischen Objekt und Subjekt aufrecht
zu erhalten ist . . . Aus dieser Sachlage folgt nicht nur die relative von der Willkür in der
Wahl des Gesichtspunktes abhängige Bedeutung eines jeden Begriffes, oder besser jeden
Wortes, sondern wir müssen im allgemeinen darauf gefaßt sein, daß eine allseitige
Beleuchtung eines und desselben Gegenstandes verschiedene Gesichtspunkte verlangen
kann, die eine eindeutige Beschreibung verhindern. Streng genommen steht ja die be-
wußte Analyse eines jeden Begriffes in einem ausschließenden Verhältnis zu seiner unmittelbaren Anwendung." Bohr, *Collected Works*, vol. 6, 204f.

252. Bohr, *Atomteori og naturbeskrivelse*, 94; trans., Bohr, *Collected Works*, vol. 6, 249.

253. Hawking, *Black Holes and Baby Universes and Other Essays*, 70.

254. Ibid., 113.

255. The three Friedmann models are exact solutions to the field equations of the general theory of relativity based on the validity of the cosmological principle. Other principles have also been proposed (e.g., by Kurt Gödel), although they have not succeeded in
gaining acceptance.

256. Fagg, *The Becoming of Time*, 98–114. Cf. also Hawking, *A Brief History of Time;*
Weinberg, *The First Three Minutes;* and Davies, *About Time*. In his article entitled "Contemporary Cosmology and Its Implications for the Science-Religion Dialogue," Stoeger
provides a condensed overview of modern cosmology and its implications.

257. Singularities can be described as space-time points with a volume of 0 and infinite
mass.

258. "Damit ist aus der Relativitätstheorie zwingend eine interne Grenze ihres Erk-
lärungspotentials abgeleitet." Mainzer, *Zeit—Von der Urzeit zur Computerzeit*, 54.

259. Cf. on this ibid., 54ff.; Coveney and Highfield, *The Arrow of Time,* 100–102. In
Black Holes and Time Warps: Einstein's Outrageous Legacy, Thorne provides a comprehensive, original history of the black holes, which combines biographical, relevant, and speculative elements.

260. Hawking, *A Brief History of Time*, 99–113, and Hawking, *Black Holes and Baby
Universes*, 101–13 and 115–25.

261. Davies, *About Time*, 120.

262. Hawking, *Black Holes and Baby Universes*, 154.

263. For a detailed background on the topic of time travel and its preconditions such
as backward curving world-lines, worm holes, etc., and their consequences, see Davies,
About Time, 233–51. In *Impossibility,* Barrow provides a brief discussion primarily of the
philosophical aspects of the possibility of time travel (199–207).

264. Cf. on this "The Future of the Universe," in Hawking, *Black Holes and Baby
Universes*, 141–55.

265. According to Richard Feynman in Hawking, *A Brief History of Time*, 134.

266. The term *imaginary* has a precise mathematical definition; see imaginary numbers ($i^2 = -1$). According to Hawking, the calculation of time with imaginary numbers is
necessary for overcoming the technical difficulties of Feynman's path integral method
(Hawking, *A Brief History of Time*, 134).

267. Ibid., 136. For a discussion of Hawking's model, see: Worthing, *God, Creation,
and Contemporary Physics*, 52–60, 62f., etc.; Esterbauer, *Verlorene Zeit*, 101–24; Ward, *Reli-*

gion and Creation, 295–300; and van Huyssteen, *Duet or Duel?*, 57ff. In *The Fire in the Equations*, Ferguson provides an easily accessible discussion on knowledge and faith that, among other things, responds to Hawking's challenge that the final triumph of human reason is the knowledge of God's plan (Hawking, *A Brief History of Time*, 138) and simultaneously aims to communicate insights from physics and biology. In the title of her book, *The Fire in the Equations*, Ferguson also alludes to Hawking's question: "What is it that breathes fire into equations . . . ?" Hawking, *A Brief History of Time*, 174.

268. Thus, for example, by Isham, "Creation of the Universe," and Grib, "Quantum Cosmology."

269. Russell, "Is Nature Creation? Philosophical and Theological Implications of Physics and Cosmology from a Trinitarian Perspective," 116.

270. "Although science may solve the problem of how the universe began, it cannot answer the question: Why does the universe bother to exist?" Hawking, *Black Holes and Baby Universes*, 99.

271. Hawking, *A Brief History of Time*, 274.

272. Cf. Davies, *About Time*, 126–29.

273. Ibid., 140–45.

274. Drees, "A Case Against Temporal Critical Realism?" esp. 328–39. For a detailed treatment of the topic of *cosmology and theology*, see also Drees, *Beyond the Big Bang*.

275. Drees, "A Case Against Temporal Critical Realism?," 339.

276. Barbour, *The End of Time*.

277. Ibid., 26ff.

278. Ibid., 323ff.

279. Coveney and Highfield, *Frontiers of Complexity*, 21 (with reference to John Barrow). See also Wertheim, *Pythagoras' Trousers*, 7f., etc.

280. Drees, "A Case Against Temporal Critical Realism?," 339.

281. Davies, *About Time*, 181f.

282. In rare cases, a *kaon* disintegrates in such a way that the symmetry of parity and charge is impaired. According to the so-called PCT principle, this also means an impairment of the symmetry of time; see Mainzer, *Zeit—Von der Urzeit zur Computerzeit*, 65f. For more details on the behavior of the *kaon*, see Davies, *About Time*, 208–13. and Coveney and Highfield, *The Arrow of Time*, 141–45.

283. It was primarily Ludwig Boltzmann (1844–1906) who worked diligently to answer this question by trying to explain the macrostates of a body (e.g., its heat) using statistical statements on the mechanical processes between molecules (i.e., their collisions). Even though this method was associated with great difficulties, the linking of thermodynamics and probability remained significant.

284. Mainzer, *Zeit—Von der Urzeit zur Computerzeit*, 74.

285. In *From Being to Becoming*, Prigogine says that "the bifurcation introduces history into physics and chemistry, an element that formerly seemed reserved for sciences dealing with biological, social, and cultural phenomena" (106).

286. For a summary of his research, see Prigogine, *The End of Certainty*. He argues that, on the narrow path between the two extremes of what is either a strictly deterministic worldview or one that is based purely on chance (183–89), he achieved at least "a noncontradictory description of nature rooted in dynamical instability" (162). It must nevertheless be mentioned that the philosophical consequences that the chemist Prigogine elaborated for his theories have often been viewed skeptically by scientists and have little practical significance for further scientific research. For critical viewpoints, see, e.g., Altner, *Die Welt als offenes System*, or Kirschenmann, "On Time and the Source of Complexity." In *Verlorene Zeit*, Esterbauer deals with Prigogine under the title "Physikalistische Annahme

Gottes im Paradigma der Selbstorganisation" (Physicalistic Assumption of God in the Paradigm of Self-Organization), 124–45. He criticizes primarily the circular mixing of scientific and ideological or philosophical conceptions. Regarding scientific overtures to theology, Esterbauer notes that the sciences all too often exceed their competence, apply methodical reductionism, and confuse categories.

287. Dissipative structures occur following a bifurcation (see below) and are distinguished by an exchange of matter and energy between a system and its environment, as well as by the system's discharge of entropy to the environment. In *Order Out of Chaos*, 12, Prigogine and Stengers assert that new types of structures can spontaneously occur far from equilibrium. Disorder (thermal chaos) can transform into order under conditions that are far from equilibrium. New dynamic states of matter can arise in which the interaction of a system with its environment is reflected. They have called these new structures *dissipative* structures, in order to emphasize the constructive role of dissipative processes during the formation of these structures.

288. Although the term *self-organization* is problematic—as Arecchi, in "A Critical Approach to Complexity and Self-Organization" (he instead recommends "hetero-organization"), and Kirschenmann, in "On Time and the Source of Complexity," have shown—I am retaining it here. First, it is relatively well known, and, second, a treatment of the philosophical difficulties that are associated with it would go beyond the framework of this study.

289. Thus, in *Zeit—Von der Urzeit zur Computerzeit*, Mainzer says that a cosmic collapse indeed means a regressive development of the universe, but not a decrease in entropy (86). For Coveney and Highfield, on the other hand, an increase in entropy coincides with the forward motion of time—thus with the time arrow (*The Arrow of Time*, 177).

290. For a lucid introduction to chaos theory, see, e.g., Huber, *Stichwort: Chaosforschung*. In *Die Chaostheorie*, Achtner deals not only with the genesis and basic concepts of chaos theory, but also with the reception of chaos theory by philosophy and theology. Both include references to secondary literature. The publication of the 26th Nobel Conference in 1990 (Holte, *Chaos: The New Science*), which contains short contributions by leading chaos researchers (such as M. Feigenbaum, J. Gleick, B. Mandelbrot, H.-O. Peitgen, and I. Prigogine), is also informative. For a detailed presentation, I refer the reader to Peitgen, Jürgens, and Saupe, *Chaos and Fractals*.

291. The so-called butterfly effect goes back to the research of the meteorologist Edward Lorenz.

292. Wild, "Wie kam die Zeit in die Welt?," 179.

293. Mainzer, *Zeit—Von der Urzeit zur Computerzeit*, 81f.; Coveney and Highfield, *The Arrow of Time*, 201.

294. Fractal geometry works with objects whose dimensions are not whole numbers, but rather fractions of whole numbers. It was facilitated by the recognition that objects occurring in nature, e.g., mountains, trees, and clouds, do not exhibit the ideal two- or three-dimensionality of the Euclidian surfaces and bodies, but, rather, lie somewhere "in-between." This is due to their self-similar structure—i.e., their structure repeats itself again and again. The diversity and beauty of the forms created by using fractal geometry has also been much discussed in the art world. Cf. the illustrations in Schroeder, *Fractals*.

295. It is no accident that one of Prigogine's books is entitled *From Being to Becoming*. Cf. also the numerous references to Whitehead in Prigogine and Stengers, *Order Out of Chaos*.

296. Similar to the theory of relativity, chaos theory has also influenced general consciousness. If chaos had a decidedly negative connotation thirty years ago, today distinctively positive associations are attached to it: chaos as the prerequisite for creativity.

297. See, e.g., Krapp and Wägenbaur, *Komplexität und Selbstorganisation*. This anthology contains contributions from the areas of mathematics, physics, biology, psychiatry, economics, sociology, and the study of German language and literature, each of which attempts to integrate chaos research into its subject matter.

298. Thus, e.g., Achtner, *Die Chaostheorie*, 36f.

299. Huber, *Stichwort: Chaosforschung*, 63 (with reference to the American physician Alan Garfinkel).

300. According to B. Mandelbrot in Holte, *Chaos: The New Science*.

301. Coveney and Highfield, *Frontiers of Complexity*, 11.

302. Ibid., 13.

303. Ibid., 7.

304. Heisenberg also speaks of a duration of the present on the basis of the theory of relativity. While in classical theory, future and past are separated from each other by an infinitely short interval of time, for a current moment, in the theory of relativity, it is correct to say: "Zukunft und Vergangenheit sind durch ein endliches Zeitintervall getrennt, dessen Dauer von dem Abstand vom Beobachter abhängt" (Future and past are separated by a limited interval of time, the duration of which is dependent upon the distance from the observer). Heisenberg, "Physik und Philosophie," 104.

305. ". . . eine zweite Zeit auftritt, die nicht an die einzelnen Moleküle oder die einzelnen Personen gebunden ist, sondern an die Beziehungen zwischen den Molekülen beziehungsweise Personen Prigogine," *Die Gesetze des Chaos*, 7.

306. Cramer, "Time of Planets and Time of Life," 75; cf. also Cramer, *Der Zeitbaum*.

307. Cramer, "Time of Planets," 77.

308. Ibid., 80.

309. Ibid., 76.

310. Ibid., 78.

311. Ibid., 79.

312. Huber, *Stichwort: Chaosforschung*, 54.

313. Cf. Prigogine and Stengers, *Dialog mit der Natur*, 287: "Jedes komplexe Wesen beinhaltet eine Vielfachheit von Zeiten, die alle durch subtile und komplexe Verbindungen miteinander verknüpft sind" (Every complex being contains a diversity of times that are all linked by means of subtle and complex ties). *Dialog mit der Natur* is based on the French *La nouvelle alliance*. However, it is not identical with the English translation of the same book, which is entitled *Order Out of Chaos: Man's New Dialogue with Nature*.

314. I owe the inspiration for this image to Davies, *About Time*, 16.

315. Prigogine and Stengers, *Dialog mit der Natur*, 287 (this section is not part of the English translation in *Order Out of Chaos*) Cf. also Prigogine's 1977 Nobel speech. After referring to the questions that should be clarified in the coming years, Prigogine continues: "But already now the development of the theory permits us to distinguish various levels of time: time as associated with classical or quantum dynamics, time associated with irreversibility through a Lyapounov function and time associated with 'history' through bifurcations. I believe that this diversification of the concept of time permits a better integration of theoretical physics and chemistry with disciplines dealing with other aspects of nature." "Time, Structure and Fluctuations," 153.

316. Prigogine and Stengers, *Order Out of Chaos*, 13.

317. Peitgen, "The Causality Principle."

318. "Hinter diesem seinem [Einsteins] 'Objektivismus' verbirgt sich m.E. die unbewußte Vorentscheidung so vieler Physiker, daß der Raum der Zeit ontologisch vorangehe,

d.h. daß die Zeit eine Art Raum, eine vierte Dimension sei. Umgekehrt enthält die Entscheidung für die Priorität der Quantentheorie eine wiederum unbewußte Vorentscheidung für die philosophische Priorität der Zeit, denn Wahrscheinlichkeit bedeutet den Zeitmodus der Zukünftigkeit (von Weizsäcker, "Notizen über die philosophische Bedeutung der Heisenbergschen Physik" 15f.). For an account (and certain amount of discussion), primarily on the theoretical approach of von Weizsäcker to time and epistemology, see Esterbauer, *Verlorene Zeit*.

319. Von Weizsäcker, "Notizen," 26.

320. Cf. on this Jüngel, *Gott als Geheimnis der Welt*, 290f.; trans., 216f., etc.

321. In *Order Out of Chaos*, Prigogine and Stengers use this expression as a characteristic for modern science as a whole, "from the level of elementary particles to cosmological models," 306.

322. Cf. to this in pp. 71–72: the dynamic view of time in classical prophesy, which sees a battlefield in the present, in contrast to the priesthood's static view of time that is oriented toward law and order.

323. Quotation according to Gustav Born, postscript to *My Life*, 298f. This quote, however, is not part of the version published at http://nobelprize.org/physics/laureates/1954/born-lecture.html.

324. Both Stoeger and Isham make similar arguments in Russell, Stoeger, and Coyne, *Physics, Philosophy, and Theology*, 242f. or 404. Cf. also Torrance, *Space, Time and Resurrection*, 23f. and 179ff. There are also areas within the natural sciences, however, that cannot be dealt with in isolation from aspects of other academic disciplines. Thus, for example, in *Duet or Duel?*, van Huyssteen stresses that the nature of cosmology is interdisciplinary (47).

325. For example, Ulf Görman has proven the importation of economic theory into biology (in the work of William Hamilton) (Görman, "Är moralen styrd av generna?").

326. Russell, Stoeger, and Coyne, *Physics, Philosophy, and Theology*, 370.

327. Thus, Lash, "Observation, Revelation, and the Posterity of Noah," 208.

328. Ibid., 209.

329. Ibid., 208.

330. Ibid., 210.

331. The expression is taken from Luther's commentary on Gal. 3:6 in his lecture on the Epistle to the Galatians from 1531 (Luther, *In epistolam S. Pauli ad Galatas Commentarius*, 360, 5ff.) Cf. Jüngel 1989 who entitles his inquiries on the first volume of Pannenberg's systematic theology: "Nihil divinitatis, ubi non fides. Ist christliche Dogmatik in rein theoretischer Perspektive möglich? Bemerkungen zu einem theologischen Entwurf von Rang" [Nihil divinitatis, ubi non fides. Is Christian dogmatics possible from a purely theoretical perspective? Comments on an outstanding theological project].

332. Wertheim, *Pythagoras' Trousers*, 117. In her book, Wertheim wishes to characterize the rise of physics in Western culture as a religiously inspired process. Using numerous examples from the history of physics, she substantiates her thesis that the rise of the "mathematical man," which was inspired by the Pythagorean ideal, has, due to its clearly religious undercurrents, substantially hindered the development of the "mathematical woman" and thwarted her effective participation in the shaping of physics.

333. Ibid., 118.

334. Barrow, *Theories of Everything,* 15f.

335. Wertheim, *Pythagoras' Trousers*, 209–10.

336. Ibid., 14ff., 238ff.

337. For a discussion of various hermeneutical challenges to the dialogue between science and theology, see also Jackelén, *The Dialogue between Religion and Science*.

338. ". . . zentrale[n] Bereich, von dem aus wir die Wirklichkeit selbst gestalten, [der aber] für die wissenschaftliche Sprache die unendlich ferne Singularität [bildet], die zwar für die Ordnung im Endlichen Entscheidendes bedeutet, die aber nie erreicht werden kann," Heisenberg, *Ordnung der Wirklichkeit*, 51.

339. Cf. Davies, *About Time*, 9, 275–83. Davies anticipates new discoveries on the topic of time as important as Einstein's. He names twelve time problems that still await solutions.

Chapter 4

1. Cf. Bayer, "Erklärung und Erzählung," who comes to the conclusion that narration without explanation would be empty, and explanation without narration, blind (13).

2. The block understanding fits, above all, a concept of eternity as being unchangeable and simultaneous at all moments for God. The model of "flowing" time is rather in harmony with the understanding of a God who can experience time, hear prayers, and act in the world.

3. Polkinghorne, *Science and Providence*, 81.

4. Ibid., 83, and ibid.: "God's perfection is not the static holding of the topmost metaphysical peak, but it lies in the total love of his unfailing action."

5. Cf. on this also Heim, "Zeit und Ewigkeit." In this article, Heim is concerned with emphasizing the "dynamischen Dualismus der neutestamentlichen Lebensanschauung" (dynamic dualism of the New Testament worldview) (427) in contrast to a static dualism that he sees in Platonism. For Heim, dynamism is expressed in a time that presses toward its abolition and consummation in a higher form of existence. Not only time's content, but also time itself, is overcome. As a result, models of the future that are based on the linear availability of time—whether as a continuation of what exists under positive or negative circumstances, or as the conception of a place of rest beyond time (403–8)—become impossible. This abolition of time is simultaneously the unveiling of the content of eternity, which already exists but is still concealed. For this dynamism, Heim accepts an antinomy. Although time must have a beginning and an end in order to express the certainty "daß die Zeitform nichts Ewiges ist, was unverändert fortdauern dürfte" (that the form of time is not something that may continue unchanged forever), 422, time must also be infinite as "ein Ausdruck dafür, daß in der Zeitform etwas Ewiges ruht, daß also die Aufhebung der Zeitform nicht eine Vernichtung, sondern eine Enthüllung ist" (an expression for the fact that something eternal is embedded in the form of time, so that the abolition of the form of time is therefore not an act of destruction, but rather an unveiling), ibid. What is seen from one side as a final point in time is viewed from the other side as eternity (423).

6. Cf. the schematic depiction of the light cone for $c \rightarrow \infty$ in Russell, "Is Nature Creation?," 96–100.

7. Ibid., 99f.

8. Cf. pp. 82–86 and 98–101 above, as well as Dalferth, "Gott und Zeit," 16, and Prigogine and Stengers, *Dialog mit der Natur*, 286f. (This passage is not part of the English translation *Order Out of Chaos*).

9. Torrance, *Space, Time and Incarnation*, 58, etc.

10. Torrance himself comes from the Reformed tradition.

11. Torrance, *Space, Time and Incarnation*, 48.

12. Ibid., 60f. For this reason, Torrance considers a program of demythologization, which transforms the space-time structures into a kind of spacelessness and timelessness, as a retreat into irrationality and meaninglessness.

13. Ibid., 65.

14. Ibid., 66.

15. Ibid., 75.

16. Ibid., 89.

17. Ibid., 68.

18. Ibid., 72.

19. Ibid., 76.

20. Ibid., 72.

21. Ibid., 73.

22. $i = \sqrt{-1}$, a = real part of z, b = imaginary part of z.

23. One should remember that *imaginary* is not synonymous with *false* or *unreal*, but is rather a precisely defined term.

24. The extent to which the model of the complex plane is also applicable to the relationship of time and eternity is something that would need to be considered. Cf. on this also Ewald, "Bemerkungen zum Begriff von Raum und Zeit," who attempts to regard the creation of the cosmos *ex nihilo* as a transformation of complex, unreal solutions of field equations into real solutions. The fact that space and time can be mathematically exceeded makes it easier to understand eternity as something that embraces space and time.

25. Cf., e.g., Link, *Schöpfung*, esp. 400–454. Within the framework of his theology of creation, Link sees the common horizon of scientific and theological thinking in the question of time.

26. As Schwöbel also emphasizes in *Trinitarian Theology Today*, in the criticism of philosophical theism, one should not forget the commendable role that it played during the seventeenth century, the century of the wars between Christian denominations (8f.). The attempt to distinguish a general, timeless conception of God from historical, secondary, denominationally shaped contents of such concepts helped to establish a common ground for society. The doctrine of the Trinity was thereby pushed into second place, however.

27. Schwöbel, "Christology and Trinitarian Thought," 141.

28. The concern here is not with a general overview of the theological discussion of the Trinity during, e.g., the second half of the twentieth century. For such an overview, cf., e.g., Peters, *GOD as Trinity*, esp. 81–145, or Schwöbel, *Trinitarian Theology Today*, 1–30, 148–56.

29. Gunton, "The Trinity, Natural Theology," 88–103.

30. Vanhoozer, "Does the Trinity Belong in a Theology of Religions?," 41–71.

31. D'Costa, "Trinitarian *Différance* and World Religions."

32. Ricoeur, *Soi-même comme un autre*, 140ff., etc.

33. Vanhoozer, "Does the Trinity Belong in a Theology of Religions?," 65.

34. Ibid., 66.

35. Gunton, "The Trinity, Natural Theology," 103.

36. Gunton, *The One, the Three and the Many*, 214.

37. Gunton, "Relation and Relativity."

38. Ibid., 101.

39. Ibid., 106.

40. Ibid.

41. Ibid., 109.

42. Ibid., 100.

43. Johnson, *She Who Is*, 192.

44. Ibid., 203.

45. Ibid., 196f.

46. Ibid., 216.

47. Ibid.

48. Even though I do not wish to dismiss a correlation between the Trinity and the structuring of society as strongly as Peters does, I do share his criticism of the attempts to create social ethics out of the Trinity; and I see a constructive alternative in his suggestion to consider the reign of God as a visionary model (*GOD as Trinity*, 184ff.).

49. Johnson, *She Who Is*, 197f.

50. Ibid., 197.

51. Ibid., 220f.

52. Ibid., 222.

53. Jenson, "What is the Point of Trinitarian Theology?" 36.

54. Ibid., 41: "God's life is narratively ordered."

55. Ibid., 37.

56. Ibid.

57. Ibid., 38.

58. Ibid., 40.

59. Ibid., 39.

60. Ibid., 41.

61. Ibid., 42.

62. See pp. 98–101 above.

63. Peters, *GOD as Trinity*, 180f. On the question of the hypostatic differentiation of the Spirit based on biblical writings, cf. also Mackey, *The Christian Experience of God*, 66–87. In summary, Mackey says: "[I]t might well be that binitarian thought is as well supported in the New Testament as is trinitarian" (87).

64. Keller, *Apocalypse Now and Then*, xiii.

65. In *Einführung in die Eschatologie,* Sauter provides an overview of the development of eschatology, as well as a depiction of its basic questions.

66. Hjelde, *Das Eschaton und die Eschata.*

67. Ibid., 498.

68. ". . . leichte Verdeutschung einer lateinisch-griechischen Vorlage," ibid., 98.

69. Ibid., 111–26.

70. See pp. 23–26 (on the quantitative over-representation of eternity terminology) and 37–41 (on the relationship of time and eternity).

71. Hjelde, *Das Eschaton und die Eschata*, 91.

72. Greshake, "Eschatologie. II," 860.

73. See Farrugia and Wagner, "Eschatologie. VI."

74. ". . . harmlosen 'eschatologischen' Kapitelchen am Ende der Dogmatik," Barth, *Der Römerbrief,* 484; trans., 500.

75. "Von ihr her steigen jene Gewitter auf, die das ganze Land der Theologie fruchtbar bedrohen: verhageln oder erfrischen." Von Balthasar, "Eschatologie," 403.

76. Holmström, "Das eschatologische Denken der Gegenwart," 314.

77. ". . . anhaltender eschatologischer Konjuktur," Vorgrimler, *Hoffnung auf Vollendung*, 9.

78. ". . . nach dem Dornröschenschlaf des 19. Jahrhunderts," Ratzinger, *Eschatologie—Tod und ewiges Leben*, 50. As the title suggests, Ratzinger is concerned only with individual eschatology; however, he simultaneously outlines, in a certain tension to this, "[d]as eschatologische Problem als Frage nach dem Wesen des Christlichen überhaupt" (the eschatological problem as a question on the essence of Christianity per se), ibid., 29. A number of additional examples for the (re)discovery of eschatology can be found in Hjelde, *Das Eschaton und die Eschata*, 15–20.

79. "Unterschwellig, nur von wenigen erfaßt, meldet sich im 19. Jh. an, was dann das 20. Jh. als die Wahrnehmung eschatologischer Bedingtheit des christlichen Glaubens insgesamt fast überschwemmt." Ratschow, "Eschatologie. VIII.," 334.

80. "Christentum, das nicht ganz und gar und restlos Eschatologie ist, hat mit *Christus* ganz und gar und restlos nichts zu tun." Barth, *Der Römerbrief*, 298; trans., 314.

81. "Das Christentum ist ganz und gar und nicht nur im Anhang Eschatologie, ist Hoffnung, Aussicht und Ausrichtung nach vorne, darum auch Aufbruch und Wandlung der Gegenwart. Das Eschatologische ist nicht etwas *am* Christentum, sondern es ist schlechterdings das Medium des christlichen Glaubens . . ." Moltmann, *Theologie der Hoffnung*, 12; trans., *Theology of Hope*, 16.

82. Cf. also the account of the motives and waves of the eschatological renewal that extends back to before 1900 in Geißer, "Grundtendenzen der Eschatologie."

83. Dalferth, "The Eschatological Roots," 156. The interest of Dalferth's article is different from that of this study. Dalferth is concerned with arguing—in light of eschatology, or, more precisely, in light of the eschatological experience of the resurrected Christ—for the necessity of a Trinitarian concept of God.

84. Cf. Hjelde, *Das Eschaton und die Eschata*, passim, who makes this linguistic confusion the starting point of his study.

85. Tillich, *Eschatologie und Geschichte*.

86. ". . . transzendenten Geschehenssinn," ibid., e.g., 77: ". . . jedes beliebig kleine oder beliebig große Geschehen nimmt Teil am Eschaton, am transzendenten Geschehenssinn" (. . . every possible insignificant or significant event participates in the *eschaton*, in the transcendent meaning of events).

87. Cf., e.g., Ott, *Eschatologie*, who sees in eschatology nothing other than the unfolding of the Christ-Kyrios confession under the aspect of God's sovereignty (10, 25). To be the *eschatos*, according to Ott, is therefore identical to being sovereign (11).

88. ". . . nicht mehr als Finale, sondern als Ferment der Theologie," Sauter, *Einführung in die Eschatologie*, 2f.

89. Ibid., 13.

90. See pp. 37–41 above.

91. Sauter, *Einführung in die Eschatologie*, 13ff.; Moltmann, *Das Kommen Gottes*, 192–202; trans., *The Coming of God*, 168–77.

92. ". . . einer unvergleichlich intensiven Wahrnehmung der Gegenwart . . . [j]eder Zeitpunkt strandet gleichsam in der Ewigkeit," Sauter, *Einführung in die Eschatologie*, 19.

93. ". . . *widerfährt* uns als das, was uns begrenzt," ibid.

94. Cf. pp. 89–92 above.

95. Cf. pp. 86–89 above.

96. Cf. pp. 93–97 above.

97. Cf., among others, Ratschow, "Eschatologie," 361–63, who, e.g., lists two titles oriented toward ecology. Greshake, "Eschatologie," 398, does indeed refer to Teilhard de Chardin, whose "attempt," however, he characterizes as marginal precisely because of his scientific ambitions, as well as other things. Ratschow, on the other hand, discusses Teilhard de Chardin in detail (together with Pannenberg and Moltmann) as an example for the eschatologization of theology ("Eschatologie," 342–48).

98. An exception here is Pannenberg. See, e.g., Pannenberg, "Theological Questions."

99. Polkinghorne and Welker, *The End of the World*.

100. ". . . nicht die allgemeinen Zukunftsmöglichkeiten der Geschichte [erforscht]," Moltmann, *Theologie der Hoffnung*, 174; trans., 192.

101. ". . . zum gnostischen Erlösermythos," Moltmann, *Das Kommen Gottes*, 285; trans., 260.

102. ". . . Synchronisierung der Geschichtszeit und der Naturzeit," Moltmann, *Gott in der Schöpfung*, 147ff.; trans., *God in Creation*, 137ff.

103. Cf. Koyré, *From the Closed World*. A reappraisal of this topic is found in Hübner, "Eschatologische Rechenschaft." On the history of the "scientific conquest of the cosmos," cf. also Schultz, *Scheibe, Kugel, Schwarzes Loch*. An interdisciplinary account of various aspects of cosmology is offered by Audretsch and Mainzer, *Vom Anfang der Welt*.

104. Weinberg, *The First Three Minutes*, 154.

105. Ibid.

106. Ibid., 155.

107. Monod, *Chance and Necessity*, 172–180.

108. The "pessimistic" scientific viewpoints addressed here are opposed, however, by more "optimistic" schemes. For example, Teilhard de Chardin's attempt to unite cosmology and theology, as well as the so-called Anthropic Principle, may be regarded as such. The latter asserts in its weak form: "Because there are observers in this universe, the universe must possess features that permit the existence of these observers." In its strong form, it says: "The laws and special structure of the universe must be created in such a way that, at one point, the universe inevitably produces an observer" (according to Breuer, *Das anthropische Prinzip*, 24).

109. Tipler's Omega Point Theory is probably the most well-known example; see Frank J. Tipler, "The Omega Point Theory," and Tipler, *The Physics of Immortality*. Another is the model developed by Freeman J. Dyson, see Dyson, "Time without End." For a more generally comprehensible version (without 137 mathematical equations), see Dyson, *Infinite in All Directions*, 79–121. Tipler assumes a closed universe, and Dyson, an open one. While Tipler reckons with the instability of protons, Dyson works primarily with the assumption that matter is stable, although he does not consider the situation hopeless in the case of instability; this would then be "the supreme test of life's adaptability" (Dyson, *Infinite in All Directions*, 111f.). Dyson's and Tipler's approaches are discussed, e.g., by Worthing in *God, Creation, and Contemporary Physics*, 159–98; and Drees in *Beyond the Big Bang*, 117–54.

110. Tipler, *The Physics of Immortality*, 3; see also 328–39.

111. Dyson, "Time without End," 447.

112. Ibid., 453: "In the open cosmology, history has no end."

113. Tipler, *The Physics of Immortality*, 12.

114. Ibid., 305–27. For Tipler, the point of contact with Pannenberg lies primarily in the emphasis on the future. On Pannenberg's reception of Tipler's Omega Point Theory, cf. Pannenberg, "Theological Appropriation," esp. 264ff., and Pannenberg, *Systematische Theologie*, vol. 2, 186ff.; trans., 159ff.

115. Tipler, *The Physics of Immortality*, 16; see also 306–27.

116. Ibid., 227.

117. Ibid., 218.

118. Ibid., 220.

119. Ibid., 225.

120. Dyson, *Infinite in all Directions*, 103f.

121. Dyson, "Time without End," 453: "It is conceivable that in another 10^{10} years life could evolve away from flesh and blood and become embodied in an interstellar black cloud (Hoyle, 1957) or in a sentient computer (Čapek, 1923)." Cf. also Dyson, *Infinite in All Directions*, 107: "If this assumption is true, that life is organization rather than sub-

stance, then it makes sense to imagine life detached from flesh and blood and embodied in networks of superconducting circuitry or in interstellar dust clouds."

122. Dyson, "Time without End," 455.

123. Ibid., 456.

124. Ibid., 459.

125. Ibid., 456. Dyson hereby specifies the complexity of a single human as $Q = 10^{23}$ bits and the complexity of the human species as $Q = 10^{33}$ bits; ibid., 454.

126. Ibid., 459.

127. Dyson, *Infinite in All Directions*, 117f.

128. What, for example, will happen in ca. 5 billion years when the energy of our sun is consumed and a "red giant" ultimately becomes a "white dwarf"—which, in turn, may well represent an extremely marginal event for the universe as a whole—can hardly have any practical significance for the lifespan of a human of this millennium or of future millennia. The perspective of what in comparison to this order of magnitude is an extremely short evolutionary history of life and of what is an even shorter history of humankind adds to this impression.

129. On the connection of cosmology and eschatology in the notion of the heavenly Jerusalem, cf. Hübner, "Eschatologische Rechenschaft," 151, as well as the literature listed therein. Cf. also the historical study of the tradition of the eschatological and heavenly Jerusalem by Söllner, *Jerusalem*. This study aims to elucidate the multilayered nature of this tradition, as well as its potential for the dialogue between Judaism, Christianity, and Islam.

130. Tipler, *The Physics of Immortality*, 14.

131. Gunton, *The Triune Creator*, 216.

132. Cf. also the critical discussion in Drees, *Beyond the Big Bang*, 128–41; Polkinghorne, *The Faith of a Physicist*, 165f.; and Worthing, *God, Creation, and Contemporary Physics*, 164–75. In *Unendliche Weiten*, Ganoczy also discusses Tipler's proposal, among others; but, in my opinion, he avoids the actual discussion by rushing prematurely to the conclusion that the theological view of the end of the world integrates, from the material perspective, a lot from scientific models but reaches beyond these models in its formal exposition (67–79).

133. Cf. Dyson, *Infinite in All Directions*, 119: "I do not make any clear distinction between mind and God. God is what mind becomes when it has passed beyond the scale of our comprehension." Here, Dyson combines a "mind" pantheism (whereby "mind" is understood as that which infiltrates and controls matter, 118) with a god-of-the-gaps model.

134. Tipler, *Physics of Immortality*, 9.

135. Polkinghorne, *The Faith of a Physicist*, 165.

136. ". . . [d]as ungelöste und stets unterdrückte Problem im Zeitverständnis der Metaphysik," Picht, "Die Zeit und die Modalitäten," 71.

137. Theunissen, *Negative Theologie der Zeit*, 360. Peter Manchester provides another example of relation in his article "Time in Christianity," in Balslev and Mohanty, *Religion and Time*, 133. Like Theunissen, he relates faith to the past, but then he describes hope as the relation to the present; and, finally, he relates love and the future to each other. This difference illustrates the dilemma of these types of classifications; they cannot escape the suspicion of arbitrariness.

138. Theunissen, *Negative Theologie der Zeit*, 340ff. He distances himself, e.g., from Heidegger by saying that Heidegger's concept of the future is "only a name for transcendental self-relatedness" [nur ein Titel für transzendentale Selbstbezüglichkeit], 344.

139. "Vergangenheit und Zukunft sind auf (mögliche) Gegenwart, Notwendigkeit und

Möglichkeit auf (mögliche) Wirklichkeit bezogen." Picht, "Die Zeit und die Modalitäten," 74. Cf. in this regard also A. M. Klaus Müller's model of the interlocking modes of
time (Müller, *Wende der Wahrnehmung,* 132–56).

140. "Die Gegenwärtigkeit *innerhalb eines Kommunikationsnetzes* macht die Wirklichkeit aus. Außerhalb der Vieldimensionalität des Bezugssystems, in dem uns Wirklichkeit erscheint, hat das Wort, Gegenwart' keinen möglichen Sinn." Picht, "Die Zeit
und die Modalitäten," 74.

141. ". . . ein vieldimensionales, offenes Gefüge mit mobilen Parametern . . . der universale Horizont der Phänomenalität der Phänomene überhaupt," ibid., 75.

142. This is due to the fact that Picht distinguishes between two levels [*Potenzen*] of
possibility. On the first level, "possible" means that which can *exist* and is therefore related
to the future. On the second level, however, "possible" means that which can be *true; in*
this sense, possibility takes precedence over the modes of time. The question whether it is
possible for a being who is situated in his or her present (time) to know time as a whole
transcends even the second level (ibid., 75f.).

143. Ibid., 76. Picht calls these forms phenomenal or transcendental time.

144. ". . . eine tiefe Umschichtung im Zeitverständnis," Ratschow, "Eschatologie," 335.

145. "Die Entwicklung wird der Schlüssel, der in alle Schlösser paßt." Ibid., 335.

146. Cf. the discussion of the ideas of these thinkers that are relevant in this context
(ibid., 337–46).

147. *Confessiones* XI .21.27.

148. Moltmann, *Gott in der Schöpfung,* 143–45; trans., 132–35; and Moltmann, *Das
Kommen Gottes,* 42–44; trans., 25–27. It is noticeable that the christological profile in
Moltmann's eschatology has become less pronounced throughout his career. If Moltmann
says in *Theology of Hope* that Christian eschatology speaks "of 'Christ and his future,'" 192,
then the Christology in *The Coming of God* primarily has the task of substantiating the
universalism of eschatological salvation. Moltmann, *Das Kommen Gottes,* 219–22 and
278–84; trans., 194–95 and 250–56.

149. Cf. Schwarz, "Eschatology or Futurology." Admittedly, Schwarz expresses a weak
theology of time by assuming an unproblematic, linear concept of time. The interesting
thing about this article, however, is its attempt to understand progress, as well as the striving for progress, as proleptic anticipation of the *eschaton* promised by God.

150. Cf. on this also Gregersen, "Gud og tilfældigheden," who, proceeding from his
theory that chance constitutes a God-given condition of existence, reflects theologically
within the context of scientific theories about God and indeterminism. Gregersen sees the
world as self-creative and multicentric (225, etc.). For chaos theory, he prefers an indeterministic interpretation. In his opinion, this corresponds to our state of knowledge, whereas a deterministic interpretation presupposes at least two suppositions that lie beyond our
knowledge, namely, that in the case of computer simulations, one is dealing with complete
descriptions of natural systems, and that every uncertainty or complexity on the micro- or
macro-level can be traced back to a mathematical formalism (198f.).

151. I have the impression that the expressions "weak causality" and "indeterminism"
are used in each instance according to the preference of the respective author. Achtner, e.g.
(cf. Achtner, *Die Chaostheorie*), as well as Achtner, Kunz, and Walter, *Dimensions of Time,*
128–30, and pp. 162–72 above), who emphasizes "order" in chaos, prefers to speak of
causality, whereas Gregersen prefers the term *indeterminism.*

152. "Zeit ist in privilegiertem Sinne Zukunft." Zimmerli, "Zeit als Zukunft," esp.
126–33. Cf. Link, *Schöpfung,* 449, who considers the future as the "source" [*Quellort*] of
time, although he thereby holds fast to linear thinking; time is unfolded as a stream directed from the future into the present. See also ibid., 500: Eternity accompanies us as the

horizon of our history, and it simultaneously (as well as in tension, though this is not thematized by Link) comes towards us "from what is ahead" [*von vorne*].

153. Cf. the theological interpretation of this connection in Gregersen, "Gud og tilfældigheden," 211f. Gregersen sees a connection between the development of diverse life forms and God's intention in the world. The interaction of natural constants, the tendencies inherent in the work of creation (which he understands, in the sense of Popper, as "propensities" [ibid., 209]), and the bubbling coincidences are God's means of realizing this intention.

154. 2 Cor. 5:17.

155. Moltmann, *Gott in der Schöpfung*, 144f.; trans., 132f., opposes extrapolation to anticipation, with which human beings adapt to what is to come (advent) by means of fear or hope. However, I believe the concept of anticipation does not go far enough, because human beings also react to the extrapolative future with anticipation. In hope and fear, human beings also adapt to that which must still be extrapolated from the present. The concept of intropolation should, in turn, make clear that, here, something new, something different, and also something completely foreign is consciously encountered and received.

156. ". . . die ewige Novität, der gemäß der ewige Gott sich selber Zukunft ist," Jüngel, *Gott als Geheimnis der Welt*, 513; trans., 375.

157. "Gott und Liebe werden niemals alt. Ihr Sein ist und bleibt im Kommen," ibid.

158. Moltmann, *Das Kommen Gottes*, 45; trans., 29.

159. Ibid., 292; trans., 265.

160. The eschatological *creatio ex vetere* is understood as *renovatio omnium* (ibid.).

161. ". . . der alte Kosmos durch den neuen und der neue durch den alten vergeschichtlicht [wird]," Hübner, "Eschatologische Rechenschaft," 154.

162. 2 Cor. 5:17.

163. On the concept of *annihilatio mundi*, cf. also Stock, *Annihilatio mundi*. Stock asserts that, despite its later rigidity, this concept is to be understood as the comprehensive metaphor for freedom. It is "a pre-critical example of critical dialogue with the thinking of the time, to the extent that it is committed to recognizing the existence of the always existing" [ein vorkritisches Beispiel kritischen Gesprächs mit dem Denken der Zeit, sofern dies eben der Erkenntnis des Seins des Immerseienden verpflichtet ist], 174. It was the tragedy of the idea of *annihilatio*, "that belief gained God but lost freedom, whereas the beginning enlightenment of human beings grasped the world, but allowed God to become a metaphor" [daß der Glaube Gott gewann, aber die Freiheit verlor, während die anhebende Aufgeklärtheit des Menschen die Welt ergriff, Gott aber zur Metapher werden ließ], 185. Ott sees a two-kingdom dualism in Luther's idea of the *abolitio et in nihilum reductio* and, correspondingly, prefers the Reformed model of a *purgatio et innovatio* as more appropriate (*Eschatologie*, 45).

164. Cf. Moltmann, *Das Kommen Gottes*, 295–302; trans., 268–76.

165. Cf. pp. 109–16.

166. "Menschliches Wesen, / was ist's gewesen? / In einer Stunde/geht es zugrunde, sobald das Lüftlein des Todes drein bläst. / Alles in allen / muß brechen und fallen, / Himmel und Erden / die müssen das werden, / was sie vor ihrer Erschaffung gewest." *EG* 449,7; text from 1666.

167. "Die Glucke führt ihr Völklein aus, / der Storch baut und bewohnt sein Haus / Die unverdroßne Bienenschar fliegt hin und her, . . . / Der Weizen wächset mit Gewalt; / darüber jauchzet jung und alt . . . / Ach, denk ich, bist du hier so schön / und läßt du's uns so lieblich gehn . . . / Welch hohe Lust, welch heller Schein / wird wohl in Christi Garten sein!" *EG* 503, 4.6.7.9.10, text from 1653.

168. Cf. on this also Hübner, "Eschatologische Rechenschaft," 150–67.

169. 1 John 3:2.

170. See pp. 115–16 above.

171. Cf., e.g., Mahlmann, "Auferstehung der Toten und ewiges Leben."

172. Mahlmann, "Auferstehung der Toten und ewiges Leben," 118.

173. See pp. 115–16 above and Jüngel, "Der Tod als Geheimnis des Lebens," 340.

174. ". . . einer unabhängig vom Wissen anderer, einer selbstgewußten Existenz des Menschen über seinen Tod hinaus," Mahlmann, "Auferstehung der Toten und ewiges Leben," 120.

175. See pp. 191–93 above and Ricoeur, *Soi-même comme un autre*, 140ff., etc.

176. Thus, e.g., Ringleben, "Gott und das ewige Leben," 56f. Jüngel also speaks of eternal life as a transformation by means of which the self forever becomes identical to its life (*Tod*, 154; the relevant sentence is missing in the English translation, 122).

177. Cf. also the presupposition of an identity constituted by relation in Ps. 104:29.

178. Theunissen, *Negative Theologie der Zeit*, 360: "Das Werden der Freiheit *zu* sich aus der Freiheit *von* sich geschieht im Grunde des Glaubens selbst als *kommunikative* Genese des Selbstseins" (The becoming of freedom *to* itself from the freedom *from* itself occurs in the ground of faith itself as the *communicative* genesis of selfhood).

179. Keller, "The Last Laugh," 389f.

180. Mahlmann, "Auferstehung der Toten und ewiges Leben," 129ff.

181. Many of the eschatological themes addressed here call for a discussion on what a person is or on what necessarily belongs to being a person. A discussion of these questions would go beyond the framework of this study, however. Here, this much should be noted: I understand personhood to be constituted by relationality. Accordingly, one of the most important traits of a person is the ability to integrate what he or she can also differentiate and keep separate: public and private, spirit and body, rationality and emotionality, faith and knowledge, etc.

182. Rom. 6:3–11 and 1 John 3:2.

183. Ratschow, "Eschatologie," 350f., 357f., 359, 361.

184. Ratschow, *Anmerkungen*, and see pp. 62–64 above. Ott also works with the idea of the unveiling of the hidden present (*Eschatologie*, 18, 41ff., 69f., etc.). The eschatological event is the apocalypse of that which previously was already established. Then, however, the continuous existence of the cosmos and of humanity means a disruption of the *eschaton* (15); and the meaning of this interim becomes, as Ott fittingly asserts, one of the most difficult problems of eschatology (26). In his work, Ott wishes to overcome an absolute, linear understanding of time (56f., 66f.), but he does not find an appropriate alternative. Instead, he dodges the issue by moving to the area of individual ethics and a qualitative description of eternity: Eternal life is the *glorificatio* of God (38), the absolute assurance of God (45), and nothing other than the revelation of our present life (41).

185. Cf. in this context also the provocative account of the role of apocalyptic thought, which has changed during the course of the ages, in the horizon of politics and the church, in Keller, *Apocalypse Now and Then;* on the subject of time, esp. 84–138.

186. Ratschow, "Eschatologie," 361.

187. In her article, "The Last Laugh," Keller similarly describes the strengths of Moltmann's book.

188. Pannenberg attempts this in *Systematische Theologie*, vol. 2, 123; trans., 101; cf. pp. 106–9 above.

189. Moltmann, *Das Kommen Gottes*, 291; trans., 264.

190. Ibid., 314; trans., 285.

191. "Reversible Zeit ist eine Art zeitlose Zeit, denn diese Zeitform ist selbst zeitlos wie die *absolute* Zeit Newtons." Ibid.

192. Ibid., 293; trans., 265.

193. Ibid., 328; trans., 298.

194. Ibid., 312; trans., 283.

195. Cf. ibid., 42–44; trans., 25–27.

196. Ibid., 316; trans., 287.

197. Ibid., 324; trans., 295.

198. ". . . ist 'das Ereignis der Ewigkeit im Sein'" (ibid., 313; trans., 285).

199. ". . . die dynamische Gegenwart der Ewigkeit in der Zeit," ibid., 292; trans., 266.

200. ". . . schwingt die irdische Schöpfung, die Menschen, die Tiere und die Erde, in der kosmischen Liturgie der Ewigkeit," ibid., 312.; trans., 283.

201. Ibid., 309; trans., 279.

202. Ibid., 316f.; trans., 286f.

203. Ibid., 291; trans., 259.

204. Ibid., 308; trans., 280.

205. Ibid., 316f.; trans., 286f.

206. Ibid., 308, 316f; trans., 280, 286f.

207. ". . . die aionische Zeit, die mit Ewigkeit erfüllte Zeit, die ewige Zeit," ibid., 324; trans., 295.

208. Ibid., 311; trans., 282.

209. Ibid., 324; trans., 295.

210. "In den aionischen Kreisläufen der Zeit regeneriert sich das geschöpfliche Leben unablässig aus der allgegenwärtigen Quelle des Lebens, aus Gott," ibid.

211. ". . . in den zyklischen Bewegungen der ewigen Daseinsfreude," ibid.

212. "[E]ntsteht auch eine wechselseitige *Perichorese* zwischen Ewigkeit und Zeit," ibid., 325; trans., 295.

213. ". . . Die ausgerollten Zeiten der Geschichte werden wie eine Buchrolle eingerollt, wie Offb 5 zu verstehen gibt." Ibid., 324; trans., 294–95.

214. Ibid., 291; trans., 259.

215. The kabbalistic notion of the original self-limiting of God—an exile in God—as it was developed by Isaak Luria. Cf. Scholem, *Die jüdische Mystik*, 285ff.

216. See pp. 198–203 above.

217. Moltmann, *Das Kommen Gottes*, 325; trans., 296.

218. Cf. on this Moltmann's explanation about his creation theology in a discussion with Christian Link: "Wenn die Schöpfung eschatologisch offen und geschichtlich im Fluß ist, kann die theologische Sprache sie nicht durch Definitionen feststellen und ihre Zukunft durch Begriffe verstellen, sondern muß sich der 'messianischen Imagination' bedienen. Ich meine damit eine Phantasie, die in der Gegenwart des Messias Jesus entsteht und die Möglichkeiten der messianischen Zeit im Blick auf die Schöpfung erkundet" (If creation is eschatologically open and historically in flux, then theological language cannot capture it with definitions and block its future with concepts; it must instead make use of the "messianic imagination." By this, I mean an imagination that arises in the presence of Jesus the Messiah and explores the possibilities of the messianic age in view of creation). Moltmann, "Zum Gespräch mit Christian Link," 93.

219. Cf. Mainzer, "Zeit als Richtungspfeil," esp. 58–68. Within the framework of his reflections on the evolution of technology and culture, Mainzer comes to the conclusion that the parallel between a political analysis of time and concepts of physics is striking. Instead of the illusionary assumption of a universal time, he says that one must speak of proper times. The talk of the proper time of political, social, and economic systems is indeed "initially only an analogy between the terminology of political science and sociology and the theory of relativity" [zunächst nur eine Analogie zwischen der Terminologie der

Politikwissenschaft und Soziologie mit der Relativitätstheorie]. The systems coming under consideration are too "slow" for real effects of the theory of relativity—but it here becomes "clear that the talk of the proper times, or internal times, of political and social systems and the criticism of universal measures of time are not postmodern relativism, but is rather suggested by the various individual scientific disciplines" [deutlich, daß die Rede von den Eigenzeiten bzw. inneren Zeiten politischer und sozialer Systeme und die Kritik univer-saler Zeitmaßstäbe kein postmoderner Relativismus ist, sondern durch verschiedene Einzelwissenschaften nahegelegt wird], 64. In comparable fashion, Prigogine and Stengers speak of internal developments: "Time is no longer merely a parameter of movement, but rather measures internal developments in a world that is out of balance. . . . We no longer are forced to choose between 'practical' freedom and 'theoretical' determinism. Tomorrow is no longer contained in today" [(D)ie Zeit ist nicht länger ein bloßer Parameter der Be-wegung, sondern mißt innere Entwicklungen in einer Welt des Nichtgleichgewichts. . . . Wir müssen nicht mehr zwischen "praktischer" Freiheit und "theoretischem" Determinis-mus wählen. Das Morgen ist nicht länger im Heute enthalten]. *Dialog mit der Natur,* 25 (this passage is not part of the English translation *Order Out of Chaos*).

220. Eccles. 3:1 NRSV; see also vv. 2–15.

221. ". . . jede einzelne *Tatsache* ist festgelegt," Hertzberg, *Der Prediger,* 103.

222. Fox, *Qohelet,* 192.

223. Seow, *Ecclesiastes,* 169.

224. Gordis, *Koheleth,* 229; similarly also Crenshaw, *Ecclesiastes,* 92.

225. Longmann, *The Book of Ecclesiastes,* 124.

226. Lauha, Kohelet, 63.

227. ". . . Betonung der schlechthinnigen Abhängigkeit alles Irdischen, mit einer starken Unterstreichung der Ausschließlichkeit Gottes," Hertzberg, *Der Prediger,* 109.

228. ". . . Musik des Unabänderlichen," ibid.

229. See in this regard the comment by Welker that it is "a theological misjudgment . . . that God is automatically active and present in *each and every* place of space and time! God, by turning away God's face, by lowering or veiling it, as the biblical texts say, can in fact leave times to the destructive dynamics of creaturely misdevelopment. This does not mean that God *has to* leave certain realms of creaturely life and thus certain times to their own destructive power. All times are *coram deo,* but God is not automatically active and present in all of them. In order to grasp and to express this, we should grasp God's relation to time as a living aggregation or relation of times that includes their *fullness, but not their totality*" ("God's Eternity," 323).

230. "Alles Ding währt seine Zeit, Gottes Lieb in Ewigkeit," *EG* 325. This contrast is impressed upon us for nine stanzas before the tenth stanza then concludes: ". . . bis ich dich nach dieser Zeit lob und lieb in Ewigkeit" (until, after this time, I praise and love you for all eternity).

231. Link, "Gott und die Zeit," 65: "Eternity must . . . be processed, so to speak; it must be 'prepared' in the process of God's transformations. . . " [Die Ewigkeit muß . . . sozusagen erarbeitet, sie muß im Prozeß der Wandlungen Gottes "zubereitet" werden].

232. Cf. ibid., 63.

233. ". . . Konstitution unserer Zeit durch Gottes Selektion aus seiner Zeit" (Herms, "Meine Zeit in Gottes Händen," 81).

234. Link, "Gott und die Zeit," 61.

235. Cf. Gronemeyer, *Das Leben als letzte Gelegenheit,* 147–58, who describes the inabil-ity to tolerate the different and the unfamiliar as the final consequence of the modern usurpation of time. Keller is thinking in the same direction when she translates the New Testament *basileia* not with "kingdom of God," but instead with "divine commonwealth,"

conceiving of this as "a spatiality constituted by the creaturely plenum of finite, spirit-filled mutualities locally congregating." *Apocalypse Now and Then*, 291. Cf. also Achtner, Kunz, and Walker, (*Dimensions of Time*), who with the aid of their theory of the tripolar time structure (endogenous time—self-relation of the human, exogenous time—world relation of the human, transcendental time—religious relation of the human), wish to point toward "ways to escape the time crisis of our 'acceleration society.'"

236. See on this, e.g., Weis, *Was treibt die Zeit?*

237. Cf. Westhelle, "The Challenge of Theology," 25: "If time is not a function of a process in which space is created, it is irrelevant."

238. Cf. Ricoeur, *Time and Narrative*, e.g., 244: "Narrated time is like a bridge set over the breach speculation constantly opens between phenomenological time and cosmological time."

239. "Im Zusammenhang mit Irreversibilität gelangen wir zu einer Beschreibung der Physik, die auf allen Ebenen ein narratives Element ins Spiel bringt." Prigogine, "Zeit, Chaos und Naturgesetze," 91.

240. Cf. also the use of the dance metaphor for the world in Moltmann, *Gott in der Schöpfung*, 306–9; trans., 304–7, and the linking of narration and liturgy/rite in Keller, *Apocalypse Now and Then*, 136–38.

241. "An den Mistral. Ein Tanzlied," in the appendix to *Die fröhliche Wissenschaft*, Nietzsche, *Werke in zwei Bänden,* 542–44; trans., *The Gay Science,* 258–260.

242. See pp. 112–15 above.

243. E.g., Gronemeyer, *Das Leben als letzte Gelegenheit;* Reheis, *Die Kreativität der Langsamkeit;* and Achtner, Kunz, and Walter, *Dimensions of Time.* From a sociological perspective, Richard Fenn presents the thesis that "time-panic" leads to an increase in fascistic tendencies in society. He develops this theory by analyzing conceptions of time that are expressed in various types of rites (Fenn, *The End of Time*).

244. Augustine, *Confessiones* IV.8.13. English translation by the author.

Bibliography

Achtner, Wolfgang. 1991. *Physik, Mystik und Christentum. Eine Darstellung und Diskussion der natürlichen Theologie bei T. F. Torrance*. Frankfurt/Main et al.: Peter Lang.

———. 1997. *Die Chaostheorie. Geschichte, Gestalt, Rezeption. EZW-Texte 1997/135*. Berlin: Evangelische Zentralstelle für Weltanschauungsfragen.

Achtner, Wolfgang, Stefan Kunz, and Thomas Walter. 1998. *Dimensionen der Zeit. Die Zeitstrukturen Gottes, der Welt und des Menschen*. Darmstadt: Wissenschaftliche Buchgesellschaft.

———. 2002. *Dimensions of Time: The Structures of the Time of Humans, of the World, and of God*. Translated by Arthur H. Williams, Jr. Grand Rapids, MI: Eerdmans.

Albrektson, Bertil. 1967. *History and the Gods: An Essay on the Idea of Historical Events as Divine Manifestations in the Ancient Near East and in Israel*. Coniectanea biblica. Old Testament Series 1. Lund: CWK Gleerup.

Alexander, H. G., ed. 1956. *The Leibniz-Clarke Correspondence: Together with Extracts from Newton's Principia and Opticks*. Manchester: Manchester University Press.

Altner, Günter. 1965. *Schöpfungsglaube und Entwicklungsgedanke in der protestantischen Theologie zwischen Ernst Haeckel und Teilhard de Chardin*. Zürich: EVZ.

———, ed. 1986. *Die Welt als offenes System. Eine Kontroverse um das Werk von Ilya Prigogine*. Frankfurt/Main: Fischer.

Anselm of Canterbury. 1962. *Proslogion. Untersuchungen. Lateinisch-deutsche Ausgabe*. Translated by Franciscus Salesius Schmitt OSB, Abtei Wimpfen. Stuttgart-Bad Cannstatt: Friedrich Frommann.

Anz, Wilhelm. 1964. "Christlicher Glaube und griechisches Denken." In *Zeit und Geschichte: Dankesgabe an Rudolf Bultmann zum 80. Geburtstag*, edited by E. Dinkler. Tübingen: Mohr (Siebeck), 531–55.

Arecchi, F. T. 1993. "A Critical Approach to Complexity and Self-Organization." In *Origins, Time and Complexity*, Part I, Studies in Science and Theology (SSTh). Vol. 1, *Yearbook of the European Society for the Study of Science and Theology*. Edited by G. V. Coyne, K. Schmitz-Moormann, and C. Wassermann. Geneva: Labor et Fides, 5–29.

Ariès, Philippe. 1977. *L'homme devant la mort*. Paris: Éditions du Seuil.

Assmann, Jan. 1989. "Das Doppelgesicht der Zeit im altägyptischen Denken." In *Die Zeit*.

Dauer und Augenblick. Veröffentlichungen der Carl Friedrich von Siemens Stiftung, edited by H. Gumin and H. Meier. München, Zürich: Piper, 2:189–223.

Audretsch, Jürgen, and Klaus Mainzer, eds. 1989. *Vom Anfang der Welt. Wissenschaft, Philosophie, Religion, Mythos.* München: Beck.

———. 1990. *Wieviele Leben hat Schrödingers Katze? Zur Physik und Philosophie der Quantenmechanik.* Mannheim, Wien, Zürich: BI Wissenschaftsverlag.

Augustinus. 1966. *Confessiones—Bekenntnisse. Lateinisch und Deutsch.* Translated by Joseph Bernhart. 3rd ed. München: Kösel.

———. 1991. *Confessions.* Translated by Henry Chadwick. Oxford: Oxford University Press.

Aurelius, Carl Axel. 1994. *Luther i Sverige. Svenska lutherbilder under tre sekler.* Skellefteå: Artos.

Balslev, Anindita Niyogi, and Jitendranath N. Mohanty, eds. 1993. *Religion and Time.* Vol. 54, *Studies in the History of Religions.* Edited by H. G. Kippenberg and E. T. Lawson. Leiden, New York, Köln: E. J. Brill.

Balthasar, Hans Urs von. 1960. "Eschatologie." In *Fragen der Theologie heute.* 3rd ed. Edited by J. Feiner, J. Trütsch, and F. Böckle. Einsiedeln, Zürich, Köln: Benziger, 403–22.

Barbour, Ian G. 1966. *Issues in Science and Religion.* Englewood Cliffs, NJ: Prentice-Hall.

———. 1976. *Myths, Models and Paradigms: A Comparative Study in Science and Religion.* San Francisco: Harper & Row.

———. 1988. "Ways of Relating Science and Theology." In *Physics, Philosophy, and Theology: A Common Quest for Understanding,* edited by R. J. Russell, W. R. Stoeger, and G. V. Coyne. Vatican City State: Vatican Observatory, 21–48.

———. 1997. *Religion and Science: Historical and Contemporary Issues.* San Francisco: HarperSanFrancisco, 1990.

Barbour, Julian. 1999. *The End of Time: The Next Revolution in Our Understanding of the Universe.* London: Weidenfeld & Nicolson.

Barr, James. 1962. *Biblical Words for Time.* Studies in Biblical Theology 33. London: SCM.

Barrow, John D. 1991. *Theories of Everything: The Quest for Ultimate Explanation.* Oxford: Clarendon Press.

———. 1994. *Theorien für Alles. Die Suche nach der Weltformel.* Translated by Anita Ehlers. Reinbek bei Hamburg: Rowohlt.

———. 1999. *Impossibility: The Limits of Science and the Science of Limits.* New York: Oxford University Press.

Barth, Karl. 1926. *Der Römerbrief.* Vierter Abdruck der neuen Bearbeitung. München: Chr. Kaiser.

———. 1933. *The Epistle to the Romans.* Translated from the 6th ed. by Edwyn C. Hoskyns. London: Oxford University Press.

———. 1945. *Die Kirchliche Dogmatik* III,1. Zollikon-Zürich: Evangelischer Verlag.

———. 1946. *Die Kirchliche Dogmatik* II,1. 2nd ed. Zollikon-Zürich: Evangelischer Verlag.

———. 1957. *Church Dogmatics* 2.1. Translated by T. H. L. Parker et al. New York: Charles Scribner's Sons.

———. 1958. *Church Dogmatics* 3.1. Translated by J. W. Edwards, O. Bussey, and H. Knight. Edinburgh: T & T Clark.

Bauman, Zygmunt. 1992. *Mortality, Immortality and Other Life Strategies.* Oxford: Polity Press.

Bayer, Oswald. 1997. "Erklärung und Erzählung. Eine Bestimmung des Verhältnisses von

Theologie und Naturwissenschaften." *Neue Zeitschrift für systematische Theologie und Religionsphilosophie* 39(1):1–13.

Belfrage, Esbjörn et al. 1996. *Guds kärlek är som stranden och som gräset. En bok om psalmdiktaren Anders Frostenson.* Stockholm: Verbum.

Benktson, Benkt-Erik. 1989. *Samtidighetens mirakel. Kring tidsproblematiken i Lars Gyllenstens romaner.* Stockholm: Bonniers.

Berg, Christian. 2002. *Theologie im technologischen Zeitalter. Das Werk Ian Barbours als Beitrag zur Verältnisbestimmung von Theologie zu Naturwissenschaft und Technik.* Stuttgart: Kohlhammer.

Bergmann, Peter G. 1979. "The Space-Time Concept in General Relativity." In *Relativity, Quanta, and Cosmology in the Development of the Scientific Thought of Albert Einstein,* edited by F. De Finis. New York: Johnson Reprint Corporation, 1:141–56.

Bergmann, Sigurd. 1995. *Geist, der Natur befreit. Die trinitarische Kosmologie Gregors von Nazianz im Horizont einer ökologischen Theologie der Befreiung.* Mainz: Grünewald.

Boethius, Anicius Manlius Severinus. 1957. *Philosophiae consolatio.* Edidit Ludovicus Bieler. Corpus Christianorum: Series Latina 94. Turnhout: Brepols.

———. 1973/1978. *The Theological Tractates with an English Translation.* Translated by H. F. Stewart, E. K. Rand, and S. J. Tester. Vol. 74, Loeb Classical Library, edited by G. P. Goold. Cambridge/London: Harvard University Press/Heinemann.

Bohm, David, and Basil J. Hiley. 1993. *The Undivided Universe: An Ontological Interpretation of Quantum Theory.* London, New York: Routledge.

Bohr, Niels. 1958a. *Atomphysik und menschliche Erkenntnis. Die Wissenschaft.* Vol. 112. Edited by W. Westphal. Translated by Sophie Hellmann and Hertha Kopfermann. Braunschweig: Vieweg.

———. 1958b. *Atomteori og naturbeskrivelse.* Kopenhagen: J. H. Schultz.

———. 1963. *Essays 1958–1962 on Atomic Physics and Human Knowledge.* New York, London: Interscience.

———. 1985. *Collected Works.* Vol. 6, *Foundations of Quantum Physics I (1926–1932).* Edited by J. Kalckar. Amsterdam, New York, Oxford, Tokyo: North-Holland Physics Publishing.

Boman, Thorleif. 1965. *Das hebräische Denken im Vergleich mit dem griechischen.* 4th ed. Göttingen: Vandenhoeck & Ruprecht.

Born, Max. 1978. *My Life. Recollections of a Nobel Laureate.* London: Taylor & Francis.

Bornkamm, Günther. 1975. Enderwartung und Kirche im Matthäusevangelium. In *Überlieferung und Auslegung im Matthäusevangelium.* 7th ed. Edited by G. Bornkamm, G. Barth, and H. J. Held. Neukirchen-Vluyn: Neukirchener Verlag, 1:13–47.

Bovon, François. 1989. *Das Evangelium nach Lukas. Evangelisch-Katholischer Kommentar zum Neuen Testament.* Vol. III.1. Zürich/Neukirchen-Vluyn: Benziger/Neukirchener.

Breuer, Reinhard. 1984. *Das anthropische Prinzip. Der Mensch im Fadenkreuz der Naturgesetze.* Frankfurt/Main, Berlin, Wien: Ullstein.

Brooke, John Hedley. 1991. *Science and Religion: Some Historical Perspectives.* Cambridge: Cambridge University Press.

Brooke, John H., and Geoffrey Cantor. 1998. *Reconstructing Nature: The Engagement of Science and Religion.* Edinburgh: T & T Clark.

Buchholtz, Klaus-Dietwardt. 1965. *Isaac Newton als Theologe. Ein Beitrag zum Gespräch zwischen Naturwissenschaft und Theologie.* Witten: Luther-Verlag.

Bühler, Pierre, and Clairette Karakash, eds. 1992. *Science et foi font système. Une approche herméneutique.* Geneva: Labor et Fides.

Bultmann, Rudolf. 1948. Heilsgeschichte und Geschichte. *Theologische Literaturzeitung,* 73:659–66.

Burtt, Edwin Arthur. 1967. *The Metaphysical Foundations of Modern Physical Science: A Historical and Critical Essay*. London: Routledge & Kegan.

Cancik, Hubert. 1989. "Die Rechtfertigung Gottes durch den 'Fortschritt der Zeiten.' Zur Differenz jüdisch-christlicher und hellenisch-römischer Zeit- und Geschichtsvorstellungen." In *Die Zeit. Dauer und Augenblick. Veröffentlichungen der Carl Friedrich von Siemens Stiftung,* edited by H. Gumin and H. Meier. München, Zürich: Piper, 2:257–88.

Clayton, Philip D. 1997. *God and Contemporary Science*. Edinburgh Studies in Constructive Theology. Edinburgh: Edinburgh University Press.

Clifford, Richard J. 1994. *Creation Accounts in the Ancient Near East and in the Bible*. Catholic Biblical Quarterly Monograph Series 26. Washington, DC: Catholic Biblical Association of America.

Cliqué, Guy M. 2001. *Differenz und Parallelität. Zum Verständnis des Zusammenhangs von Theologie und Naturwissenschaft am Beispiel der Überlegungen Günter Howes*. Frankfurt am Main: Peter Lang.

Colpe, Carsten. 1989. "Die Zeit in drei asiatischen Hochkulturen (Babylon–Iran–Indien)." In *Die Zeit. Dauer und Augenblick. Veröffentlichungen der Carl Friedrich von Siemens Stiftung,* edited by H. Gumin and H. Meier. München, Zürich: Piper, 2:225–56.

Concilium. 1993. *Reinkarnation oder Auferstehung?* 29:5.

Conzelmann, Hans. 1954. *Die Mitte der Zeit*. Studien zur Theologie des Lukas. Beiträge zur historischen Theologie 17. Tübingen: Mohr (Siebeck).

Coveney, Peter, and Roger Highfield. 1991. *The Arrow of Time*. New York: Fawcett Columbine.

———. 1995. *Frontiers of Complexity: The Search for Order in a Chaotic World*. New York: Ballantine Books.

Coyne, George V., Karl Schmitz-Moormann, and Christoph Wassermann, eds. 1993. *Origins, Time and Complexity. Part 1, Studies in Science and Theology (SSTh). Vol. 1, Yearbook of the European Society for the Study of Science and Theology*. Geneva: Labor et Fides.

———. 1994. *Origins, Time and Complexity. Part 11, Studies in Science and Theology (SSTh). Vol. 2, Yearbook of the European Society for the Study of Science and Theology*. Geneva: Labor et Fides.

Cramer, Friedrich. 1993. *Der Zeitbaum. Grundlegung einer allgemeinen Zeittheorie*. Frankfurt/Main, Leipzig: Insel.

———. 1994. "Time of Planets and Time of Life. The Concept of a 'Tree of Times.'" In *Origins, Time and Complexity*, Part 11, Studies in Science and Theology (SSTh). Vol. 2, *Yearbook of the European Society for the Study of Science and Theology*. Edited by G. V. Coyne, K. Schmitz-Moormann, and C. Wassermann. Geneva: Labor et Fides, 74–81.

Crenshaw, James L. 1988. *Ecclesiastes: A Commentary*. London: SCM.

Cullmann, Oscar. 1962. *Christus und die Zeit: Die urchristliche Zeit- und Geschichtsauffassung*. 3rd ed., Zürich: EVZ.

———. 1964. *Christ and Time: The Primitive Christian Conception of Time and History*. Rev. ed. Translated by Floyd V. Filson. Philadelphia: Westminster.

———. 1965. *Heil als Geschichte. Heilsgeschichtliche Existenz im Neuen Testament*. Tübingen: Mohr (Siebeck).

———. 1967. *Salvation in History*. Translated by Sidney G. Sowers and SCM Press. New York: Harper & Row.

Dalferth, Ingolf U. 1994. "Gott und Zeit." In *Religion und Gestaltung der Zeit*, edited by D. Georgi, H.-G. Heimbrock, and M. Moxter. Kampen: Kok Pharos, 9–34.

———. 1995. "The Eschatological Roots of the Doctrine of the Trinity." In *Trinitarian Theology Today: Essays on Divine Being and Act*, edited by C. Schwöbel. Edinburgh: T & T Clark, 147–70.

Daly, Gabriel. 1988. *Creation and Redemption*. Dublin: Gill & Macmillan.

Davies, Paul. 1984. *God and the New Physics*. New York: Simon & Schuster.

———. 1995. *About Time: Einstein's Unfinished Revolution*. New York: Simon & Schuster.

Davies, P. C. W., and J. R. Brown, eds. 1986. *The Ghost in the Atom: A Discussion of the Mysteries of Quantum Physics*. Canto edition, 1993. Cambridge: Cambridge University Press.

D'Costa, Gavin. 1998. "Trinitarian *Différance* and World Religions: Postmodernity and the 'Other.'" In *Faith and Praxis in a Postmodern Age*, edited by Ursula King. London: Cassell, 28–46.

Delling, Gerhard. 1940. *Das Zeitverständnis des Neuen Testaments*. Gütersloh: Bertelsmann.

———. 1970. *Zeit und Endzeit. Zwei Vorlesungen zur Theologie des Neuen Testaments*. Biblische Studien 58. Edited by H. Gollwitzer, F. Hahn, and H.-J. Kraus. Neukirchen-Vluyn: Neukirchener Verlag.

Den Svenska Psalmboken [*Sv ps*]. 1986. Stockholm: Verbum.

Den Svenska Psalmboken av Konungen gillad och stadfäst år 1937 [*Svps1937*].

Dinter, Astrid. 1999. *Vom Glauben eines Physikers. John Polkinghornes Beitrag zum Dialog zwischen Theologie und Naturwissenschaften*. Mainz: Grünewald.

Drees, Willem B. 1990. *Beyond the Big Bang: Quantum Cosmologies and God*. La Salle: Open Court.

———. 1996. "A Case Against Temporal Critical Realism? Consequences of Quantum Cosmology for Theology." In *Quantum Cosmology and the Laws of Nature: Scientific Perspectives on Divine Action*. 2nd ed. Edited by R. J. Russell, N. Murphy, and C. J. Isham. Vatican City State/Berkeley, CA: Vatican Observatory Publications/The Center for Theology and the Natural Sciences, 327–60.

Duchrow, Ulrich. 1966. "Der sogenannte psychologische Zeitbegriff Augustins im Verhältnis zur physikalischen und geschichtlichen Zeit." *Zeitschrift für Theologie und Kirche* 63:267–88.

Dyson, Freeman J. 1979. "Time without End: Physics and Biology in an Open Universe." *Reviews of Modern Physics* 51(3):447–60.

———. 1990. *Infinite in All Directions*. London: Penguin Books.

Ebeling, Gerhard. 1964. "Zeit und Wort." In *Zeit und Geschichte: Dankesgabe an Rudolf Bultmann zum 80. Geburtstag*, edited by E. Dinkler. Tübingen: Mohr (Siebeck), 341–56.

Eichrodt, Walther. 1956. "Heilserfahrung und Zeitverständnis im Alten Testament." *Theologische Zeitschrift* 12:103–25.

———. 1963. *Theologie des Alten Testaments* 1. 7th ed. Berlin: Evangelische Verlagsanstalt.

Einstein, Albert. 1934. *The World as I See It*. Translated by Alan Harris. New York: Friede Publishers.

———. 1950a. *Out of My Later Years*. New York: Philosophical Library.

———. 1950b. "Physics and Reality" (1936). In *Out of My Later Years*. New York: Philosophical Library, 59–97.

———. 1950c. "The Fundaments of Theoretical Physics" (1940). In *Out of My Later Years*. New York: Philosophical Library, 98–110.

———. 1950d. "The Theory of Relativity" (1949). In *Out of My Later Years*. New York: Philosophical Library, 41–48.

———. 1984. *Mein Weltbild*. Edited by C. Seelig. Rev. ed. Frankfurt/Main, Berlin, Wien: Ullstein.

————. 1996a. *The Collected Papers of Albert Einstein*. Vol. 6, *The Berlin Years: Writings, 1914–1917*. Edited by A. J. Kox, M. J. Klein, and R. Schulmann. Princeton: Princeton University Press.

————. 1996b. *Die formale Grundlage der allgemeinen Relativitätstheorie* [Königlich Preußische Akademie der Wissenschaften, Berlin: Sitzungsberichte, 1914]. In *The Collected Papers of Albert Einstein*, vol. 6, *The Berlin Years: Writings, 1914–1917*, edited by A. J. Kox, M. J. Klein, and R. Schulmann. Princeton: Princeton University Press, 72–130.

————. 1996c. *Die Grundlage der allgemeinen Relativitätstheorie* [*Annalen der Physik* 49, 1916]. In *The Collected Papers of Albert Einstein*, vol. 6, *The Berlin Years: Writings, 1914–1917*, edited by A. J. Kox, M. J. Klein, and R. Schulmann. Princeton: Princeton University Press, 283–339.

————. 1996d. *Über die spezielle und die allgemeine Relativitätstheorie (Gemeinverständlich)* [Braunschweig: Vieweg, 1917]. In *The Collected Papers of Albert Einstein*, vol. 6, *The Berlin Years: Writings, 1914–1917*, edited by A. J. Kox, M. J. Klein, and R. Schulmann. Princeton: Princeton University Press, 420–539.

Einstein, Albert, and Hedwig and Max Born. 1969. *Briefwechsel 1916–1955, kommentiert von Max Born*. München: Nymphenburger Verlagshandlung.

————. 1971. *The Born-Einstein Letters*. Translated by Irene Born. New York: Walker.

Einstein, Albert, and Leopold Infeld. 1938. *The Evolution of Physics*. New York: Simon & Schuster.

Eliade, Mircea. 1967. *From Primitives to Zen: A Thematic Sourcebook of the History of Religious Ideas*. Vol. 4, *A History of Religious Ideas*. New York: Harper & Row.

————. 1974. *The Myth of the Eternal Return or, Cosmos and History*. Translated by Willard R. Trask. 2nd ed. Bollingen Series 46. Princeton: Princeton University Press.

————. 1978. *Geschichte der religiösen Ideen*. Vol. 1: *Von der Steinzeit bis zu den Mysterien von Eleusis*. Translated by Elisabeth Darlap. Freiburg: Herder.

————. 1978–1985. *A History of Religious Ideas*. 3 vols. Translated by Willard R. Trask. Chicago: University of Chicago Press.

————. 1979. *Geschichte der religiösen Ideen*. Vol. 2: *Von Gautama Buddha bis zu den Anfängen des Christentums*. Translated by Adelheid Müller-Lissner and Werner Müller. Freiburg: Herder.

————. 1981. *Geschichte der religiösen Ideen*. Vol. 4: *Quellentexte*. Translated by Günter Lanczkowski. Freiburg: Herder.

————. Ellingsen, Svein. 1990. *Skjult som vind i treets krone: Studiehefte til seks salmer i Norsk Salmebok*. Oslo: Verbum.

Esterbauer, Reinhold. 1996. *Verlorene Zeit—wider eine Einheitswissenschaft von Natur und Gott*. Stuttgart: Kohlhammer.

Evangelischer Erwachsenenkatechismus. 1975. 2nd ed. Gütersloh: Gütersloher Verlagshaus Gerd Mohn.

Evangelisches Gesangbuch: Ausgabe für die Evangelische Kirche im Rheinland, die Evangelische Kirche von Westfalen und die Lippische Landeskirche [*EG*]. 1995. Gütersloh, Bielefeld, Neukirchen-Vluyn.

Evangelisches Gesangbuch: Ausgabe für die Evangelische Kirche im Rheinland, die Evangelische Kirche von Westfalen, die Lippische Landeskirche; in Gemeinschaft mit der Evangelisch-reformierten Kirche (Synode evangelisch-reformierter Kirchen in Bayern und Nordwestdeutschland); in Gebrauch auch in den evangelischen Kirchen im Großherzogtum Luxemburg [*EG1996*]. 1996. Gütersloh, Bielefeld, Neukirchen-Vluyn: Gütersloher Verlagshaus, Luther-Verlag, Neukirchener Verlag.

Ewald, Günter. 1980. "Bemerkungen zum Begriff von Raum und Zeit in der Physik." In

Gott–Geist–Materie. Theologie und Naturwissenschaft im Gespräch, edited by H. Dietz-felbinger and L. Mohaupt. Hamburg: Lutherisches Verlagshaus, 79–86.

Fagg, Lawrence W. 1995. *The Becoming of Time: Integrating Physical and Religious Time*. At-lanta, GA: Scholars Press.

Farrugia, Edward G., and Harald Wagner. 1995. "Eschatologie. VI. Im ökumenischen Gespräch." In *Lexikon für Theologie und Kirche*. 3rd ed. Freiburg, Basel, Rom, Wien: Herder, 3:876–78.

Fenn, Richard K. 1997. *The End of Time: Religion, Ritual, and the Forging of the Soul*. Lon-don: SPCK.

Ferguson, Kitty. 1994/1997. *The Fire in the Equations: Science, Religion, and the Search for God*. Philadelphia: Templeton Foundation Press.

Flasch, Kurt. 1993. *Was ist Zeit? Augustinus von Hippo. Das XI. Buch der Confessiones. His-torisch-philosophische Studie. Text—Übersetzung—Kommentar*. Frankfurt/Main: Klostermann.

Fölsing, Albrecht. 1994. *Albert Einstein. Eine Biographie*. 3rd ed. Frankfurt/Main: Suhrkamp.

———. 1997. *Albert Einstein: A Biography*. Translated by Ewald Osers. New York: Viking.

Ford, David F., ed. 1997. *The Modern Theologians: An Introduction to Christian Theology in the Twentieth Century*. 2nd ed. Oxford: Blackwell.

Fox, Michael V. 1989. *Qohelet and His Contradictions*. Journal for the Study of the Old Tes-tament: Supplement Series 71 (Bible and Literature Series 18). Edited by D. J. A. Clines and P. R. Davies. Sheffield: Almond Press.

Fraser, Julius T. 1991. *Die Zeit. Auf den Spuren eines vertrauten und doch fremden Phänomens*. Translated by Anita Ehlers. München: dtv.

Frere, W. H. 1909. "Introduction." In *Hymns Ancient and Modern: Historical Edition*. Lon-don: n.p., ix–xc.

Frey, Jörg. 1998. *Die johanneische Eschatologie*. Vol. II: *Das johanneische Zeitverständnis*. Wissenschaftliche Untersuchungen zum Neuen Testament 110. Edited by M. Hengel and O. Hofius. Tübingen: Mohr Siebeck.

Fuchs, Ernst. 1960a. "Christus das Ende der Geschichte (1949)." In Fuchs, *Zur Frage nach dem historischen Jesus*. Gesammelte Aufsätze 2. Tübingen: Mohr (Siebeck), 79–99.

———. 1960b. "Das Zeitverständnis Jesu." In Fuchs, *Zur Frage nach dem historischen Je-sus*. Gesammelte Aufsätze 2. Tübingen: Mohr (Siebeck), 304–76.

Ganoczy, Alexandre. 1992. *Suche nach Gott auf den Wegen der Natur. Theologie, Mystik, Naturwissenschaften—ein kritischer Versuch*. Düsseldorf: Patmos.

———. 1998. *Unendliche Weiten . . . Naturwissenschaftliches Weltbild und christlicher Glaube. Technik und Weisheit* (Schriftenreihe der Klaus Hemmerle Gesellschaft). Vol. 1. Freiburg, Basel, Wien: Herder.

Geißer, Hans Friedrich. 1994. "Grundtendenzen der Eschatologie im 20. Jahrhundert." In *Die Zukunft der Erlösung. Zur neueren Diskussion um die Eschatologie. Veröffentlichun-gen der Wissenschaftlichen Gesellschaft für Theologie 7*, edited by K. Stock. Gütersloh: Chr. Kaiser/Gütersloher Verlagshaus, 13–48.

Geister, Philip. 1996. *Aufhebung zur Eigentlichkeit. Zur Problematik kosmologischer Escha-tologie in der Theologie Karl Rahners*. Uppsala Studies in Faiths and Ideologies 5. Edit-ed by A. Jeffner and C. R. Bråkenhielm. Uppsala: Department of Studies in Faiths and Ideologies.

Gerhardt, C. J., ed. 1890. *Die philosophischen Schriften von Gottfried Wilhelm Leibniz*. Vol. VII. Berlin: Weidmannsche Buchhandlung.

Gese, Hartmut. 1958. "Geschichtliches Denken im Alten Orient und im Alten Testa-ment." *Zeitschrift für Theologie und Kirche* 55:127–45.

Gimmler, Antje, Mike Sandbothe, and Walther Ch. Zimmerli, eds. 1997. *Die Wiederentdeckung der Zeit. Reflexionen–Analysen–Konzepte*. Darmstadt: Wissenschaftliche Buchgesellschaft.

Gnilka, Joachim. 1978. *Das Evangelium nach Markus. Evangelisch-Katholischer Kommentar zum Neuen Testament*. Vol. II.1. Zürich/Neukirchen-Vluyn: Benziger/Neukirche-ner.

Gordis, Robert. 1968. *Koheleth—the Man and His World: A Study of Ecclesiastes*. 3rd ed. New York: Schocken Books.

Gorman, Frank H., Jr. 1990. *The Ideology of Ritual: Space, Time and Status in the Priestly Theology*. Journal for the Study of the Old Testament: Supplement Series 91. Sheffield: JSOT Press.

Görman, Ulf. 1997. "Är moralen styrd av generna?" *Svensk Teologisk Kvartalskrift* 73(1):1–10.

Gotteslob: Katholisches Gebet- und Gesangbuch mit dem Anhang für das Erzbistum Paderborn [GL]. 1975. Stuttgart/Paderborn.

Gowan, Donald E. 1987. *Eschatology in the Old Testament*. Edinburgh: T & T Clark.

Gregersen, Niels Henrik. 1992. "Gud og tilfældigheden—et teologisk forsøg med indeterminismen." In *Kaos og kausalitet. Om kaos-teorien og dens betydning for filosofi og teologi*, edited by N. H. Gregersen and A. W. Nielsen. Aarhus: Aarhus Universitetsforlag, 151–230.

Gregersen, Niels Henrik, and J. Wentzel van Huyssteen, eds. 1998. *Rethinking Theology and Science: Six Models for the Current Dialogue*. Grand Rapids: Eerdmans.

Greshake, Gisbert. 1995. "Eschatologie. II. Die Geschichte des Traktates." In *Lexikon für Theologie und Kirche*. 3rd ed. Vol. 3. Freiburg, Basel, Rom, Wien: Herder, 860–65.

———. 1998. "Eschatologie." In *Dictionnaire critique de Théologie*, edited by J.-Y. Lacoste. Paris: Presses Universitaires de France, 396–400.

Grib, Andrej A. 1996. "Quantum Cosmology, the Role of the Observer, Quantum Logic." In *Quantum Cosmology and the Laws of Nature: Scientific Perspectives on Divine Action*, edited by R. J. Russell, N. Murphy, and C. J. Isham. 2nd ed. Vatican City State/Berkeley, CA: Vatican Observatory Publications/The Center for Theology and the Natural Sciences, 165–84.

Gronemeyer, Marianne. 1993. *Das Leben als letzte Gelegenheit. Sicherheitsbedürfnisse und Zeitknappheit*. Darmstadt: Wissenschaftliche Buchgesellschaft.

Gumin, Heinz, und Heinrich Meier, ed. 1989. *Die Zeit. Dauer und Augenblick. Veröffentlichungen der Carl Friedrich von Siemens Stiftung*. Vol. 2. München, Zürich: Piper.

Gunton, Colin E. 1993. *The One, the Three and the Many: God, Creation and the Culture of Modernity*. Cambridge: Cambridge University Press.

———. 1995. "Relation and Relativity: The Trinity and the Created World." In *Trinitarian Theology Today: Essays on Divine Being and Act*, edited by C. Schwöbel. Edinburgh: T & T Clark, 92–112.

———. 1997. "The Trinity, Natural Theology, and a Theology of Nature." In *The Trinity in a Pluralistic Age: Theological Essays on Culture and Religion*, edited by K. J. Vanhoozer. Grand Rapids/Cambridge: Eerdmans, 88–103.

———. 1998. *The Triune Creator: A Historical and Systematic Study*. Edinburgh Studies in Constructive Theology. Grand Rapids: Eerdmans.

Hafstad, Kjetil. 1985. *Wort und Geschichte. Das Geschichtsverständnis Karl Barths*. Beiträge zur evangelischen Theologie 98. Edited by E. Jüngel and R. Smend. München: Chr. Kaiser.

Haught, John F. 1995. *Science and Religion: From Conflict to Conversation*. Mahwah, NJ: Paulist Press.

Hawking, Stephen W. 1988a. *Eine kurze Geschichte der Zeit. Die Suche nach der Urkraft des Universums*. Translated by Hainer Kober. Reinbek bei Hamburg: Rowohlt.

———. 1988b. *A Brief History of Time: From the Big Bang to Black Holes*. Toronto, New York: Bantam Books.

———. 1993. *Black Holes and Baby Universes and Other Essays*. New York: Bantam Books.

Heim, Karl. 1926. "Zeit und Ewigkeit, die Hauptfrage der heutigen Eschatologie." *Zeitschrift für Theologie und Kirche* NF 7:403–29

Heisenberg, Werner. 1984a. "Physik und Philosophie" [Stuttgart: S. Hirzel, 1959]. In *Gesammelte Werke/Collected Works. Abteilung C: Allgemeinverständliche Schriften. Philosophical and Popular Writings, II. Physik und Erkenntnis 1956–1968*, edited by W. Blum, H.-P. Dürr, and H. Rechenberg. München, Zürich: Piper, 3–201.

———. 1984b. "Sprache und Wirklichkeit in der modernen Physik." In *Gesammelte Werke/Collected Works. Abteilung C: Allgemeinverständliche Schriften. Philosophical and Popular Writings, II. Physik und Erkenntnis 1956–1968*, edited by W. Blum, H.-P. Dürr, and H. Rechenberg. München, Zürich: Piper, 271–301.

———. 1985a. "Bemerkungen über die Entstehung der Unbestimmtheitsrelation." In *Gesammelte Werke/Collected Works. Abteilung C: Allgemeinverständliche Schriften. Philosophical and Popular Writings, III. Physik und Erkenntnis 1969–1976*, edited by W. Blum, H.-P. Dürr, and H. Rechenberg. München, Zürich: Piper, 514–17.

———. 1985b. "The Development of Concepts in Physics of the 20th Century." In *Gesammelte Werke/Collected Works. Abteilung C: Allgemeinverständliche Schriften. Philosophical and Popular Writings, III. Physik und Erkenntnis 1969–1976*, edited by W. Blum, H.-P. Dürr, and H. Rechenberg. München, Zürich: Piper, 447–63.

———. 1987. *Der Teil und das Ganze. Gespräche im Umkreis der Atomphysik.* 10th ed. München: dtv.

———. 1971. *Physics and Beyond: Encounters and Conversations.* Translated by Arnold J. Pomerans. New York: Harper & Row.

———. 1989. *Ordnung der Wirklichkeit. Mit einer Einleitung von Helmut Rechenberg.* München, Zürich: Piper.

Held, Carsten. 1998. *Die Bohr-Einstein-Debatte. Quantenmechanik und physikalische Wirklichkeit.* Paderborn, München, Wien, Zürich: Schöningh.

Heller, Bruno. 1970. *Grundbegriffe der Physik im Wandel der Zeit.* Braunschweig: Vieweg.

Helm, Paul. 1988. *Eternal God: A Study of God without Time.* New York: Oxford University Press.

Hermann, Armin. 1979. *Die neue Physik. Der Weg in das Atomzeitalter.* München: Moos.

Herms, Eilert. 1997. "Meine Zeit in Gottes Händen." In *Zeit und Schöpfung. Veröffentlichungen der Wissenschaftlichen Gesellschaft für Theologie 12,* edited by K. Stock. Gütersloh: Chr. Kaiser/Gütersloher Verlagshaus, 67–90.

Herrmann, Siegfried. 1977. *Zeit und Geschichte.* Stuttgart: Kohlhammer.

Hertzberg, Hans Wilhelm. 1963. *Der Prediger.* Kommentar zum Alten Testament 17:4–5. Gütersloh: Gütersloher Verlagshaus Gerd Mohn.

Hjelde, Sigurd. 1987. *Das Eschaton und die Eschata. Eine Studie über Sprachgebrauch und Sprachverwirrung in protestantischer Theologie von der Orthodoxie bis zur Gegenwart.* Beiträge zur evangelischen Theologie 102. Edited by E. Jüngel and R. Smend. München: Chr. Kaiser.

Holmström, Folke. 1935. "Das eschatologische Denken der Gegenwart. Die weltanschaulichen Hemmungen der eschatologischen Renaissance in ideengeschichtlicher und prinzipieller Beleuchtung." *Zeitschrift für systematische Theologie* 12(2):314–59.

Holte, John, Hg. 1993. *Chaos: The New Science.* Nobel Conference 26. Lanham, MD: University Press of America.

Hornung, Erik. 1993. *Geist der Pharaonenzeit.* 2nd ed. München: dtv.

Huber, Andreas. 1996. *Stichwort: Chaosforschung.* München: Wilhelm Heyne.

Hübner, Jürgen. 1966. *Theologie und biologische Entwicklungslehre. Ein Beitrag zum Gespräch zwischen Theologie und Naturwissenschaft.* München: Beck.

———. 1994. "Eschatologische Rechenschaft, kosmologische Weltorientierung und die Artikulation von Hoffnung." In *Die Zukunft der Erlösung. Zur neueren Diskussion um die Eschatologie. Veröffentlichungen der Wissenschaftlichen Gesellschaft für Theologie 7,* edited by K. Stock. Gütersloh: Chr. Kaiser/Gütersloher Verlagshaus, 147–75.

———, ed. 1987. *Der Dialog zwischen Theologie und Naturwissenschaft. Ein bibliographischer Bericht.* München: Chr. Kaiser.

Hymns Ancient and Modern: Historical Edition [Hymns]. 1909. London.

Isham, Chris J. 1988. "Creation of the Universe as a Quantum Process." In *Physics, Philosophy, and Theology: A Common Quest for Understanding,* edited by J. Russell, W. R. Stoeger, and G. V. Coyne. Vatican City State: Vatican Observatory, 375–408.

———. 1996. "Quantum Theories of the Creation of the Universe." In *Quantum Cosmology and the Laws of Nature: Scientific Perspectives on Divine Action.* 2nd ed. Edited by R. J. Russell, N. Murphy, and C. J. Isham. Vatican City State/Berkeley, CA: Vatican Observatory Publications/The Center for Theology and the Natural Sciences, 51–89.

Jackelén, Antje. 1996. "Vom Erobern des Selbstverständlichen und dem Willen zur Berührung. Überlegungen zum Gespräch zwischen Theologie und Naturwissenschaften." In *What Does it Mean Today to Be a Feminist Theologian?* Vol. 4, *Yearbook of the European Society of Women in Theological Research.* Edited by A. Günter and U. Wagener. Mainz/Kampen: Grünewald/Kok Pharos, 28–41.

———. 1997. "Förlorad evighet som orsak till kronisk tidsbrist?" *Svensk Teologisk Kvartalskrift* 73(1):23–32.

———. 2004. *The Dialogue between Religion and Science: Challenges and Future Directions.* Edited by Carl Helrich. Kitchener, Ontario: Pandora Press.

Jammer, Max. 1969. *Concepts of Space: The History of Theories of Space in Physics.* 2nd ed., Cambridge, MA: Harvard University Press.

———. 1999. *Einstein and Religion.* Princeton: Princeton University Press.

Jeanrond, Werner G. 1991. *Theological Hermeneutics: Development and Significance.* New York: Crossroad.

———. 1995. *Call and Response: The Challenge of Christian Life.* Dublin: Gill & Macmillan.

———. 1998. "Correlational Theology and the Chicago School." In *Introduction to Christian Theology: Contemporary North American Perspectives,* edited by R. A. Badham. Louisville, KY: Westminster John Knox, 137–53.

Jenson, Robert W. 1995. "What is the Point of Trinitarian Theology?" In *Trinitarian Theology Today: Essays on Divine Being and Act,* edited by C. Schwöbel. Edinburgh: T & T Clark, 31–43.

Johnson, Elizabeth A. 1994. *She Who Is: The Mystery of God in Feminist Theological Discourse.* New York: Crossroad.

Jüngel, Eberhard. 1973. *Tod.* 3rd ed. Stuttgart, Berlin: Kreuz-Verlag.

——— 1974. *Death, the Riddle and the Mystery.* Translated by Iain and Ute Nicol. Philadelphia: Westminster.

———. 1977. *Gott als Geheimnis der Welt. Zur Begründung der Theologie des Gekreuzigten im Streit zwischen Theismus und Atheismus.* Tübingen: Mohr (Siebeck).

———. 1980. "Der Tod als Geheimnis des Lebens." In *Entsprechungen: Gott–Wahrheit–Mensch. Theologische Erörterungen.* München: Chr. Kaiser, 327–54.

———. 1983. *God as the Mystery of the World.* Translated by Darrell L. Guder. Grand Rapids: Eerdmans.

———. 1989. "Nihil divinitatis, ubi non fides. Ist christliche Dogmatik in rein theoretischer Perspektive möglich? Bemerkungen zu einem theologischen Entwurf von Rang". *Zeitschrift für Theologie und Kirche* 86:204–35.

Kant, Immanuel. 1974. *Kritik der reinen Vernunft*. Vol. 1. Frankfurt/Main: Suhrkamp.

———. 1996. *Critique of Pure Reason*. Translated by Werner S. Pluhar. Indianapolis: Hacket.

Katechismus der Katholischen Kirche. 1993. München et al.: Oldenbourg et al.

Keller, Catherine. 1996. *Apocalypse Now and Then: A Feminist Guide to the End of the World*. Boston: Beacon Press.

———. 1997. "The Last Laugh: A Counter-Apocalyptic Meditation on Moltmann's *Coming of God*." *Theology Today* 54(3):381–91.

Kemp, Peter. 1992. *Lévinas. En introduktion*. Translated by Rikard Hedenblad. Göteborg: Daidalos.

Kessler, Rainer. 1994. "Das Sabbatgebot. Historische Entwicklung, kanonische Bedeutung und aktuelle Aspekte." In *Religion und Gestaltung der Zeit*, edited by D. Georgi, H.-G. Heimbrock, and M. Moxter. Kampen: Kok Pharos, 92–107.

Kirschenmann, P[eter]. P. 1994. "On Time and the Source of Complexity: Criticism of Certain Views Meant to Humanize Science." In *Origins, Time and Complexity*, Part II, Studies in Science and Theology (SSTh). Vol. 2, *Yearbook of the European Society for the Study of Science and Theology*. Edited by G. V. Coyne, K. Schmitz-Moormann, and C. Wassermann. Geneva: Labor et Fides, 89–95.

Koyama, Kosuke. 1979. "Wird Gott vom Monsunregen naß? Eine Sicht der Geschichte als aufsteigende Spirale." In *Wie Christen in Asien denken. Ein theologisches Quellenbuch*, edited by D. J. Elwood. Frankfurt/Main: Otto Lembeck, 89–100.

Koyré, Alexandre. 1994. *From the Closed World to the Infinite Universe*. Baltimore, London: Johns Hopkins University Press.

Krapp, Holger, and Thomas Wägenbaur, eds. 1997. *Komplexität und Selbstorganisation. "Chaos" in den Natur- und Kulturwissenschaften*. München: Fink.

Kroll, Richard, Richard Ashcraft, and Perez Zagorin, eds. 1992. *Philosophy, Science, and Religion in England 1640–1700*. Cambridge: Cambridge University Press.

Krolzik, Udo. 1979. *Umweltkrise—Folge des Christentums?* Stuttgart, Berlin: Kreuz Verlag.

Kronholm, Tryggve. 1989. עת. In *Theologisches Wörterbuch zum Alten Testament*. Stuttgart: Kohlhammer, 6:463–82.

Kümmel, Werner Georg. 1972. *Die Theologie des Neuen Testaments nach seinen Hauptzeugen: Jesus, Paulus, Johannes*. 2nd ed. *Grundrisse zum Neuen Testament. Das Neue Testament Deutsch. Ergänzungsreihe* 3. Edited by G. Friedrich. Göttingen: Vandenhoeck & Ruprecht.

———. 1973. *The Theology of the New Testament according to Its Major Witnesses: Jesus–Paul–John*. Translated by John E. Steely. Nashville: Abingdon Press.

Küng, Hans. 1984. *Eternal Life?* Translated by Edward Quinn. New York: Doubleday.

———. 1988. *Ewiges Leben?* 7th ed. München, Zürich: Piper.

Kuschel, Karl-Josef. 1990. *Geboren vor aller Zeit? Der Streit um Christi Ursprung*. München, Zürich: Piper.

———. 1992. *Born before All Time*. Translated by John Bowden. New York: Crossroad.

Larson, Duane H. 1995. *Times of the Trinity: A Proposal for Theistic Cosmology*. Bern, New York: Peter Lang.

Lash, Nicholas. 1988. "Observation, Revelation, and the Posterity of Noah." In *Physics, Philosophy, and Theology: A Common Quest for Understanding*, edited by R. J. Russell,

W. R. Stoeger, and G. V. Coyne. Vatican City State: Vatican Observatory, 203–15. Also in N. Lash. 1996. *The Beginning and the End of "Religion."* Cambridge: Cambridge University Press, 75–92.

Lauha, Aarre. 1978. *Kohelet.* Biblischer Kommentar. Altes Testament 19. Neukirchen-Vluyn: Neukirchener Verlag.

Leaver, Robin A., James H. Litton, and Carlton R. Young, eds. 1985. *Duty and Delight: Routley Remembered.* Norwich: Canterbury Press.

Leftow, Brian. 1991. *Time and Eternity.* Cornell Studies in the Philosophy of Religion. Edited by W. P. Alston. Ithaca, London: Cornell University Press.

Lévinas, Emmanuel. 1987. *Time and the Other (and additional essays).* Translated by Richard A. Cohen. Pittsburgh: Duquesne University Press.

———. 2000. *God, Death, and Time.* Translated by Bettina Bergo. Stanford: Stanford University Press.

Levine, Étan. 1986. "The Jews in Time and Space." In *Diaspora. Exile and the Contemporary Jewish Condition*, edited by É. Levine. New York: Shapolsky Books, 1–11.

Link, Christian. 1991. *Schöpfung. Schöpfungstheologie angesichts der Herausforderungen des 20. Jahrhunderts. Handbuch Systematischer Theologie.* Vol. 7.2. Edited by C. H. Ratschow. Gütersloh: Gütersloher Verlagshaus Gerd Mohn.

———. 1997. "Gott und die Zeit. Theologische Zugänge zum Zeitproblem." In *Zeit und Schöpfung.* Veröffentlichungen der Wissenschaftlichen Gesellschaft für Theologie 12. Edited by K. Stock. Gütersloh: Chr. Kaiser/Gütersloher Verlagshaus, 41–66.

Linnemann, Eta. 1975. "Zeitansage und Zeitvorstellung in der Verkündigung Jesu." In *Jesus Christus in Historie und Theologie. Neutestamentliche Festschrift für Hans Conzelmann zum 60. Geburtstag,* edited by G. Strecker. Tübingen: Mohr (Siebeck), 237–63.

Lohse, Eduard. 1974. *Grundriß der neutestamentlichen Theologie.* Theologische Wissenschaft 5. Edited by C. Andresen, W. Jetter, W. Joest, O. Kaiser, and E. Lohse. Stuttgart: Kohlhammer.

Longman, Tremper, III. 1998. *The Book of Ecclesiastes.* New International Commentary on the Old Testament. Edited by R. K. Harrison and R. L. Hubbard Jr. Grand Rapids: Eerdmans.

Luther, Martin. [1531] 1535. *In epistolam S. Pauli ad Galatas Commentarius.* WA [Weimarer Ausgabe]. Vol. 40.I.

Lutheran Book of Worship. 1978. Minneapolis: Augsburg Publishing House and Philadelphia: Board of Publication, Lutheran Church in America.

Mackey, James P. 1983. *The Christian Experience of God as Trinity.* London: SCM.

Mahlmann, Theodor. 1994. "Auferstehung der Toten und ewiges Leben." In *Die Zukunft der Erlösung. Zur neueren Diskussion um die Eschatologie.* Veröffentlichungen der Wissenschaftlichen Gesellschaft für Theologie 7. Edited by K. Stock. Gütersloh: Chr. Kaiser/Gütersloher Verlagshaus, 108–31.

Maier, Hans. 1996. "Eine Zeit in der Zeit? Die christliche Zeitrechnung." In *Was ist Zeit? Zeit und Verantwortung in Wissenschaft, Technik und Religion.* 2nd. ed. Edited by K. Weis. München: dtv, 101–26.

Mainzer, Klaus. 1995. *Zeit. Von der Urzeit zur Computerzeit.* München: Beck.

———. 1998. "Zeit als Richtungspfeil. Die Entwicklung unumkehrbarer Zeit in Selbstorganisationsprozessen von der kosmisch-physikalischen über die biologische bis zur soziokulturellen Evolution." In *Was treibt die Zeit? Entwicklung und Herrschaft der Zeit in Wissenschaft, Technik und Religion,* edited by K. Weis. München: dtv, 27–69.

Manzke, Karl Hinrich. 1992. *Ewigkeit und Zeitlichkeit. Aspekte für eine theologische Deutung der Zeit.* Göttingen: Vandenhoeck & Ruprecht.

McGrath, Alister E. 1999. *Science and Religion: An Introduction*. Oxford: Blackwell.

Merchant, Carolyn. 1989. *The Death of Nature: Women Ecology and the Scientific Revolution*. San Francisco: HarperSanFrancisco.

Metz, Johann Baptist. 1992. *Glaube in Geschichte und Gesellschaft. Studien zu einer praktischen Fundamentaltheologie*. 5th ed. Mainz: Grünewald.

Mittelstaedt, Peter. 1966. *Philosophische Probleme der modernen Physik*. 2nd ed. Mannheim: Bibliographisches Institut.

Moltmann, Jürgen. 1967. *Theology of Hope: On the Ground and Implications of a Christian Eschatology*. Translated by James W. Leitch. London: SCM.

———. 1973. *Theologie der Hoffnung. Untersuchungen zur Begründung und zu den Konsequenzen einer christlichen Eschatologie*. 9th ed. München: Chr. Kaiser.

———. 1985. *Gott in der Schöpfung. Ökologische Schöpfungslehre*. 2nd ed. München: Chr. Kaiser.

———. 2003. *God in Creation: A New Theology of Creation and the Spirit of God*, Translated by Margaret Kohl. Minneapolis: Fortress.

———. 1987. "Zum Gespräch mit Christian Link." *Evangelische Theologie* 47(1):93–95.

———. 1995. *Das Kommen Gottes. Christliche Eschatologie*. Gütersloh: Chr. Kaiser/Gütersloher Verlagshaus.

———. 1996. *The Coming of God: Christian Eschatology*. Translated by Margaret Kohl. Minneapolis: Fortress.

Monod, Jacques. 1972. *Chance and Necessity*. Translated by Austryn Wainhouse. New York: Vintage Books.

Morenz, Siegfried. 1960. *Ägyptische Religion*. Stuttgart: Kohlhammer.

———. 1973. *Egyptian Religion*. Translated by Ann E. Keep. Ithaca: Cornell University Press.

Mortensen, Viggo. 1989. *Teologi og naturvidenskab. Hinsides restriktion og ekspansion*. Kopenhagen: Munksgaard.

Muilenburg, James. 1961. "The Biblical View of Time." *Harvard Theological Review* 54(4): 225–52.

Müller, A. M. Klaus. 1978. *Wende der Wahrnehmung. Erwägungen zur Grundlagenkrise in Physik, Medizin, Pädagogik und Theologie*. München: Chr. Kaiser.

Newton, Isaac. 1729. *Mathematical Principles of Natural Philosophy*. Translated by Andrew Motte. London.

———. 1964. *Opera Quae Exstant Omnia. Faksimile-Neudruck der Ausgabe von Samuel Horsley in 5 Bänden, London 1779–1785*. Vol. 2. Stuttgart-Bad Cannstatt: Friedrich Frommann (Günter Holzboog).

———. 1972. *Isaac Newton's Philosophiae Naturalis Principia Mathematica. The Third Edition (1726) with Variant Readings*. Vols. I and II. Edited by A. Koyré and B. I. Cohen. Cambridge: Harvard University Press.

———. 2003. *Opticks*. Amherst, NY: Prometheus.

Nietzsche, Friedrich. 1967. *Werke in zwei Bänden*. Vol. 1. Edited by I. Frenzel. München: Carl Hanser [Lizenzausgabe für Bertelsmann, Gütersloh].

———. 2001. *The Gay Science*, Edited by Bernard Williams. Translated by Josefine Nauckhoff and Adrian Del Caro. Cambridge: Cambridge University Press.

Nivenius, Olle. 1991. *Psalmer och människor*. Stockholm: Verbum.

Ott, Heinrich. 1958. *Eschatologie. Versuch eines dogmatischen Grundrisses*. Theologische Studien 53. Edited by K. Barth and M. Geiger. Zollikon: Evangelischer Verlag.

Otto, Eberhard. 1966. "Zeitvorstellungen und Zeitrechnung im Alten Orient." *Studium Generale* 19(12):743–51.

Padgett, Alan G. 1992. *God, Eternity and the Nature of Time*. New York: St. Martin's Press.

Pagels, Heinz R. 1984. *Cosmic Code. Quantenphysik als Sprache der Natur*. Translated by Ralf Friese. 2nd ed. Berlin, Frankfurt/Main, Wien: Ullstein.

Pais, Abraham. 1982. *'Subtle is the Lord . . . ': The Science and the Life of Albert Einstein*. Oxford, New York: Oxford University Press.

Pannenberg, Wolfhart. 1975. "Das Wirklichkeitsverständnis der Bibel." In Pannenberg, *Glaube und Wirklichkeit. Kleine Beiträge zum christlichen Denken*. München: Chr. Kaiser, 18–30.

———. 1981. "Theological Questions to Scientists." *Zygon* 16(1):65–77.

———. 1988. *Systematische Theologie*. Vol. 1. Göttingen: Vandenhoeck & Ruprecht.

———. 1989. "Theological Appropriation of Scientific Understandings: Response to Hefner, Wicken, Eaves, and Tipler". *Zygon* 24 (2):255–71.

———. 1991a. *Systematic Theology*. Vol. 1. Translated by Geofffrey W. Bromiley. Grand Rapids: Eerdmans.

———. 1991b. *Systematische Theologie*. Vol. 2. Göttingen: Vandenhoeck & Ruprecht.

———. 1993. *Systematische Theologie*. Vol. 3. Göttingen: Vandenhoeck & Ruprecht.

———. 1994. *Systematic Theology*. Vol. 2. Translated by Geoffrey W. Bromiley. Grand Rapids: Eerdmans.

———. 1998. *Systematic Theology*. Vol. 3. Translated by Geoffrey W. Bromiley. Grand Rapids: Eerdmans.

Peacocke, Arthur R. 1993. *Theology for a Scientific Age*. Second, enlarged edition. London: SCM Press.

Peitgen, Heinz-Otto. 1993. "The Causality Principle, Deterministic Laws and Chaos." In *Chaos: The New Science*. Nobel Conference 26. Edited by J. Holte. Lanham, MD: University Press of America, 35–43.

Peitgen, Heinz-Otto, Hartmut Jürgens, and Dietmar Saupe. 2004. *Chaos and Fractals: New Frontiers of Science*. New York: Springer.

Perdue, Leo G. 1994. *The Collapse of History: Reconstructing Old Testament Theology*. Overtures to Biblical Theology. Minneapolis: Fortress.

Peters, Ted. 1993. *GOD as Trinity: Relationality and Temporality in Divine Life*. Louisville: Westminster/John Knox.

———. 1996. "Theology and Science: Where Are We?" *Zygon* 32(2):323–43.

———, ed. 1998. *Science and Theology: The New Consonance*. Boulder, CO: Westview Press.

Petry, Michael John. 1994. "Newton, Isaac (1643–1727)." In *Theologische Realenzyklopädie*. Berlin, New York: de Gruyter, 24:422–29.

Picht, Georg. 1971. "Die Zeit und die Modalitäten." In *Quanten und Felder. Physikalische Betrachtungen zum 70. Geburtstag von Werner Heisenberg*, edited by H. P. Dürr. Braunschweig: Vieweg, 67–76.

Plato. 1952. *Timaios*. Translated by R. G. Bury. Vol. 7, Loeb Classical Library. London/ Cambridge: Heinemann/Harvard University Press.

Polkinghorne, John. 1988. "The Quantum World." In *Physics, Philosophy, and Theology: A Common Quest for Understanding*, edited by R. J. Russell, W. R. Stoeger, and G. V. Coyne. Vatican City State: Vatican Observatory, 333–42.

———. 1989. *Science and Providence: God's Interaction with the World*. London: SPCK.

———. 1994. *The Faith of a Physicist: Reflections of a Bottom-Up Thinker*. Princeton, NJ: Princeton University Press.

Polkinghorne, John, and Michael Welker. 2000. *The End of the World and the Ends of God: Science and Theology on Eschatology*. Harrisburg, PA: Trinity Press International.

Predel, Gregor. 1996. *Sakrament der Gegenwart Gottes. Theologie und Natur im Zeitalter der*

Naturwissenschaften. Freiburger Theologische Studien 158. Freiburg, Basel, Wien: Herder.

Preuß, H. D. 1986. עוֹלָם. In *Theologisches Wörterbuch zum Alten Testament*, vol. 5. Stuttgart: Kohlhammer, 1144–59.

Prigogine, Ilya. 1977. "Time, Structure and Fluctuations." Nobel Lecture, December 8, 1977. In *Les Prix Nobel 1977*. Stockholm: Almqvist & Wiksell, 132–53.

———. 1980. *From Being to Becoming: Time and Complexity in the Physical Sciences*. San Francisco: W. H. Freeman.

———. 1997. "Zeit, Chaos und Naturgesetze." In *Die Wiederentdeckung der Zeit. Reflexionen–Analysen–Konzepte*, edited by A. Gimmler, M. Sandbothe, and W. Ch. Zimmerli. Darmstadt: Wissenschaftliche Buchgesellschaft, 79–94.

———. 1998. *Die Gesetze des Chaos*. Translated by Friedrich Griese. Frankfurt/Main, Leipzig: Insel.

———. 1984. *Order out of Chaos: Man's New Dialogue with Nature*. New York: Bantam Books.

Prigogine, Ilya, in collaboration with Isabelle Stengers. 1997. *The End of Certainty: Time, Chaos, and the New Laws of Nature*. New York: Free Press.

Prigogine, Ilya, and Isabelle Stengers. 1990. *Dialog mit der Natur. Neue Wege naturwissenschaftlichen Denkens*. Translated by Friedrich Griese. 6th ed. München, Zürich: Piper.

Pröpper, Thomas. 1991. *Erlösungsglaube und Freiheitsgeschichte. Eine Skizze zur Soteriologie*. 3rd ed. München: Kösel.

Psalmer i 90-talet [Ps90]. 1994. Stockholm: Verbum.

Psaltaren: Bibelkommissionens provöversättning. 1995. Örebro/Stockholm: Libris/Verbum.

Quispel, Gilles. 1951. "Zeit und Geschichte im antiken Christentum." In *Eranos-Jahrbuch*, vol. 20. Zürich: Rhein-Verlag, 115–40.

Rahner, Karl. 1964a. "Das Leben der Toten." In *Schriften zur Theologie*. 4th ed. Einsiedeln, Zürich, Köln: Benziger, 4:429–37.

———. 1964b. "Theologische Prinzipien der Hermeneutik eschatologischer Aussagen." In *Schriften zur Theologie*. 4th ed. Einsiedeln, Zürich, Köln: Benziger, 4:401–28.

———. 1965. "Die Einheit von Geist und Materie im christlichen Glaubensverständnis." In *Schriften zur Theologie*. Einsiedeln, Zürich, Köln: Benziger, 6:185–237

———. 1966a. "The Hermeneutics of Eschatological Assertions." In *Theological Investigations*, vol. 4. Translated by Kevin Smyth. London: Darton, Longman & Todd, and Baltimore: Helicon Press, 323–46.

———. 1966b. "The Life of the Dead." In *Theological Investigations*, vol. 4. Translated by Kevin Smyth. London: Darton, Longman & Todd, and Baltimore: Helicon Press, 347–54.

———. 1969. "The Unity of Spirit and Matter in the Christian Understanding of Faith." In *Theological Investigations*, vol. 6. Translated by Karl-H. and Boniface Kruger. London: Darton, Longman & Todd, and Baltimore: Helicon Press, 153–77.

———. 1970a. "Theologische Bemerkungen zum Zeitbegriff." In *Schriften zur Theologie*. Einsiedeln, Zürich, Köln: Benziger, 9:302–22.

———. 1970b. "Theologische Erwägungen über den Eintritt des Todes." In *Schriften zur Theologie*. Einsiedeln, Zürich, Köln: Benziger, 9:323–35.

———. 1974a. "Observations on the Concept of Time." In *Theological Investigations*, vol. 11. Translated by David Bourke. New York: Seabury, 288–308.

———. 1974b. "Theological Considerations on the Moment of Death." In *Theological Investigations*, vol. 11. Translated by David Bourke. New York: Seabury, 309–21.

Ratschow, Carl Heinz. 1954. Anmerkungen zur theologischen Auffassung des Zeitproblems. *Zeitschrift für Theologie und Kirche* 51:360–87.

———. 1982. "Eschatologie. VIII. Systematisch-theologisch." In *Theologische Realenzyklopädie.* Berlin, New York: de Gruyter, 10:334–63.

Ratzinger, Joseph. 1990. *Eschatologie—Tod und ewiges Leben. Kleine Katholische Dogmatik.*
6th ed. Vol. 9. Edited by J. Auer and J. Ratzinger. Regensburg: Friedrich Pustet.

Reheis, Fritz. 1996. *Die Kreativität der Langsamkeit. Neuer Wohlstand durch Entschleuni-
gung.* Darmstadt: Wissenschaftliche Buchgesellschaft.

Rendtorff, Rolf. 1975. "Genesis 8,21 und die Urgeschichte des Jahwisten." In Rendtorff,
Gesammelte Studien zum Alten Testament. München: Chr. Kaiser, 188–97.

Richardson, W. Mark, and Wesley J. Wildman, eds. 1996. *Religion and Science: History,
Method, Dialogue.* New York and London: Routledge.

Ricoeur, Paul. 1984. *Time and Narrative,* vol. 1. Translated by Kathleen McLaughlin and
David Pellauer. Chicago, London: University of Chicago Press.

———. 1985. *Time and Narrative,* vol. 2. Translated by Kathleen McLaughlin and David
Pellauer. Chicago, London: University of Chicago Press.

———. 1988. *Time and Narrative,* vol. 3. Translated by Kathleen Blamey und David Pellauer. Chicago, London: University of Chicago Press.

———. 1990. *Soi-même comme un autre. L'ordre philosophique.* Edited by F. Wahl. Paris:
Éditions du Seuil.

———. 1993. *Från text till handling. En antologi om hermeneutik redigerad av Peter Kemp
och Bengt Kristensson.* Translated by Margareta Fatton, Peter Kemp and Bengt Kristensson. 4th ed. *Moderna franska tänkare,* edited by B. Östling. Stockholm/Stehag:
Symposion.

Ringgren, Helmer. 1963. *Israelitische Religion.* Die Religionen der Menschheit. 26. Edited
by C. M. Schröder. Stuttgart: Kohlhammer.

Ringleben, Joachim. 1994. "Gott und das ewige Leben. Zur theologischen Dimension der
Eschatologie." In *Die Zukunft der Erlösung. Zur neueren Diskussion um die Eschatologie.* Veröffentlichungen der Wissenschaftlichen Gesellschaft für Theologie 7. Edited
by K. Stock. Gütersloh: Chr. Kaiser/Gütersloher Verlagshaus, 49–87.

Rochberg-Halton, Francesca, and James C. Vanderkam. 1992. "Calendars." In *The Anchor
Bible Dictionary.* New York: Doubleday, 1:810–20.

Ronnås, John. 1990. *Våra gemensamma psalmer. Kommentarer till psalmbokens 325 första
psalmer.* Stockholm: Verbum.

Rudolph, Kurt. 1980. *Die Gnosis. Wesen und Geschichte einer spätantiken Religion.* 2nd ed.
Göttingen: Vandenhoeck & Ruprecht.

———. 1987. *Gnosis—The Nature and History of Gnosticism.* San Francisco, CA: Harper-
SanFrancisco.

Russell, Robert J. 1988. "Quantum Physics in Philosophical and Theological Perspective."
In *Physics, Philosophy, and Theology: A Common Quest for Understanding,* edited by R.
J. Russell, W. R. Stoeger, and G. V. Coyne. Vatican City State: Vatican Observatory,
343–74.

———. 1997. "Is Nature Creation? Philosophical and Theological Implications of Physics
and Cosmology from a Trinitarian Perspective." In *The Concept of Nature in Science
and Theology,* Part I, *Studies in Science and Theology (SSTh).* Vol. 3, *Yearbook of the European Society for the Study of Science and Theology.* Edited by N. H. Gregersen, M. W.
S. Parsons, and C. Wassermann. Geneva: Labor et Fides, 94–124.

Russell, Robert J., Nancey Murphy, and Chris J. Isham, eds. 1996. *Quantum Cosmology
and the Laws of Nature: Scientific Perspectives on Divine Action.* 2nd ed. Vatican City

State/Berkeley, CA: Vatican Observatory Publications/The Center for Theology and the Natural Sciences.

Russell, Robert J., William R. Stoeger, and George V. Coyne, eds. 1988. *Physics, Philosophy, and Theology: A Common Quest for Understanding*. Vatican City State: Vatican Observatory.

Sasse, Hermann. 1933. αἰών, αἰώνιος. In *Theologisches Wörterbuch zum Neuen Testament*. Stuttgart: Kohlhammer, 1:197–209.

Sauter, Gerhard. 1995. *Einführung in die Eschatologie*. Darmstadt: Wissenschaftliche Buchgesellschaft.

Schelkle, Karl Hermann. 1973. *Theologie des Neuen Testaments*. Vol. 2. Düsseldorf: Patmos.

Schleiermacher, Friedrich. 1948. *The Christian Faith*. 2nd ed. Edited by H. R. Mackintosh and J. S. Stewart. Edinburgh: T & T Clark.

———. 1960. *Der christliche Glaube nach den Grundsätzen der Evangelischen Kirche im Zusammenhange dargestellt*. 7th ed. Vol. 1. Edited by M. Redeker. Berlin: Walter de Gruyter.

———. 1994. *On Religion: Speeches to Its Cultured Despisers*. Translated by John Oman. Louisville: Westminster John Knox.

———. N.d. *Über die Religion. Reden an die Gebildeten unter ihren Verächtern*. Edited by M. Rade. Berlin: Deutsche Bibliothek.

Schmid, Hans Heinrich. 1975. "Das alttestamentliche Verständnis von Geschichte in seinem Verhältnis zum gemeinorientalischen Denken." In *Wort und Dienst*. Jahrbuch der Kirchlichen Hochschule Bethel. NF 13. Edited by H. Krämer. Bethel bei Bielefeld: Verlagshandlung der Anstalt Bethel, 9–21.

Schneider, Erwin Eugen. 1958. "Die Bedeutung der Begriffe Raum, Zeit und Ewigkeit in der christlichen Verkündigung und Lehre." *Kerygma und Dogma* 4:281–86.

Scholem, Gershom. 1957. *Die jüdische Mystik in ihren Hauptströmungen*. Frankfurt/Main: Alfred Metzner.

Schroeder, Manfred. 1991. *Fractals, Chaos, Power Laws: Minutes from an Infinite Paradise*. New York: W. H. Freeman.

Schultz, Uwe, ed. 1990. *Scheibe, Kugel, Schwarzes Loch. Die wissenschaftliche Eroberung des Kosmos*. München: Beck.

Schulz, Siegfried. 1970. *Die Stunde der Botschaft. Einführung in die Theologie der vier Evangelisten*. 2nd ed. Hamburg/Zürich: Furche/Zwingli.

Schwarz, Hans. 1971. "Eschatology or Futurology? On the Interdependence Between Christian Eschatology and Secular Progress." *Theologische Zeitschrift* 27:347–64.

Schwöbel, Christoph. 1995a. "Christology and Trinitarian Thought." In *Trinitarian Theology Today: Essays on Divine Being and Act*, edited by C. Schwöbel. Edinburgh: T & T Clark, 113–46.

———, ed. 1995b. *Trinitarian Theology Today: Essays on Divine Being and Act*. Edinburgh: T & T Clark.

Segerbank, Catharina. 1993. *Dödstanken i svensk romantik. Odödlighetstanke och uppståndelsetro hos tre svenska diktare: Per Daniel Amadeus Atterbom, Johan Olof Wallin, Erik Johan Stagnelius*. Bibliotheca historico-ecclesiastica Lundensis 31. Lund: Lund University Press.

Selander, Inger. 1980. *O hur saligt att få vandra: Motiv och symboler i den frikyrkliga sången*. Stockholm: Gummessons.

Seow, C. L. 1997. *Ecclesiastes: A New Translation with Introduction and Commentary. Anchor Bible* 18C. New York: Doubleday.

Sherrard, Philip. 1992. *Human Image: World Image. The Death and Resurrection of Sacred Cosmology.* Ipswich: Golgonooza Press.

Sigurdson, Ola. 1996. *Karl Barth som den andre. En studie i den svenska teologins Barth-reception.* Stockholm/Stehag: Symposion.

Sing Alleluia: A Supplement to the Australian Hymn Book [SA]. 1987. London/Blackburn: Collins.

Smith, Jonathan Z. 1987. *To Take Place: Toward Theory in Ritual.* Chicago Studies in the History of Judaism. Edited by J. Neusner, W. S. Green, and C. Goldscheider. Chicago/London: University of Chicago Press.

Söllner, Peter. 1998. *Jerusalem, die hochgebaute Stadt. Eschatologisches und Himmlisches Jerusalem im Frühjudentum und im frühen Christentum.* Texte und Arbeiten zum neutestamentlichen Zeitalter 25. Tübingen, Basel: Francke.

Southgate, Christopher, et al., eds. 1999. *God, Humanity and the Cosmos: A Textbook in Science and Religion.* Edinburgh: T & T Clark.

Stendahl, Krister. 1977. "The Apostle Paul and the Introspective Conscience of the West." In *Paul Among Jews and Gentiles and Other Essays.* London: SCM, 78–96.

———. 1984. "Immortality Is Too Much and Too Little." In *Meanings.* Philadelphia: Fortress, 193–202.

Stenmark, Mikael. 1995. *Rationality in Science, Religion, and Everyday Life: A Critical Evaluation of Four Models of Rationality.* Notre Dame: University of Notre Dame Press.

Stinissen, Wilfrid. 1992. *Evigheten mitt i tiden.* Örebro: Libris.

Stock, Konrad. 1971. *Annihilatio mundi. Johann Gerhards Eschatologie der Welt.* Forschungen zur Geschichte und Lehre des Protestantismus 10. Reihe, 42. Edited by E. Wolf. München: Chr. Kaiser.

———, ed. 1994. *Die Zukunft der Erlösung. Zur neueren Diskussion um die Eschatologie.* Veröffentlichungen der Wissenschaftlichen Gesellschaft für Theologie. Vol. 7. Gütersloh: Chr. Kaiser/Gütersloher Verlagshaus.

———, ed. 1997. *Zeit und Schöpfung. Veröffentlichungen der Wissenschaftlichen Gesellschaft für Theologie.* Vol. 12. Gütersloh: Chr. Kaiser/Gütersloher Verlagshaus.

Stoeger, William R. 1988. "Contemporary Cosmology and Its Implications for the Science-Religion Dialogue." In *Physics, Philosophy, and Theology: A Common Quest for Understanding,* edited by R. J. Russell, W. R. Stoeger, and G. V. Coyne. Vatican City State: Vatican Observatory, 219–47.

Streib, Heinz. 1994. "Erzählte Zeit als Ermöglichung von Identität." In *Religion und Gestaltung der Zeit,* edited by D. Georgi, H.-G. Heimbrock, and M. Moxter. Kampen: Kok Pharos, 181–98.

Stuhlmacher, Peter. 1967. "Erwägungen zum Problem von Gegenwart und Zukunft in der paulinischen Eschatologie." *Zeitschrift für Theologie und Kirche* 64:423–50.

Stump, Eleonore, and Norman Kretzmann. 1981. "Eternity." *Journal of Philosophy* 78(8): 429–58.

Swinburne, Richard. 1968. *Space and Time.* London, New York: Macmillan, St. Martin's Press.

———. 1993. *The Coherence of Theism.* Rev. ed. Clarendon Library of Logic and Philosophy. Edited by L. J. Cohen. Oxford: Clarendon.

The Australian Hymnbook with Catholic Supplement [AHB]. 1977. Sydney: Collins.

Theunissen, Michael. 1997. *Negative Theologie der Zeit.* 3rd ed. Frankfurt/Main: Suhrkamp.

Thomas von Aquin. 1964. *Summa Theologiae: Latin Text and English Translation.* Vol. 2. Translated by Timothy McDermott, OP. London: Blackfriars.

Thorne, Kip S. 1994. *Black Holes and Time Warps: Einstein's Outrageous Legacy.* New York: W. W. Norton.

Tillich, Paul. 1951. *Systematic Theology.* Vol. 1. Chicago: University of Chicago Press.

———. 1963. "Eschatologie und Geschichte." In *Der Widerstreit von Raum und Zeit. Schriften zur Geschichtsphilosophie, Gesammelte Werke,* edited by R. Albrecht. Stuttgart: Evangelisches Verlagswerk, 6:72–82.

———. 1973. *Systematische Theologie.* 4th ed. Vol. 1. Stuttgart: Evangelisches Verlagswerk.

Tipler, Frank J. 1988. "The Omega Point Theory: A Model of an Evolving God." In *Physics, Philosophy, and Theology: A Common Quest for Understanding,* edited by R. J. Russell, W. R. Stoeger, and G. V. Coyne. Vatican City State: Vatican Observatory, 313–31.

———. 1994. *The Physics of Immortality.* New York: Doubleday.

Torrance, Thomas F. 1997. *Space, Time and Incarnation.* Rev. ed. Edinburgh: T & T Clark.

———. 1998. *Space, Time and Resurrection.* Rev. ed. Edinburgh: T & T Clark.

Toulmin, Stephen. 1985. *The Return to Cosmology. Postmodern Science and the Theology of Nature.* Berkeley, Los Angeles, London: University of California Press.

Tracy, David. 1987. *Plurality and Ambiguity: Hermeneutics, Religion, Hope.* San Francisco: Harper & Row.

Tysk, Karl-Erik. 1990. *Evigt liv.* Stockholm: Verbum.

van Huyssteen, J. Wentzel. 1998. *Duet or Duel? Theology and Science in a Postmodern World.* London: SCM.

———. 1999. *The Shaping of Rationality: Toward Interdisciplinarity in Theology and Science.* Grand Rapids: Eerdmans.

Vanhoozer, Kevin J. 1997a. "Does the Trinity Belong in a Theology of Religions? On Angling in the Rubicon and the 'Identity' of God." In *The Trinity in a Pluralistic Age: Theological Essays on Culture and Religion.* Grand Rapids/Cambridge: Eerdmans, 41–71.

———, ed. 1997b. *The Trinity in a Pluralistic Age: Theological Essays on Culture and Religion.* Grand Rapids/Cambridge: Eerdmans.

von Rad, Gerhard. 1965. *Old Testament Theology.* Vol. 2. Translated by D. M. G. Stalker. Louisville: Westminster John Knox.

———. 1972. *Genesis: A Commentary.* Rev. ed. Translated by John H. Marks. London: SCM.

———. 1975. *Theologie des Alten Testaments.* 6th ed. Vol. 2: *Die Theologie der prophetischen Überlieferungen Israels.* München: Chr. Kaiser.

———. 1987. *Das erste Buch Mose. Genesis. Das Alte Testament Deutsch.* Teilbd. 2/4. 12th ed. Göttingen, Zürich: Vandenhoeck & Ruprecht.

von Weizsäcker, Carl Friedrich. 1971. "Notizen über die philosophische Bedeutung der Heisenbergschen Physik." In *Quanten und Felder. Physikalische Betrachtungen zum 70. Geburtstag von Werner Heisenberg,* edited by H. P. Dürr. Braunschweig: Vieweg, 11–26.

———. 1995. *Zeit und Wissen.* München: dtv.

Vorgrimler, Herbert. 1980. *Hoffnung auf Vollendung. Aufriß der Eschatologie.* Quaestiones disputatae 90. Edited by K. Rahner and H. Schlier. Freiburg, Basel, Wien: Herder.

Walker, Benjamin. 1987. *Gnosticism: Its History and Influence.* San Bernardino, CA: Borgo Press.

Ward, Keith. 1996. *Religion and Creation.* Oxford: Clarendon.

Weidlich, Wolfgang. 1974. "Zeit und Raum als Beispiele naturwissenschaftlicher Begriffsbildung." In *Naturwissenschaft und Theologie. Texte und Kommentare,* edited by H. Aichelin and G. Liedke. Neukirchen-Vluyn: Neukirchener Verlag, 62–72.

Weinberg, Steven. 1988. *The First Three Minutes: A Modern View of the Origin of the Universe.* Rev. ed. New York: Basic Books.

Weis, Kurt, ed. 1996. *Was ist Zeit? Zeit und Verantwortung in Wissenschaft, Technik und Religion.* 2nd ed. München: dtv.

———, ed. 1998. *Was treibt die Zeit? Entwicklung und Herrschaft der Zeit in Wissenschaft, Technik und Religion.* München: dtv.

Welker, Michael. 1998. "God's Eternity, God's Temporality, and Trinitarian Theology." *Theology Today* 55(3):317–28.

Wendorff, Rudolf. 1980. *Zeit und Kultur. Geschichte des Zeitbewußtseins in Europa.* 2nd ed. Opladen: Westdeutscher Verlag.

Werner, Martin. 1959. *Die Entstehung des christlichen Dogmas.* Stuttgart: Kohlhammer.

Wertheim, Margaret. 1997. *Pythagoras' Trousers: God, Physics, and the Gender Wars.* New York, London: W. W. Norton.

Westermann, Claus. 1974. *Genesis.* Biblischer Kommentar, Altes Testament. Vol. 1.1. Neukirchen-Vluyn: Neukirchener Verlag.

———. 1984a. *Genesis 1–11: A Commentary.* Translated by John J. Scullion, SJ. Minneapolis: Augsburg Publishing House.

———. 1984b. "Erfahrung der Zeit im Alten Testament." In *Erfahrung der Zeit. Gedenkschrift für Georg Picht,* edited by C. Link. Stuttgart: Klett-Cotta. 113–118.

Westfall, Richard S. 1980. *Never at Rest: A Biography of Isaac Newton.* Cambridge: Cambridge University Press.

Westhelle, Vítor. 1989. "The Challenge of Theology to Science and the Church." In *The New Faith-Science Debate: Probing Cosmology, Technology, and Theology,* edited by J. M. Mangum. Minneapolis and Geneva: Fortress and WCC Publications, 23–35.

White, Lynn, Jr. 1967. The Historical Roots of Our Ecological Crisis. *Science* 155:1203–7.

Whitrow, Gerald James. 1989. *Time in History: Views of Time from Prehistory to the Present Day.* Oxford, New York: Oxford University Press.

Wilch, John R. 1969. *Time and Event: An Exegetical Study of the Use of 'eth in the Old Testament in Comparison to Other Temporal Expressions in Clarification of the Concept of Time.* Leiden: E. J. Brill.

Wild, Wolfgang. 1996. "Wie kam die Zeit in die Welt? Der Zeitbegriff der Physik." In *Was ist Zeit? Zeit und Verantwortung in Wissenschaft, Technik und Religion.* 2nd ed. Edited by K. Weis. München: dtv, 153–79.

Wittgenstein, Ludwig. 1963. "Tractatus logico-philosophicus." *Schriften (1).* Frankfurt/Main: Suhrkamp, 7–83.

Worthing, Mark William. 1996. *God, Creation, and Contemporary Physics.* Theology and the Sciences. Edited by K. Sharpe. Minneapolis: Fortress.

Würthwein, Ernst. 1984. "Chaos und Schöpfung im mythischen Denken und in der biblischen Urgeschichte." In *Zeit und Geschichte: Dankesgabe an Rudolf Bultmann zum 80. Geburtstag,* edited by E. Dinkler. Tübingen: Mohr (Siebeck), 317–27.

Zimmerli, Walther Ch. 1997. "Zeit als Zukunft." In *Die Wiederentdeckung der Zeit. Reflexionen – Analysen – Konzepte,* edited by A. Gimmler, M. Sandbothe, and W. Ch. Zimmerli. Darmstadt: Wissenschaftliche Buchgesellschaft, 126–47.

Index